VAUGHAN WILLIAMS
AND HIS WORLD

EDITED BY
BYRON ADAMS AND DANIEL M. GRIMLEY

D1600272

THE UNIVERSITY OF CHICAGO PRESS
CHICAGO AND LONDON

The University of Chicago Press, Chicago 60637
The University of Chicago Press, Ltd., London
© 2023 by The Bard Music Festival
Published 2023
Printed in the United States of America

32 31 30 29 28 27 26 25 24 23   1 2 3 4 5

ISBN-13: 978-0-226-83044-5 (cloth)
ISBN-13: 978-0-226-83045-2 (paper)
ISBN-13: 978-0-226-83046-9 (e-book)
DOI: https://doi.org/10.7208/chicago/9780226830469.001.0001

This publication has been produced by the Bard College Publications Office:
Irene Zedlacher, project director
Karen Spencer, design
Text edited by Paul De Angelis and Erin Clermont
Music typeset by Christopher Deschene
Indexed by Scott Smiley

This publication has been underwritten in part by a grant from
Roger and Helen Alcaly

Thank you also to the Vaughan Williams Foundation for their support

Library of Congress Control Number: 2023932613

To Tiffany Stern and Diana McVeagh

How many things by season season'd are
To their right praise and true perfection.

—William Shakespeare,
The Merchant of Venice (5.1.116–17)

Contents

Permissions and Credits

The following copyright holders, institutions, and individuals have graciously granted permission to reprint or reproduce the following materials:

British Library Board for Figure 1 (MS Mus. 1714/10/3) in Rushton, "Vaughan Williams and Cambridge."

Master and Fellows of Trinity College, Cambridge for Figure 2 in Rushton, "Vaughan Williams and Cambridge."

Historic England & Monuments Commission for Figures 1 and 2 in Siegel, "Vaughan Williams and the Royal College of Music."

National Portrait Gallery, London © National Portrait Gallery, London, for Figure 3 in Siegel, "Vaughan Williams and the Royal College of Music."

Vaughan Williams Foundation for Figure 4 in Siegel, "Vaughan Williams and the Royal College of Music."

Oxford University Press © Oxford University Press by permission of the Secretary to the Delegates of Oxford University Press, for Figure 5 in Siegel, "Vaughan Williams and the Royal College of Music"; for Music Examples 1–10, © 1934, in Rupprecht, "Modernist Image in Vaughan Williams's *Job*," used by permission; for Music Examples 1 © 1960, and 2a and 2b © 1945 in Forkert, "'Finest of the Fine Arts': Vaughan Williams and Film," used by permission; for Music Examples 1 © 1946 and 3 © 1956 in Neighbour, "'His own idiom': Vaughan Williams's Violin Sonata and the Development of His Melodic Style." All rights reserved.

Lebrecht Authors/Bridgeman Images for Figures 2 and 3 in Rupprecht, "Modernist Image in Vaughan Williams's *Job*."

The Vaughan Williams Charitable Trust © 1948 & 2018 for Music Example 3 in Forkert, "'Finest of the Fine Arts': Vaughan Williams and Film," exclusively licensed to Oxford University Press; all rights reserved; and © 2008 for Music Examples 1 and 2 in Collins and Grimley, "Vaughan Williams's Common Ground," used by permission of Hal Leonard, LLC, and Faber Music Ltd., London.

Alamy Stock Photo for Figure 1 in Adams, "Pilgrim in a New-Found-Land: Vaughan Williams in America."

Tully Potter/Bridgeman Images for Figure 2 in Adams, "Pilgrim in a New-Found-Land: Vaughan Williams in America."

Dorking Museum and Heritage Centre, Dorking, Surrey for Figures 1, 2, and 3 in Collins and Grimley, "Vaughan Williams's Common Ground."

The Estate of Michael Kennedy and John Rylands Library, University of Manchester for letters from Michael Kennedy in "Tracing a Biography: Michael Kennedy's Correspondence Concerning *The Works of Ralph Vaughan Williams*."

Britten Pears Arts for the letter from Benjamin Britten and the letters from Imogen Holst; **Bertrand Russell Foundation and the Bertrand Russell Archives, McMaster University** for the letter from Bertrand Russell; **Anthony Powers** for the letters from Steuart Wilson and Adrian Boult; **Hugh Howes** for letters from Frank Howes; © **Oxford University Press** for the letter from Alan Frank (by permission of the Secretary to the Delegates of Oxford University Press); **Cherese Scherbak** for the letter from Jani Strasser; **Association of Family Members of Julius Röntgen** for the letter from Julius Röntgen; all of the foregoing to be found in Kennedy, "Tracing a Biography: Michael Kennedy's Correspondence Concerning *The Works of Ralph Vaughan Williams*."

Nicolas Bell, executor of the estate of Oliver Neighbour for the text of Neighbour, "'His own idiom': Vaughan Williams's Violin Sonata and the Development of His Melodic Style."

Hal Leonard LLC, and Faber Music Ltd., London, for Music Example 2 in Neighbour, "'His own idiom': Vaughan Williams's Violin Sonata and the Development of His Melodic Style," © 2002 Joan Ursula Penton Vaughan Williams.

The Vaughan Williams Foundation, for all quotations from Vaughan Williams Letters, which are reproduced by kind permission. Numbering of the letters (for example VWL 3959) follows the format used by the Foundation as listed in their online catalogue (https://vaughanwilliamsfoundation.org/discover/letters/ [accessed 28 December 2022]), which includes annotated transcriptions of the correspondence.

The authors, editors, and publisher have made every effort to trace holders of copyright. They much regret if any inadvertent omissions have been made.

Acknowledgments

First, the editors thank Leon Botstein, whose unflagging enthusiasm, erudition, determination, and love of music pervade the Bard Music Festival. He is ably assisted by the Festival's codirector, Christopher H. Gibbs, James H. Ottoway Jr. Professor of Music at Bard College, and its executive director, the perennially resourceful Irene Zedlacher. Like all editors of these volumes, we owe a debt of gratitude to the sagacity, expertise, and industry of Paul De Angelis and we give thanks for the attentive copyediting of Erin Clermont. Chris Deschene copied the musical examples for this volume with care and professionalism.

Second, we are grateful to our contributors: Julian Rushton, Erica Siegel, Ceri Owen, Philip Rupprecht, Annika Forkert, Sarah Collins, Eric Saylor, and Alain Frogley. These scholars began their research during the dark year of 2020, moving forward with resolve in the face of massive uncertainty. They all have made invaluable contributions to an enhanced understanding of Vaughan Williams's life and music. We are indebted to Nicolas Bell, executor of the estate of Oliver Neighbour, for giving us permission to publish Neighbour's essay, all but finished at his death in 2015, on Vaughan Williams's late Violin Sonata.

Finally, we express our thanks to a number of institutions and individuals whose assistance was vital for the preparation of *Vaughan Williams and His World*: Chris Scobie, Lead Curator, Music Manuscripts and Music Collections, and the Music Reference Team at the British Library; Rosalba Varallo Recchia and the staff of the Seely G. Mudd Manuscript Library, Princeton University; the staff of the Bodleian Library, Oxford; the staff of the Fitzwilliam Museum, Cambridge University; the Master and Fellows of Trinity College, Cambridge; the Royal College of Music; Bryn Mawr College; the staff of the John Rylands Library at the University of Manchester; Oxford University Press; conductor and scholar Alan Tongue; Benjamin Nicholas, Reed Rubin Director of Music at Merton College, Oxford; Peter Gilliver of the Oxford Bach Choir; the composer Anthony Powers; and, especially, Hugh Cobbe, director of the Vaughan Williams Charitable Trust.

Byron Adams
Los Angeles

Daniel M. Grimley
Oxford

Ralph Vaughan Williams: Man and Music
An Introduction

BYRON ADAMS AND DANIEL M. GRIMLEY

In Elias Canetti's memoir *Party in the Blitz*, which recalls his years in London during the Second World War, he is often sharply critical of members of the British intelligentsia such as Bertrand Russell, Iris Murdoch, and especially T. S. Eliot. Canetti's disapproval did not, however, extend to Ralph Vaughan Williams:

> It has often puzzled me that great musicians are not better people than they are. In my young days I used to think that the activity by and of itself would make them better people, but this one man, whom I knew for ten or twelve years, remained alive and bright to a great age, and was incapable of a mean thought, let alone a mean action. Such a remark from someone like myself, who takes a sharp view of his fellow men, may seem implausible. But I insist on it: whatever notions one might have of a great-souled man had become truth in this one musician, and that in spite of a fame that lasted for four decades or more. . . . If, after some time, you reach the unshakeable conviction that the man really is as he appears to be, he stays alive for another dozen years, and then is buried in Westminster Abbey.[1]

Canetti, who was not especially interested in music, is not the only exacting author to have praised Vaughan Williams's character. E. M. Forster, the composer's near neighbor who collaborated on pageants meant to protest the destruction of the British countryside by shoddy development, called him "noble." Characteristically, Forster did qualify his praise, observing that in matters of judgment Vaughan Williams could be a "goose."[2]

Canetti and Forster both admired Vaughan Williams in part due to his ethical convictions, which were broadly progressive for his time and yet simultaneously concerned with preserving what he considered the finest and most authentic of English traditions. In their essay titled "Vaughan Williams's Common Ground," Sarah Collins and Daniel M. Grimley observe that the composer was one of those "Victorian radical liberals" like Forster, "who saw themselves charged with a public responsibility to continue a tradition of incremental democratic reform set in motion by their forebears." Although these ideals became more difficult to sustain in the face of two world wars and massive generational shifts in British society, by the early 1930s Vaughan Williams had embraced the political internationalism that he found in Walt Whitman's Transcendentalist vision of a united humanity. In his essay on Vaughan Williams's journeys to the United States, Byron Adams notes that the composer did not merely rhapsodize about Whitman's "vast similitude" that encompassed all of humanity. He also did the hard work of proselytizing for the Federal Union, a pro-democracy organization founded in 1938 to promote the political and economic union of all European states.[3] Philip Rupprecht provides further context for Vaughan Williams's relationship to modernity through a searching examination of his "masque for dancing," *Job* (1930), while Leon Botstein's magisterial concluding essay illuminates the ways in which the composer's aesthetics and ethical convictions were shaped by the British philosophical, historical, and literary currents of his era.

Vaughan Williams was implacably opposed to dictatorships, whether Fascist or Communist. He made his opposition clear in his correspondence, in lectures and essays, and, as Annika Forkert reveals in her essay, in his music for propaganda films during the Second World War. Just after the start of the war he wrote to Frederick Ogilvie, Director-General of the BBC: "It appears to me that one of the things we are fighting for is a free as opposed to a regimented culture."[4] Late in his life, Vaughan Williams's contempt for totalitarianism can be seen in his letter to the equally elderly composer Rutland Boughton, who had rejoined the Communist Party in 1945: "I believe in freedom and that is why I will not be bullied by Nazis, Fascists and Russians."[5] And in a letter to Jean Sibelius in 1950, as the clouds of the Cold War were descending across Europe, he wrote of music's ability to bring comfort and solace at times of intense crisis and upheaval: "You have lit a candle that shall never be put out."[6]

There was a less flattering side to Vaughan Williams's personality, however, that Canetti never witnessed, though Forster surely must have glimpsed it. O. W. Neighbour, whose essay on Vaughan Williams's late Violin Sonata appears in this volume posthumously, used to imitate Forster's pronounced exasperation with the composer's stubbornness: "If he got an idea in his head, *you – could –* NOT get it out!"[7] Along with this truculence, Vaughan Williams's flashes of anger could be incandescent. Writing to the composer shortly after the premiere of his Fourth Symphony in 1935, Elizabeth Trevelyan declared, "I found your poisonous temper in the Scherzo, contrasted with that rollicking lovable opening of the Trio, *most* exciting."[8] Introducing Vaughan Williams's notes for a lecture that preceded a performance that he conducted of Bach's *St. Matthew Passion* at the Leith Hill Festival, Eric Saylor alludes to his insistence that the smallest details be mastered, such as when he found the choral singers wanting: "Generations of Surrey musicians sweated, swore, and struggled along with Vaughan Williams as they worked to unlock the magic and mystery of the piece under his guidance, inspired by his devotion to the work and its effective realization."

Vaughan Williams's anger was not roused just at musical imperfections, however. He despised cruelty, especially to animals. Henry T. Steggles, who became one of Vaughan Williams's close friends when they both served in the Royal Army Medical Corps during the First World War, recalled, "On one occasion he went and straffed [*sic*] a native in French for alleged ill treatment of a donkey."[9] All of these aspects of the man—perfectionism, righteous indignation, compassion, romanticism, warmth of heart, and aspiration—are reflected in his music, not, however, in an autobiographical manner, but rather through a multiplicity of genres, occasions, and inspirations. Even in his most introspective compositions, his music is never solipsistic. As he wrote to Trevelyan, "A true musician cannot divorce music from real life."[10]

Other elements of Vaughan Williams's character were inculcated by his strict mother, who stressed the virtue of modesty. Vaughan Williams was a tall man, which embarrassed him. The distinguished harpsichordist Ruth Dyson noted:

> Vaughan Williams was a towering figure on the platform. Like many tall people who are modest, he tried to reduce his height by bending his shoulders. He was 6 feet 2 inches in his socks. He made a practice of not being a "great man" in his life as well as in his appearance. If he was talking to people, he would make them feel his equal.[11]

Vaughan Williams was brought up by his mother in a manner that stressed courtesy (especially toward servants and the poor), duty, hard work, and self-discipline. Margaret Vaughan Williams was a niece of Charles Darwin through his wife, Emma (née Wedgwood). Writers have made much of this lineage, but *Period Piece*, a memoir by Gwendolyn "Gwen" Raverat (née Darwin), reveals, inadvertently perhaps, that most of the Darwin-Wedgwoods were philistines regarding art, music, and literature. They insisted that Vaughan Williams take a purely academic degree from Trinity College, Cambridge, which he did with some success. In his essay about the composer's relationship with Cambridge, Julian Rushton notes how much of Vaughan Williams's time as an undergraduate was taken up with music, an art in which most of the Darwin-Wedgwoods evinced little interest. As Raverat writes, "Darwins never cared enough about Art or Fashion, to be much interested in what was Right and Highbrow."[12] Raverat's portrayal of her uncle Leonard Darwin's second wife illustrates the impediments to Vaughan William's musical career that his Darwin-Wedgwood relatives created: "She had a deep distrust of art in all its forms, but particularly of music. . . . Mildred, in her horror of the Arts, was driven into the definite statement, that a man who successfully held a small job at the post office was worth more than the greatest artist in the world!" Raverat's memoir glosses over even more unsavory aspects of the Darwin clan. The drawings scattered throughout the book, and its easy, entertaining prose, can distract from Leonard Darwin's aggressive belief in the pseudo-science of eugenics, although Raverat remarks that she was shocked and "depressed" by his convictions.[13]

Despite the lack of support from most of his mother's side of the family, Vaughan Williams persisted in his musical studies from an early age. Luckily, his mother's sister, Katherine Elizabeth Sophy Wedgwood ("Aunt Sophy," 1842–1911), was interested in music, at least insofar as it should constitute a part of any child's basic education. His later career was conditioned in large part by his early musical experiences: taking violin lessons as a little boy; studying theory through a correspondence course assisted by Aunt Sophy; struggling with the piano and organ; and, above all, singing.[14] His experiences as a choral singer and as a violist encouraged a lifelong habit of thinking in terms of melodic lines. His melodic thought was not confined to fashioning memorable tunes, however. It informed the unfolding of extended structures through thematic metamorphosis, such as occurs during the first movement of his Third Symphony (*A Pastoral Symphony*, 1921). Melodic motifs are spun into paragraphs that in turn create entire sustained formal designs. Herbert Howells wrote that "'tune' never ceases. One after another come tributary themes, short in themselves, and so fashioned as to throw one into doubting their being new; one suspects that, in them, what was a part has become a whole."[15] In other words, Vaughan Williams espoused the formal concept of the *grande ligne* taught by Gabriel Fauré to Nadia Boulanger and to Maurice Ravel (Vaughan Williams's own teacher), both of whom attended Fauré's composition class at the Paris

Conservatory. Vaughan Williams was already adept at extended linearity and modal inflection before he began to study with Ravel in December 1907. While Ravel introduced him to new ways of scoring—"He showed me how to orchestrate in points of colour rather than in lines"—and thinking about music, those lessons confirmed his predilection for the modes he found in British folksongs as well as his deep engagement with Tudor composers such as William Byrd and Thomas Tallis.[16] Ravel's tutelage, allied to an appreciation of Debussy's empiricism, provided Vaughan Williams with a fresh approach to harmony: chords were no longer bound by the techniques of "common practice" as he had been taught at the Royal College of Music, but could instead be related through new patterns of association and transformation based on color, interval, and tone.

Having experienced censure and discouragement as a composition student, Vaughan Williams was respectful of his students at the Royal College of Music. In her essay on Vaughan Williams's long relationship with the RCM, Erica Siegel writes that the composer believed in the importance of encouragement, a marked contrast to the denigrating critiques favored by his teacher there, Charles Villiers Stanford. Vaughan Williams's 1897 lessons in Berlin with the far more genial Max Bruch enabled him to assimilate the post-Beethovenian techniques that characterized much nineteenth-century German music. This accomplishment has only come to light in recent years with the publication of early chamber music scores, such as his suavely assured String Quartet in C Minor (1898). As a pedagogue, Vaughan Williams followed Bruch's kindly and positive example, which resulted in his encouraging several of his women pupils who would become superb composers, such as Elizabeth Maconchy and Grace Williams. As Siegel observes, Vaughan Williams's staunch support of these women was an anomaly during that era, both at the RCM in particular and in the male-dominated British musical establishment in general.

None of this would matter whatsoever if Vaughan Williams had not achieved great and lasting success as a composer. Simply put, he is the most important British composer of symphonies of the last century, and his nine works in this genre are comparable to those of Sibelius, Nielsen, Shostakovich, and Roussel. Throughout Vaughan Williams's career, each new symphony was greeted with keen attention on the part of performers, listeners, and the press, both in Britain and abroad. In this volume, Alain Frogley traces the critical reception of the Ninth Symphony, which was premiered just weeks before Vaughan Williams's death in 1958. In addition to symphonies, concertos, and other orchestral music, Vaughan Williams composed five operas, one of which, *Riders to the Sea* (1925–32), is ensconced in the repertory, and he produced many fine pieces of choral music (both unaccompanied and accompanied, from oratorio to anthem), chamber music, and songs. These scores sit alongside music that transcends the established boundaries of genre: the *Fantasia on a Theme of Thomas Tallis* for string quartet and double string orchestra (1910, revised 1913 and 1919); *Flos campi* for viola solo, wordless chamber chorus, and small orchestra (1925); and the popular *The Lark Ascending* (1914; revised 1920), which Vaughan Williams called a "romance," for violin and small orchestra.

Vaughan Williams has an additional legacy, however, as a composer whose hymns, such as "For All the Saints" (SINE NOMINE) and "Come Down, O Love Divine" (DOWN AMPNEY), are sung constantly in churches around the world.[17] Bianco da Siena's text of "Come Down, O Love Divine," has been translated into Spanish and has become popular with Spanish-speaking Roman Catholic parishes, and millions of people have sung Vaughan Williams's tunes, many unaware of the composer's name or status in the concert hall.[18] Most of the hymns were written especially for *The English Hymnal* (1906, revised and expanded in 1933), which was the project of a group of leftist Anglo-Catholics headed by Rev. Percy Dearmer, who, like Vaughan Williams, espoused what might be called "socialist tendencies." In addition, his anthems, such as *O Taste and See*, composed for the 1953 coronation of Queen Elizabeth II, are popular with church choirs and their directors.

Considering the substantial number of sacred texts set by Vaughan Williams during his lifetime, the composer's thoughts on metaphysics have become a topic of speculation. His second wife, Ursula (née Lock, formally Wood, 1911–2007), engaged with this question in her biography of her husband:

> Although a declared agnostic, he was able, all through his life, to set to music words in the accepted terms of Christian revelation as if they meant to him what they must have meant to George Herbert or to Bunyan. He had returned [from active service in the First World War] to *Pilgrim's Progress*, and was writing a one-act opera, *The Shepherds of the Delectable Mountains* as well as the unaccompanied *Mass in G minor* for Gustav [Holst] and his Whitsuntide singers. He said cheerfully, "There is no reason why an atheist could not write a good Mass."[19]

Earlier in the book, she made the much-quoted observation, "He was an atheist during his later years at [his school] Charterhouse and at Cambridge, though he later drifted into a cheerful agnosticism; he was never a professing Christian."[20] But organist William Cole, who succeeded

Vaughan Williams as the conductor of the Leith Hill Festival and knew him well—and doubtless was aware of Ursula Vaughan Williams's own implacable atheism—recalled in 1996: "As to religion, I am completely at odds with Ursula on this. She was trying to prove that he was an agnostic, and it is completely wrong. . . . He had a certain feeling."[21]

Vaughan Williams rarely discussed religious matters openly. On those rare occasions when he did so, his language was often subtly qualified: in his statement that there is no reason why "an atheist could not write a good Mass," he avoided overtly declaring himself an atheist as he had done when he was an undergraduate at Cambridge.[22] However, there is plenty of evidence to support Ursula Vaughan Williams's assertion that "he was never a professing Christian," such as her husband throwing cold water on a possible informal offer made in 1931 on behalf of the Archbishop of Canterbury to bestow a Lambeth Doctorate in Church Music upon him: "I feel that such things are really not for me—I have no real connection with anything ecclesiastical & no longer count myself a member of the Church of England."[23]

Michael Kennedy wrote that "the religion of Vaughan Williams's life was music," but this observation does not fully take into account the mystical, supernal, and, in the broadest possible sense, "religious" aspects of his devotion to music.[24] In a 1920 article "The Letter and the Spirit," introduced and annotated in this volume by Ceri Owen, Vaughan Williams writes, "The human, visible, audible and intelligible media which artists (of all kinds) use, are symbols not of other visible and audible things but of what lies beyond sense and knowledge."[25] In the first of the Mary Flexner Lectures that Vaughan Williams delivered at Bryn Mawr in 1932, later printed as the opening chapter of *National Music*, he declared, "A work of art is like a theophany which takes different forms to different beholders," a statement replete with both philosophical and theological implications—and he just leaves it there, explaining no further.[26]

Music was not just the love of Vaughan Williams's life, it was his all-consuming passion. He worked hard to master the intricacies of the technique of composition and often spent eight hours a day at his desk writing music. He was profoundly self-critical and thought nothing of revising scores after their premieres.[27] He listened to new music even if he did not especially like what he heard; he habitually attended concerts and the opera; he taught and encouraged younger composers; he conducted at the annual Leith Hill Musical Festival, which he founded with his sister Margaret ("Meggie"), from 1905 to 1953. His musical and aesthetic opinions were often forthright and at times recall Forster's words about his intransigence.

The trait that probably most endeared Canetti to Vaughan Williams was the selflessness of his devotion to music. He lived in music as saints are said to live in God, and, like them, he was immune to self-aggrandizement. Vaughan Williams knew the Authorized Version—that is, the "King James Version"—of the Bible in detail and committed many passages to memory. The composer's father, Arthur Vaughan Williams (1835–1875), was a member of the Anglican clergy who died when his youngest son was three years old. Arthur and his wife, Margaret (née Wedgwood, 1843–1937), were married in Christ Church, Coldharbour, Surrey, a church whose origins were decidedly evangelical.[28] But, as noted above, Vaughan Williams did not follow his parents' fervent Anglican faith. Like St. Paul the Apostle, allusions to whose epistles are scattered throughout his writings, Vaughan Williams was an evangelist, not for any particular religious faith, but for music. Possessor of a sharp wit, far from pious, a lover of good food and drink who relished the company of beautiful, accomplished women, Vaughan Williams was no ascetic and no saint in the accepted sense of that term.[29] He was modest and courteous, but not humble, for he knew his worth. Vaughan Williams strove to realize fully his vision of the kingdoms and multitudes that he intuited lay beyond the boundaries of "sense and knowledge." Less than a fortnight before his death, the musicologist and author Sylvia Townsend Warner (1893–1978) playfully asked Vaughan Williams how he would choose to be reincarnated in the world to come. Warner quotes the octogenarian composer's serious reply: "Music, he said, music. But in the next world, I shan't be doing music, with all the striving and disappointments, I shall be being it."[30]

NOTES

1. Elias Canetti, *Party in the Blitz: The English Years*, trans. Michael Hoffmann (New York: New Directions Books, 2005), 178. Canetti (1905–1994), who lived in London from 1938 until the 1970s, is best remembered for his volume *Crowds and Power* (1960). He won the Nobel Prize for Literature in 1981. In the course of his brief chapter titled "Vaughan Williams," Canetti alludes to the unconventional domestic arrangements that existed in Vaughan Williams's London home, Hanover Terrace, for the last six years of the composer's life (177).

2. Philip Nicholas Furbank, *E. M. Forster: A Life,* vol. 2: *Polycrates' Ring (1914–1970)* (London: Secker and Warburg, 1978), 226.

3. For a revisionist view of this topic, see Michael Burgess, *The British Tradition of Federalism* (London: Leicester University Press, 1995), 142.

4. Vaughan Williams to Frederick Ogilvie, Director General of the BBC, 18 October 1939, Vaughan Williams Letters (henceforth "VWL") 1609.

5. Ralph Vaughan Williams to Rutland Boughton, VWL2448. In 1956, Boughton repudiated Soviet communism in reaction to the Hungarian Uprising; for Boughton's complicated relationship to the Communist Party, see Michael Hurd, *Rutland Boughton and the Glastonbury Festivals* (Oxford: Clarendon Press, 1995), 229–31.

6. Vaughan Williams to Sibelius, 3 December 1950, Finnish National Archive, Sibelius Collection Kansio 31. Vaughan Williams wrote to Sibelius directly on at least six separate occasions between 1946 and 1955, though his admiration for Sibelius's work had begun much earlier in his career. Sibelius died in 1957, the year before Vaughan Williams.

7. Furbank, *E. M. Forster,* 226n1. Byron Adams attests that the way in which Furbank transcribes Neighbour's anecdote is not whatsoever an exaggeration.

8. Quoted in Michael Kennedy, *The Works of Ralph Vaughan Williams*, 2nd ed. (Oxford: Oxford University Press, 1980), 245.

9. Henry T. Steggles, "Dr. Ralph Vaughan Williams, O.M.," *The R.C.M. Magazine* 55/1 (February 1959): 22.

10. Ralph Vaughan Williams, *The Letters of Ralph Vaughan Williams: 1895–1958*, ed. Hugh Cobbe (Oxford: Oxford University Press, 2008), 288.

11. Ruth Dyson (1917–1997), quoted in Stephen Connock, *Toward the Sun Rising: Ralph Vaughan Williams Remembered* (Tonbridge, Kent: Albion Music, 2018), 127.

12. Gwen Raverat, *Period Piece: A Cambridge Childhood* (London: Faber and Faber, 1952, repr. 1960), 126.

13. Ibid., 199–200. Discussing population control, Leonard Darwin opined that "those who believe that venereal diseases may injuriously affect the inborn qualities of all the descendants of the diseased for many generations must hold that the lethal and sterilizing effects of these diseases are a blessing in disguise on account of their influence in stamping out such harmful hereditary effects." See Leonard Darwin, *The Need for Eugenic Reform* (London: John Murray, 1926), 77–78.

14. For an account of Vaughan Williams's early musical education, see Byron Adams, "Vaughan Williams's Musical Apprenticeship" in *The Cambridge Companion to Vaughan Williams*, ed. Alain Frogley and Aidan J. Thomson (Cambridge: Cambridge University Press, 2013), 29–38.

15. Herbert Howells, "Vaughan Williams's 'Pastoral Symphony,'" *Music & Letters* 3/2 (April 1922): 122–32, at 125. Elsewhere, Howells wrote of the second movement and finale as "'visible silence' . . . as if great distances were overlooked" (130). The phrase is of course a reference to the end of the first verse of Dante Gabriel Rossetti's sonnet "Silent Noon": "'Tis visible silence, still as the hour-glass," which Vaughan Williams set as part of his song cycle *The House of Life*.

16. Ralph Vaughan Williams, "A Musical Autobiography," in Ralph Vaughan Williams, *National Music and Other Essays*, ed. Michael Kennedy, 2nd ed. (Oxford: Oxford University Press, 1986), 191.

17. In hymnody, tunes can be separated from their original texts. Therefore, a convention has arisen to designate text and identify tune: the first few words of the text are cited in quotation marks ("For All the Saints"); the tune is named, in this case by Vaughan Williams, and that name is designated in capital letters (SINE NOMINE). Furthermore, this convention includes the practice of completely citing the first few words of the text in quotation marks, followed by the name of the tune in capital letters surrounded by parentheses. For example, this text, "For All the Saints" was written by William Walsham How (1823–1897) and published in 1864. It was first set to music by Joseph Barnby (1838–1896) to a tune called SARUM. To identify this hymn unequivocally, it should be cited as "For All the Saints" (SARUM). DOWN AMPNEY was named after the Gloucestershire village where Vaughan Williams was born on 12 October 1872.

18. Bianco da Siena (ca. 1350–ca.1434) was an Italian woolworker and a member of the Order of Jesuati. His poem was translated into English by Frederick Littlemore (1833–1890), an Anglo-Irish member of the Anglican clergy.

19. Ursula Vaughan Williams, *R.V.W.: A Biography of Ralph Vaughan Williams* (London: Oxford University Press, 1964, repr. with corrections 1984), 138. Although dedicated to Holst and his Whitsuntide Singers, when he composed the Mass in G Minor Vaughan Williams doubtless had in mind the choir of men and boys at Westminster (Roman Catholic) Cathedral in London trained by the Master of Music, Richard Runciman Terry (1878–1938). Vaughan Williams dedicated his a cappella motet *O vos omnes* to Terry; this motet was first sung under his direction on 13 April 1922 during the liturgy for Maundy Thursday. As Terry's biographer observes, "The crown of those modern works was, of course, the *Mass in G Minor* by Vaughan Williams, last and greatest of liturgical pieces written specially for Terry's performance at Westminster . . . the Mass was first sung on 12 March 1923." See Hilda Andrews, *Westminster Retrospect: A Memoir of Sir Richard Terry* (London: Oxford University Press, 1948), 134.

20. Ursula Vaughan Williams, *R.V.W.*, 29.

21. Stephen Connock, *Toward the Sun Rising*, 101. Ruth Dyson remembered, "Agnostic as he was, Vaughan Williams would often creep into [William Cole's] contributions [as organist] to Choral Evensong." See Connock, *Toward the Sun Rising*, 130.

22. Bertrand Russell, quoted in Kennedy, *The Works of Ralph Vaughan Williams*, 42. Russell's letter is quoted again in the documents chapter, "Tracing a Biography: Michael Kennedy's Correspondence Concerning *The Works of Ralph Vaughan Williams*," in the current volume.

23. Vaughan Williams to Frederick Dwelly, Dean of Liverpool (Anglican) Cathedral, VWL1148; see Vaughan Williams, *Letters of Ralph Vaughan Williams*, 199. The editor of this volume, Hugh Cobbe, dates this missive as "after October 1931." The Archbishop of Canterbury at the time of this exchange was Cosmo Gordon Lang (1864–1945), 1st Baron Lang of Lambeth, for whose 1928 enthronement Vaughan Williams composed his Te Deum in G Major.

24. Kennedy, *The Works of Ralph Vaughan Williams*, 42.

25. Ralph Vaughan Williams, "The Letter and the Spirit," *Music & Letters* 1/2 (April 1920): 88.

26. Ralph Vaughan Williams, *National Music* (Oxford: Oxford University Press, 1934), 6. See also Byron Adams, "Scripture, Church, and culture: biblical texts in the works of Ralph Vaughan Williams," in *Vaughan Williams Studies*, ed. Alain Frogley (Cambridge: Cambridge University Press, 1996), 109-17.

27. Concerning Vaughan Williams's extensive revisions to his Sixth Symphony, see Byron Adams, "The Stages of Revision of Vaughan Williams's Sixth Symphony," in

Vaughan Williams Essays, ed. Byron Adams and Robin Wells (Aldershot: Ashgate, 2003), 1–16.

28. Celia Newbury, ed., *Vaughan Williams in Dorking: A collection of personal reminiscences of the composer Dr. Ralph Vaughan Williams* (Dorking, Surrey: The Local History Group of the Dorking & Leith Hill District Preservation Society, 1979), 1.

29. The composer Roger Quilter (1877–1953) once expounded to Vaughan Williams how difficult it was to compose songs, to which Vaughan Williams replied that Quilter ought to try writing a symphony, as "they're ever so easy." See Valerie Langfield, *Roger Quilter: His Life and Music* (Woodbridge, Suffolk: Boydell Press, 2002), 236.

30. Sylvia Townsend Warner, *Letters of Sylvia Townsend Warner*, ed. William Maxwell (London: Chatto & Windus, 1982), 168. Like many writers, Warner kept a diary; the entry for 13 August 1958 tells of the visit by Ralph and Ursula Vaughan Williams to the house in Frome Vauchurch, Dorset, that she shared with her lover, the poet Valentine Ackland. In her diary, Warner tells the same story that she relates in her letter to the American composer Paul Nordoff, which is dated the same day and cited above, recalling the composer's words with only slightly different wording. Warner also recorded Ursula Vaughan Williams's observation, "Ralph only dreams music." See Sylvia Townsend Warner, *The Diaries of Sylvia Townsend Warner* (London: Chatto & Windus, 1994), 248–49. On 19 September, Warner listened in to the BBC broadcast of the Vaughan Williams memorial service in Westminster Abbey, noting that "the BBC delayed the weather & news. Almost as grand as the Abbey burial itself." See Warner, *Diaries*, 250.

Vaughan Williams and Cambridge

JULIAN RUSHTON

The University of Cambridge played a substantial role in Vaughan Williams's life beyond his years of student residence (1892–95), during which he would have been required to "keep terms" in Trinity College. His father had studied at Christ Church, Oxford, but Cambridge may have been chosen because his mother had relatives living there, including three of her cousins, sons of "Uncle Charles" Darwin. Their children were Ralph's second cousins, although some years younger. Two of the Darwin cousins were artistically gifted: the poet Frances Cornford and the artist and theater designer Gwen (Gwendolen) Raverat.[1]

Gwen's memoir, *Period Piece*, includes a Darwin family tree but does not include the Wedgwood connections that linked the Darwins to Vaughan Williams. (The composer was a great-nephew of Charles Darwin, whose mother was a Wedgwood.) One Wedgwood relation who visited the family home, to Gwen's great delight, was Ralph Wedgwood (addressed in the composer's letters by the nickname "Randolph"). It was Gwen who reported the family view that "that foolish young man, Ralph Vaughan Williams" would never go far with his music. "Aunt Etty" (Charles Darwin's daughter Henrietta) wrote in a letter that "he can't play the simplest thing decently." This would imply that the family thought of him as a performer rather than as a possible composer.[2] Vaughan Williams seems not to have set any of Frances's poems, but he collaborated more than once with Gwen.

Also living in Cambridge was the elder daughter of Herbert William Fisher, formerly a friend of Vaughan Williams's father. Florence Fisher had married Frederick William Maitland, medieval historian and professor of English law at Downing College, where the Historical Society later bore his name. Vaughan Williams renewed this family connection and played chamber music with friends at Downing; Fisher's younger daughter Adeline was an occasional participant playing piano and cello. She and Vaughan Williams became engaged to be married soon after he left Cambridge. Two Maitland daughters were bridesmaids at their wedding, and Vaughan Williams set poems by one of them, Fredegond Shove.[3]

Nicknames seem to have been common among friends in the academic community. In a letter to them both from 1897, the composer addressed the Maitland sisters as "Dear Gaga and Vuff."[4]

At the time, there was no formal program of musical study at Cambridge leading to the standard first-degree qualification, Bachelor of Arts; what is now the "Music Tripos" was established only in 1947. Vaughan Williams's program of study for the BA was History, and his musical activities may have been regarded by Trinity College as extracurricular, including some that would now be considered academic. He was, however, permitted to work toward the nominally inferior degree of Bachelor of Music (BMus), which may have negatively affected his historical studies. The BMus program, which included exercises in strict composition, may have been his principal motivation for studying at Cambridge because at that time university degrees were of higher social and professional status than a diploma from a music college. Vaughan Williams achieved a respectable Second Class BA in History. This was technically a higher degree than his teacher Charles Villiers Stanford had obtained: the Cambridge Professor of Music had received only Third Class Honours in Classics.[5]

Most senior Cambridge musicians were nominally lecturers, despite the absence of a BA course in music, but they mainly worked as college organists. Some were in charge of a full choral foundation, with boy trebles educated in a choir school; Trinity had its own school, like King's and St. John's Colleges today.[6] Alto and lower voices were then sung by "lay clerks"; these singers, who were not students, could spend a longer time in the choir than the three years typical of today's choral scholars. Stanford was organist of Trinity until 1892. He was succeeded by Alan Gray, Vaughan Williams's organ teacher, who was somewhat dubious about his pupil's musical future. Like most college organists, Gray was also a composer. The works of these organist-composers enlarged the repertoire of chapel music, and some of it is still in use today.[7] The organist of King's was A. H. Mann, and the elderly George Garrett was organist of St. John's College as well as being the "University organist." There is no reason to suppose that these two had much to do with an obscure BMus student from another college, but one music lecturer who did was a composer from Ireland, Charles Wood, who had been teaching at Gonville and Caius College since 1888, having earlier taught at the Royal College of Music (RCM). Wood succeeded Garrett as "university lecturer in harmony and counterpoint" in 1897, and he succeeded Stanford as the university's Professor of Music; his tenure lasted until his death in 1926.

Stanford was Professor of Music from 1887 to 1924, but he did not teach Vaughan Williams as an undergraduate. The professor's duties were not onerous, and Stanford retained his connection with the RCM in London. Such pluralism was not unusual; William Sterndale Bennett had been professor at Cambridge and Principal of the Royal Academy of Music, and Hubert Parry combined the equivalent appointments at Oxford and the RCM. Stanford loosened his Cambridge connections in the 1890s without resigning the professorship, visiting Cambridge to deliver lectures or tutorials at Trinity—there was no music faculty building at the time. However, early in his tenure Stanford had been busily engaged in the reform of music degrees. Prior to that, Vaughan Williams could have studied for the BMus without having to live in Cambridge; Stanford insisted on three years' residence, which was possible if the student was registered to take another subject for the BA.[8] Hence, despite passing the BMus examination in 1894, Vaughan Williams could only graduate formally as Bachelor of Music the following year, alongside his BA in History.

Vaughan Williams explained his BMus qualification to a friend, the philosopher G. E. Moore, who was perhaps puzzled that he was not yet allowed to proceed to a degree:

> The examination I have passed is supposed to certify my knowledge of 4 and 5 part counterpoint and fugue as well as harmony and all kindred subjects. I learned fugue under Bridge and, at Cambridge, with Charles Wood, who to my mind had the most intelligent idea of what a fugue should be.[9]

Vaughan Williams's BMus submission included a four-movement "Hymn," *Vexilla Regis*, with canonic writing in the first movement and a concluding fugue. This is now held in the Cambridge University Library.[10]

Vaughan Williams's first year coincided with the fiftieth anniversary of the Cambridge University Musical Society (CUMS), which the university honored in June 1893 by conferring honorary Doctor of Music degrees on Tchaikovsky, Saint-Saëns, Arrigo Boito, and Max Bruch (who later taught Vaughan Williams).[11] These composers each conducted one of their own works for CUMS; a professional orchestra had been hired for the occasion and had been rehearsed in London. The exception was Saint-Saëns, who played the solo piano part of his fantasy *Africa* with Stanford as conductor.[12] The celebration concluded with a banquet in King's College for a hundred paying guests, Vaughan Williams among them, perhaps invited because Maitland was host to Tchaikovsky at Downing College; there the Russian composer met Adeline Fisher, who, according to the composer's second wife Ursula, "pinned roses in his buttonhole" before he joined his distinguished colleagues at the ceremony where "they all received their honorary degrees."[13] After this anniversary celebration, Stanford, who had conducted CUMS for many years, resigned his position, no doubt because of pressure of work in London.

Nowadays members of the CUMS orchestra and chorus are almost all drawn from the much larger student body, but they originally included both "town" (Cambridge residents) as well as "gown" (students and university staff) members. The orchestra required professional support that Stanford was in a good position to recruit from London, only fifty miles away. For many years after the 1890s male students heavily outnumbered female students, for whom two colleges had been founded shortly before Vaughan Williams's birth. Women could study and take the same examinations as their male peers, but were not allowed to proceed to degrees until after the Second World War. Stanford admitted women to "associate" membership of CUMS, perhaps less from any principle of equality than out of necessity, especially for the chorus. Women were tolerated in the orchestra, at least for rehearsal purposes; Gwen Darwin (Raverat), then about eighteen, played second flute under the kindly direction of "Mr. Dent and Clive Carey."[14] Carey, a versatile musician and man of the theater, and Edward J. Dent, the musicologist and composer who succeeded Charles Wood as professor of music, became friends of Vaughan Williams over many years. Vaughan Williams's chief contribution to CUMS seems to have been as a timpanist; he also collected funds to hire the contrabassoon for Beethoven's Fifth Symphony. His most important practical music making was conducting a small choir on Saturday evenings, prior to Sunday performances of a Mass, for instance by Schubert; this experience was a valuable part of his preparation for life after leaving university.[15]

Few of Vaughan Williams's works were heard during his time at Cambridge. He was a member of the Cambridge University Musical Club (CUMC) and attended its concerts regularly. His four-part male-voice setting of Shelley's "Music When Soft Voices Die" (1891) was heard twice at a CUMC concert in 1893, but the performance was not repeated by audience demand: at the first attempt one of the tenors perseveringly carried on despite having lost his place. Another performance was of "The Virgin's Cradle Song" (1894; the text translated from the Latin "Dormi Jesu" by Samuel Taylor Coleridge), which was presented at a CUMC concert on 3 November 1894; the composer himself accompanied the singer.[16] Vaughan Williams attended these concerts mostly in order to hear chamber music performed by students and local amateurs, but he also enjoyed the sessions devoted to comic songs that occasionally concluded the evening's entertainment.[17]

Figure 1. Ralph ("Randolph") Wedgwood and his cousin Vaughan Williams at Cambridge, mid-1890s.

At Cambridge, Vaughan Williams made several acquaintances who became distinguished in later life, though not as musicians. Through his cousin Ralph ("Randolph") Wedgwood he met members of the intellectual "conversazione" known as the Apostles. Vaughan Williams was not himself an Apostle, but he knew the philosopher Moore, the mathematician, philosopher, and pacifist Bertrand Russell, and the economist John Maynard Keynes, whose brother Geoffrey married another Darwin, Gwen's sister Margaret. No doubt to prepare for his final examinations for his History BA, Vaughan Williams joined reading parties of Trinity friends on the Isle of

Skye, in Cornwall, and at the village of Seatoller, Borrowdale, in Cumberland. Participants included Moore and the historian G. M. Trevelyan, later Master of Trinity (known as "Trevy").[18] The Seatoller visitors' book in March 1895 contains the signature "R. Vaughan-Williams" (*sic*); it seems he had left the party early, and the signature—hyphenated in a manner that he never employed—was added as a well-meaning but clumsy forgery by a member of the reading party.

As Byron Adams has pointed out, these acquaintances, all members of the Apostles, had an unsurprising effect on Vaughan Williams's religious convictions during this period. Bertrand Russell informed Michael Kennedy that at Cambridge Vaughan Williams was open about his atheism.[19] Nevertheless, he liked to hear the music of Anglican services in the college chapels and the magnificent cathedral in nearby Ely, which he easily reached on a bicycle due to the very flat terrain. Sometimes he was on horseback, and when the rivers froze he reached Ely on skates.[20]

Having obtained his bachelor's degrees and fulfilled the residence requirement, Vaughan Williams was qualified after a prescribed lapse of time—"eight years standing from admission" to the BA—to "supplicate" the University for the degree of Doctor of Music.[21] This was not done out of vanity, although he did like to be addressed as "Dr. Vaughan Williams." Despite earlier family scepticism and Stanford's sometimes denigrating comments, he never doubted that he was a composer; but since he was newly married and settled in London, and was not an advanced performer, he needed the credibility of a doctorate to establish himself within the profession. There was no British equivalent to the Prix de Rome, which Berlioz, Debussy, and others attempted for the same reason. Vaughan Williams set to work well in advance of the earliest date at which he could take the degree, which was 1900. He passed the examination in March 1899, when he paid a short visit to Cambridge, asking Moore to book accommodation at Trinity, no doubt for the formalities that included an oral examination and tests in counterpoint. His examiners were Stanford, Precentor of Eton College Charles Harford Lloyd, and Master of the Queen's Music Walter Parratt.[22] Later that month he wrote to Gustav Holst: "I have good reason to believe my counterpoint and viva (Mus. Doc.) were satisfactory."[23] He proceeded to the degree in 1901.

To obtain his doctorate Vaughan Williams had only to compose one work, but it had to be large; the genre, form, and content were not left entirely to the composer's free will. The work had to fulfil specific requirements, unlike today when the requirement for the DMus is submission of "a portfolio of compositions" with none of the stipulations with which Vaughan Williams had to wrestle. While the text chosen for setting could be sacred or secular, the doctoral exercise had to be a vocal composition involving solo voices and a chorus written in eight parts for at least some of the time; and it must be scored for "full band" (then the academic term for "symphony orchestra").

Within this substantial choral and orchestral work Vaughan Williams had to demonstrate mastery of techniques he had studied earlier with Frederick Bridge at the RCM and with Wood at Cambridge for the BMus: strict canonic imitation and fugue. This was an open invitation to model parts of the work on techniques from the Baroque period or earlier. Another requirement was to compose a movement, overture, or interlude for the orchestra alone; this had to be in classical first-movement sonata form, which had become increasingly rule-bound since becoming defined by theorists such as Anton Reicha and A. B. Marx. A later acquaintance of Vaughan Williams, W. H. Hadow, who wrote and lectured on music at Oxford from 1890, even alludes to "the laws of form," while admitting they were not immutable.[24]

For his text Vaughan Williams chose sections from the Ordinary of the Mass. The Latin Mass and Requiem had long been treated as musical forms not necessarily intended for the Roman Catholic liturgy; the texts were set by non-believers such as Verdi (whose Requiem Vaughan Williams admired) and Protestants such as Stanford who wrote both a Mass in G (1893) and a Requiem (1897). Vaughan Williams may have preferred a Latin text because its conventionality enabled him to concentrate on displays of musical competence. As he wrote to Ralph Wedgwood, "They're such fine words, and you get such good climaxes out of them." But setting texts that engaged him emotionally—the poetry of Swinburne, Rossetti, or Whitman—could never be damned with the epithet "academic."

Vaughan Williams's later Mass in G Minor (1922) sets the entire Ordinary, but what has come to be known as "A Cambridge Mass" sets about half the text: the long Credo in G, and the shorter Sanctus, Benedictus, and Hosanna in D. He had already set the Gloria, with organ accompaniment, at the RCM—"done with Dr Parry."[25] His Credo setting includes a four-part canon as a suitably disciplined technique to evoke the Church ("Et unam sanctam catholicam et apostolicam ecclesiam") and ends with a massive "Amen" fugue, emulating numerous composers who have taken this opportunity to expand on the vocally grateful syllable "*A*" without the need to consider its liturgical context. When the work was recorded, the *Vaughan Williams Society Journal* ran a set of reviews: one writer asked "Why . . . the interminably long fugue?"[26] The widely modulating fugue is some two hundred measures out of nearly six hundred in the whole Credo, but this was an academic exercise, not something Vaughan Williams would otherwise have composed. The glowing climax to the Credo of the Mass in G Minor expands the last words ("Et vitam venturi saeculi. Amen") but not as a fugue. Finally, the "Cambridge" Credo reaches its end with a fanfare and a massive G-major chord for orchestra and full organ. Much of the choral writing in the Credo and the Sanctus is in eight parts, and the two four-part choirs are used antiphonally to good effect.

Some liturgical Mass settings include an Offertory—in the Requiem, "Domine Jesu Christe"—or a motet to fit a date in the Church calendar. Vaughan Williams instead called the orchestral interlude in sonata form "Offertorium." Including such a movement in the regulations was no doubt intended to display orchestration skills, freed from the task of accompanying voices. Vaughan Williams's effort is suitably competent and has imaginative touches. The first theme, derived from the setting of "et resurrexit" in the preceding Credo, is presented on strings, then on woodwind after a brass intervention, and again as a *tutti*. A syncopated accompaniment, as in Schubert's "Unfinished" Symphony, prepares a second theme group, more lyrical and lightly scored as was customary at this stage in sonata-form movements. The second thematic group begins with a short canon between cellos and violins. Brass and timpani interrupt, but serenity is restored for the required cadences in the dominant. The exposition is repeated, a practice that had not yet quite fallen out of favor. By way of "development" the second theme is presented in new harmonic guises before a vigorous fugal passage. The return to the opening theme is economically handled, with no literal return to the opening. The point of recapitulation is marked by the brass intervention (originally measure 5, now measure 196) followed by the woodwind version of the theme. The second theme area and coda rework the material inventively, showing the composer's acquaintance with the finest classical models. The Sanctus powerfully evokes the "Lord God of Hosts," followed by a lengthy fugal "Hosanna." The gentler Benedictus uses only the solo vocal quartet, making a fine contrast with the repeat of the "Hosanna."

With hindsight, one might conclude that the whole work is thoroughly worthy of a doctorate. The autograph, having followed his BMus work into Cambridge University Library, was forgotten perhaps even by its composer.[27] In 1964, Michael Kennedy noted its existence in the first edition of his survey, *The Works of Ralph Vaughan Williams*.[28] In his catalogues of the composer's oeuvre, Kennedy listed the sections and instrumentation. After Kennedy's initial inspection of the score, it returned to the shelves until 2007, when its quality, which Kennedy described as "the real Vaughan Williams on the way to greatness," was recognized by the conductor and scholar Alan Tongue.[29] Tongue edited the published score and also conducted a performance at Fairfield Hall, Croydon, on 3 March 2011 that was recorded and issued as a compact disc distributed by Albion Records.[30] Unlike some other composers, Vaughan Williams seems not to have been unduly troubled by the survival of works he may have considered uncharacteristic or simply juvenile, but he also showed no interest in reviving them. For a time his widow, Ursula, prohibited modern performances of these works, an interdict that she withdrew before her death.

Compositions and Premieres in and for Cambridge

Vaughan Williams was keenly involved in helping to organize the activities of CUMS, even serving as secretary for three terms. After his period of residence, most large-scale performances of his music at Cambridge were organized by CUMS, but they were not commissioned by the society. In 1909, however, incidental music and choruses for Aristophanes's *The Wasps* were commissioned by the Greek Play Committee, which selected dramas from the fifth-century BCE Athenian repertoire, both comic and tragic, to be performed in the original language.[31] In the tradition, which continues as a triennial event, performances are directed by senior staff or professionals, and the actors are students. Until after the Second World War Athenian practice was adhered to in that the cast was all male, with few exceptions. The play is put on in winter, well ahead of the examination season, and no attempt is made to replicate the original performing conditions: outdoors, with a cast of three actors doubling roles by wearing masks.

Arguments over how much was sung in the Athenian theater affected the origins of opera. The Cambridge society commissioned settings of the choruses (with solo contributions), but all the dialogue is spoken; Athenian dramas were not yet operas. As in many nineteenth-century theaters, an orchestra was available. The venue for the Greek plays was then Cambridge's New Theatre. Composers for earlier plays included Parry, who supplied music for Aristophanes's satire *The Birds* in 1883. Parry had served that year as an examiner for Cambridge music degrees, received the honorary DMus, and had his second symphony, "Cambridge," premiered by CUMS in the Guildhall on 12 June. Vaughan Williams slyly quoted Parry's music in his own score. Stanford and Wood also composed scores for Greek plays. Stanford trained the chorus in some early productions, and Wood's music for Euripides's tragicomedy *Iphigenia in Tauris* was heard in 1894, during Vaughan Williams's period of residence. To invite the most successful pupil of these three composers was a natural step.[32] Roger Savage has noted that Vaughan Williams's cousin Frances Darwin had just married a Fellow of

Trinity, the classicist and Aristophanes specialist Francis Cornford.[33] Wood conducted in 1909, although it appears that Vaughan Williams directed a couple of performances.

The entertaining history of the Greek plays by L. P. Wilkinson, Fellow of King's College, reminds us that *The Wasps* "featured two distinguished Trinity figures, the future economist Sir Dennis Robertson and the future historian Sir James Butler, as Philocleon the jury-mad Athenian and the son who has to lock him up to restrain him—piquancy being added for the Cambridge audience by the knowledge that Butler's father was in real life the venerable Master of Trinity."[34] This surely delighted the former Trinity student Vaughan Williams. Among the chorus was the tenor Steuart Wilson, who called his friend Vaughan Williams "the hero of young Cambridge."[35] Others were Heathcote Statham, later a long-serving organist of Norwich Cathedral, and the promising composer Denis Browne, who cradled the poet Rupert Brooke as he was dying; Browne was himself killed in battle soon afterward.

The Wasps has been perceived as a pivotal work in Vaughan Williams's development, taking full advantage of the enthusiasm of young performers for something new, to be heard by an audience largely of students and scholars. The overture has become a popular concert item. Although based in part on tunes from the rest of the incidental music, it is no mere potpourri. Instead, it is a lively and well-designed form, with thematic development, a central *cantabile*, a jolly new tune as the tempo quickens, and a reprise of earlier material for the closing section. Vaughan Williams clearly relished the excuse for musical onomatopoeia, opening with the buzzing of insects by way of introduction. One theme suggests a whole-tone scale, another a diatonic idiom with modal inflections; the former (a sly allusion to Debussy) reflects his recent studies in Paris with Ravel. Nevertheless, early reviews noticed that the music also proclaimed its composer's national identity, although the supposed folksongs, with one exception, are original tunes. The Greek play also encouraged Vaughan Williams to deploy his occasionally mischievous humor, most obviously in a march for kitchen utensils, which is reminiscent of piquant marches by Gounod and Bizet. Such broad comedy catches the spirit of Aristophanes, and anticipates later works such as *Sir John in Love* and *Five Tudor Portraits*. Vaughan Williams's other incidental music for Greek plays was for performances of tragedies in English and was not intended for Cambridge.[36]

A year before the first performance of *The Wasps*, CUMS had performed *Toward the Unknown Region* on 12 June 1908. The Society's performance of *A Sea Symphony*, commissioned for the 1910 Leeds Festival, preceded its London premiere.[37] Vaughan Williams's next Cambridge premiere was *Old King Cole*, a ballet presented under the auspices of the Cambridge branch of the English Folk Dance Society, with CUMS performers. This effervescent score, filled with what Ursula Vaughan Williams described as "romantic and gay" music, was first performed in the open air on 5 June 1923.[38] The venue was Nevile's Court in Trinity College. This beautiful space is surrounded on all sides by stone walls, helpful for the clear projection of sound. The staging exploited the architecture: one end held the library designed by Christopher Wren, with cloisters beneath; at the opposite end was the dining hall, from which stairs descend into the court. Like *The Wasps* this is a lightweight piece, although less satirical; it elaborates on a children's rhyme by amalgamating it with the legend of Saint Helena, mother of the Emperor Constantine the Great, as the daughter of Cole (or Coel), king of the East Saxons. After an arresting opening like that of *The Wasps*, the music of *Old King Cole* is melodically inflected with the language of English folksong and rustic fiddles. The delightful music closely follows the scenario, partly suggested by the nursery rhyme in which the king "called for his pipe, he called for his bowl, and he called for his fiddlers three." Like Midas in Greek myth, he favors the livelier third fiddle over the sentiment of the second, whose playing Helena prefers; as everyone else leaves for a banquet, the second fiddler's lonely solo ends the ballet. Vaughan Williams implies that the music was rather too difficult for the amateur players.[39] The conductor, Bernhard ("Boris") Ord, was already the founder of the University's Madrigal Society. He succeeded Mann as organist of King's College Chapel in 1929.[40]

Prior to his next Cambridge premiere, *The Poisoned Kiss*, Vaughan Williams had produced a serious ballet score: *Job, a Masque for Dancing*. The stage premiere of *Job* (1931) was at the Cambridge Theatre, which, however, is in London. The work does have actual Cambridge connections, however: the initial scenario was by John Maynard Keynes's brother Geoffrey, a distinguished surgeon and literary scholar, and is based as much—if not more—on William Blake's illustrations as on the biblical story; the designs, also based on Blake, were by Keynes's sister-in-law and Vaughan Williams's cousin Gwen Raverat.[41]

Perhaps urged by his friend Dent as well as Stanford's example, Vaughan Williams was eager to contribute to the slender repertory of opera in English. For this the 1920s were a significant decade, although few of its most ambitious productions, such as the operas of Rutland Boughton, have been staged in recent years. Following the 1924 premiere of *Hugh the Drover*, Vaughan Williams worked on three dramatic works in the 1920s, although only *Sir John in Love* was performed at the time. His most ambitious project,

The Pilgrim's Progress, was already mooted; an episode, *The Shepherds of the Delectable Mountains*, was performed at the RCM in 1922. The "Romantic extravaganza" *The Poisoned Kiss* was composed in 1927–29, but Vaughan Williams, or those who counseled him, felt it needed revision, leading to much correspondence with the librettist, Evelyn Sharp.[42] The opera took time to reach even a provisionally final form, as the composer and librettist were at odds—albeit politely—about its tone and genre, which wound up somewhere between the extremes of satirical comedy and romance. As Stephen Connock has pointed out, *The Poisoned Kiss* may have been affected not only by its literary sources in the work of Nathaniel Hawthorne and Richard Garnett, but by recent opera revivals. One was the 1911 Cambridge production in English of Mozart's *The Magic Flute*, staged by Carey and Dent. Vaughan Williams himself in an article had identified *The Beggar's Opera* as a foundation stone of opera in English; it was revived in London in the early 1920s, as was its less successful sequel, *Polly*.[43]

The Poisoned Kiss had been intended for a London premiere, but instead ran for a week in Cambridge, followed by a single performance in the capital. After this, it was subjected to further revision, up until nearly the end of Vaughan Williams's life. Like *The Wasps* and *Old King Cole*, it is among his lighter works, an attempt to revive the type of fantasy operetta, with magical elements, that Gilbert and Sullivan had tried out in *The Sorcerer* and, due to its satirical bite, the more effective *Iolanthe*. Vaughan Williams's music, with its rambunctious opening and passages contrasting tart modernism with diatonic lyricism, is perhaps not unlike what Sullivan might have written had he been born thirty-five years later. Cambridge is not a large city, but its cultural life remained vigorous, and the opera's casting and Vaughan Williams's tuneful music made participation easier for young singers.

In the 1930s, in addition to CUMS and CUMC, the Madrigal Society was active in the revival of the Elizabethan and early Jacobean music that Vaughan Williams loved. The Society sang on the river Cam at the end of "May Week" (Cambridge's name for celebratory events that followed examinations; despite its name, May Week is in early June), and also toured, possibly performing something by Vaughan Williams in France.[44] So in 1936, CUMS was allotted the delayed premiere of *The Poisoned Kiss* in Cambridge's newly established Arts Theatre (a project masterminded by John Maynard Keynes). The premiere was 18 May 1936, directed by Cyril Rootham, organist of St. John's College, in his last year as conductor of CUMS; Boris Ord succeeded him as conductor a year later. Gwen Raverat was again the designer, and the director, Camille Prior, was a prominent figure in Cambridge's theatrical activities for many years.

Two years later, CUMS under Ord included Vaughan Williams's one-act opera *Riders to the Sea* in an operatic triple bill, following its premiere the previous year at the RCM. When Ord returned from military service after the war, he wrote to Vaughan Williams, who replied on Christmas Day, 1946. It appears that Ord may have asked for music for the choir of King's College Chapel, but the composer felt unable to comply. Vaughan Williams did, however, offer suggestions to overcome "the almost entire absence of English carols" in the traditional Christmas Eve service broadcast of nine lessons and carols. [45]

Ord was still the conductor when the society mounted the second production of *The Pilgrim's Progress* in February 1954. CUMS did not routinely present staged performances, but the idea was no doubt encouraged by Vaughan Williams's Cambridge connections, including Dent and Carey who were involved in the discussions that preceded both productions.[46] Dent had retired from the professorship some years earlier and was living in London; the fascinating exchange of letters between him and Vaughan Williams that followed the London premiere (1951) may have been a factor in inducing CUMS to undertake *The Pilgrim's Progress*. Vaughan Williams was prepared to listen to constructive criticism, and Dent's letters inspired revisions that were presumably implemented in 1954.[47]

The second production proved more to the composer's satisfaction than the first; Ursula Vaughan Williams reports him saying "*This* is what I meant." It was resourcefully directed by Dennis Arundell, and was staged in Cambridge's Guildhall which allowed more scope for the large cast than the Arts Theatre. However, the stage, which is above floor level, must have created access problems, which seem to have been resolved despite what Ursula Vaughan Williams refers to as "the difficult, steep stage."[48] She may have been referring to the steps needed for access, as the stage is actually flat, and capable of accommodating a symphony orchestra. There are rising seats behind, used for the chorus in oratorios and concert performances of opera. For staged operas the orchestra has to be placed on the floor, reducing audience accommodation. If the stage sloped it must have been fixed that way for the production, perhaps to improve sight lines from the remaining floor space; in addition, there is also gallery seating. The alternative large-scale performance space, King's College Chapel, would have been inappropriate given Vaughan Williams's insistence that *The Pilgrim's Progress* is a true opera, not intended for church performance. In any case, the acoustics of that vast edifice are difficult, and most of the audience would have been unable to see the proceedings.

Ursula Vaughan Williams also reports that after a difficult start in freezing weather—"The wind seemed to come straight from Siberia"—Ord obtained excellent results from both orchestra and chorus. Like *The Poisoned Kiss*, *The Pilgrim's Progress* proved well suited to performance involving students, with its large number of relatively small roles. Even Pilgrim himself, John Noble, was still a student; he reports interestingly on difficulties in preparing the production, does not mention a sloping stage, and also recalls Arundell's resourceful use of curtains and "shadows and lighting."[49]

This production met with greater critical success than the London premiere. Ralph and Ursula Vaughan Williams were unable to stay for the whole week of performances, but they did receive reports from those present or involved, such as Humphry Trevelyan (son of "Trevy" and a Fellow of King's), who sang Lord Hate-Good. The weather remained icy, and Ord slipped on steps in King's and dislocated his right shoulder. Allen Percival, one of his assistants and the director of music at Homerton College, stepped into the breach for three performances before Ord returned for the final performance, conducting left-handed. Percival "acquitted himself with distinction" according to Patrick Hadley, who had been appointed Professor of Music in 1946 in succession to Dent.[50] When Ord eventually retired from the direction of CUMS, he was replaced by his successor as organist of King's, David Willcocks, who conducted works by Vaughan Williams in Cambridge before his move to London as director of the RCM in the 1970s.[51]

If Vaughan Williams felt he had a debt to Cambridge, he assuredly repaid it over many years. He generously offered assistance to refugees from Germany, funding the studies of Paul Cohn to read mathematics at Trinity and assisting the musical education of the singer Ruthala ("Ruth") Salaman.[52] Vaughan Williams may have come to know of her needs through his cousin Frances Cornford, who lived in a substantial property in Conduit Head Road about one and a half miles from the center of Cambridge. This house was divided into two homes, one occupied by the Salaman family. Ruth married Darwin's great-grandson, the distinguished scientist Horace Barlow.

Cambridge in its turn remained conscious of having nurtured a great man, and Vaughan Williams's academic connections with the university did not end with his Doctor of Music degree. In 1935 he was awarded the Order of Merit and he also received the signal distinction of an Honorary Fellowship at Trinity. Curiously, the college fellowship included the classical scholar A. E. Housman, the author of *A Shropshire Lad* who notoriously deplored Vaughan Williams's cutting a stanza from "Is my team ploughing" in *On Wenlock Edge*; a 1911 Cambridge performance of this song cycle was attended by the composer.[53] Housman died in 1936, and was probably not involved with new appointments, even of honorary fellows.

The Darwin and Trinity network of connections was further extended through another Fellow, Edgar (later Lord) Adrian, who succeeded "Trevy" as Master in 1951. His daughter Ann, a fine pianist, married the scientist Richard Keynes, son of Geoffrey and thus another Darwin great-grandson. As an Honorary Fellow, Vaughan Williams had no need to reside, still less to make the college his home, as E. M. Forster eventually did in King's. Despite having proclaimed a degree of religious scepticism, even while a student resident in Trinity, Vaughan Williams was greatly concerned with musical standards within the Anglican Communion. It is therefore appropriate that his connection to the college is recorded on a brass plaque in its chapel, something not usually accorded to "rustici" Honorary Fellows.[54] As Ursula Vaughan Williams wrote, no doubt following a hint from her husband, it was at Cambridge that "his independence and emancipation started, and his real life began."[55]

Figure 2.

Warm thanks to Eric Saylor, Hugh Cobbe, and Alan Tongue, who each offered valuable suggestions as I was preparing this article. In addition, special thanks to Mr. Nicolas Bell for providing Figure 2, which is reproduced here by kind permission of the Master and Fellows of Trinity College.

1. Frances Cornford's 1959 memoir of Vaughan Williams for the Royal College of Music, reproduced in Stephen Connock, *Toward the Rising Sun: Ralph Vaughan Williams Remembered* (Tonbridge, Kent: Albion Music, 2018), 261–64; Gwen Raverat, *Period Piece: A Cambridge Childhood* (London: Faber and Faber, 1952); Frances Spalding, *Gwen Raverat: Friends, Family & Affections* (London: Harvill, 2001).

2. Raverat, *Period Piece*, 13, 233, 273.

3. Fredegond Maitland married Gerald Shove, economist and friend of J. M. Keynes. See Roger Savage, "'While the Moon Shines Gold': Vaughan Williams and Literature: An Overview," in Julian Rushton, ed., *Let Beauty Awake: Elgar, Vaughan Williams and Literature* (Rickmansworth: Elgar Editions, 2010), 43–64; on the Maitland connection, see 43–45, 49–52.

4. Hugh Cobbe, ed., *Letters of Ralph Vaughan Williams 1895–1958* (Oxford: Oxford University Press, 2008), 17.

5. In connection with Stanford's student years, Paul Rodmell refers to Trinity as "a body which did not take music seriously from an academic standpoint." See Paul Rodmell, *Charles Villiers Stanford* (Aldershot: Ashgate, 2002), 39.

6. Although there is no longer a choir school attached to Trinity, Vaughan Williams would surely have been delighted by the recent achievements of its chapel choir, with female membership, under the direction of Richard Marlowe and Stephen Layton.

7. Gray was commissioned for the 1898 Leeds Festival alongside Elgar, who wrote resentfully to A. J. Jaeger that "that fool Gray" was allowed as much rehearsal time as he was for his much longer work (*Caractacus*). Jerrold Northrop Moore, ed., *Elgar and His Publisher: Letters of a Creative Life* (Oxford: Clarendon Press, 1987), 87.

8. Rodmell, *Charles Villiers Stanford*, 171.

9. Hugh Cobbe dates the letter "1895?" as it falls between Vaughan Williams passing the BMus and receiving the BA; see *Letters of Ralph Vaughan Williams*, 13.

10. Cambridge University Library, Anderson Room, Mus. B.103. See Michael Kennedy, *A Catalogue of the Works of Ralph Vaughan Williams*, 2nd ed. (Oxford: Oxford University Press, 1996), 4–5.

11. Gerald Norris, *Stanford, the Cambridge Jubilee, and Tchaikovsky* (Newton Abbot, Devon: David and Charles, 1980). In 1897, Vaughan Williams traveled to Berlin to study with Bruch.

12. Rodmell, *Charles Villiers Stanford*, 170.

13. Jill Vlasto, "A Cambridge Occasion," *The Musical Times* 109/1505 (July 1968): 616–18; Ursula Vaughan Williams, *R.V.W.: A Biography of Ralph Vaughan Williams* (Oxford and London: Oxford University Press, 1964), 36.

14. Raverat, *Period Piece*, 170.

15. Michael Kennedy, *The Works of Ralph Vaughan Williams*, 2nd ed. (Oxford: Clarendon Press, 1992), 18.

16. Kennedy, *Catalogue*, 3–4; and *Works of Ralph Vaughan Williams*, 18.

17. Memories of Dr. G. F. McCleary, in Stephen Connock, *Toward the Rising Sun*, 301–3.

18. Vaughan Williams to G. E. Moore, dated by Cobbe to October 1897 in *Letters of Ralph Vaughan Williams*, 18.

19. Byron Adams, "Scripture, Church, and culture: biblical texts in the works of Ralph Vaughan Williams," in *Vaughan Williams Studies*, ed. Alain Frogley (Cambridge: Cambridge University Press, 1996), 99–117; Kennedy, *Works of Ralph Vaughan Williams*, 42.

20. Ursula Vaughan Williams, *R.V.W.*, 37. The river Cam is a tributary of the Ouse which flows through Ely.

21. Statutes of the University, see https://www.cambridgestudents.cam.ac.uk/your-course/examinations/graduate-exam-information/higher-degrees/higher-doctorates. It is sometimes implied that his doctorate was from Trinity, but Oxford and Cambridge colleges have never had the power to award degrees.

22. Special thanks to Alan Tongue for this information.

23. Letter from Ralph Vaughan Williams to G. E. Moore [early March 1899], VWL279, letter from Ralph Vaughan Williams to Gustav Holst, VWL 233.

24. W. H. Hadow, *Studies in Modern Music*, first series (London: Seeley, Service & Co., 1893–95, frequently reissued, 11th impression 1926), 140.

25. Kennedy, *Catalogue*, 3.

26. *Ralph Vaughan Williams Society Journal* 51 (June 2011): 31.

27. Mass for SATB soloists, mixed double chorus and orchestra, Cambridge University Library, Anderson Room, Mus.D. 26. This score was given the title "A Cambridge Mass" in the twenty-first century. For basic information, see Michael Kennedy, *Catalogue*, 10.

28. Michael Kennedy, *The Works of Ralph Vaughan Williams*, 1st ed. (Oxford: Oxford University Press, 1964), 42.

29. Kennedy, *Catalogue*, 10; Alan Tongue, "A Significant Find," *Ralph Vaughan Williams Society Journal* 49 (October 2010): 14–15.

30. Full score and vocal scores: Ralph Vaughan Williams, *A Cambridge Mass*, ed. Alan Tongue (London: Stainer & Bell, 2012). I am grateful to Alan Tongue for a view of Michael Kennedy's messages to him, agreeing with his estimate of the Mass following its performance.

31. For *The Wasps*, Kennedy (*Catalogue*, 45) names a translator, but this was for the "libretto." Parallel Greek and English texts were available to the audience.

32. See Michael Kennedy, *The Works of Ralph Vaughan Williams*, 121–23; Colin Lees, "The Wasps," *Ralph Vaughan Williams Society Journal* 72 (June 2018): 9–12.

33. Roger Savage, "Vaughan Williams, the Romany Ryes, and the Cambridge Ritualists," *Music & Letters* 83 (2002): 383–418; on *The Wasps*, see 392–95.

34. L. P. Wilkinson, https://www.cambridgegreekplay.com/the-history-of-the-cambridge-greek-play.

35. Kennedy, *Works of Ralph Vaughan Williams*, 108.

36. Ralph Vaughan Williams, *Beyond My Dream: Music for Greek Plays*, cond. Alan Tongue, Compact Disc, Albion Records. ALBCD 033 (2017). This disc includes music from Vaughan Williams's scores to *The Bacchae*, *Elektra*, and *Iphigenia in Tauris*.

37. Kennedy mentions that the timpanist in *Toward the Unknown Region* was none other than Edward J. Dent (*Works of Ralph Vaughan Williams*, 100).

38. Ursula Vaughan Williams, *R.V.W.*, 151.

39. Kennedy, *Works of Ralph Vaughan Williams*, 93–96.

40. For more information on both Mann and Ord, see Timothy Day, *I Saw Eternity the Other Night: King's College, Cambridge, and an English Singing Style* (London: Allen Lane, 2018).

41. Apart from *Job*, few of Raverat's stage designs survive; they included Greek plays and other work for CUMS. Spalding, *Gwen Raverat*, 338.

42. Evelyn Sharp was a suffragist and writer who specialized in literature for children; her brother Cecil Sharp was a noted collector of folksongs and dances and an associate of Vaughan Williams.

43. Stephen Connock, "'Sheer early morning loveliness': Ralph Vaughan Williams and *The Poisoned Kiss*," in *A Special Flame: The Music of Elgar and Vaughan Williams*, ed. John Norris and Andrew Neill (Rickmansworth: Elgar Editions, 2004), 116–29.

44. This supposition I have from my mother, who sang with the Madrigal Society, and told me that their French hosts pronounced the composer's name "Voggen Villiums."

45. *Letters of Ralph Vaughan Williams*, 408–9.

46. John Noble, "Primary Memories," and Leonard Hancock, "Primary Memories," in Connock, *Toward the Rising Sun*, 151–52, 190–92. The conductor Leonard Hancock remembers the 1951 Covent Garden performance of *The Pilgrim's Progress*; baritone John Noble recalls the 1954 production at Cambridge.

47. Kennedy, *Catalogue*, 192–206.

48. Ursula Vaughan Williams, *R.V.W.*, 343–44.

49. Connock, *Toward the Rising Sun*, 190–92. John Noble may be heard on the first recording, conducted by Adrian Boult.

50. Ursula Vaughan Williams, *R.V.W.*, 344. Allen Percival was later principal of the Guildhall School of Music and Drama and a director of Stainer & Bell, one of Vaughan Williams's publishers before he moved to Oxford University Press. As a student in the 1960s, I played bass clarinet for Percival in a performance of Stravinsky's *Perséphone*. My mother, who served as CUMS secretary from 1940 to 1955, told me that the orchestra did not like him very much.

51. In the 1960s I played clarinet for David Willcocks in *A Sea Symphony* with CUMS, and *In Windsor Forest*, the cantata extracted from *Sir John in Love*, in a King's May Week concert. See interview with Willcocks in Connock, *Toward the Rising Sun*, 233–37.

52. Neil Wenborn, "'A desirable end': Vaughan Williams and the refugee relief effort of the 1930s and 1940s," *Ralph Vaughan Williams Society Journal* 76 (October 2019): 10.

53. Arthur Bliss, "Ralph Vaughan Williams," and Edward J. Dent, "Ralph Vaughan Williams" in Connock, *Toward the Sun Rising*, 246–47, 266–67.

54. Nicolas Bell, librarian of Trinity College, informs me that these are posthumous tributes. It has been suggested that Vaughan Williams queried the word *rustici*, but the objection could have only come from his widow; however, it clearly does not mean "pastoral" in the mildly derogatory sense used of certain English composers, but refers to the collection of folksongs.

55. Ursula Vaughan Williams, *R.V.W.*, 34.

Vaughan Williams and
the Royal College of Music

ERICA SIEGEL

Toward the end of a speech delivered at the opening ceremony of the Royal College of Music on 7 May 1883, Edward, Prince of Wales, declared:

> The establishment of an institution such as I open to-day is not the mere creation of a new musical society. The time has come when class can no longer stand aloof from class, and that man does his duty best who works most earnestly in bridging over the gulf between different classes which it is the tendency of increased wealth and increased civilization to widen. I claim for music the merit that it has a voice which speaks, in different tones, perhaps, but with equal force, to the cultivated and the ignorant, to the peer and the peasant. I claim for music a variety of expression which belongs to no other art, and therefore adapts it more than any other art to produce that union of feeling which I much desire to promote. . . . What more, gentleman, can I say on behalf of the art for the promotion of which we are to-day opening this institution—an institution which I trust will give to music a new impulse, a glorious future, and a national life.[1]

Prince Edward's speech, which the *Times* quoted in its entirety, is indicative of the heavy promotion of the Royal College of Music at the time. As the *Times* stated, the RCM was so significant that "in the history of English music it may without exaggeration be said to mark an epoch. . . . When a nation is, as it were, wedded to the genius of art the fierce light of publicity must needs beat upon the union from its very beginning."[2] Given that Britain was suffering from an overabundance of musical conservatories during this era, other publications were far less generous in their optimism.[3] The RCM was routinely mocked in satirical publications such as *Punch*, *Moonshine*, *Judy*, and *Funny Folks*, with the latter publishing a parody of the RCM's opening ceremony:

> H.R.H. rose and addressed the assembly as follows: "Ladies and gentlemen,—I congratulate you on the opening of the Royal College of Music—the most comprehensive Musical School of this or any age. . . . A baritone will not have to pay more than a 'tenor,' and though contraltos will be expected to pay 'treble' fees, a fiver will probably cover the whole. You must remember, too, that in *our* school all the work-hours will be 'play hours.' I will only add that each resident pupil will be expected to bring with him or her a musical-box, a tuning-fork, and fiddle-spoon, a composing draught, and a copy of Dr. Grove's 'Dictionary of Music.'" (Loud cheers.)
>
> H.R.H. then declared the Royal College of Music open, on which the doors were immediately shut, to prevent any one coming in without paying fees.[4]

The College's origins can be traced back to nationalist ideologies that emerged in the wake of the Great Exhibition in 1851, when the state of music in Britain became the source of societal anxieties in the press, in educational institutions, and in the halls of power. Disturbed by ever-present financial difficulties that plagued the Royal Academy of Music, Albert of Saxe-Coburg and Gotha, Queen Victoria's musically accomplished Prince Consort, believed that Britain would benefit from a new music school that would enjoy adequate and consistent financial support.[5] At Albert's urging, the Society of Arts produced a report on the state of music education in 1865, completing their task four years after the Prince Consort's death. Albert's son, Alfred, Duke of Edinburgh, took up his father's cause by founding the National Training School of Music. The NTSM failed to thrive, however. Its financial basis was unsound from the beginning, and Arthur Sullivan was a conscientious Principal only for the first few years of his tenure, becoming increasingly distracted by the production of his operettas with W. S. Gilbert for the impresario Richard D'Oyly Carte. In January of 1881, Sullivan tendered his resignation to the Duke of Edinburgh.[6] Almost immediately, plans were put in motion to establish the RCM, as it was easier to raise enthusiasm and money for a new institution that promised decisive, innovative change.[7]

From its inception, the Royal College of Music was designed to do what no other music conservatory in Britain had been able to accomplish: train native-born performers and composers who could compete on an equal

Figure 1. National Training School of Music, ca. 1876.

footing with their continental peers. As a student and later teacher who found widespread international success as a composer, Vaughan Williams was not only a product of the pedagogical revolution's ethos, but also a deeply engaged participant and advocate for its aims and activities. This essay explores Vaughan Williams's involvement with the RCM, from his student years to his return as teacher, within a broader consideration of the vast changes that occurred at the College during the interwar years, and Vaughan Williams's legacy as one of the "most eminent and well loved of [the] College's many distinguished sons."[8]

Vaughan Williams the Student

Vaughan Williams first entered the RCM in September 1890. At the time, the College was still housed in the former National Training School of Music building (Figure 1). Located to the west of Royal Albert Hall, this building was designed by Henry Hardy Cole and constructed in 1874–75 with funds provided by Charles James Freake.[9] The building, meant to provide a stark contrast to its concert hall neighbor, was intended to evoke "the Old English style of the sixteenth century."[10] In reality, however, the building's facade, featuring flat oriel windows and decorative sgraffito panels designed by Francis Wollaston Moody, owed much to foreign as opposed to native influence.[11] The cramped interior was plagued by poor acoustics; composer C. Hubert Parry (1848–1918) later described it as "about the worst building ever constructed for any purpose."[12] This building eventually proved unsuitable for a conservatory and instead became the headquarters of the Royal College of Organists.

Vaughan Williams's decision to attend the RCM was motivated by his desire to study with Parry, whose music he had first become acquainted with as a teenager.[13] As he recounted in "A Musical Autobiography" (1950):

> I remember my cousin, Stephen Massingberd, coming into the room full of that new book *Studies of Great Composers*. "This man, Parry," he said, "declares that a composer must write music as his musical conscience demands." This was quite a new idea to me, the loyalty of the artist to his art. Soon after that I got to know some of his music, especially parts of "Judith" and I remember, even as a boy, my brother saying to me that there was something, to his mind, peculiarly English about his music. So I was quite prepared to join with the other young students of the R.C.M. in worshipping at that shrine, and I think I can truly say that I have never been disloyal to it.[14]

Before Vaughan Williams was allowed to study with Parry, however, he first had to achieve a Grade 5 in harmony. Thus, for his first two terms, Vaughan Williams studied with Francis Edward Gladstone (1845–1928).[15] Under Gladstone's direction, Vaughan Williams completed all the exercises in George Macfarren's *The Rudiments of Harmony*, a dogmatic but nevertheless useful resource for beginners. He found his early studies profitable, later remarking that working through Macfarren's textbook under Gladstone's tutelage was "a discipline for which I have ever since been grateful."[16]

After achieving his Grade 5 in 1891, Vaughan Williams was at last able to begin lessons with Parry. Given the reverence Vaughan Williams later expressed toward Parry, it is hardly surprising that the young composer quite easily fell "under his spell."[17] As Jeremy Dibble observes, Vaughan Williams was undoubtedly drawn to Parry's evolutionary views of music history and the ability of music to serve a higher democratic purpose.[18] (In 1896, Parry published a book titled *The Evolution of the Art of Music*, which is informed by the philosophy of Herbert Spencer as well as the broad outline of Darwin's *On the Origin of Species*.)[19] Indeed, as Vaughan Williams characterized it, Parry's ability to "never . . . divorce art from life" surely inspired his young pupil as he struggled with opposition from his mother's family to his chosen career path.[20] Reflecting upon Parry's influence decades later, Vaughan Williams remarked:

> Parry once said to me, "Write choral music as befits an Englishman and a democrat." We pupils of Parry have, if we have been wise, inherited from Parry the great English choral tradition which Tallis passed on to Byrd, Byrd to Gibbons, Gibbons to Purcell, Purcell to Battishill and Greene, and they in their turn through the Wesleys to Parry. He has passed on the torch to us and it is our duty to keep it alight.[21]

While Vaughan Williams's statements might imply that the RCM's curriculum was predicated upon a rediscovery of the nation's musical past, it was German rather than British music that formed the foundation of the RCM's curriculum. Over the course of his studies with Parry, Vaughan Williams gained increasing familiarity with the three Bs— Brahms, Beethoven, and J. S. Bach. Parry encouraged Vaughan Williams to study Beethoven's quartets "as a religious exercise."[22] Despite Vaughan Williams's distaste for the hero-worship that surrounded Beethoven, he willingly obliged his teacher.[23] Through Parry's generous practice of loaning scores to his pupils, Vaughan Williams also became familiar with a wealth of relatively contemporary works, including *Siegfried* and *Tristan und Isolde* by Wagner as well as Brahms's *Ein deutsches Requiem*.[24] Parry, who came late to the serious study of both piano and composition, was not adept enough to provide a strict technical foundation for his students. In other words, though Parry lacked a secure technique as a composer, he achieved impressive results through sheer willpower and hard-won practical experience. As Vaughan Williams stated:

> The secret of Parry's greatness as a teacher was his broad-minded sympathy; his was not that so called broadmindedness which comes of want of conviction; his musical antipathies were very strong, and sometimes, in the opinion of those who disagreed with them, unreasonable; but in appraising a composer's work he was able to set these on one side and see beyond

Figure 2. Royal College of Music, Prince Consort Road, 1894.

them. And it was in this spirit that he examined the work of his pupils. A student's compositions are seldom of any intrinsic merit, and a teacher is apt to judge them on their face-value. But Parry looked further than this; he saw what lay behind the faulty utterance and made it his object to clear the obstacles that prevented fullness of musical speech. His watchword was "characteristic"—that was the thing which mattered.[25]

At the insistence of his mother and her Darwin and Wedgwood relations, Vaughan Williams left the RCM in 1892 to study at Trinity College, Cambridge. He took the BMus examination in 1894, followed by a Bachelor of Arts in History in 1895, for which he received an impressive Second Class.[26] Having satisfied familial demands, Vaughan Williams returned to the RCM in the summer term of 1895. In the interim, the institution had gone through a transformation. In contrast to his earlier period of study, Vaughan Williams found that the College was now housed in its new, well-designed building on Prince Consort Road, with two grand staircases designed to separate the male and female students (Figure 2). The director was his erstwhile teacher, Parry, who had succeeded George Grove at the beginning of the year.

Former pupils at the RCM tended to remember their time there before the First World War as a halcyon period. For example, Herbert Howells (1892–1983) recalled it as a "cosy family."[27] Unsurprisingly, the reality was more complicated. One of the College's principal voice teachers, Albert Visetti (1846–1928), was notorious for sexually harassing his women students.[28] Some pupils who studied with the Irish-born composer Charles Villiers Stanford (1852–1924) remembered his severity and tempestuous personality. In a recorded conversation with Howells, Arthur Bliss (1891–1975) recalled, "Well, of course, there was a galaxy of very talented people there, quick, professional, and it was tremendously stimulating." While this sort of memory was common among those who studied at the RCM during this period, Bliss qualified his praise with a tart remark: "The only thing that didn't stimulate me, I'm afraid, was the teaching. . . . I didn't feel that the College was exciting. What I felt was exciting was what was happening outside," by which he meant the London seasons of the Ballets Russes and modernist developments in Russian and French music.[29]

During his second period at the RCM, which lasted roughly a year, Vaughan Williams studied composition under Stanford. Teacher and pupil did not get along whatsoever. Always an admirer of Parry, he surely sympathized with Bliss's negative assessment of Stanford's teaching: "I prefer to forget the hours I spent with Stanford."[30] Vaughan Williams later recounted:

> He was intolerant and narrow-minded, and it was this, I think, which made him a good teacher. If a thing was wrong, it was wrong; if it was right it was right, and there was no question about it. It is fatal for a teacher to say, even mentally, to a pupil, "well perhaps you are right after all." Stanford was often cruel in his judgements and the more sensitive among his pupils wilted under his methods and found comfort under a more soft-hearted teacher. I remember I once showed Stanford the slow movement of a string quartet. I had worked feverishly at it, and, like every other young composer, thought not only that it was the finest piece that had ever been written, and that my teacher would fall on his knees and embrace me, but that it was also my swan song. Now what would Parry have done in a case like this? He would have pored over it for a long time in hopes of finding something

characteristic and, even if he disliked the piece as a whole, would try to find some point of praise. Stanford dismissed it with a curt "All rot, me boy!" This was cruel but salutary.[31]

As Byron Adams once observed, Stanford's brutal dismissiveness may have been rooted in his own aims for his students: he wanted them to be able to earn a living within the rough-and-tumble commercialized musical world of late Victorian and Edwardian Britain.[32] A few of Stanford's students (including Howells) remembered his teaching with gratitude and the man with affection, and it is to Stanford's credit that he taught and promoted the Afro-British composer Samuel Coleridge-Taylor (1875–1912). Other students, such as Arthur Benjamin (1893–1960) and Bliss, remained ambivalent or unimpressed. Writing in 1950, Benjamin recalled:

> Opinionated though he was to the point of bigotry, Stanford never undermined a pupil's personality. Musically (and not only musically) he certainly was a bigot. Those of us who, having indulged in a spice of "modern" harmony, were not angrily ejected from his room, were considered by our fellows, after all, mere fogeys. Displeased, Stanford would foam with rage, stab viciously with his pencil at an offending chord, point to the door with a long arm and utter the command: "Leave the room, me bhoy [*sic*], and don't come back till ye can write something beautiful!" A few days later he might see one in a corridor, throw an arm round one's shoulders and enquire: "And how is the masterpiece going?"
>
> He was bigoted in his dislikes—in his antipathy towards Elgar and still more towards Debussy and Ravel. He would speak of the Frenchmen's "eunuch music." Yet he included their works in College programmes.[33]

Though Vaughan Williams's recollections of his teacher painted him in a more forgiving light than those of Bliss and Benjamin—according to Adams, Stanford's students often "succumbed to a kind of institutional 'Stockholm syndrome' peculiar to the composition graduates of the Royal College"[34]—the damage that Stanford wrought on his self-confidence was lasting.[35]

Aside from his fraught lessons with Stanford, Vaughan Williams's second period of study at the RCM allowed him to develop long-lasting friendships that helped his musical development. The nucleus of Vaughan Williams's social activities was the College's Literary and Debating Society.

Though the all-male club's existence lasted for one year, from 1896 to 1897, its members, which included the composers Gustav Holst (1874–1934), Fritz Hart (1874–1949), Thomas Dunhill (1877–1946), and John Ireland (1879–1962), provided a much-needed sense of camaraderie.[36] Given that a chief criticism often leveled at the RCM was its failure to foster any meaningful social life, it is perhaps all the more remarkable that such a feat was achieved at all.[37] Vaughan Williams remarked about these bonds: "The benefit that one obtains from an academy or college is not so much from one's official teachers as from one's fellow students."[38]

Return of the Prodigal Son

In 1919, Vaughan Williams returned once again to the RCM, this time as a member of its teaching staff. In the twenty-three years that had elapsed since his student days, Vaughan Williams had maintained contact with the College. He attended concerts; contributed an inflammatory article, "Who Wants the English Composer?" to *The R.C.M. Magazine* in 1912; and served a brief stint on the RCM's Council.[39]

During the First World War, the simmering tensions between Stanford and Parry erupted into the open. Stanford resented his modest salary as a teacher compared to that of Parry's as director. Stanford envied Parry's inherited wealth, while Parry was jealous of Stanford's fluent compositional technique and wider reputation.[40] Adding to Parry's misery, the wartime deaths of former students such as Francis Purcell Warren (1895–1916) and Ernest Farrar (1885–1918) called into question the Germanic emphasis of the institution itself. In his 1914 Christmas address to RCM students, Parry made what must have seemed a startling *mea culpa*:

> I have my own confession to make. For I have been a quarter of a century and more a pro-Teuton. I owed too much to their music and their philosophers and authors of former times to believe it possible that the nation at large could be imbued with the teaching of a few advocates of mere brutal violence and material aggression; with the extravagance of those who talked about super-morality; with the ruthless implications of their insistence that the State is power, and nothing but power, and has no concern with honour, right, justice, or fair play.[41]

Vaughan Williams's return occurred at a pivotal moment in the College's history. The RCM was undergoing a period of expansion and change that radically transformed the nature of musical training there and enhanced

Figure 3. Portrait of Hugh Allen, 1920s.

its stature as an innovative center for British musical developments. With Parry's death in October of 1918, it was clear that the prewar Germanic bias was outmoded and reforms were urgently required. At the helm of this transfiguration was the RCM's new director, Hugh Allen (1869–1946), who

Figure 4. Ralph Vaughan Williams, ca. 1921.

had been appointed to the position after Parry's death (Figure 3). Allen faced immense challenges, upon which music critic H. C. Colles (1879–1943) elaborated in *The Royal College of Music: A Jubilee Record* (1933):

> The College, in common with every other educational institution in the country, began in those years a new chapter in its history. Those who ruled its policy were quick to see that it must be made ready for service on a far larger scale than formerly, and be able to accommodate itself to educational needs which were partly the result of a social reaction after the war, and partly affected by the mechanisation of music through the gramophone and the wireless. The R.C.M.'s mission was no longer to induce a careless world to take an interest in the art of music, but to direct into profitable channels an exuberant but uninstructed popular enthusiasm.[42]

Impulsive, disorganized, astonishingly rude, uncommonly kind, and at times utterly devoid of rationality, Allen nevertheless possessed an almost inconceivable brilliance for administration combined with an unwitting genius for politics, musical and otherwise.[43] His appointment, however, initially raised some eyebrows, as Colles later remarked:

> The appropriateness of the appointment was by no means so obvious to the outer world. Hugh Allen was very little known to the generality of London musicians beyond the organist circle and those who had had some connection with the Universities. . . . There was a general impression that he was a man of superabundant energy whose methods with a choir were forcible rather than subtle, and whose musical experience was chiefly that of the choral conductor's rostrum and the organ-loft. There were stories going about his unconventional behaviour in both these capacities. They were supported by some caricatures made by a clever young graduate, or perhaps undergraduate, of Oxford, one of which showed Allen as a street organ-grinder; another, truer to life, portrayed him in his shirt-sleeves balanced precariously on the edge of a table and assuming a threatening attitude towards an unseen choir.
>
> Such a reputation was hardly the complete introduction of him to a post which Parry had adorned with his own original work as a composer, the high scholarship of his

historical books on music, and a natural dignity of presence never relaxed, however much he might unbend in congenial surroundings. One could not imagine a caricature of Parry being true enough to be amusing. Even those who thought they knew Allen pretty well may have wondered whether he would ever quite "fill the bill." Those who really knew him (and fortunately there were some members of the Council among them), who had known Parry and were aware of the intimate friendship which had united these two very different men, had no doubts.[44]

At the time of his appointment, Allen had already established a vigorous reputation as an educational reformer. As a fellow of New College, Oxford, he implemented changes to the music curriculum there to raise the study of music to the same level as other academic subjects. He implemented similar measures during his periods directing music at University College, Reading (1908–18) and Cheltenham Ladies College (1910–18)—posts that he held simultaneously with his activities in Oxford.[45]

Over the course of his RCM tenure from 1919 to 1937, Allen made a number of changes. In order to address financial challenges, the RCM dramatically increased the number of paying pupils it admitted.[46] The resulting increase in students enabled Allen to restructure the teaching staff; in his first year as director, he made twenty-six new appointments including Vaughan Williams, Holst, Howells, Colles, Adrian Boult (1889–1983), Percy Buck (1871–1947), Harold Darke (1888–1976), and Kathleen Long (1896–1968), among others.[47] An overwhelming majority of the new appointments were former RCM pupils who had already established successful professional careers, and a substantial number were drawn from Allen's friends or his former students at Oxford. As a result, the College soon began to exude an atmosphere of "congenial Oxford liberalism" with a broader outlook and a more modern repertory.[48] Vaughan Williams and Allen were close friends. The composer first encountered Allen during his matriculation at Cambridge when the latter was an organ scholar at Christ's College. Allen was heavily involved in musical activities, including conducting some early performances of Vaughan Williams's music.

Unsurprisingly, these new appointments had a significant pedagogical impact. To raise the level of technical training, Allen worked with the faculty to address many of the gaps in the College's curriculum that had left students without the vital practical skills they needed to pursue careers in the musical world beyond the school. In 1903, Holst once complained to Vaughan Williams, "As for conducting (which we ought to learn) it is impossible to attain in England and I fear we must give up all hopes of it."[49] When Allen assumed the helm of the College, one of the first courses to be added was one in conducting, taught by Boult. Other additions included the creation of two new orchestras, an array of remedial courses in aural skills and musical appreciation for students entering the College with marginal training, as well as classes in ballet, folk dancing, a teacher's training course, and an opera training program.[50]

One of Allen's particular strengths as an administrator was his ability to capitalize on the burgeoning interest in British music that came in the wake of the First World War. Like Grove, Allen had a knack for fundraising through his powerful friendships with the monied "great and good." These administrative gifts enabled him to leverage a great deal of power and influence within the music profession in England.[51]

In addition to reviving earlier programs designed to promote music by British composers, such as the Patron's Fund, Allen invested heavily in British opera.[52] Allen's operatic vision started with a proposal to turn a room under the concert hall into a theater for the RCM's opera class. To generate funding and enthusiasm, Allen announced that the theater would serve as a tribute to his beloved predecessor, Parry. Allen's ploy worked beautifully, and so the Parry Opera Theatre came into being as an ironic tribute to a composer who had at times voiced withering disdain for the genre.[53]

While the Parry Opera Theatre was intended to serve the needs of the College's students, it also played a vital role by providing the composition faculty with opportunities to have their operas rehearsed and staged. Vaughan Williams in particular benefited from this welcome development; the College mounted several productions of his operas, beginning with *The Shepherds of the Delectable Mountains* in 1922, followed by the first five performances of *Hugh the Drover* in 1924, *Sir John in Love* in 1929, and *Riders to the Sea* in 1937. Beyond staging his operas, the College provided Vaughan Williams with ample opportunities for his scores to be performed in the College's concerts. In addition, Vaughan Williams was able to avail himself of Boult and the orchestra in order to try out new works before they were performed in public.[54]

Allen's changes to the College, which, according to Colles, "amounted to a complete reformation and came near to being a revolution" were not without critics.[55] At times the RCM was perceived as encouraging an amateur rather than an exclusively professional atmosphere.[56] Indeed, Allen and Vaughan Williams shared a respect for both amateur and professional musicianship. Intermingling amateur and professional music making was crucial to Vaughan Williams's convictions about musical citizenship. As he observed in "Making Your Own Music" (1939): "In a healthy musical commonwealth we want both—the professional and the amateur, not as rivals but as partners."[57] Although Vaughan Williams undoubtedly benefited from the musical network of the RCM, the most lasting legacy he bequeathed to the College was his students.

Vaughan Williams as Teacher

Vaughan Williams's pedagogy and personal warmth contrasted sharply with many of the other professors at the RCM. Belinda Norman-Butler, who studied with him in the late 1920s, recalled, "None of the other professors looked at us as people—he did."[58] According to Ruth Gipps, Vaughan Williams "was the first person who ever called me 'a musician.'"[59] Beyond the kindness and respect for their dignity, however, many students found it challenging to discuss his methodology in detail. Elizabeth Maconchy (1907–1994), who studied with Vaughan Williams from 1925 to 1929, wrote in an obituary tribute:

> I find it difficult to describe his teaching, and his other pupils may feel the same difficulty. They would all agree, I think, that he was an inspiring teacher (by which I mean that he inspired them to write better music than they would otherwise have written) and that he set them a standard of absolute musical integrity. But he had little respect for the rules and conventional methods of teaching composition, and never followed a formal scheme.
>
> The reason for this apparent lack of method was his complete rejection of ready-made solutions. All through his life he chose the laborious method of "working out his own salvation"—his own phrase. And this is what he encouraged his pupils to do. His teaching, though he never said it in so many words—was always directed towards making his pupils think for themselves in their own musical language. He fully recognised the importance of an adequate technique, but for him the purpose of technique was how to give the clearest expression to the musical ideas of each individual composer in his own way. It is something for which there is no formula, and which cannot be learnt at second hand. He taught one to learn direct from the great music of the past—Bach, in particular, but many others too, and never from books. He liked to play the works he was discussing on the piano, often as piano duets: and very odd they sounded at times.[60]

In "working out his own salvation" as a teacher, Vaughan Williams drew upon his own varied experiences as a student of Parry, Stanford, Max Bruch, and Maurice Ravel whom he studied with for several months beginning in early December 1907. One principle, however, remained consistent throughout his teaching: his belief that encouragement was the best foundation for intellectual growth. Reflecting on his pedagogy, Vaughan Williams remarked, "With my own pupils now I always try to remember the value of encouragement. Sometimes a callow youth appears who may be a fool or may be a genius, and I would rather be guilty of encouraging a fool than of discouraging a genius."[61] This belief that encouragement served as a solid foundation for intellectual growth was surely a reaction to his dispiriting experience as a student of Stanford. Vaughan Williams explained, "I believe that every composer can achieve something, even a small song, which no one else could do as well."[62] Given the positive light that Vaughan Williams cast on his time with Parry, it might be easy to assume that Parry was the only source of his emphasis on encouragement, but his studies with Max Bruch (1838–1920) in 1897 were recalled with similar gratitude. Of his experience under Bruch's tutelage, which took place not long after his dismal time with Stanford, he remarked, "I only know that I worked hard and enthusiastically and that Max Bruch encouraged me, and I had never had much encouragement before."[63]

Student recollections offer insights into the evolution of Vaughan Williams's teaching and his unconventional approach. Unsurprisingly, it was his early years of teaching in the "gloomy crypt assigned to him by the authorities . . . filled with the smoke of his perpetual pipe, and littered with the matchboxes he had stolen from his pupils" that were the most haphazard.[64] Gordon Jacob (1895–1984), who was one of Vaughan Williams's students in the early 1920s, remarked disparagingly that his teacher "was then going through a revulsion against 'technique' in favour of untrammelled imagination."[65] Ultimately, Jacob felt that he benefited more substantially from his theory lessons with Howells.[66] Constant Lambert (1905–1951) also detected a certain disregard for technique on Vaughan Williams's part. In contrast to Jacob, however, Lambert intuited that there was an underlying logic to his teacher's approach: "Vaughan Williams was above all a psychologist and realised that a strict and suddenly imposed course of theory would have been fatal to a student such as myself at that moment. Instead, he encouraged me to go on composing, at an alarming rate I admit."[67] According to Jacob, Vaughan Williams eventually realized that this approach was not altogether successful and later modified his teaching methods. Jacob noted that "his later pupils were put through the mill or, as he put it, 'made to do their stodge' methodically."[68]

Vaughan Williams's suspicion of overemphasizing technique—surely in part a reaction against Stanford's fetishization of rigorous training—nonetheless lasted only a few years. Another of Vaughan Williams's students, Michael Mullinar,[69] wrote an article demonstrating that this shift to emphasizing technical training was firmly entrenched in his teaching by 1926:

> He corrects all technical errors, of course. If your harmony does not seem to be going well in a definite direction, he asks you what you want it to do; and then, after you have told him (if you can) what you are trying to work out, he shows where the progression is doubtful or weak. And if your part-writing has no character, or if your rhythms seem to get tired or change their shape without reason, he makes clear what is wrong.
>
> He queries all weak passages, and asks you to think over them for a few days, until you yourself arrive at the conclusion that they actually are weak. If after all you cannot realise that they are weak, and so cannot think his way, he does not wish them to be altered.
>
> If he considers that a work which falls short of being satisfactory could possibly be improved, he will offer his ideas, but only as suggestions, and he will not allow you to adopt them unless you really feel that way and can make the ideas your own.[70]

Mullinar's remarks illustrate that Vaughan Williams was searching for a balance between the openness of Parry and ensuring a certain level of technical rigor.

Vaughan Williams's unconventional approach—initial misgivings about the value of traditional teaching methods, especially the use of textbooks—has often been a point of discussion.[71] Given that composition students at the RCM were expected to have a firm grasp of harmony and counterpoint by the time they began their studies with him, it is not entirely surprising that Vaughan Williams did not see the need for spending an excessive amount of time on these topics in their lessons. An absence of textbooks did not mean an absence of structured exercises, as Vaughan Williams often instructed students to practice writing in the style of other composers, exercises that he had undertaken during his studies with Ravel.[72] Of the importance of these exercises, Mullinar attests:

> Dr. Vaughan Williams advises his students to write in forms for which they have no liking. If you want to write songs, and are disinclined towards fugues or concert overtures, he says

Figure 5. Studio photograph of Elizabeth Maconchy, 1925.

that while you are a student you must master the technique of every sort of composition, and then sets you to the task of writing the fugue or the overture. At the same time he says that no doubt you will never use these unwelcome forms when you have become a professional composer, because a composer can only create music successfully in the forms that naturally attract him. But while you are a student of composition, you must learn all you can, and exercise your-self in every direction that is likely to be of help in the end.[73]

Many of these exercises were of course tailored to the individual needs of each student. Vaughan Williams often referred perplexed students in need to other teachers who specialized in harmony, counterpoint, or orches-tration, such as Howells, Jacob, Holst, or R. O. Morris (1886–1948).[74]

A composer whose legacy is deeply entwined with a cultural nationalism as expressed through an interest in folk music and a rediscovery of Tudor com-posers might be expected to steer his students into similar areas of inquiry.[75] Yet Vaughan Williams strongly cautioned students against imitating his idiom, as he wanted them to develop their own voice, even if it differed greatly from his own.[76] In Maconchy's case, he supported her strong inter-est in Bartók, whose music helped her to discover her own style. Having benefited from studying abroad with Bruch and Ravel, Vaughan Williams encouraged his students to do the same, sending Maconchy to study in Prague with Karel Jirák (1891–1972), and Grace Williams (1906–1977) to Vienna for lessons with Egon Wellesz (1885–1974), a celebrated musicologist and composer who had been taught by Schoenberg (Figure 5).[77]

In addition to formal lessons, Vaughan Williams was an insistent advo-cate for his students, encouraging them to seek out as many performance opportunities as possible. Furthermore, Vaughan Williams encouraged his students to develop a social network such as the one that had played such a vital role during his second period of study at the RCM. As Grace Williams recalled:

> We learnt from the first to be self-critical; and in order to encour-age us to take criticism from each other, he got us to form a composers' club, which worked well and did us a lot of good. He was all for having our works played over by fellow-students and kept telling us to go and talk nicely to so-and-so and so-and-so because it was essential for us to hear what we'd written. When orchestral scores and parts were ready he did all he could to get them tried over by one or other of the College orchestras.[78]

In marked contrast to Stanford's views on women's inferiority as composers, Vaughan Williams championed the music of his female pupils. Over the course of his teaching career at the RCM, he taught a number of women who went on to develop successful professional careers. Jenny Doctor's research has shown that this support was not limited to their period of study and continued well after they left the College. Vaughan Williams frequently offered advice on scores, attended rehearsals and performances of his students' works, and lobbied on their behalf when they struggled to secure performances, broadcasts, and publication.[79]

A partial list of Vaughan Williams's better-known women students includes Maconchy, Williams, Ruth Gipps (1921–1999), Imogen Holst (1907–1984), Dorothy Gow (1892–1982), Peggy Glanville-Hicks (1912–1990), Jean Coulthard (1908–2000), and Anna Claudia Russell-Brown (1911–2006), who was more commonly known by her stage name, Anna Russell. In addition to compositions, Gipps founded a number of orchestras during her career, enabling her to promote the works of younger composers and women composers who struggled to obtain performances in the face of the male-dominated British musical establishment. Many of Maconchy's works garnered awards and prizes. Early in her career, her Quintet for Oboe and Strings was awarded third prize in the *Daily Telegraph*'s Chamber Music Competition in 1933. In 1953, her *Proud Thames* won the London County Council's competition for a coronation overture. Later in her career, she was made a Dame Commander of the British Empire, becoming the second female composer after Ethel Smyth to receive this honor. Williams became one of the most lauded Welsh composers of her generation. Ina Boyle (1889–1967), who studied privately with Vaughan Williams, became the first resident Irishwoman to write a symphony. Glanville-Hicks, who spent a significant portion of her life in the United States, enjoyed a distinguished career as a composer. She received a number of high-profile grants and awards, including two Guggenheim fellowships. Coulthard became a prominent Canadian composer and pedagogue, teaching composition at the University of British Columbia. Russell enjoyed a highly successful career in comedy, becoming well-known for her parodies of Gilbert and Sullivan and Wagner's *Der Ring des Niebelungen*.[80]

Vaughan Williams's reputation for encouraging his female pupils led him to take on students in whom other teachers had little faith. This may explain, at least in part, his undeserved posthumous reputation as a mediocre teacher. The case of Anna Russell is illuminating in this regard. She initially studied with Howells, whom she described as having "nothing but contempt for my considerable output of compositions."[81]

Discouraged, Russell decided to switch to Vaughan Williams; she supplied vivid details of those lessons in her autobiography:

> He said my compositions weren't bad, but very derivative. "For instance," he said, "that one is quite a creditable piece of Debussy." This got to be rather a joke: "Who are we going to be today," he'd ask, "Mozart or Wagner?" One day he asked me to please restrain the urge to be Gilbert and Sullivan, as he found himself humming my pieces, which interfered with his own musical thinking. After that he always referred to me as "Gilbert and Sullivan Russell-Brown." This was another portent of what I was to become, although nothing was further from my mind at the time.[82]

Aside from Jacob and Lambert, it is notable that Vaughan Williams's most successful students were women. While they faced gender-based discrimination during their lifetimes, in recent years the expressive and accomplished scores of Boyle, Glanville-Hicks, Maconchy, and Williams have begun to receive greater recognition and an increasing number of performances and recordings.

During the late 1930s at the RCM, Vaughan Williams taught the Aotearoa/New Zealand composer Douglas Lilburn (1915–2001), who studied with him from 1937 to 1939. Lilburn's influence on the musical life of his native country was both enlivening and profound.[83]

At the beginning of the Second World War, the aging Vaughan Williams decided to retire from full-time teaching, although he continued to work during the war due to the number of teaching staff who had enlisted. He also continued to adjudicate at the RCM up to his death. Of his lasting influence, Maconchy stated: "An immense number of musical people owe him a debt of gratitude: for his music, for his generosity, and for the example of his complete devotion to music. But his pupils perhaps owe him most of all. We measure our musical achievements by his standards, and his inspiration keeps us writing."[84] As Parry passed the torch to Vaughan Williams, so Vaughan Williams passed a legacy to a succeeding generation of the composers he trained at the RCM. These composers have left their indelible mark on the musical life and repertory of Great Britain, thereby fulfilling the vision articulated by Prince Edward at the opening ceremony of the RCM: "an institution which I trust will give to music a new impulse, a glorious future, and a national life."

1. "The Royal College of Music," *Times* (London), 8 May 1883.

2. Ibid.

3. For a detailed study of this subject, see Cyril Ehrlich, *The Music Profession in Britain Since the Eighteenth Century* (Oxford: Clarendon Press, 1985).

4. "Opening of the Royal College of Music," *Funny Folks*, 12 May 1883.

5. Guy Warrack, "The Royal College of Music: The First Eighty-five Years," typescript draft (British Library, ca. 1977, General Reference Collection X.431/11358), 2–5. Also see David Wright, "The South Kensington Music Schools and the Development of the British Conservatoire in the Late Nineteenth Century," *Journal of the Royal Musical Association* 130/2 (2005): 236–82; and G. W. E. Brightwell, "In Search of a Nation's Music: The Role of the Society of Arts and the Royal Academy of Music in the Establishment of the Royal College of Music in 1883," in *Nineteenth-Century British Music Studies* 3, ed. Peter Horton and Bennett Zon (Aldershot: Ashgate, 2003), 251–72.

6. Arthur Jacobs, *Arthur Sullivan: Victorian Musician*, 2nd ed. (Aldershot: Ashgate, 1992), 103–6, 111–12. For the acrimonious end of Sullivan's tenure as Principal, see 155.

7. H. C. Colles, *The Royal College of Music: A Jubilee Record, 1883–1933* (London: Macmillan, 1933), 8.

8. Edwin Benbow, "Preface," *The R.C.M. Magazine* 55/1 (February 1959): 3.

9. Henry Hardy Cole (1843–1916) was the son of Henry Cole (1808–1882). A civil servant by profession, Henry Cole was heavily involved with the Society for the Encouragement of the Arts, Manufactures, and Commerce. In addition to playing a vital role in both the planning and execution of the Great Exhibition of 1851, he also served as the first director of the South Kensington Museum (later renamed the Victoria and Albert Museum) with his advocacy of the arts extending to the development of the National Training School for Music. For his services, he received a knighthood in 1875. H. H. Cole's involvement in designing the National Training School for Music presumably came through his father. At the time of the project, H. H. Cole was a lieutenant in the Royal Engineers, having spent much of his career overseeing archaeological surveys in India. Though he served as the project's principal designer, the Science and Art Department appeared to have played a role as well. The building's funder, Charles James Freake (1814–1884), was a property developer by profession, working primarily in South Kensington. Like Henry Cole, Freake was a well-known patron of the arts and received a baronetcy in 1882. For further details, see John Skidmore, "The Society and the National Training School for Music," *RSA Journal* 140/5426 (February 1992): 205; "Royal College of Organists," in *Survey of London,* vol. 38: *South Kensington Museums Area,* ed. F. H. W. Sheppard (London: London County Council, 1975), 217–19; and "Princes Gate and Princes Gardens: The Freake Estate, Development by C. J. Freake," in *Survey of London,* vol. 45: *Knightsbridge,* ed. John Greenacombe (London: London County Council, 2000), 191–205.

10. "National Training School of Music, South Kensington," *Building News and Engineering Journal* 29 (29 October 1875): 489.

11. Francis Wollaston Moody (1824–1886) was a well–known decorative artist and teacher. He enjoyed a long association with the South Kensington Museum, designing its well-known Ceramic Staircase at the request of Henry Cole. See Skidmore, "Royal College of Organists," 217–19; and Owen Gibbons, "An Art Teacher: The Late F. W. Moody," in *The Magazine of Art,* (1893): 404–8.

12. Quoted in Colles, *The Royal College of Music: A Jubilee Record*, 2–3. For a brief discussion of the building's failings, see F. E. Gladstone, "The Royal College of Music from Within," *The R.C.M. Magazine* 4/1 (1907): 12.

13. Ralph Vaughan Williams, "A Musical Autobiography," in *National Music and Other Essays*, ed. Michael Kennedy (Oxford: Oxford University Press, 1963), 180.

14. Ibid. Stephen Massingberd (1869–1925) was related to Vaughan Williams through the Darwins. Massingberd and his wife were enthusiastic promoters of music in Lincolnshire and Vaughan Williams often visited their estate at Gunby Hall near Spilsby.

15. F. E. Gladstone taught both organ and harmony at the RCM.

16. Vaughan Williams, "A Musical Autobiography," 181. George Alexander Macfarren (1813–1887) was a composer whose music was admired by both Mendelssohn and Wagner. Despite his blindness, Macfarren was appointed professor of music at Cambridge University in 1875. *The Rudiments of Harmony* was first published in 1860 by Cramer, Beale, and Chappell.

17. Ralph Vaughan Williams, "The Teaching of Parry and Stanford," in *Vaughan Williams on Music*, ed. David Manning (Oxford: Oxford University Press, 2008), 315.

18. Jeremy Dibble, "Parry, Stanford and Vaughan Williams: The Creation of Tradition," in *Vaughan Williams in Perspective*, ed. Lewis Foreman (London: Albion Music, 1998), 35–36.

19. See Byron Adams, "Scripture, Church, and culture: biblical texts in the works of Ralph Vaughan Williams," in *Vaughan Williams Essays*, ed. Alain Frogley (Cambridge: Cambridge University Press, 1996), 101–2.

20. Vaughan Williams, "Teaching of Parry and Stanford," 316.

21. Vaughan Williams, "A Musical Autobiography," 182.

22. Ibid., 181.

23. Ibid.

24. Ibid., 181–82.

25. Ralph Vaughan Williams, "Sir Hubert Parry," in *Vaughan Williams on Music*, 296. Vaughan Williams was fortunate to have been deeply liked by Parry, which surely led to the more favorable deference that his compositions received, as opposed to the outright condemnation experienced by others. See Jeremy Dibble, *C. Hubert Parry: His Life and Music* (Oxford: Clarendon Press, 1992), 283–84; and Byron Adams, "Vaughan Williams's Musical Apprenticeship," in *The Cambridge Companion to Vaughan Williams*, ed. Alain Frogley and Aidan J. Thompson (Cambridge: Cambridge University Press, 2013), 34.

26. For further discussion on Vaughan Williams's student years at Cambridge, see Julian Rushton's essay in this volume. —Ed.

27. Quoted in Christopher Palmer, *Herbert Howells: A Celebration*, 2nd ed. (London: Thames Publishing, 1996), 16.

28. See Diana Souhami, *The Trials of Radclyffe Hall* (New York: Doubleday, 1999), 17–25.

29. See "Herbert Howells Talking to Sir Arthur Bliss," in Palmer, *Herbert Howells*, 372–73.

30. Arthur Bliss, *As I Remember*, rev. ed. (London: Thames Publishing, 1989), 28–29.

31. Vaughan Williams, "The Teaching of Parry and Stanford," 320.

32. Adams, "Vaughan Williams's Musical Apprenticeship," 36.

33. Arthur Benjamin, "A Student in Kensington," *Music & Letters* 31/3 (July 1950): 201.

34. Adams, "Vaughan Williams's Musical Apprenticeship," 36.

35. Despite keeping up a facade of admiration for Stanford in public, Vaughan Williams could be scathing in private; see Adams, "Vaughan Williams's Musical Apprenticeship," 35–37.

36. Thomas Dunhill, "The Royal College of Music from Within: The R.C.M. Literary and Debating Society," *The R.C.M. Magazine* 5/1 (Christmas Term, 1908): 17–21.

37. Frank Howes, "A Chapter of Autobiography," *The R.C.M. Magazine* 72/2 (1978): 81.

38. Vaughan Williams, "A Musical Autobiography," 185.

39. Ralph Vaughan Williams, "Who Wants the English Composer?," *The R.C.M. Magazine* 9/1 (1912): 11–15. For the disapproving reactions of both Stanford and Parry to this essay, see Jeremy Dibble, *Charles Villiers Stanford: Man and Musician* (Oxford: Oxford University Press, 2002), 389n9. Vaughan Williams's brief period on the RCM Council is mentioned in George Dyson, "Tributes to Vaughan Williams," *The Musical Times* 99/1388 (October 1958): 538.

40. See Paul Rodmell, *Charles Villiers Stanford* (Aldershot: Ashgate Publishing, 2002), 305–9.

41. Dibble, *Parry*, 470.

42. Colles, *The Royal College of Music: A Jubilee Record*, 46.

43. H. C. Colles, "Directors of the R.C.M.: Sir Hugh Allen and Dr. George Dyson," *The Musical Times* 78/1136 (October 1937): 862; Percy Scholes's comments in Thomas Armstrong, "Sir Hugh Allen," *The Musical Times* 87/1237 (March 1946): 76; and Frank Howes, "Sir Hugh Allen," *Monthly Musical Record* 60/711 (1 March 1930): 66–67.

44. See Colles, "Directors of the R.C.M.": 861–62.

45. See Cyril Bailey, *Hugh Percy Allen* (London: Oxford University Press, 1948), 7–9 and 98–101. Allen also continued to hold his post at Oxford while at the RCM.

46. For an updated examination of Allen's directorship, see David C. H. Wright, *The Royal College of Music and Its Contexts: An Artistic and Social History* (Cambridge: Cambridge University Press, 2020), 133–86.

47. Kathleen Long was born in Brentford and studied piano at the RCM with Herbert Sharpe from 1910 to 1916. As a pianist, she was well-known for her interpretations of Fauré and Mozart, recording several of the latter's piano concertos. She also frequently collaborated with French ensembles such as the Loewenguth Quartet and Pasquier Trio. In 1950 she was awarded the Palmes académiques from the French Republic for her contributions to French music. A CBE followed in 1957. After several decades on the teaching staff of the RCM, she retired in 1964. See Gordon Stewart and John Russell, "Farewell to Kathleen Long," *The R.C.M. Magazine* 30/1 (1965): 15–16; Diana McVeagh, "Long, Kathleen," *Grove Music Online*, https://www.oxfordmusiconline.com/grovemusic/view/10.1093/gmo/9781561592630.001.0001/omo–9781561592630–e–0000016947; and Warrack, "The Royal College of Music: The First Eighty-five Years," 141.

48. Frank Howes, "A Chapter of Autobiography," 82.

49. Ralph Vaughan Williams and Gustav Holst, *Heirs and Rebels: Letters Written to Each Other and Occasional Writings on Music*, ed. Ursula Vaughan Williams and Imogen Holst (London: Oxford University Press, 1959), 12.

50. Interestingly enough, Stanford had previously recommended the creation of a full-blown opera class to no avail; see Rodmell, *Stanford*, 306.

51. See Bailey, *Hugh Percy Allen*, 103–5.

52. The Patron's Fund was founded in 1903 through the financial support of Lord Ernest Palmer to foster interest in British music by supporting native composers and musicians. Although the Patron's Fund activities were managed by the RCM, it was open to all British composers. During Allen's directorship, the Fund's focus expanded beyond performances to also include a series of rehearsals open to the public. For further discussion of the Patron's Fund, see Wright, *The Royal College of Music and Its Contexts*, 93–97.

53. See ibid. 175–81. For Parry's attitude to opera, see Dibble, *Parry*, 243.

54. Michael Kennedy, *The Works of Ralph Vaughan Williams* (Oxford: Clarendon Press, 1964), 156.

55. Colles, "Directors of the R.C.M.": 862.

56. See Wright, *The Royal College of Music and Its Contexts*, 187.

57. Ralph Vaughan Williams, "Making Your Own Music," in *Vaughan Williams on Music*, 76.

58. Stephen Connock, *Toward the Sun Rising: Ralph Vaughan Williams Remembered* (London: Albion Music, 2018), 193.

59. Ruth Gipps, "Dr. Ralph Vaughan Williams, O.M.," *The R.C.M. Magazine* 55/1 (February 1959): 50.

60. Elizabeth Maconchy, "Vaughan Williams as a Teacher," *Composer* 2 (March 1959): 18–19.

61. Vaughan Williams, "A Musical Autobiography," 187.

62. Vaughan Williams, "The Teaching of Parry and Stanford," 318.

63. Vaughan Williams, "A Musical Autobiography," 187.

64. Quoted in Stephen Lloyd, *Constant Lambert: Beyond the Rio Grande* (Woodbridge: Boydell Press, 2014), 32.

65. Eric Wetherell, *Gordon Jacob—A Centenary Biography* (London: Thames Publishing, 1995), 26.

66. Ibid.

67. Lloyd, *Constant Lambert*, 32.

68. Gordon Jacob, "Dr. Ralph Vaughan Williams, O.M.," *The R.C.M. Magazine* 55/1 (February 1959): 31.

69. Michael Mullinar (1895–1973) was born in northern Wales and developed into a brilliant pianist who taught score reading at the RCM. Vaughan Williams dedicated his Sixth Symphony to him. For Mullinar's role in the creation of that score, see Byron Adams, "The Revisions of Vaughan Williams's Sixth Symphony," in *Vaughan Williams Essays*, ed. Byron Adams and Robin Wells (Aldershot: Ashgate Press, 2003), 3–4.

70. Michael Mullinar, "Dr. Vaughan Williams as Teacher," *The Midland Musician* 1/1 (January 1926): 9.

71. Michael Mullinar, "Dr. Ralph Vaughan Williams, O.M.," *The R.C.M. Magazine* 55/1 (February 1959): 32.

72. See Adams, "Vaughan Williams's Musical Apprenticeship," 41.

73. Mullinar, "Vaughan Williams as Teacher," 9.

74. R. O. Morris, who was Vaughan Williams's brother-in-law, was celebrated for his mastery of counterpoint, especially that of the sixteenth century.

75. For a discussion of Vaughan Williams's legacy in relation to nationalism, see Alain Frogley, "Constructing Englishness in music: national character and the reception of Ralph Vaughan Williams," in *Vaughan Williams Studies*, ed. Alain Frogley (Cambridge: Cambridge University Press, 1996): 1–22.

76. Mullinar, "Vaughan Williams as Teacher," 9.

77. Wellesz is chiefly remembered for his magisterial volume *A History of Byzantine Music and Hymnography* (Oxford: Clarendon Press, 1960). One of Schoenberg's early students, Wellesz completed nine symphonies, and operas such as *Incognita*, Op. 69 (1950). In 1940, the British government interned Wellesz and other German and Austrian refugees on the Isle of Man as "enemy aliens." Wellesz was released after five months due to insistent lobbying by Vaughan Williams and H. C. Colles, longtime chief music critic of the *Times*.

78. Grace Williams, "Dr. Ralph Vaughan Williams, O. M.," *The R.C.M. Magazine* 55/1 (February 1959): 36.

79. For further discussion of Vaughan Williams's support of women composers, see Jenny Doctor, "'Working for Her Own Salvation': Vaughan Williams as Teacher of Elizabeth Maconchy, Grace Williams and Ina Boyle," in *Vaughan Williams in Perspective*, ed. Lewis Foreman (London: Albion Music, 1998), 181–201; Jenny Doctor, "Intersecting Circles: The Early Careers of Elizabeth Maconchy, Grace Williams, and Ina Boyle," *Women & Music* 2 (1998): 90–109; and Erica Siegel, "'I'm not making this up, you know!': The Success of Two of Vaughan Williams's Students in America," *The Musical Quarterly* 99/3–4 (Fall–Winter 2016): 356–85.

80. For information on the careers of Vaughan Williams's female pupils, see Rhiannon Mathias, *Lutyens, Maconchy, Williams and Twentieth-Century British Music: A Blest Trio of Sirens*

(Farnham: Ashgate, 2012); Ita Beausang and Séamas de Barra, *Ina Boyle (1889–1967): A Composer's Life* (Cork: Cork University Press, 2018); Suzanne Robinson, *Peggy Glanville-Hicks: Composer and Critic* (Urbana: University of Illinois Press, 2019); Anna Russell, *I'm Not Making This Up, You Know* (New York: Continuum, 1985); and Jill Halstead, *Ruth Gipps: Anti–Modernism, Nationalism and Difference in English Music* (Aldershot: Ashgate, 2006).

81. Russell, *I'm Not Making This Up, You Know,* 75.

82. Ibid.

83. For a comprehensive introduction, see Philip Norman, *Douglas Lilburn: His Life and Music* (Christchurch, NZ: Canterbury University Press, 2006).

84. Elizabeth Maconchy, "Dr. Ralph Vaughan Williams, O.M.," *The R.C.M. Magazine* 55/1 (February 1959): 34.

Vaughan Williams's
"The Letter and the Spirit" (1920)

INTRODUCED AND ANNOTATED
BY CERI OWEN

According to Ursula Vaughan Williams, in her husband's 1920 essay "The Letter and the Spirit" Vaughan Williams "summed up what he believed, both then and for the rest of his life."[1] The essay provides insights into many aspects of his mature ideas, among them the importance of practical music-making within a musical culture; an understanding of beauty as the content of music and a condition of its value; an emphasis on music's purpose as communication; and an exploration of musical creativity as a collective endeavor. Of particular significance is the emphasis Vaughan Williams placed here upon the "revelatory" capacities of art—the first time he grappled explicitly with the spiritual nature of music in his published writings. This topic was to appear persistently in his essays and lectures thereafter, and was a lifelong theme of his music.[2]

Yet, what Vaughan Williams meant by the "spirit" and "spiritual" in this essay bears further discussion. He borrowed his title from an idiom derived, in turn, from the Bible, specifically one of St. Paul's epistles: "The letter killeth, but the Spirit giveth life."[3] Transposing the scripture to a musical context, the "letter" of musical notation is not simply held in tension with the "spirit" of musical sound and experience; rather, the essay becomes a discourse on the relationship between the two. As such, Vaughan Williams explores how music "lives," asking where and how it exists and where its meaning inheres: in its text or in its act?

Vaughan Williams had apparently been moved to broach his topic in response to post–First World War developments in music education and renewed debates about music appreciation. He makes a somewhat scathing reference near the essay's opening to the views of "some of our acknowledged leaders of musical thought," quoting from a number of sources including Henry Hadow's 1918 pamphlet *The Needs of Popular Musical Education*, which, Vaughan Williams notes, bore "the *imprimatur* of the President of the Board of Education."[4] Following a successful 1919 campaign to persuade the Board of Education to appoint Cecil Sharp as occasional inspector of training colleges in folk song and dancing, Vaughan Williams here returned to the matter of education reform. Though he would likely have agreed with much of Hadow's manifesto, especially the proposed expansion of music's role within schools and universities, Vaughan Williams took issue with what he considered to be a disproportionate emphasis upon music history, biography, and other contextual matters, and above all on musical literacy. This, Vaughan Williams believed, betrayed a misunderstanding of the nature of music, promoting the misapprehension that musical notation contains the essence of music, and that fostering musical ability proceeds from learning to read silently from a musical score, akin to reading a book, rather than learning "to *hear*." To hear music, Vaughan Williams explains, requires a different kind of interpretative process:

> To be really musical one must be able to *hear*. The ear must be sensitive, the mind must be quick to grasp what the ear has heard and see its connection with what has gone before, and to be prepared for what is to come, and above all the imagination must be vivid, to see the glimpses of the heart of things which the composer has crystallized into earthly sound.
>
> To educate a child in music is to teach him to hear; then and then only he is a musician.

Vaughan Williams arrives at this theory of musical listening, and his priority for music education, having first offered the following definition of art's nature and purpose: "Before going any further may we take it," he asks,

> that the object of an art is to obtain a partial revelation of that which is beyond human senses and human faculties—of that, in fact, which is spiritual? and that the means which we employ to induce this revelation are those very senses and faculties themselves?
>
> The human, visible, audible and intelligible media which artists (of all kinds) use, are symbols not of other visible and audible things but of what lies beyond sense and knowledge.

To make sense of this well-known but rather opaque passage, it is useful to consider Vaughan Williams's earlier articles, to whose territory "The Letter and the Spirit" returned. In 1903, Vaughan Williams had argued that "music is not a 'symbol' of anything else, it has no 'meaning,'" by which he suggested not that music is unmeaningful, rather that music's meaning cannot be approached through verbal language, and that music does not refer to anything outside itself.[5] His position did not change substantially in "The Letter and the Spirit," for though he now argued that music does have a symbolic quality, he held that it symbolizes something more than what is human and knowable: "a sign standing for something that cannot itself be expressed."[6] Furthermore, given that Vaughan Williams elaborates in "The Letter and the Spirit" that "the symbols of the musical composer are those of the ear—musical sounds in their various combinations," he evoked an earlier ideal of musical autonomy, previously expounded in his 1902 article "Palestrina and Beethoven."

Here, when discussing the qualities of "beauty" and "emotion" that music must possess—qualities he similarly emphasized in "The Letter and the Spirit"—he argued:

> All music, strictly speaking, is emotional, because every impression produced by music is an emotion. . . . It is a great mistake to suppose, as many people do, that music is a sort of phonograph into which the composer speaks his emotions, and that these are in their turn reproduced in the hearer.
>
> The emotion felt by anyone listening to music is *purely aesthetic*, that is to say, the emotion is purely that of pleasure in the perception of beauty . . . with our emotions in listening to the music the composer's intention has nothing to do. Art is to be judged not by intention but by the results. . . . There is but one really musical emotion, and it is produced by the music composed, and not by the agency which composed the music.[7]

Vaughan Williams therefore holds that music's content and meaning resides at least in part in the experience of the listener. He makes a similar point in "The Letter and the Spirit," but explains that in order to realize music's beauty fully, acts of listening must be conducted through a sensual, physical experience of the body in response to "actual sound." Only through the experience of those sounds—and crucially, by learning to "hear" them, which also involves the "mind," "memory," and "imagination"—can music be "understood," eliciting an emotional reaction and inducing the spiritual "revelation" to which he refers.

It is because "the art of music is essentially one of sound" that Vaughan Williams considers learning to read music silently from the page to be a problematic agenda for music education. Whereas in a poem, he reasons,

"The poet writes his poem, and there it is ready for everyone who has learnt to read and who understands the meaning of words"; in contrast, "a musical composition when invented is only half finished, and until actual sound is produced that composition *does not exist*." "How then is the musical composer to make his invention live in actual sound?" he asks, and then provides both an answer as well as a theory of musical notation:

> [The composer] must seek out others who are capable of making the sounds he desires and must instruct them when and where to make these sounds. For this purpose a clumsy and unprecise code of signals has been evolved which by conven- tion indicate that certain sounds are to be made . . . .
>
> What the musical composer, in effect, says to his performers is:—"I desire to produce a certain spiritual result on certain people; I hope and believe that if you blow, and scrape, and hit in a particular manner this spiritual effect will result."

Significant here is Vaughan Williams's overt preoccupation just after the First World War with the material quality of what he also calls "the actual shock of sound," which carries music's capacity for inducing that "spiritual effect." Notable as well is the collective idea of musical creativity unfolded here, for he argues that a composer "wishes to be in spiritual commu- nication with his hearers. To do that certain sounds are necessary; and until those sounds are heard the spiritual contact is not established." He also explains that the composer "must seek out others who are capable of making the sounds he desires," later describing "that twin-mind [of the performer] which will translate his imaginings into sound, and consum- mate that 'marriage of true minds' which alone can give his music life."

This principle of collective expression, subjectivity, and authorship was one he invoked elsewhere.[8] It was an ideal that developed partly through contact with traditional music cultures, in which, he observed, music evolved collectively through oral transmission in performance, in a manner different to "the written music of definite composers."[9] One of the noteworthy features of "The Letter and the Spirit" is the way in which Vaughan Williams dwells upon the role of the performer within a con- ception of co-creation and perhaps even co-authorship in notated music. This is in part due, Vaughan Williams explains, to the inadequacy of nota- tion to "indicate what [the composer] wanted with any precision." As he rightly observes, "Two singers or players may follow faithfully the compos- er's intentions as given in the written notes and produce widely different results." In this way, the potential distance between a composer's intention and the performer's realization may perhaps have widened in Vaughan Williams's mind, compared with his earlier writings; thus, the opportunity for a performer's "individual rendering" has also arguably expanded.[10] At the same time, a composer's desire and capability to communicate has also perhaps intensified in 1920, for in "The Letter and the Spirit" Vaughan Williams imagines that "actual sound" has the power "to produce in [the composer] that spiritual state which he hopes to induce in others."

The possibility of communication and the role of sound was to become one of the most pressing cultural, social, and political concerns of the interwar years, reshaping understandings of modernity and constructions of the self.[11] In essays published after "The Letter and the Spirit," Vaughan Williams returned persistently to the relationship between musical notation, sound, and experience, and to the questions of how a composer communicates with others through their music and whose authorship and subjectivity "the musical composition" projects. In considering how far Vaughan Williams's aesthetics anticipated poststructuralism's "death of the author," as Aidan J. Thomson has argued, it may be significant that when Vaughan Williams reprinted "The Letter and the Spirit" in his 1953 book *Some Thoughts on Beethoven's Choral Symphony with writings on other musical subjects* (London: Oxford University Press, 1953), he removed the paragraph in which he originally emphasized the importance of hearing a piece of music "as it was intended—then, and then only, can we get into absolute communion with the composer."[12] Equally pertinent is how, by the end of his life, Vaughan Williams was more explicit about the "creative" role taken by the listener as well as the performer in the act of making music: "When we listen to a symphony as we should do," he declared in 1954, "we are actually taking part in it, together with the composer and the performers. We are taking part in the creation of that symphony."[13] Vaughan Williams's preoccupation with the possibility of a community drawn together through communication in music, and his belief that music's meaning and very existence inheres at least in part through acts of interpretation conducted through the medium of "actual sound," are developed within "The Letter and the Spirit." As he concludes, "While music is the art of sound, it is the ear which must be taught its language."

When "The Letter and the Spirit" was republished in *Some Thoughts on Beethoven's Choral Symphony with writings on other musical subjects*, various revisions were made by Vaughan Williams. The original, inconsistent punctuation from its 1920 appearance in *Music & Letters* has been retained in the body of the text below, with notations about the changes made as the essay was reprinted. These emendations are detailed in footnotes to the 1920 text, reproduced below. They include editorial changes of punctuation and the addition or removal of inconsequential words. Although some of these revisions may have been the work of a copy editor, they were authorized by Vaughan Williams and indicate the level of detail with which he approached the task of editing his own writings. Other revisions to "The Letter and the Spirit" included the correction of errors and the removal and inclusion of other more substantial details, as well as two more substantial revisions.

The first of these was the substitution of the paragraph beginning "It was Lord Rosebery (I believe) who once said that when he could not go for a holiday he bought a guide book and trusted to his imagination for the rest" (found as the second full paragraph on page 67 below), by this paragraph:

> A musical score is like a map. The expert map reader can tell fairly exactly what sort of country he is going to visit, whether it is hilly or flat, whether the hills are steep or gradual, whether it is wooded or bare, what the roads are likely to be; but can he experience from a map the spiritual exaltation when a wonderful view spreads before his eyes, or the joy of careering downhill on a bicycle or, above all, the sense of rest and comfort induced by the factual realization of those prophetic letters "P.H."? [14]

The second substantial revision—the excision of the section of text in which Vaughan Williams cites an ideal way in which to judge a piece of music "as it was intended"—assumes more significance when viewed in the context of his aesthetics more broadly as has been touched upon above. In this excised passage Vaughan Williams insists on the necessity of a "certain shock of sound which will help us to a certain extent to obtain a glimpse of the vision which the composer is trying to convey to us."

As an epigraph before his essay, Vaughan Williams affixed a quotation drawn from a poem by the Tudor author and courtier Thomas Vaux, Second Baron Vaux of Harrowden (1509–1556). The punctuation in this quotation was later modified to render "Whereto serve ears if that there be no sound?," with the comma after "ears" removed as is found in the poem from which the quotation is excerpted.[15]

The Letter and the Spirit

"Whereto serve ears, if that there be no sound?"
Lord Vaux.

That the art of music is essentially one of sound is a proposition which would seem too obvious to need proof.

Yet it is the opinion of many people that the really musical man prefers not to hear music, but gets at his music silently by reading it to himself as he would a book.

Many years ago there appeared in *Punch* a picture illustrating the supposed growth in the near future of musical appreciation; the barrel organ was to be replaced by itinerant conductors turning over the leaves of scores and beating time. The picture represents two street-boys reading the score and watching the conductor, while the following conversation takes place:[1]—"'Eavenly adagio ain't it, Bill?" "Yes, but he takes the *tempo* too *accelerato*."[2]

Now Mr. Punch may be taken as always representing faithfully the average point of view. This then[3] is the average opinion, that when the street-boy becomes really musical he will no longer want to hear music but will be content to look at it. And this theory has the sanction of some of our acknowledged leaders of musical thought.

Sir Henry Hadow, in an address lately published with the *imprimatur*[4] of the President of the Board of Education, says:[5]—" . . . It is a very low order of education which does not enable a person to read a page or write a letter without reading the words aloud. The same degree of education which enables us to read a page of Shakespeare to ourselves would enable us equally well to read a page of Beethoven."

Again Dr. Arthur Somervell is reported to have said the other day[6] at an educational conference:[7]—"When we go into a shop to buy a book we do not ask the salesman to read over a few passages to us, in order that we may see if we like it: we read for ourselves. Yet with music how many there are who ask that the piece shall be 'tried over'

---

1. Em dash removed in 1953.
2. No italicization.
3. Comma was inserted after this word.
4. No italicization.
5. Em dash removed.
6. "The other day" removed but the comparable reference to "an address lately published" by Hadow retained.
7. Em dash removed.

for them before they buy. They ought instead to be able to read it for themselves, without playing or singing."

And,[8] to quote once again, the very distinguished amateur musician, Alexander Ewing, in a letter to Dr. Ethel Smyth wrote as follows:[9]—"A work of Bach's . . . .[10] exists for us on paper and in performance: two kinds of existence, differing in degree perhaps, but the one as real as the other."

I venture to believe that the opinions quoted above are founded on a fallacy—namely, that to read silently a page of Beethoven is the exact counterpart of reading silently a page of Shakespeare.

Before going any further may we take it that the object of an art is to obtain a partial revelation of that which is beyond human senses and human faculties—of that, in fact, which is spiritual? and[11] that the means which[12] we employ to induce this revelation are those very senses and faculties themselves?

The human, visible, audible and intelligible media which artists (of all kinds) use, are symbols not of other visible and audible things but of what lies beyond sense and knowledge.

The symbols of the painter are those which can be appreciated by the eye—colour, shape[13] and the appearance of natural objects; the symbols of the poet are words and their meaning; and the symbols of the musical composer are those of the ear—musical sounds in their various combinations. To say that poetry when read aloud uses the symbol of sound is only to say that poetry then borrows to a slight extent from the sister art of music. But to realize how little part the ear plays in the poetic scheme one has only to imagine the spiritual effect of (say)[14] Homer declaimed aloud to two listeners, one who did, and the other who did not[15] understand Greek. If sound[16] was a large factor in poetry the spiritual effect on both hearers would be nearly equal;[17] as it is,[18] we know that the effect of declamation in an unknown language is almost negligible, and the reaction to the stimulus must be referred to music rather than to poetry. To a listener who understands the meaning of the words the actual sound of

---

8. Comma after "And" removed.
9. "As follows" and em dash removed.
10. Ellipsis rendered as ". . ."
11. Capitalization added.
12. "which" removed.
13. "shape" pluralized.
14. Parentheses replaced by commas.
15. Comma added after "who did not".
16. Rendered "If the sound".
17. Semi-colon replaced with a colon.
18. Comma removed.

those words doubtless[19] has a powerful emotional effect but only in connection with the meaning and association of the words spoken. When a poem is read in silence the sound is absent, but the meaning of the words with all that[20] they symbolize is still there.

Where is the symbolic effect of a printed page of music? Can a page of musical notes and a page of poetry be compared in any way? It seems absurd to ask such a question; yet it is necessary, because there is a widespread notion (shared as we have seen by some of the most distinguished musical thinkers) that a printed page of music is the exact parallel of a painted picture or a printed poem.

The art of music differs from poetry and painting in this, that it involves two distinct processes—that of invention and that of presentation. It is just possible that in very primitive kinds of musical improvisation the acts of invention and presentation may be simultaneous. But it is difficult to say that[21] there are any cases in which the act of invention did not slightly precede the act of presentation; at all events in the ordinary case of a composer singing or playing his own compositions[22] he is simply acting in a dual capacity, first that of composer and then that of performer; the two processes are quite distinct.

In the other arts this is not so; the invention and presentation are one process. The painter paints his picture, and it is a complete work of art; all that is needed further is a pair of eyes and the heart and mind to realize what one sees. The poet writes his poem, and there it is ready[23] for everyone who has learnt to read and who understands the meaning of words. But a musical composition when invented is only half finished, and until actual sound is produced that composition *does not exist*.

How then is the musical composer to make his invention live in actual sound? If it is a single line of melody or capable of being played on one instrument he may be able to complete the work himself. But how if his invention requires more than one voice or instrument? Then he must seek out others who are capable of making the sounds he desires and must instruct them when and where to make these sounds.[24] For this purpose a clumsy and unprecise code of written signals has been evolved, which by convention indicate that certain sounds are to be made.

---

19. "doubtless" removed.
20. "that" removed.
21. "that" removed.
22. "composition" (singular) used here.
23. "ready" removed.
24. "These" replaced with "the".

This code of signals or series of orders is known as a musical score, and has about as much to do with music as a time-table has to do with a railway journey.

What the musical composer, in effect, says to his performers is:[25]— "I desire to produce a certain spiritual result on certain people; I hope and believe that if you blow, and scrape, and hit in a particular manner this spiritual effect will result. For this purpose I have arranged with you a code of signals in virtue of which, whenever you see a certain dot, or dash, or circle,[26] you will make a particular sound; if you follow these directions closely my invention will become music, but until you make the indicated sounds my music *does not exist*."

So a musical score is merely an indication of potential music, and moreover it is a most clumsy and ill-devised indication. How clumsy it is may be seen from the importance of the "individual renderings" of any piece of music. If the[27] composer could indicate what he wanted with any precision there would be no room for this; as it is, two singers or players may follow faithfully the composer's intentions as given in the written notes and produce widely different results.

Under our present system of musical notation the composer can give only the most general indication of what he wishes. Perhaps future generations will devise something more precise; though whether this will be an advantage is doubtful.

The art of music[28] requires two minds (or one mind acting in two distinct ways) to produce the final result[29]—the inventor and the presenter (in other words the composer and the performer).[30] If the composer is wise he will not try to make his score "fool-proof"[31] but will wait for that twin-mind which will translate his imaginings into sound, and consummate that 'marriage of true minds'[32] which alone can give his music life.

It is, of course, not to be denied that the power to realize to a certain extent by visual inspection what sounds will result from this code of signals (in other words to read a score) is an almost necessary part of the

---

25. Em dash removed.
26. Punctuation rendered as "a certain dot or dash or circle,".
27. "the" replaced with "a".
28. "then" inserted after "the art of music".
29. Em dash replaced by a colon.
30. In 1953, the clause in parentheses was removed and the text emended to read "or, in other words, the composer and the performer."
31. Inverted commas removed and a comma inserted after "fool-proof".
32. Original single quotation marks removed. Vaughan Williams quotes from Shakespeare's Sonnet 116: "Let me not to the marriage of true minds/Admit impediments."

expert musician's equipment;[33] but this power will not make him musical, any more than the knowledge of machinery which is necessary to a watchmaker enables him to tell the time.[34]

It is also true that[35] pleasure and exaltation of spirit of a certain kind is the result of this power; more especially is this true of the pleasure of memory evoked by reading the score of a well known[36] and often heard work.

It was Lord Rosebery (I believe) who once said that when he could not go for a holiday he bought a guide book and trusted to his imagination for the rest. Certainly if you have once been to the Malvern Hills you can to a certain extent re-live your impressions by reading in the guide-book that "300 yards further on a small footpath leads off to the right (difficult, but fine *view*); guide unnecessary; milk (l*d*. per glass) can be obtained at the cottage on the right"—but who can pretend that the emotions roused by this are the same as those he experienced when he first climbed the hill and saw all England spread at his feet?[37]

So it is with music; the pleasure and profit of reading a score silently is at the best purely intellectual, at the worst[38] is nothing more than the satisfaction of having accomplished a difficult task successfully. It is not the pleasure of music. This can be achieved through the ear only.

In what does being "musical" consist? It should be possible to be a first-rate musician and yet not be able to read a note of music, never to have heard of Bach or Beethoven, nor to know by sight the difference between an oboe and an organ; and,[39] conversely it is possible to be able to do[40] all these things and yet be no musician.

To be really musical one must be able to *hear*. The ear must be sensitive, the mind must be quick to grasp what the ear has heard and see its connection with what has gone before, and to be prepared for what is to come, and above all the imagination must be vivid, to see the glimpses of the heart of things which the composer has crystallized into earthly sound.

---

33. "the expert musician's equipment" replaced simply with "a musician's equipment".
34. In 1953, the line break here was removed and the two paragraphs run together.
35. "the" inserted before "pleasure".
36. "well known" hyphenated.
37. In 1953, this paragraph was replaced by the one discussed at the end of the introduction.
38. "it" inserted after "worst".
39. Comma removed after "and".
40. "to be able to do" replaced with "to know".

To educate a child in music is to teach him to hear; then and then only he is a musician.[41] I am far from saying that the power to read music, the knowledge of musical history, an intelligent interest in the technique of instruments will not be a great help to him when once he has learnt to love music, but they must never be allowed to take the place of music; we must first seek the Kingdom of God and all these things will be added unto us.[42]

How does the composer invent? Does he not[43] hear the melodies and harmonies which[44] he makes with the mind's ear only? But what is it which he invents? Not the little black dots which he puts down on paper but the actual sounds which[45] those black dots represent. He wishes to be in spiritual communication with his hearers. To do that certain sounds are necessary; and until those sounds are heard the spiritual[46] contact is not established. And does not the composer also need actual sound to produce in him that spiritual state which he hopes to induce in others? Does not the actual shock of sound help to fertilize his imagination and lead him on to still further musical invention? The text books,[47] of course, are horrified at the idea of "composing at the piano"[48] and hold it to be the sign of the incompetent amateur. The answer is that everyone must use the means which enable him to do the best. If a[49] composer finds inspiration in the bass trombone or the accordion, by all means let him use them. There is fairly conclusive evidence that Beethoven, Wagner[50] and Elgar used the pianoforte in the course of composition and that Rheinberger[51] did not. The inference is obvious.

In primitive times the intervention of the written note between the composer and the performer did not exist. The primitive composer either sang his simple melodies himself or[52] taught them orally to

---

41. The second half of this sentence emended to read: "then, and then only, is he a musician."
42. Vaughan Williams alludes to Matthew 6:33.
43. "not" removed.
44. "which" removed.
45. "which" removed.
46. "spiritual" removed.
47. "text books" hyphenated.
48. In 1953, Vaughan Williams inserted the following here: "(as R. O. Morris writes, 'it is always considered as not quite playing the game')," quoting his brother-in-law, the composer and musicologist Reginald Owen Morris (1886–1948).
49. "a" replaced with "the".
50. A comma inserted after "Wagner".
51. Emended to read "Berlioz and Rheinberger".
52. "else" inserted after "or".

others; and there is, theoretically, no reason why a composer should not invent a symphony and teach it to an orchestra of performers without writing down a note, provided both he and they could cope with such a prodigious feat of mind and memory. The writing of notes is merely a convenience, necessary owing to the comparative feebleness of our memories and the want of concentration in our minds. To hold up this mere convenience as an ideal to be aimed at, is, surely, to put the cart before the horse.[53]

We have taken it for granted up to now that an expert musician can mentally bear[54] exactly the sound of any piece of music—that, though he cannot actually feel the emotion he can realize exactly what the effect on him of every harmony, melody or rhythm which he sees written, would be if he heard it. But how far is this true?[55] Doubtless when the music is simple or of an accustomed type, the musician is on sure ground; but when anything in an unaccustomed idiom comes his way, is he not often out of his depth when trusting to the eye alone? Even in the case of comparatively simple music is it not possible to realize mentally the whole sound and yet miss the beauty? Any fairly equipped musician can look through a piece, say, of Purcell and realize exactly how all the notes would sound, but can he be sure whether he has realized its beauty? Or to take a simpler example still—is it not a common experience with anyone to look through a single line of melody like a folk-song and be entirely deaf to its emotional appeal until he has heard it sung?

But a musician may answer:[56]—"I can trust my powers of score reading[57] enough to judge a piece as beautiful if I can see beauty in it by a silent reading of the score."

"Yes," I should answer, "but how if you cannot see beauty in it? Will you then trust your judgment? Will you not feel bound to hold it up to the test of the ear? If not, you have not given it a fair judgment." Why is it that it is always the dull unimaginative music which gains the prize in a competition? Is it not because the adjudicators are content to look at the music and not to hear it?[58]—with the result that anything which *looks* right on paper is judged to be good, and everything which[59] *looks*

---

53. Punctuation emended to read: "To hold up this mere convenience as an ideal to be aimed at is surely to put the cart before the horse."
54. "bear" replaced with "hear" and "exactly" removed.
55. In 1953, the following text occupied a paragraph of its own, ending with "sung."
56. Em dash removed.
57. "score reading" hyphenated.
58. Question mark removed.
59. "which" replaced with "that".

unfamiliar and awkward is rejected?[60] A pianoforte arrangement should be demanded with every score which is sent in for a competition; then the adjudicator can have the music played through to him and become familiar with the *sound* of the work before he proceeds to criticize it in detail. What an amateurish way of setting to work! Yes, but the only way of getting at the truth.

I foresee an objection here. It may be said that to play over an orchestral piece on the pianoforte is not to give the true sound and is no nearer the truth of music than the inspection of the score. The ideal way, of course, to judge of a piece of music is to hear it as it was intended—then, and then only, can we get into absolute communion with the composer; but even from such an unsympathetic medium as the pianoforte we do get a certain shock of sound which will help us to a certain extent to obtain a glimpse of the vision which the composer is trying to convey to us.

Are we than[61] to be slaves of our bodies? Will not the mind be able eventually to free itself from all bodily trammels and get to the essence of things without physical intermediaries.[62] It may indeed be argued that when we are actually hearing music the physical ear plays only a small part in our understanding of it. The physical ear can do no more than receive one moment of sound at a time, and our grasp of even the simplest tune depends on our power of remembering what has gone before and of co-ordinating it with what comes after. So that it seems that the mind and the memory play even a more important part than the ear in appreciating music. Why not go one step further and eliminate the physical ear altogether? Let us hear music with the mind's ear only.

Perhaps in future years this will happen—a new art will be evolved in which the mind of the composer will be in direct touch with the mind of his audience.[63] But this art will not be music—it will be a new art; and with the new art a new set of means of communication will have to be devised. Our old system of dots and dashes which go to make up a music-score[64] are, as we have seen, no more than a code

---

60. "looks" not italicized (both times). The following passage from "a pianoforte arrangement" as far as "to convey to us," inclusive, was removed in 1953.
61. "than" is replaced with "then".
62. The period replaced by a question mark.
63. "the mind of" removed. The 1953 revision of this sentence thus reads: "Perhaps in future years this will happen—a new art will be evolved in which the mind of the composer will be in direct touch with his audience."
64. "music-score" unhyphenated, and a comma added after "score".

of directions to[65] makers of musical sounds; if the sounds are not to be made, the code of directions will no longer be necessary, and our score-reader's occupation will be gone.

Certain types of musical thinkers seem to have inherited the medieval fear of beauty—they talk about "mere beauty" and "mere sound,"[66] as if they were something to be feared and avoided. But in our imperfect existence what means have we of reaching out to that which is beyond the senses but through those very senses?[67] When Plato praises the Dorian Mode as inspiring courage, does he mean the Dorian mode written out on paper? When the trumpet sounding the charge rouses the soldier to frenzy, does anyone suggest that it would have just the same effect if he took a surreptitious glance at a copy of[68] *Military sounds and signals?*[69] Would any amount of study of his own score have led Haydn to declare that his "Let there be Light" came straight from Heaven?

Surely, while music is the art of sound, it is the ear which must be taught its language; when a new art supersedes it, a new language will necessarily follow in its train.

R. Vaughan Williams

---

65. "the" inserted after "directions to".
66. Comma removed.
67. The following sentence replaced with this one: "Would Ulysses have been obliged to be lashed to the mast if the sirens instead of singing to him had shown him a printed score?"
68. "a copy of" removed.
69. "*Military sounds and signals*" capitalized.

1. Ursula Vaughan Williams, *R.V.W.: A Biography of Ralph Vaughan Williams* (London: Oxford University Press, 1964), 163. "The Letter and the Spirit" was first published in *Music & Letters*, 1/2 (April 1920): 87–93. Vaughan Williams published it again, with revisions, in *Some Thoughts on Beethoven's Choral Symphony with writings on other musical subjects* (London: Oxford University Press, 1953), 53–63. The essay also appeared in its revised form in both the 1963 and 1987 editions of *National Music and Other Essays* (London: Oxford University Press), 121–28. The 1963 and 1987 editions of *National Music and Other Essays* were both edited by Michael Kennedy.

2. For an introduction to the themes of Vaughan Williams's writings, see David Manning, "The public figure: Vaughan Williams as writer and activist," in *The Cambridge Companion to Vaughan Williams*, ed. Alain Frogley and Aidan J. Thomson (Cambridge: Cambridge University Press, 2013), 231–48, esp. 239–46. For a discussion of Vaughan Williams's aesthetics see Aidan J. Thomson, "'Es klang so alt und war doch so neu': Vaughan Williams, Aesthetics and History," in *British Musical Criticism and Intellectual Thought, 1850–1950*, ed. Jeremy Dibble and Julian Horton (Woodbridge, Suffolk: Boydell, 2018), 255–77. On the spiritual in Vaughan Williams's music and aesthetics, see Byron Adams, "Scripture, Church, and culture: biblical texts in the works of Ralph Vaughan Williams," in *Vaughan Williams Studies*, ed. Alain Frogley (Cambridge: Cambridge University Press, 1996), 99–117.

3. "And such trust have we through Christ to God-ward: not that we are sufficient of ourselves to think anything as of ourselves: but our sufficiency is of God: who also hath made us able ministers of the new testament, not of the letter, but the spirit: for the letter killeth, but the spirit giveth life." 2 Corinthians 3:4–6.

4. W. Henry Hadow, *The Needs of Popular Musical Education* (London: Oxford University Press, 1918), 9. William Henry Hadow (1859–1937) was a musicologist and a leading figure in the reform of music education in Britain during the interwar years. The other sources from which Vaughan Williams quotes are a letter from the musician, composer, and translator Alexander Ewing (1830–1895) to the composer, writer, and suffragist Ethel Smyth (1858–1944), reproduced in Smyth's *Impressions that Remained: Memoirs*, vol. 1 (London: Longmans, Green, and Co., 1919), 146; and a speech made by Arthur Somervell (1863–1937), the composer and Chief Inspector of Music to the Board of Education from 1920 (having been Inspector of Music since 1901). I have not been able to locate the speech made by Somervell "the other day at an educational conference," as Vaughan Williams puts it, nor the source through which Vaughan Williams consulted it. Before these quotations, Vaughan Williams describes a cartoon by George du Maurier that had appeared in *Punch* 75 (December 28, 1878), 298.

5. Vaughan Williams, "*Ein Heldenleben*" (1903), in *Vaughan Williams on Music*, ed. David Manning (Oxford: Oxford University Press, 2008), 159–63, at 162.

6. Benedict Taylor, "Romanticism," in *Vaughan Williams in Context*, ed. Julian Onderdonk and Ceri Owen (Cambridge: Cambridge University Press, forthcoming).

7. Vaughan Williams, "Palestrina and Beethoven" (1902), in *Vaughan Williams on Music*, 125–28.

8. I have explored this theme of Vaughan Williams's aesthetics in "On Singing and Listening in Vaughan Williams's Early Songs," *19th-Century Music* 40/3 (Spring 2017): 257–82.

9. Vaughan Williams, "English Folk-Songs" (1912), in *Vaughan Williams on Music*, 185–200, at 188, and 194–95.

10. Consider, for instance, his argument in 1912 that "even in the case of music which is printed, we know well that three separate players will make the same piece of music sound very different according to their different temperaments. But in the case of printed music [in contrast to orally/aurally transmitted music] the divergencies can

never get very far, as each successive player goes back to the original printed copy." Vaughan Williams, "English Folk-Songs," 194. It should be remembered that in spite of—or perhaps because of—his ambivalence toward the inadequacies of notation, Vaughan Williams still expected a performer to pay heed to the "letter" of his music; see Ralph Vaughan Williams, *National Music*, 1st ed. (London: Oxford University Press, 1934), 26–27, where he discusses how a performer must "work back to the composer's vision" in grappling with notation. However, "he does not suggest that the listener has to perceive the composer's vision in the performance," as Thomson has pointed out in "'Es klang so alt und war doch so neu,'" 261–62n30.

11. See, for example, James G. Mansell, *The Age of Noise in Britain: Hearing Modernity* (Urbana: University of Illinois Press, 2017).

12. Thomson, "'Es klang so alt und war doch so neu,'" 261.

13. Vaughan Williams, "Howland Medal Lecture" given at Yale University in 1954, and published in *Vaughan Williams on Music*, 99–109, at 100. Interestingly, Vaughan Williams later in this lecture seems to hint at the possibility that during a performance, a listener may perceive the same "vision" as the composer and performer; see 102–3. However, he removed this passage when the lecture appeared in published form, after a number of substantial revisions, under the title "Making Your Own Music," an Epilogue to *The Making of Music* (Ithaca, NY: Cornell University Press, 1955), 53–61.

14. In this revised paragraph, Vaughan Williams drew upon material published earlier in *National Music*, in which he had incorporated ideas, in turn, from "The Letter and the Spirit." For the first version of this revised paragraph, see "Some Tentative Ideas on the Origins of Music," a chapter in *National Music*, 1st ed. (1934), 24. This paragraph was further revised in 1953 and is the one quoted here; see Vaughan Williams, *Some Thoughts on Beethoven's Choral Symphony*, 58–59. On a British map, "P.H." is an abbreviation for "Public House"—in other words, a pub.

15. See *English Renaissance Poetry: A Collection of Shorter Poems from Skelton to Jonson*, ed. John Williams (Garden City, NY: Doubleday, 1963), 43. Vaughan Williams had set Vaux's line in his song "How can the tree but wither" in 1896.

Modernist Image in Vaughan Williams's *Job*

PHILIP RUPPRECHT

Defining a "Modern Outlook"

In an expansive three-part profile published in 1920, Edwin Evans introduced Vaughan Williams to *Musical Times* readers as a leading modern British composer. In the course of this essay, Evans moves from sketching his subject's "cosmopolitan" training—his studies with Bruch and Ravel—to asserting his place in "our musical tradition." By "congenital characteristics," the critic argues, Vaughan Williams faced less risk of "becoming denationalized" than many younger colleagues.[1] It is hardly surprising that the subject of nation would figure prominently in writing about British music in the wake of the 1918 Armistice. Evans speaks bluntly of the "placid mediocrity" of English musical tradition in the previous century; the "intense reverence" for Brahms at the Royal College of Music was "more destructive of individuality," he argues, than Wagnerism.[2] Vaughan Williams is named as the senior figure within a generation that finally achieved artistic independence. Defining the forty-seven-year-old composer's "characteristically English" elements—an affinity for folksong and a "restorationist" movement toward past tradition[3]—Evans presents a familiar image of an already significant oeuvre. It is only in *A London Symphony*, just reaching print by 1920, that Evans touches on a "modern outlook," commenting specifically on formal features—development sections rich in "new incident" and "curtailed" recapitulations.[4] From a later perspective, Evans's fleeting references to musical modernity are intriguing. He mentions relatively little about innovations in pitch or rhythm, two conventional touchstones of musical modernism. Austerity and an "ascetic mood" are hallmarks of Vaughan Williams's harmony, but Evans does not elaborate further.[5] The composer's "healthy literary taste," however, and a characteristic "economy of speech," loom large in Evans's account.[6] It is through the interplay of these two motifs—Vaughan Williams's response to literary sources, and his characteristic mode of artistic "speech"—that this essay will approach the score of *Job: A Masque for Dancing*, first heard in 1930 and staged the following year. *Job* is central to understanding the perception least precisely articulated in Evans's discussion: namely, that Vaughan Williams was often recognized as a genuinely *modern* composer.

The view of Vaughan Williams in the 1920s was rich in tropes of the national, rural, and mystical, but to recall these alone is to miss other facets of an evolving understanding of his art. True, this music was associated—as in A. E. F. Dickinson's 1928 study—with "an increasing reaction against modern 'civilization,' or (in plainer words) against urbanization, in favour of the simpler, yet richer, life of the countryside."[7] With the arrival of *Job*, however, the discussion shifts. As music critic Frank Howes wrote effusively in 1937, *Job* was "wholly characteristic, profoundly English, and unflinchingly modern."[8] Howes made a comparable claim for the 1925 suite *Flos campi*, this time with more direct reference to compositional technique: "from a technical point of view . . . decisively modern."[9] He was not alone in identifying Vaughan Williams as modern: his senior colleague at the *Times*, H. C. Colles, writing for a 1934 *Oxford History of Music* volume, directly quoted the bitonal oboe and viola duet with which *Flos campi* opens to exemplify the latest word in musical style, a "rejection of every technical principle which the nineteenth century held to be inviolable."[10] Michael Kennedy suggested that by the 1920s Vaughan Williams and Holst found the chromaticism and neoclassical idioms of Stravinsky and Bartók "more to their liking than they had done before the war."[11] Approaching *Job*, we can recuperate a sense of Vaughan Williams's position as an established but progressive voice in British music. That a score of a composer in his fifties was received as "unflinchingly modern" is not the whole issue, however. This stylistic denomination, in Kennedy's comments, refers primarily to the realm of pitch materials or rhythmic texture, yet there is room for historical interpretation to acknowledge other facets of the modern "outlook." Beyond the narrow realm of the score itself, given the distributed and composite authorship of a ballet production, we can take in the perspective of historians of modernism in other fields, above all dance. The 1931 Camargo Society premiere of *Job*, Rishona Zimring notes, was an event framed by Bloomsbury literary and visual modernism, and the choreographic and dramatic innovations of Ninette de Valois. Fusing experimental and primitivist strands of modernism and folk dance revivalism, *Job* is an "emblematic and innovative" interwar modernist text.[12] In its eclectic array of choreographic resources—movement and poses, expressionist gesture, masking—de Valois drew on "every trend of the time," as Kathrine Sorley Walker observes.[13]

It is significant that the two scores Howes and Colles regarded as most "modern" are literary in origin, though neither involves direct setting of words to music (*Flos campi* has a wordless chorus treated in a manner similar to both Debussy's *Nocturnes* and Ravel's *Daphnis et Chloé*). That Vaughan Williams publicly downplayed programmatic reference in his works need not discount the presence of a "nexus of associations" between specific scores and prior literary sources.[14] In the case of *Job*, William Blake's famous illustrations were a self-evident source for musical elaboration: the resulting score embodies the "intensification of . . . mystical and symbolic elements" perceptible in Vaughan Williams's music of the post–World War I decade.[15] Since the composer was working consciously within the directly mimetic framework of a ballet scenario, interpreting specific musical gestures in *Job* as "images" of the stage action is an obvious hermeneutic possibility. Before doing so, it is worth considering in closer detail some concepts of image familiar to critics of the period.

The interplay of unheard words with instrumental music in *Flos campi* had initially elicited negative criticism. At the premiere, Colles found the Latin Vulgate epigraphs in the score (all quotations from the biblical Song of Songs) merely confusing: "The composer has wilfully surrounded the flowers of his musical thought with a thorny hedge of riddles."[16] In a later detailed analysis, however, Howes finds the opening move from keyless arabesque to a diatonic march-like theme to embody something quite directly illustrative of the verse. His comments elaborate a working theory of the musical image:

> The purpose of a symbol is to embody an idea, and the idea in the lily was the providence of God. But . . . they may be sensuously enjoyed for what they are and provide the considerer of lilies with a sensuous experience. This when held fast in recollection is called an image. . . . In so far as music is a phenomenon of mind and not merely of ear the composer is perpetually translating ideas into images, aural images.[17]

Focusing intently on the moment of translation between linguistic or visual symbol—as the token of an external referent or idea—and the sensuous experience of image, Howes speaks across the semiotic divide between the linguistic and the sonic.

While music criticism hardly lacks for concepts of semantic reference—in tone poem or operatic genres—Howes's evasion of conventional talk of thematic "transformation" or "leitmotifs" is striking. Referring to image, memory, and perceptual-psychological operations, his comments recall the lexicon of prewar poetic modernism. It is quite possible that Howes read aesthetic formulations such as those of T. E. Hulme, which were first published in 1924: "Creation of imagery is needed to force language to convey over this *freshness* of impression . . . something which ordinary language and ordinary expression lets slip through."[18] In a later text, Hulme observes, "The direct language is poetry, it is direct because it deals in images. The indirect language is prose, because it uses images that have died and become figures of speech. . . . While one arrests your mind all the time with a picture, the other allows the mind to run along with the least possible effort."[19]

Aesthetic ideas such as Hulme's, initially the property of a select avant-garde circle, achieved wider dissemination in early twentieth-century poetic theory.[20] The distance from Verlaine's *Art Poétique* exhortation "Take eloquence and wring its neck!" to Hulme's writings is a short one indeed.[21] Arthur Symons's account of a Symbolist revolt "against exteriority, against rhetoric" was for many younger writers—including T. S. Eliot—a definitive text.[22] A no less iconoclastic manifesto was propounded by Ezra Pound in the 1910s under the slogan of "Imagism." He defines the new mode of writing in three quick points: "Direct treatment of the 'thing' whether subjective or objective"; a restriction of words to "presentation"; and retreat from "metronome" prosody.[23] Pound also formulates a point crucial to poetry and music as time-bound arts, the image's fleeting quality: "An 'Image' is that which presents an intellectual and emotional complex in an instant of time."[24] Advancing a theory of the image as condensed and direct, the poets, as Sarah Collins observes, exhibited "Symbolist-inspired veneration" of music's lack of semantic or linguistic reference.[25]

As Howes's account of "aural image" in *Flos campi* suggests, by the 1920s composers and musician-critics were responding to aesthetic debates in literary and visual arts circles. While a period of "revolutionary" modernism in painting, for example, was over by the 1920s, a return to traditional representation among British artists was accompanied, paradoxically, by "critical attention to formal properties."[26] Cecil Gray's rejection of stylistic evolution or progress in favor of cyclical concepts of music history, meanwhile, presented affinities with modernist historical thought, whether unconsciously or following contacts with the poets D. H. Lawrence and H.D. in 1917.[27] Was Vaughan Williams himself working within imagist paradigms? Recalling one of Evans's observations—that "among his manifold musical interests theories occupy no place"—the case appears unlikely at first. Parsing the emergent artistic currents of the interwar period, though, including the multiple aesthetic commitments of the *Job* ballet project, for example, a broader aesthetic prospect opens, in which the blunt, instantaneous quality of modernist poetic images bears on musical developments. The question of Vaughan Williams's "modernity," I will argue, in the mimetic context of staged ballet, reflects the workings of a direct and transition-free musical discourse redolent of the ideals and theorizing of the poetic imagists.

With the Hulmean poetic notion of the image as direct presentation "in an instant of time," another thread of Evans's 1920 portrait of Vaughan Williams takes on new meaning. The composer's characteristic mode of musical expression, Evans notes, lacks "circumlocution," avoids "argumentative resources," and shows minimal concern for "the connection between successive ideas." The resulting music conveys seeming "disjointedness," by a typical mode of expression that Evans calls "blunt and to the point."[28] Many modern composers, he goes on to note, are adopting "elliptical methods" of thematic presentation; it is by "power of concentration," above all, that *A London Symphony* makes its formal effect.[29] Dickinson, a few years later, writing of "the most downright composer who ever lived," echoes this line; the music eschews "every form of rhetorical address."[30] An emphasis on instantaneousness, directness, and the unmediated juxtaposition of isolated ideas was early recognized as a trait of Vaughan Williams's musical language.[31] It was also, by the mid-1920s, an obvious point of contact with modernist aesthetics in other media.

Job and Balletic Modernism

At an early stage of its genesis, a scenario for a *Job* ballet was created by the Blake scholar Geoffrey Keynes, working in tandem with the artist and scenic designer Gwendolen Raverat. This scenario was first offered to the Ballets Russes. Keynes himself wrote to Diaghilev in French on 29 June 1927 proposing *"une esquisse d'un ballet"* drawn from Blake engravings, which were also sent. Keynes mentioned Raverat's preparation of a miniature theater with drawings and costume designs.[32] A scenario text in French, translated by Raverat, was presented to Diaghilev's secretary Boris Kochno; this was quickly rejected as "too English" and "too old-fashioned."[33] Though Vaughan Williams had likely begun sketching a score by this point, news of Diaghilev's rejection may well have come as a disappointment. Writing to Raverat, he took a revealingly different line: "My dear Gwen . . . it really wdnt have suited the sham serious really decadent & frivolous attitude of the R[ussian] B[allet] towards everything—can you imagine Job sandwiched in between 'Les Biches' and 'Cimarosiana'. . . No—I think we are well out of it—I don't think this is sour grapes."[34]

One can understand the composer's reaction while observing that the decadence and frivolity of the Ballets Russes represented only a part of their artistic trajectory. From annual visits to England dating back to 1911, London's intellectual circles had flocked to the company. Vaughan Williams, in 1913, had himself discussed a Cupid and Psyche scenario with Nijinsky and Gordon Craig over lunch at the Savoy.[35] To literary observers, meanwhile, the major prewar productions—Nijinsky's *Jeux*, *L'après-midi d'un faune*, and *Le sacre du printemps*—were not merely opulent Orientalist or primitivist spectacle, but innovative for "vigour in pattern," expressing ideas "in moving forms."[36] The company's *décor* excited visual modernists with "movement in masses of colour" and "fusion of theatrical elements."[37] For the art critic Roger Fry, Diaghilev's 1926 production of Stravinsky's *Les noces* afforded reflections on the "mixture of plastic and illustrative elements" and the difficulty of "perfect cooperation" between two arts, dance and music.[38]

After the long hiatus of war, Diaghilev's return to London in 1919 marked a cultural rebirth. Booked in venues such as the London Coliseum, ballet found a wider audience appeal.[39] The prima ballerina Tamara Karsavina, in 1920, even starred in a whimsical play, J. M. Barrie's *The Truth About the Russian Dancers*, with music by Arnold Bax. Playing a ballerina who marries an English aristocrat, Karsavina danced *en pointe* (even in a golf-playing scene) while other characters spoke and acted conventionally.[40] For more elitist viewers, including the economist John Maynard Keynes, who in 1925 had married the Ballets Russes dancer Lydia Lopokova, classical ballet was a reminder, as Jennifer Homans notes, of "the lost civilization" of prewar times.[41]

The modernist image of the Ballets Russes remained clear in Massine's choreography for *La boutique fantasque* and *Le tricorne*, both performed to great acclaim in London during the 1919 season. For critics such as Edward J. Dent, the angularity of the dance was emblematic: "His movements are always dehumanized and conventional. He seems to be expressing in his own art what one finds in a good deal of contemporary music and poetry."[42] In Satie's *Parade*, however, Dent heard only "glorified silliness."[43] The *Dancing Times* editor Philip Richardson, by mid-decade, critiqued the *en pointe* choreography as effeminate, especially given that the male soloist Anton Dolin had controversially danced *en pointe* as the Dandy in *Les fâcheux*; of the 1925 London season, the paper summarily concluded, "We have had enough of this sort of thing."[44] As Lynne Garafola observes, "Preciousness was never entirely absent from the Ballets Russes. . . . in the period following Diaghilev's return to London in late 1924 the dandy element would come to the fore among his cultivated public."[45]

The *Job* project was at once a part of London's modernist ballet scene of the 1920s, and a reaction against Diaghilev's central presence within that scene. Its origins lay with a member of the close-knit Bloomsbury social and intellectual circle, Geoffrey Keynes, Maynard's younger brother, who was friendly with Lydia Lopokova, Maynard's wife. As mentioned above, the idea of a translation of Blake's *Illuminations of the Book of Job* to the ballet stage was developed initially by Keynes and his sister-in-law, Raverat.[46] (Gwendolen Raverat, née Darwin, was the sister of Geoffrey Keynes's wife, Elizabeth.) The *décor* models and an early five-act scenario in Raverat's hand were established before another family connection, Vaughan Williams, who was her cousin by marriage, was invited to compose a score. Assuming a 1927 beginning, the musical sketches stand in close proximity to another of his stage projects, *The Poisoned Kiss* (1927–28), for which Raverat later provided the mise-en-scène. The Raverat-Keynes scenario embodied some structural features that endured into the finished ballet, including the basic spatial opposition of Earth and Heaven and the framing symmetry of Introduction and Epilogue.[47]

That the Camargo Society's eventual 1931 production of *Job* was received as modernist in outlook owed much to Ninette de Valois. She came to the project as a choreographer of broad sympathies, from the expressionist movement of *Rout* (1926, score by Arthur Bliss) to Noh-inspired and lighter demi-caractère dances.[48] For ballet critics, the careful groupings of her choreography and Raverat's *décor* captured a "surface simplicity" true to Blake: the relative stasis of Job and his family was a foil to Anton Dolin's Satan, "a whirlwind in the pastoral atmosphere."[49] To the *Dancing Times* editor, de Valois's success was a matter of "dignity and restraint."[50] De Valois's experience working with actors led her to a dramatic form close to Keynes's original impulse—a dance piece inspired by static pictures.[51] That some attacked *Job* for a lack of classical balletic steps—the dancing was barefoot—was a criticism she robustly defended.[52] Cyril Beaumont saw Central European school influence in the "simple . . . angular archaic stylisation" of movements by Job and his family, and the "cold and austere" actions of the Godhead and angels.[53] To Beryl de Zoete, the "imperfectly eurhythmic" moves were unconvincing.[54] The figures of War, Pestilence, and Famine were masked; the Godhead himself, after Blake, is named "Job's Spiritual Self."[55] The Camargo *Job* as a whole, Beaumont commented, is Blakean in conception, rather than biblical: "The whole action is *symbolic*, not *material*," a "purely mental" struggle "between self-love personified by the figure of Satan and true humanity symbolised by Job's spiritual self." The stage separation of heavenly/earthly realms, divided by a flight of broad steps, represented two "domains of the mind,"[56] a theatrical vision of significant bearing on Vaughan Williams's score.

"Pageant for Orchestra" and "Masque for Dancing":
Musical and Balletic Reactions

Without Diaghilev's interest in a *Job* ballet, the composer had gone ahead and completed his score, using a large orchestra: it was premiered as a "pageant for orchestra" at the Norwich Festival on 23 October 1930. A radio broadcast on London wavelengths from the BBC's Savoy Hill studios followed on 13 February 1931. As the Camargo Society launched its first season, discussions for a staging were underway, with support from Edwin Evans, a founding member of the managing committee, and Gustav Holst.[57] The Camargo's production opened on 5 and 6 July 1931, then traveled to the ISCM (International Society for Contemporary Music) meeting in Oxford, for a matinee on 24 July.[58] For the Camargo's modest pit, its conductor, Constant Lambert, prepared a reduced orchestration at the composer's request. Concert performances of the full-orchestral *Job* followed at the Gloucester Three Choirs Festival (10 September) and in London, conducted by Basil Cameron (3 December).[59]

The reactions to *Job* in the musical press stressed Vaughan Williams's long-standing interests in folk traditions, yet sensed something new. After the Norwich premiere, Richard Capell, while reporting the ad hoc orchestra's technical limitations, caught the score's "great spaciousness"; the *Telegraph* mentioned "the antiquity of national tunes" in the first scene's round dances.[60] To Colles, *Job* was Blakean in its "acceptance of form and . . . rejection of formalism."[61] For Ernest Newman, scarcely a Vaughan Williams admirer, the BBC relay conveyed music of "grave beauty" with "a touch of fascinating strangeness"; though unconvinced by Satan's music, Newman hailed the composer's advance to a language "new for him and for us."[62] Eric Blom allowed that music so "austere, archaic, almost ascetic" might not appeal to all tastes.[63] Reviewers of the 1931 Camargo staging heard music of "nobility," with direct bearing on each situation, and matching Blake's mysticism, but also a "stiffness" due to "self-conscious striving after archaic formulae."[64] The young Henry Boys praised the composer's "lack of bombast in the face of great issues."[65] Colles, writing again in 1934, recalled that "ISCM Continentals" at Oxford found *Job* lacking "musical novelty"—"This, they said, is not modern music"—but argued for the work's originality as a fusing of "unsophisticated folk art" with a modern theatrical concept.[66] Music commentators made few observations about the choreographic and visual aspects of the staging, or else lamented a lack of classical ballet steps. Herbert Hughes, for example, quipped that a work with "so little Terpsichore . . . must be very modern indeed."[67] The *Times* was more positive, noting that lighting effects enhanced the impression of stage groupings, while the score captured "the ecstasy of Blake."[68]

"Dramatic Meanings" and Musical Form

Press reactions revealed competing responses to *Job*: music writers rarely mentioned de Valois's choreography or Raverat's costumes and *décor*, while dance critics mostly ignored the music.[69] The work's modernist credentials were more apparent to commentators on ballet than musicians. A *Dancing Times* profile of de Valois's "theatrical sense" observed that the lighting cues created "swift and continuous" action.[70] The scenario as a whole reflected Keynes's admiration for "a fundamental simplicity" in Blake's pictures, and the idea of converting figures and groupings "into actuality and movement."[71] Vaughan Williams had his own decided views, having completed *Job* as an orchestral score before plans for the Camargo staging had even begun. De Valois excluded him from early dance rehearsals in 1931. Composer and choreographer experienced "some difficult situations": their relationship remained tense, with a degree of rancor on both sides.[72] As Vaughan Williams's first wife, Adeline, reported, "The stage is such a real thing to him and every bit of music has its dramatic meaning."[73]

One need not insist on univocal intentions in a work of distributed authorship and multimedia performance, however. Claims of "unification" or theatrical synthesis are not necessary to an understanding of *Job* as music, and one can rightly assume that the *Job* score conveys richly detailed "dramatic meanings" as purely sounding orchestral gestures.[74] Julian Rushton notes that Vaughan Williams's dramatic scenario, while effective, is "theologically less complex"[75] than Blake's or the symbolic interpretations of Joseph Wicksteed, whose 1910 book was important to Keynes.[76] If the composer pointedly avoided close fidelity to Wicksteed's arguments concerning visual symmetry, he was even more so after his own intrinsically musical approach to Blake's visual imagination.[77] Particularly on the level of the formal and sectional unfolding of its scenes, *Job*—like *Flos campi*, among other 1920s scores—is essentially sui generis.[78] From Blake's twenty-one engraved illuminations Keynes and Raverat conceived a scenario of nine balletic scenes; while respecting their basic divisions of the action, Vaughan Williams's score unfolds its own evolving continuity: many scenes are marked "*segue*," to follow without articulated pause between dances. Despite its expansive forty-minute duration, *Job* exhibits none of the traditional three- or four-movement symphonic divisions. Whatever else it may be, it is not in any sense a symphony. Its idiosyncratic design of dances alternating with actions defines the terms for an original notion of musical image-making. As detailed below, steering this time-bound sequence is a tonal pattern by which individual scenes mostly fail to achieve anything like a conventional cadence. Scenes do not often close in a single home key. The traditional markers of "rest" or closure are displaced by very different tonal motions—successions that embody a sense of boldly unmediated juxtaposition, rupture, or brutal destruction of key, entirely evocative of the struggle Blake had imagined visually.

As Keynes reminded Evans, Vaughan Williams cultivated "a complex about the word 'ballet,'"[79] so both the Camargo ballet and the published score were titled *Job: A Masque for Dancing*. For twentieth-century English audiences the word *masque* in relation to Vaughan Williams's score invoked a historical antecedent in the seventeenth-century allegorical genre, itself derived from older folk ritual; significant elements of pageantry; and, with Satan's scenes, functioning as antimasque.[80] The composer himself had firsthand familiarity with a Victorian-Edwardian masque revival.[81] But the folkloric strains in *Job* also stand, along with the self-evident neoclassicism of its courtly dances—a Minuet of "charming Ravelian clarity"[82] as well as a Sarabande and a Galliard—among its claims to a 1920s modernity found in Ravel's *Le tombeau de Couperin* (1919) and other pieces of the postwar period. Stravinsky's *Le sacre* re-created round dances—the *khorovod*—in a historically researched visual framework in a Ballets Russes sensation London had seen in both 1913 and in 1921, and more recently in *Les noces* (1926).[83] In the woodwind opening of *A Pastoral Symphony,* as Daniel M. Grimley suggests, one hears a stylized round dance, as English May Day rite, but one that echoes both Stravinsky and Debussy.[84] Vaughan Williams may have disparaged Poulenc's *Les biches* and *Cimarosiana*, but *Job* also reanimated archaic dance patterns; the contrast, in the end, was less technical than a matter of subject and tone.

As is well known, the composer's scenario sharply diverges at several points from that of Keynes and Raverat.[85] The latter, often credited to Keynes alone, was printed in program books for ballet audiences; Vaughan Williams's variant scenario appears in both the published piano and orchestral scores of *Job*. Keynes adapted Wicksteed's view of Blake's symmetry to the larger temporal movement of his and Raverat's plot: the framing parallelism is of Job's appearance in the first scene "in the sunset of his material prosperity" and the closing "sunrise of a new and different prosperity," placing the dramatic climax at the ballet's center—a larger rhythm that Vaughan Williams's score also follows.[86]

To what extent, however, does the *Job* score present a succession of musical "images," as opposed to a more conventional sequence of patterned dances or the dramatic actions of a plot? Are not the musical gestures in *Job* dynamic enactments of the Blake illustrations that are meticulously listed as cues in the score? A central argument, recalling the modernist poets, will be to listen for the image's directness of address—its instantaneous quality. The musical image, while bounded by the medium's time-logic, affords moments of singular, almost static revelation, fragmentation, or the dissolution of local sequence. As in the "spatial forms" of poetic modernism, post-Mallarmé, one recognizes musical images as specific moments at which the art form's innate temporality is subject to passing "dislocation."[87]

Eschewing discursive symphonic "development" of motifs or themes, *Job* deals in gestures that are abrupt, brief, and often shocking, especially in the music assigned to Satan. The musical image, in orchestral garb, asserts a sonic density borne of music's potential for polyphonic stratification, simultaneity, and harmonic reinterpretations. There is, too, a sense of musical stasis that, according to photographic evidence, was aptly realized in the Blake-inspired symmetries and groupings of de Valois's modernist stage movements.[88] The *musical* directness of *Job* did not escape critical notice. In 1934, the composer Edmund Rubbra singled out the score's sudden and "daring" shifts between plain triads. Describing Job's terror before the enthroned Satan in Scene 6, Percy Young observes: "The composer's delineation is formal . . . his utterance is blunt; his serenity of purpose reflected in absence of secondary comment." James Day recognizes the work's reliance on brief melodic "embryo elements" and imposing "*coups de théâtre*."[89] What each writer discerns in passing is a characteristic mode of presentation and dramatic continuity that one might define explicitly as imagist.

With a category of musical image at its center, the present reading moves from a traditional account of the score based on thematic material and drama to one that gives more attention to moments at which musical continuity is subject to disconcerting disruptions of imagist directness. Even Howes, whose *Flos campi* commentary is imagist in vocabulary, reverts to a virtually leitmotific listing of themes to account for each balletic scene when discussing *Job*.[90] The thematic view is ultimately misleading, first because the drama's psychological interiority argues an overdetermination of roles: Satan's musical interactions with Job and God are complex and bound by parody rather than deeper thematic independence. Second, one senses in *Job* a cumulative interplay of "versions" of a tune, redolent of the layers of variants of a given folksong, rather than the telos of "thematic transformation" of opera or tone poem.[91] Cataloguing only melodic themes overlooks other elemental facets of the musical images in *Job*—the sonic shock of massive orchestral utterances, and the tonal and harmonic dimensions of gesture.

As noted earlier, the Wicksteedian symmetry of the Introduction and Epilogue (Scenes 1 and 9) of *Job* is partly a matter of long-range

Table 1. Principal actions and tonal shifts, *Job*, Scenes 1–9.

Scene 1	2	3	4	5	6	7	8	9
Blake I (II, V)	[none]	III	VI (ix)	IV	VII, X, VIII	XII, XIV	V, XVI XXI, XVIII	XIX, XX
Job sits; Blessing;	Satan's Dance	Minuet: Sons and Wives	Job's Dream	Messengers and Comforters; Curse		Elihu; Pavane	Galliard; Satan banished;	Job, old: Blessing
Sarabande							Altar Dance	
G- A+	F*	E- C-	E+ C#- E-	D- C#-	C#- C+ A+ C*	B- G+	C+ D+ G+	G- B♭+

[+ major; - minor; *mode fluid]

tonal framing, the two movements elaborating a tonality of G minor (G Dorian), albeit without much diatonic cadence. (Modal ascriptions define respective tonic triads; eschewing raised leading-tone sevenths, the pitch collectional emphases of Scene 1 are G Dorian and A Mixolydian.) For many listeners, however, long-range recurrence of pitch levels will be less telling than more local effects: *how* harmonies arrive or vanish, the characteristic *way* of moving around tonal space within individual scenes or moments of the action. A schematic overview of *Job* (Table 1) reveals a cardinal feature of the score: scenes rarely end with rounded return to their opening key. The exceptions prove the rule: Satan's Dance (Scene 2), with its dourly asserted F tonic amid chaotic octatonic divagations, and brusque, whirling ostinatos, remains tonally closed. Thus Scene 1 moves upward from earthly G minor to heavenly A major. Job's Dream (Scene 4), beginning and ending with a clear E tonic, offers a stark modal blighting, from luminous major to cold minor.

In every scene in *Job*, a tonal shift creates the bold gestural motion. The very suddenness of the shift is crucially important to the schematic effect. What the key scheme reveals is an underlying transformational impulse, not by thematic-motivic means, but by more elemental changes of tonal center. That influence is visible in rising or sinking motions that are dramatically telling. The rise of Scene 1 from G is followed by sinking motions within later scenes. On a broader level of motion *between* scenes, the prominence of C♯ in the Dream scene, as well as those featuring the Messengers and Comforters (Scenes 4–6), defines a contrast between the ballet's framing G tonality and a C-sharp tritonal counterpole that signals Satan's influence.[92] Satan's exceptional tonal presence is, however, achieved parasitically, in relation to the larger key identities of others, as Howes (briefly moving beyond thematic questions) observes. Evil is represented by "clashes, distractions, and self-contradictions . . . within the order of harmony."[93] The underlying perception—that Vaughan Williams's *Job* creates the action of scenes by the virtual motion between keys—deserves fuller exploration.

An account of the tonal discourse of *Job* as one facet of the delineation of "aural images" furthers an understanding of its modernism on levels beyond obvious intervallic dissonances or the sonic modernity of, for instance, Vaughan Williams's use of saxophone in the Comforters' music. The modernist aesthetics of image, meanwhile, encompass both a static and dynamic conception. Pound's notion of the image's self-sufficient, proto-physical stasis evolved, as Daniel Albright recalls, into the energetic shaping of motion in the prewar English avant-garde: in Vorticism, the image was figured as "radiant node or cluster."[94] A fuller reading of the painterly imagism of Vorticism is beyond the scope of this essay, but for the remaining discussion bear in mind the complementary notions of centrifugal and centripetal energy in seeking out musical forms of the image. In the balletic context of *Job*, perhaps, the centrifugal aspect of musical images corresponds to the gestural or mimetic features of individual musical utterances within the unfolding sequence of dances and actions. In observing music that is more static or tableau-like, we access the centripetal, clenched density of the musical image. This duality is best exemplified by reference to two specific segments of *Job*: first, the Scene 1 "Introduction" comprising several distinct actions; and, second, Satan's fatal Scene 3 appearance, in the "Minuet of Job's Sons and Daughters."

Pastoral Stasis and Heavenly Dance (Scene 1)

Job sits in "the sunset of prosperity" (as Keynes has it), or in "quiet contentment surrounded by flocks and herds" (as in the composer's scenario). The two texts subtly convey different views of Job's state, but the elemental separation of an earthly pastoral realm below and heaven above is found in both scenarios. The division on stage is spatial; in the score, the same metaphysical scheme finds form in images that are sonic-orchestral, rhythmic, and tonal—to speak of keys as they are defined and as areas traversed by signature moves. Like a succession of tableaux, the stage groupings of Scene 1 arrive musically as a series of self-contained images, with minimal or no transition: autonomous blocks of color, tonality, and sound. Two tonal images frame the scene, the G minor of Job and his family (see Example 1) and the bright A major of the Sarabande of the Sons of God that supersedes it. Job's key is abandoned; there is no return for now; his travails have begun. The absolute musical dichotomy, apart from basic tonal level, is articulated by mode (minor then major), tempo (a languid Largo, a determined Sarabande), orchestral color, and

Example 1. *Job*, Scene 1, Job's prosperity theme.

Example 2. *Job*, Scene 1, prosperity theme, inner voice.

sheer sonic force. Vaughan Williams places Job in a sunset landscape redolent of the modernist pastoral cultivated by a number of British artists in the 1920s.[95] The orchestral palette encompasses softly diffuse flutes, harp, and divisi string doublings, all low in register, *piano*. The closing Sarabande breaks into a thundering brass-led and cymbal-crowned tutti, *fortissimo*. Each passage is an aural flash of meaning—a single, direct, and concentrated image accompanying dancers fixed in space. (In *Job*, only Satan has the capacity to move between earth and heaven.) As a sequence, moreover, Scene 1 works by block-like montage or overlay; there are virtually no musical transitions. The concentrated immediacy of each single image, meanwhile, merits further comment (Examples 1 and 2).

One might link the unruffled surface of Job's opening "Prosperity" music to his physical stasis in Scene 1. Raverat's cloth backdrop reproduces the symbols of spiritual and material wealth of Blake's first illumination—a Gothic church to the left, lavish dwellings to the right, his flocks, and musical instruments hanging from a large tree in the center (Figures 1 and 2).[96] Job himself, central, moves only once, standing to bless his children. His family kneels, then move to the sides, leaving him and his wife "in meditation." According to Wicksteed, the silent instruments are Blake's symbol of Job's spiritual side "not yet waked,"[97] whereas in the early Keynes-Raverat scenario his sin is materialism—two hints, if any were needed, that this opening is no idyll.[98] The "modernist pastoral" of Vaughan Williams's interwar music is deceptive. Daniel M. Grimley observes that it is a quietism of "loss and withdrawal," not inner peace.[99] As Eric Saylor notes, in both *A Pastoral Symphony* and *Job* Vaughan Williams engages themes of sacrifice and redemption, in an idiom of "quiet intensity."[100]

The G minor music of Example 1, superficially a kind of endless folkish "tune" with steady rising or falling accompaniment, is tonally unmoored, directionless.[101] Rising triads in parallel motion cloud, rather than confirm, key centers. Over shifting bass or heavy drones of fifths—an unmistakable musical signifier of the pastoral—traditional sighing figures (the violins, mm. 4–5, for example) fail to resolve intervallically. The Bach-like textural density of Job's "prosperity" stands in sharp contrast with the clear, bass-driven key and unadulterated triads of the later Sarabande. The harmonic rhythm, meanwhile, is unpredictable, and with the sudden incursion of new drone-fifths (first on B, then E♭) tonal stability gives way to impassioned chromatic arabesques (Example 2). The returning theme, now an inner voice, is at odds tonally with a new ostinato figure (F and C contradicting F♯ and C♯).

According to Keynes, Job's sons and daughters join in "a pastoral dance." Vaughan Williams's score now specifies folk dance models.[102] The first is for the women alone (to the piping of two flutes), then joined by the men (adding bassoons), both in a plaintive G Dorian. A round dance follows (Example 3); the key shift to B Dorian is absolutely abrupt. In the two seven-measure phrases (the tune varied in the repeat), Vaughan Williams's drone-fifths and melodic dissonances recall the astringency

Figure 1. Gwendolen Raverat, watercolor design for *Job*, Scene 1.

of Stravinsky's music in the 1920s, especially of *Les noces*. The melodic hemiolas ending each phrase create lilting cross-rhythms. When the two tunes are superposed contrapuntally as "the dance becomes general," the previous music is transposed to G (Example 4), returning listeners, tonally, to an earlier "home," albeit with a newly chromatic undertow (drone-fifths, over E♭ and E♮) denying the possibility of genuine cadence. To approach the "instant of time" captured in Pound's modernist image, the musical image here fuses—vertically, by montage—two moments previously juxtaposed in time. In the schematic patterning of its folk dances, *Job* claims the paradoxical temporal stasis of gestures "turning in circles, movement without progression."[103]

The event of Job's blessing intensifies the process of textural overlay of musics previously heard separately (Example 5). Above the Prosperity theme (returning in the tenor register), an anguished chromatic counter-melody appears, while the women's nimble pastoral dance (to piping winds) continues impassively. The blessing itself sounds as a single, novel musical image—a forceful orchestral tutti, instantly *forte* after previously hushed sounds, but quickly subsiding. Tonally, the moment of blessing

Figure 2. William Blake, *Illustrations of the Book of Job*, Illustration I.

arrives without transition, by abrupt tritone succession of bass-register roots (E♭ displacing A).[104]

"Satan enters unperceived." With bounding string pizzicato figure, then a brash trumpet fanfare, Satan's arrival is sharply profiled, yet his Scene 1 presence is less an autonomous force than a reflection of Job—or God, whom Satan will displace in Scene 2. Satan's fanfare, distorting Job's G minor, finds a smooth voice-leading link to the A major tonic of the Sarabande of the Sons of God, for his attention is directed toward

Example 3. *Job*, Scene 1, men's round dance.

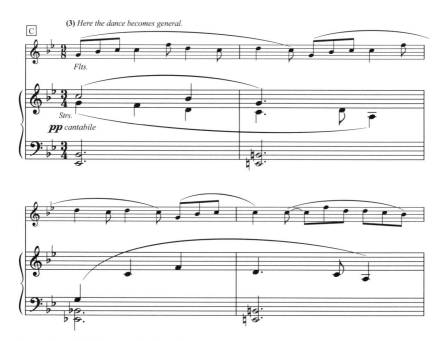

Example 4. *Job*, Scene 1, the dance becomes general.

Example 5. *Job*, Scene 1, Job stands up and blesses his children.

heaven. For the spectacle of heaven's "opening," two harps present a new figure, rising from the depths: "the line of Angels stretches from Earth to Heaven." After the Sarabande, Satan parodies the gesture, his obedient-cum-mechanical rising-fourths cycle (F–B♭–E♭–A♭–D♭) failing—three times in a row—to match the angelic A major or the still-brighter B-major sonority of God's presence.

For the closing Scene 1 actions, the *Job* score traces a swift sequence of events, as if miming the direct-speech of the biblical account (see Examples 6 and 7). The snatch of the returning Prosperity theme is distanced through distinctive timbre (muted strings, mm. 144–48), for we are looking down on Job from heaven. The stage actions are described by Beaumont: "The Children of God kneel and raise their arms in homage to the Godhead. He extends his arm towards Satan, who is unmoved. Then the Dark Angel appears to dispute with the Godhead."[105] Musically, Satan's "words" (Example 6, opening) are a snarling parody of Job's Blessing, twisting the repeated G–C♯ tritone (in garish triadic garb) of his earlier melody. God's answer to Satan ("All that he hath is in thy power"; Example 6, close) recasts this "speech" in a majestic tutti. That

Example 6. *Job*, Scene 1, Satan says, "Put forth thy hand now . . ."; God says, "All that he hath . . ."

Example 7. *Job*, Scene 1, return of closing dance of homage, "Sarabande of the Sons of God."

the divine utterance transforms both Job's and Satan's musical speech serves to advance the plot; musically, God's words introduce an essentially fresh idea, over a bright, Lydian-inflected C tonic—a tonality that has not appeared until this point. The phrase bursts in after notated silence (measure 157)—and in this kind of abruption, one hears the characteristic aural image of *Job*. Silence demarcates the moment as rhetorically independent while furthering a discursive chain by thematic-gestural affinities. The moment of divine speech is followed immediately by a *fortissimo* reprise of the two eight-measure strains of the Sarabande of the Sons of God (Example 7)—an image massive in sonority yet compact in form. Scene 1's closing blackout retraces the vast registral distance between piccolos and the lowest orchestral bass. In stark, imagistic terms, the music charts the great gulf fixed between earth and heaven.

Minuet of the Sons of Job and Their Wives (Scene 3)

Geoffrey Keynes's scenario for Satan's first attack on Job describes a simple cause and effect: "Job's sons and daughters are feasting and dancing when Satan appears and destroys them." Blake's Illustration III (Figure 3) depicts the very instant of destruction, with Satan raining lightning and flames down on Job's family. In Vaughan Williams's score, the catastrophe is marked with a verbal cue (measure 71): "Enter Satan above. The dance stops suddenly. The dancers fall dead. Tableau as in Blake III." Prior to the catastrophe, the "Minuet of the Sons of Job and their Wives" unfolds musically as a genteel, upper-class indoor dance—"formal, statuesque, and slightly voluptuous." The dancers' clashing of golden cups (to orchestral cymbals) on the second downbeat of each three-measure phrase is a folkloric touch (following Wicksteed, the cups are "in their left hands").[106]

The whole scene unfolds from Satan's perspective, as Beaumont's description reveals: "With Satan's eyes we look down on Earth and see Job's sons and daughters."[107] Job himself is absent from the feast, and will not learn of his family's destruction until Messengers arrive in Scene 4.[108] Both the audience and listeners meanwhile will witness Satan's split-second slaughter of Job's children in grim dramatic irony. A solo cello, harp, and oboe sound some luxurious banquet music, yet the doomed celebration is strangely hushed. Two unison flutes, as at the very opening of *Job*, again play in their low register, a sonority that Mellers argues has connotations of antiquity or a "preciously archaic Arcadianism."[109] But it is by fashioning a patently intricate and subtly corrupt harmonic surface that Vaughan Williams creates the most sharply defined aural images in Scene 3.

As in the first scene, the largest level of action is traced by a schematic motion between two triads. The Minuet dancers inhabit a precarious realm of E minor, destroyed by Satan's C minor. The two tonal presences achieve their effect within a carefully balanced network of triads across the scene as a whole (Example 8 gives a synopsis). The deadly conclusion is foretold, tonally, by the oboe's introductory phrase ("stage lights up"): even before the dancers enter, their E minor is challenged by the oboe's C-minor tonic note, floating high above (an unresolved sixth, contradicting B, the dominant of E minor). Tonal peace is withheld by this opening friction; one hears in the Minuet proper (Example 9) a musical image of Job's sin: a common chord blighted by a telltale fault. In a manner that

Figure 3. William Blake, *Illustrations of the Book of Job*, Illustration III.

recalls Job's Prosperity music in Scene 1, the Minuet wanders listlessly, then sinks gradually to a trio-like section claiming a C-sharp-minor drone as tonic (the key signature is marked). This key is compromised as well, now by a high-register A-major layer.[110] The trio's animation aspires to the heavenly brightness of the Sons of God, though here too, conflated pitch claims produce an oblique tonal image.

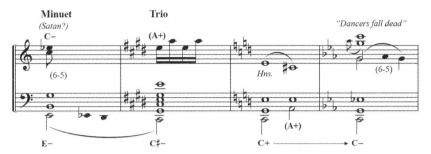

Example 8. *Job,* Scene 3, Minuet tonal synopsis.

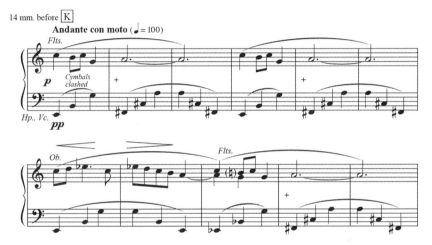

Example 9. *Job,* Scene 3, opening phrases: "Enter Job's sons and their wives."

Example 10. *Job,* Scene 3, local triadic motions.

With the Minuet's return, unsullied triads played by the harp—C and A major—briefly eradicate corrupting tensions, but the vision is cruelly destroyed by Satan's C minor. The awful moment of his triumph, a vast explosion of the full orchestral tutti, has been explained, thematically, as a variant of Job's earlier Blessing music.[111] If the internal pairing of the Minuet's E minor and C-sharp minor rooted musics is a Blakean contrary encapsulating the gist of Job's experience, the musical articulation of its climax—a translation, the score note reminds us, of Blake's third illustration—presents the shock of a single, indelible image. The two moments—Job's Scene 1 blessing of his children, and Satan's Scene 3 slaughter of Job's sons and their wives—share a wailing chromatic descent from on high, but the effect of Satan's entrance is a Beethovenian terror, underscored orchestrally by the violence of the bass drum. Harmonically, Vaughan Williams blights C major (to C minor, E to E-flat) and the tonal fault is expunged (by resolving an A-flat sixth to a G fifth). The Minuet's triadic motions (see Example 10), on local levels, evade traditional root movement by a discourse of displacements traversing the shifting tonics, E, C♯, and C. In this scene, Satan alone claims the power of an imposing dominant pedal (with timpani roll, mm. 86–94), a signature diatonic security eluding Job's family.

Conclusion: Time-Logic and the Image

Impressed by de Valois's ability to create a ballet derived from pictorial sources, the critic Arnold L. Haskell called *Job* a true "dance-drama" comprising "a thousand pictures," each one Blakean.[112] Haskell's phrasing could by the 1930s evoke cinematic models, yet he elsewhere links *Job* to older conventions of theatrical storytelling: in de Valois's staging, he observed, Satan's "grand aria" stood apart from chorus or recitative numbers.[113] The pictures in Blake's art were also visions: pictorial counterparts, as Roger Fry put it, to "vast elemental forces."[114] Translating stark visions to the stage, de Valois favored movements of hieratic simplicity. In the Camargo *Job*, one critic wrote that "the Heavenly Throne at the top of a flight of steps suggested the spirit of a medieval mystery play."[115]

However central the moral and spiritual symbolisms of the Job legend may have been for Keynes, Raverat, or Vaughan Williams, it is with the score as a sonic presentation—its fundamentally musical vision, as it were—that this essay has sought meanings. Colles's passing remark (cited earlier) on the *Job* score's Blakean "acceptance of form and . . . rejection of formalism" is consonant with the primary musical dimensions of its visionary scenario.[116] Following Frank Howes's comment on *Flos campi*, *Job* presents listeners with its own characteristic genre of "aural images." The precise outlines of given images in *Job* can be traced, on the one hand, to the directly visual source of the Blake illustrations, which are referenced in Vaughan Williams's score. But the composer's concept of musical "image" also offers broader affinities to an aesthetic crux of literary and visual modernism.

Both Colles's talk of "form" and Howes's notion of composers "translating ideas into images" mobilize a modernist aesthetic lexicon—a vocabulary common to literary and visual critics before 1914, and Bloomsbury's heightened fascination with Diaghilev's Ballets Russes productions of the postwar decade. For de Valois in *Job*, as for Bronislava Nijinska in *Les noces*, the choreography of stage motions and groupings achieved a new constructivism of abstract geometrical forms and taut symmetries.[117] For Haskell, *Job* was an "intensely serious" piece that had been staged by de Valois and Raverat in "the grand-manner-simple."[118] In the uncluttered, almost photographic modernism of Anglophone writers from Pound and Eliot to Evelyn Waugh and Sylvia Townsend Warner, meanwhile, reality was transmitted in direct images, blunt montage, and sudden shifts of temporal sequence. Eschewing elaborate transitions and carefully prepared modulations, *Job* does the same. Vaughan Williams's score moves between musical events without mediation. In its brevity, speed, and in moments of shocking orchestral force, *Job* presents aural images of a directness approaching those of modernist literary, visual, or choreographic ideals.

Vaughan Williams's reputation as a musical modernist is not easily reduced to structural notions of emancipated dissonance or rhythmic complexity (though later scores, including the Fourth and Sixth symphonies, offer boldly personal responses to such developments). With *Job* in view, we resituate the composer's position in relation to other facets of 1920s artistic modernism, defamiliarizing in the process some aspects of his music often deemed most characteristic. For example, one can realize that the composer's affinity for folk dance parallels—rather than contradicts—the theatrical modernism of the Ballets Russes. The palpable layering of historical epochs in *Job*, similarly—beyond its ties to musical neoclassicism—reflects an overtly modernist outlook. Like a palimpsest, this fusion of contemporary events with "mythological prototypes"—so central for literary modernism[119]—finds direct echoes in *Job*'s "tradition and modernity, blended together."[120] As the midcentury critic Burnett James remarked, *Job* appears to obliterate historical time: "The past is active in the present . . . in a single point of time which is neither historical nor cyclical, but existential."[121]

What Edwin Evans, and many of the composer's contemporaries, heard as a characteristic mode of musical continuity—a disjointedness or an absence of rhetorical address—finds particularly direct realization at several moments in *Job*. The clearest signs of what Howes termed Vaughan Williams's "unflinching modernity" were given to listeners through the interplay, juxtaposition, and placement of ideas in time. A hearing of *Job* as modernist will foreground the density of the aural image, and its massed resistance to the time-logic of musical performance. Placing single, indelible gestures at the center of its sounding continuity, Vaughan Williams's *Job* communicates visions defined by the sheer novelty of each arriving moment.

For responses to an earlier draft, I am grateful to Byron Adams, Daniel M. Grimley, and Jung-Min Mina Lee.

1. Edwin Evans, "Modern British Composers. IX. Ralph Vaughan Williams," *Musical Times* 61/926 (April 1920): 232–34; "Modern British Composers. X. Ralph Vaughan Williams (Continued)," *The Musical Times* 61/927 (May 1920): 302–5; "Modern British Composers. X. Ralph Vaughan Williams (Concluded)," *The Musical Times* 61/928 (June 1920): 371–74. The roman numerals used by *The Musical Times* for this series of articles are confusing, but generally denote both the particular composer under discussion and the progression of the series. A contemporary of Holst and Vaughan Williams, Edwin Evans was a music critic for the *Pall Mall Gazette* and later for the *Daily Mail*; he was particularly interested in contemporary French and British composers.

2. Evans, "Modern British Composers. IX, Ralph Vaughan Williams": 233; Edwin Evans, "Modern British Composers (Introductory Article)," *Musical Times* 60/911 (January 1919): 10–13, at 11.

3. Evans, "Modern British Composers (Introductory)": 12.

4. Evans, "Modern British Composers. X. Ralph Vaughan Williams (Concluded)": 372.

5. Evans, "Modern British Composers. X. Ralph Vaughan Williams (Continued)": 304.

6. Evans, "Modern British Composers. IX": 233, 232.

7. A .E. F. Dickinson, *An Introduction to the Music of R. Vaughan Williams* (London: Oxford University Press, 1928), 8.

8. Frank Howes, *The Dramatic Works of Ralph Vaughan Williams* (London: Oxford University Press, 1937), 45.

9. Frank Howes, *The Later Works of R. Vaughan Williams* (London: Oxford University Press, 1937), 3.

10. H. C. Colles, *Oxford History of Music*, vol. 7: *Symphony and Drama, 1850–1900* (London: Oxford University Press, 1934), 13.

11. Michael Kennedy, *The Works of Ralph Vaughan Williams*, 2nd ed. (Oxford: Clarendon Press, 1980), 210. Bartók, for his part, admired Vaughan Williams's Piano Concerto, which he heard Harriet Cohen play in a performance under Hermann Scherchen at the Strasbourg Festival in August 1933 (237).

12. Rishona Zimring, "Ballet, Folk Dance, and the Cultural History of Interwar Modernism: The Ballet *Job*," *Modernist Cultures* 9 (2014): 99–114, at 100.

13. Kathrine Sorley Walker, *Ninette de Valois: Idealist Without Illusions* (1987; London: Dance Books, 1998), 112.

14. For subtle consideration of the composer's complex attitude to programmatic reference, see "Salisbury, Hardy, and Bunyan: The Programmatic Origins of the Symphony," in Alain Frogley, *Vaughan Williams's Ninth Symphony* (Oxford: Oxford University Press, 2001), 256–94, at 276.

15. Byron Adams, "Scripture, Church, and culture: biblical texts in the works of Vaughan Williams," in *Vaughan Williams Studies*, ed. Alain Frogley (Cambridge: Cambridge University Press, 1996), 99–117, at 112.

16. Colles, *Times* (12 October 1925). For the Scottish music critic Cecil Gray, *Flos campi* was "devoid of programmatic implications." Gray's observation appeared in an article published in *The Nation and the Athenaeum* 38/8 (21 November 1925): 290, cited in Kennedy, *The Works of Ralph Vaughan Williams*, 191.

17. Howes, "*Flos campi*," *Later Works*, 5.

18. T. E. Hulme, "Bergson's Theory of Art," in *Speculations*, ed. Herbert Read (1924; London: Routledge, 1960), 163.

19. T. E. Hulme, "Lecture on Modern Poetry," in *Further Speculations,* ed. Sam Hynes (Minneapolis: University of Minnesota Press, 1955), 74.

20. For a valuable study, see Ronald Bush, "Modernist Poetry and Poetics," in *Cambridge History of Twentieth-Century English Literature*, ed. Laura Marcus and Peter Nicholls (Cambridge: Cambridge University Press, 2004), 232–50.

21. On Verlaine, see Arthur Symons, *The Symbolist Movement in Literature* (1899; rev. ed. New York: E. P. Dutton, 1958), 46.

22. Ibid., 5. Eliot's comments on Symons are quoted in Bush, "Modernist Poetry," 235–36.

23. Bush, "Modernist Poetry," 235; Pound, "A Retrospect" (1918), in *Literary Essays of Ezra Pound*, ed. T. S. Eliot (New York: New Directions, 1968), 3.

24. Pound, "A Retrospect," 4.

25. Sarah Collins, *Lateness and Modernism: Untimely Ideas About Music, Literature and Politics in Interwar Britain* (Cambridge: Cambridge University Press, 2018), 144.

26. Frances Spalding, *British Art Since 1900* (London: Thames & Hudson, 1986), 63.

27. On imagist threads in Gray's music-historical writings, see Collins, *Lateness*, 123–58, esp. 147–48.

28. Evans, "Modern British," 232.

29. Ibid., 372.

30. Dickinson, *An Introduction*, 6. The composer's compositional-expressive bluntness is sometimes compared to his personal manner: for a record of Vaughan Williams's "British downrightness" in conversation, see Gerald Cumberland, *Set Down in Malice: A Book of Reminiscences* (New York: Brentano's, 1919), 255–57, at 255.

31. On Vaughan Williams's "linking together of heterogenous fragments" see, more recently, analysis of the opening of *A Pastoral Symphony* in Ben Earle, "Modernism and Reification in the Music of Frank Bridge," *Journal of the Royal Musical Association* 141 (2016): 335–402, esp. 364–71.

32. Keynes to Diaghilev, 29 June 1927, Dance Collection, New York, quoted in Walker, *Ninette de Valois*, 109. "Dance Collection, New York" became the Jerome Robbins Dance Division at the New York Public Library of the Performing Arts at Lincoln Center. See https://archives.nypl.org/dan/19642#c336311.

33. Quoted in Howes, *Dramatic Works*, 47; see also Geoffrey Keynes, *Blake Studies: Notes on His Life and Works* (London: Rupert Hart-Davis, 1949), 153. Diaghilev was visiting London for Ballets Russes performances at Prince's Theatre, 13 June to 23 July 1927.

34. Vaughan Williams to Raverat, undated, in Ralph Vaughan Williams, *The Letters of Ralph Vaughan Williams 1895–1958,*, ed. Hugh Cobbe (Oxford: Oxford University Press, 2008), 158–59; Cobbe dates the letter to October 1927. On chronology, see also Ursula Vaughan Williams, *R.V.W.: A Biography of Ralph Vaughan Williams* (London: Oxford University Press, 1964), 183–84.

35. Vaughan Williams, *R.V.W.*, 93–94; Stephen Lloyd, *Constant Lambert: Beyond the Rio Grande* (Woodbridge, Suffolk: Boydell and Brewer, 2014), 139.

36. Anon., "The Russian Ballet II," *New Statesman* (19 July 1913): 469–70, quoted in Susan Jones, "Diaghilev and British Writing," *Dance Research* 27 (2003): 65–92, at 69.

37. Anne Estelle Rice, *Rhythm* 2/3 (August 1912): 107, quoted in Jones, "Diaghilev," 70, 71.

38. Roger Fry, "Some Questions in Aesthetics," in *Transformations: Critical and Speculative Essays on Art* (London: Chatto & Windus, 1926), 1–57, at 45. Fry's discussion includes a long quotation from Cecil Gray's review of Stravinsky's *Les noces*, in *The Nation and the Atheneum* (10 July 1926); see Fry, *Transformations: Critical and Speculative Essays on Art*, 33–34.

39. Gareth Thomas, "Modernism, Diaghilev and the Ballets Russes in London, 1911–1929," in *British Music and Modernism, 1895–1960*, ed. Matthew Riley (Farnham: Ashgate, 2010), 75.

40. It was Edwin Evans who first suggested Bax compose the score. See Lewis Foreman, *Arnold Bax: A Composer and His Times*, 3rd. ed. (Woodbridge, Suffolk: Boydell Press, 2007), 189–92.

41. Jennifer Homans, *Apollo's Angels: A History of Ballet* (New York: Random House, 2010), 410.

42. E. J. Dent, "Music: 'La Boutique Fantasque,'" *Athenaeum* (13 June 1919), quoted in Thomas, "Modernism," 77. *La Boutique Fantasque* featured music by Rossini arranged by Respighi, while the music for *Le tricorne* was composed by Falla; both ballets were choreographed by Massine.

43. E. J. Dent, "Music: A Parade of Silliness," *Athenaeum* (21 November 1919), quoted in Thomas, "Modernism," 78. *Parade* (1917) was a surrealist ballet with music by Satie; choreography by Massine, and cubist sets and costumes designed by Picasso.

44. Philip Richardson, *Dancing Times* (July 1925 and January 1926), quoted in Thomas, "Modernism," 86. With music by Georges Auric and choreography by Bronislava Nijinska, *Les fâcheux* was premiered in Monte Carlo on 12 January 1924; this is the ballet in which Anton Dolin danced *en pointe*. See Colin Roust, *Georges Auric: A Life in Music and Politics* (Oxford: Oxford University Press, 2021), 79–81 and Richard Buckle, *Diaghilev* (New York: Atheneum, 1984), 428.

45. Lynn Garafola, *Diaghilev's Ballets Russes* (New York: Oxford University Press, 1989), 343.

46. On *Job*'s chronology, see Howes, *Dramatic Works*, 46–47; Keynes, *Blake Studies*, 146–56; Frank W. D. Ries, "Sir Geoffrey Keynes and the Ballet *Job*," *Dance Research* 2 (1984): 19–34; Walker, *Ninette de Valois*, 109; and Frances Spalding, *Gwen Raverat: Friends, Family, and Affections* (London: Harvill Press, 2001), 333–37.

47. The five-act draft is reprinted in Ries, "Sir Geoffrey Keynes," 30–32; and in Alison Sanders McFarland, "A Deconstruction of William Blake's Vision: Vaughan Williams and *Job*," *Vaughan Williams Essays*, ed. Byron Adams and Robin Wells (Aldershot: Ashgate Publishing Ltd., 2003), 29–53, at 45–46. Ries credits this scenario to Keynes; McFarland treats it as written by Raverat.

48. Beth Genné, *The Making of a Choreographer: Ninette de Valois and "Bar aux Folies-Bergère"* (Madison, WI: Society of Dance History Scholars, 1996), 60–61.

49. Richard Jennings, "Job," *The Spectator* (11 July 1931): 47.

50. Philip Richardson, "The Sitter Out," *Dancing Times* (August 1931): 416. Richardson's column also quotes from Richard Capell's *Daily Mail* review: "The whole representation had a beauty both strange and dignified." To Haskell, de Valois's "remarkable simplicity of grouping" matched the atmosphere of the biblical story; see Arnold L. Haskell, "Some Recent Choreography," *Dancing Times* (September 1931): 535–37, at 536.

51. On de Valois and *Job*, see Arnold L. Haskell, *Ballet* (rev. ed., Harmondsworth: Penguin, 1945), 118–25, 161–62; and Arnold L. Haskell, *The National Ballet: A History and a Manifesto* (London: Adams and Black, 1944), 23–25, 48–50.

52. Ninette de Valois, "Modern Choreography," part 3, *Dancing Times* (March 1933): 669–70. On Vaughan Williams's stipulation to avoid "toe-dancing" in *Job*, Kathrine Sorley Walker remarks, "De Valois had no intention of using pointes in her choreography." *Ninette de Valois*, 112. See also Genné, *Making of a Choreographer*, 62–63.

53. Cyril W. Beaumont, *The Sadler's Wells Ballet* (London: C. W. Beaumont, 1947), 103.

54. Beryl de Zoete, "The Camargo Ballet Season," *Monthly Musical Record* (July–August 1932): 132–33, at 133.

55. "Blake's Jehovah is really an aspect of Job himself." Keynes, *Blake Studies*, 147. Keynes also recalled the "possible controversy" of representing Divine Persons on stage. Ries, "Sir Geoffrey Keynes," 23. See also Howes, *Dramatic Works*, 49.

56. Beaumont, *Sadler's Wells*, 102. For photos of the 1931 production, see Walker, *Ninette de Valois*, 110–13.

57. See Kathrine Sorley Walker, "The Camargo Society," *Dance Chronicle* 18 (1995): 1–114, esp. 28–30.

58. Holst paid for one extra dress rehearsal; see Ninette de Valois, *Come Dance with Me: A Memoir 1898–1956* (Cleveland: World Publishing, 1957), 119–20.

59. On performance history, see Kennedy, *The Works of Ralph Vaughan Williams*, 203–4, 227–29; and Lloyd, *Constant Lambert*, 139–42. The piano score was published in 1931, a full score in 1934.

60. Richard Capell, "The Norwich Festival," *Monthly Musical Record* 60 (December 1930): 364–65; F. B., "Modern Music at Norwich," *Daily Telegraph*, 24 October 1930; see also "The Norwich Festival," *Musical Times* 71/1054 (December 1930): 1081–82.

61. Our Music Critic, "Norwich Musical Festival," (London) *Times*, 24 October 1930: 12.

62. Newman, "The Week's Music," *Sunday Times*, 15 February 1931.

63. Eric Blom, "Music of the Month," *Listener*, 11 March 1931: 414.

64. "The New Music: Oxford Festival," *Times*, 25 July 1931; E. E., "The Camargo Society," *Musical Times* (August 1931): 745; H. F., "The Week's Music," *Sunday Times*, 26 July 1931.

65. Henry Boys, "The Oxford Festival," *Monthly Musical Record* (September 1931): 266–67, at 266.

66. "'Job, A Masque': The Published Score," *Times*, 1 December 1934. Colles's "Continentals" included visiting Parisian and Viennese pianists, and conductors Hermann Scherchen and Alfredo Casella. See Edwin Evans, "The Oxford Festival," *Musical Times* 72 (1 September 1931): 803–6.

67. H. H., "The Ballet of 'Job,'" *Daily Telegraph*, 6 July 1931.

68. "Camargo Society," *Times*, 6 July 1931. The "ecstasy" trope recurs in [A. H. Fox Strangways], "Washing in Jordan," *Music & Letters* 12 (October 1931): 323; and D. H. [Dyneley Hussey], "London Concerts: Philharmonic Society," *Musical Times* 73 (January 1932): 68. A. H. Fox Strangways was a British music critic, editor, and music historian who wrote for the *Times* (London), the *Observer*, and founded the journal *Music & Letters*.

69. De Zoete admired the choreography but found the score "dull," in "Camargo Ballet Season," *Monthly Musical Record*: 133.

70. P. J. S. R., "The Theatrical Sense in Ballet," *Dancing Times* (December 1931): 251–52, at 252.

71. Keynes, *Blake Studies*, 149.

72. Ursula Vaughan Williams, *R.V.W.*, 187. Keynes recalled Vaughan Williams's approval of "some of the folk dance ideas Ninette used" and his fear *Job* "would become 'too theatrical,'" quoted in Ries, "Sir Geoffrey Keynes," 24. One detects a certain *froideur* in de Valois's later assertion that the Camargo's conductor, Lambert, was "no real admirer" of the *Job* score. De Valois, *Step by Step: The Formation of an Establishment* (London: W. H. Allen, 1977), 54.

73. Adeline Vaughan Williams, 1931 letter, quoted in Ursula Vaughan Williams, *R.V.W.*, 187.

74. See also Howes, *Dramatic Works*, 45; or Hubert Foss, *Ralph Vaughan Williams: A Study* (London: George G. Harrap, 1950), 185.

75. Julian Rushton, "Preface," in *Job: A Masque for Dancing*, ed. Julian Rushton (Oxford: University Press, 2018), v.

76. Joseph H. Wicksteed, *Blake's Vision of the Book of Job: A Study* (London: J. M. Dent, 1910).

77. "I've got the Wicksteed book—but I'm not going to worry about the left foot & the right foot," Vaughan Williams wrote to Raverat in August 1927, *Letters*, 158. In the autograph score, the composer interpolated small reproductions of the Blake images; see Rushton, "Preface," v.

78. The "romantic extravaganza" *The Poisoned Kiss* avoids grand-opera conventions in a style reminiscent of a *Singspiel* or operetta.

79. Keynes to Evans, 16 December 1930, VWL883.

80. Deborah Heckert, *Composing History: National Identities and the English Masque Revival, 1860–1920* (Woodbridge, Suffolk: Boydell Press, 2018), 204n12; Percy M. Young, *Vaughan Williams* (London: Dennis Dobson, 1953), 113–15.

81. On Vaughan Williams and Holst's music for Jonson's *Pan's Anniversary* (1905), see Heckert, *Composing History*, 122–30.

82. Young, *Vaughan Williams*, 117.

83. On the composer's admiration for *Les noces*, see Kennedy, *The Works of Ralph Vaughan Williams*, 390.

84. Daniel M. Grimley, "Landscape and Distance: Vaughan Williams, Modernism, and the Symphonic Pastoral," in Riley, *British Music*, 147–74, at 153.

85. Howes (*Dramatic Works*, 45–65) prints the Keynes and Vaughan Williams scenarios side by side.

86. Keynes, *Blake Studies*, 151.

87. In developing a concept of musical image, I draw on Joseph Frank's classic account of literary imagism in the modernist poetry and novel, "Spatial Form in Modern Literature," in Frank, *The Widening Gyre: Crises and Mastery in Modern Literature* (Bloomington: Indiana University Press, 1963), 3–62. On "dislocation" of temporality in Mallarmé, Pound, and Eliot, see 12–13.

88. For photos of the 1931 Camargo *Job* (and 1940s Sadler's Wells revivals), see Walker, *Ninette de Valois*, 110–13; Ries, "Sir Geoffrey Keynes," 24–29; Beaumont, *Sadler's Wells*, facing 97.

89. Edmund Rubbra, "Vaughan Williams: Some Technical Characteristics," *Monthly Musical Record* 64 (February 1934): 27–28, at 27; Young, *Vaughan Williams*, 119; James Day, *Vaughan Williams* (London: J. M. Dent, Farrar, Straus, and Cudahy, 1961), 129, 130.

90. Howes, *Dramatic Works*, 50–65; see also Young, *Vaughan Williams* 111–20; Day, *Vaughan Williams*, 128–31; A. E. F. Dickinson, *Vaughan Williams* (London: Faber, 1963): 336–57; and Wilfrid Mellers, *Vaughan Williams and the Vision of Albion* (London: Pimlico, 1991), 146–57; O. Alan Weltzien, "Notes and Lineaments: Vaughan Williams's *Job: A Masque for Dancing* and Blake's Illustrations," *The Musical Quarterly* 76 (1992): 301–36.

91. In a 1919 "Dance Tunes" essay, the composer writes that "Liszt and Wagner did not 'invent' this device"; see David Manning, ed., *Vaughan Williams on Music* (Oxford: Oxford University Press, 2008), 210.

92. McFarland reads minor-third and tritone relations as symbolic; see McFarland, "Deconstruction," 42–43. The bold tritonal shifts in *Job* suggest a Mephistophelian spirit of tonal negation, one that persists—even after Satan's downfall—in both strophes of the G-centered Pavane of the Sons of Morning (Scenes 7 and 8). See Dickinson, *Vaughan Williams*, 353.

93. Howes, *Dramatic Works*, 54.

94. Pound, cited in Daniel Albright, "Imagism," in *Putting Modernism Together: Literature, Music, and Painting, 1872–1927* (Baltimore: Johns Hopkins Press, 2015), 144–56, at 151.

95. Derwent Lees, Charles Cundall, and Ben Nicholson all embraced landscape painting during and after the war. On Paul Nash's war art as an iconographic context for *A Pastoral Symphony*, see Grimley, "Landscape and Distance," 160–64. On sunrise and sunset tropes in war writing, see Paul Fussell, *The Great War and Modern Memory* (Oxford: Oxford University Press, 2000), 57.

96. Beaumont describes the same backcloth; see Beaumont, *Sadler's Wells*, 97.

97. Wicksteed, *Blake's Vision*, 50.

98. As Rishona Zimring notes, *Job*'s critique of materialism, by 1930–31, had assumed obvious social resonance amid the global economic crisis. Zimring, *Social Dance and the Modernist Imagination in Interwar Britain* (Farnham: Ashgate, 2013), 122.

99. Grimley, "Landscape and Distance," 147–74, at 149.

100. Eric Saylor, *English Pastoral Music* (Urbana: University of Illinois Press, 2017), 87.

101. Compare Herbert Howells's observations in "Vaughan Williams's 'Pastoral Symphony,'" *Music & Letters* 3 (1922): 122–32, at 125.

102. John Playford, *The English Dancing Master* (London, 1651). In the published piano score of *Job* (11 measures after rehearsal letter A), a note specifies "Jenny Pluck Pears," "Hunsdon House," and the "Munich glyptothek"—a votive frieze showing three graces—as models for "the figures of this dance." The note is absent from the manuscript score and Julian Rushton's 2018 edition of *Job*.

103. Theodor W. Adorno, *Philosophy of New Music*, trans. and ed. Robert Hullot-Kentner (Minneapolis: University of Minnesota Press, 2006), 143.

104. Rushton, *Job*, Scene 1, measure 72; piano score, 10 after rehearsal letter C. Scene 1, at this moment, offers pitch-specific premonitions of a prominent tritonal shift within Scene 2, Satan's Dance of Triumph.

105. Beaumont, *Sadler's Wells*, 98.

106. The published score names the Morris dance "Winster Processional" as a model.

107. Beaumont, *Sadler's Wells*, 98.

108. The biblical Job receives four messengers, each declaring: "I only am escaped alone to tell thee" (Job 1:15–19).

109. Mellers, *Vaughan Williams*, 150. Simona Pakenham compares the Minuet's "suggestion of the East" to the idiom of *Flos campi*; see Simona Pakenham, *Vaughan Williams: A Discovery of His Music* (London: Macmillan, 1957), 90. Other writers overlook the drama of Scene 3.

110. The biquintal displacement of tonal layers—here, a local vertical pairing C♯ and A tonics—recalls comparable textures in Stravinsky. See Joseph N. Straus, "Harmony and Voice Leading in the Music of Stravinsky," *Music Theory Spectrum* 36 (2014): 1–33.

111. Mellers speaks of a "blessing-curse" theme; *Vaughan Williams*, 151.

112. Haskell, *National Ballet*, 23.

113. Haskell, *Ballet*, 164.

114. Roger Fry, "Three Pictures in Tempera by William Blake" (1904), in *Vision and Design* (1924; New York: Peter Smith, 1947), 141.

115. Janet Leeper, *English Ballet* (London: King Penguin, 1945), 21.

116. Our Music Critic, "Norwich Musical Festival," *Times*, 24 October 1930.

117. On Nijinska's spatial architecture in *Les noces*, see esp. Garafola, *Diaghilev's Ballets Russes*, 126–28.

118. Haskell, *National Ballet*, 23.

119. On literary palimpsest, see Frank, "Spatial Form," 58–60.

120. Foss, *Vaughan Williams*, 186.

121. Burnett James, liner notes for Ralph Vaughan Williams, *Job: A Masque for Dancing*, "Sir Adrian Boult conducting the London Philharmonic Orchestra," LP, London LL 1003 (1954).

"Finest of the Fine Arts":
Vaughan Williams and Film

ANNIKA FORKERT

As was so often the case in the annals of mid-twentieth-century film music, Vaughan Williams's career in the industry began with a phone call. In the 1945 essay "Composing for the Films," Vaughan Williams recalled:

> Some years ago I happened to say to the composer, Arthur Benjamin, that I should like to have a shot at writing for the films. . . . He mentioned my curious wish to a well-known film conductor. The result was that, one Saturday evening, I had a telephone call asking me to write some film music.[1]

Most British composers active during this time created music for film, radio, or television at some point in their careers.[2] In 1935 alone, for example, Benjamin Britten collaborated with W. H. Auden on *Night Mail* for Basil Wright's GPO Film Unit; William Walton wrote the score of *As You Like It*, the first of four high-prestige cinematic adaptations of Shakespeare; and Arthur Bliss scored *Things to Come*, a science-fiction film with a screenplay by H. G. Wells. Jeffrey Richards notes that this trend accelerated during the Second World War, as a range of composers, including Arnold Bax, John Ireland, Lord Berners, and Constant Lambert sought to contribute to the war effort through providing film music.[3] Vaughan Williams shared this patriotic motivation. In 1940 his name was entered, along with many of his composer colleagues, into the address books of influential musical directors, conductors, and producers in the British film industry. The musical protocols developed by that industry were often varied and unconventional. British film composers sometimes worked from cue sheets, sometimes from rough cuts, sometimes just conversations, in contrast to the more formal protocols used in Hollywood. Such a haphazard approach frequently resulted in drastic cuts and revisions made shortly before a recording.[4] After their use by the studio, the relevant manuscripts and scores were often lost or discarded.

Vaughan Williams enjoyed certain privileges and exceptions to this rather slapdash practice in his work with the film industry.[5] For one thing, he did not rely on film music for his primary income. Other composers' motivations for writing film scores were often less lofty than Vaughan Williams's—they needed money because the war had sharply curtailed their previous sources of revenue.[6] Even Walton admitted that he was lured by the "filthy lucre" and complained about Vaughan Williams's lack of a pressing financial motive: "It is not a help for the rest of the composers if someone of his calibre & reputation is asking half what most of us get."[7] Vaughan Williams's music and reputation had the potential to draw a large audience to mostly big-budget and middlebrow films, even though he was not above criticism from certain authors (for example, his future musical collaborator Ernest Irving). He could afford to approach film scoring with his "ever-youthful spirit," as his colleague William Alwyn described it, and spend time openly musing upon the industry's structures, challenges, and benefits. He also enjoyed a high level of respect and consideration from collaborators on the film sets, including orchestral musicians, which was not always afforded to less famous composers.[8]

Historically, scholars have approached Vaughan Williams's film work in two ways. Some have charted common elements between the two worlds of his film music and concert works, hoping to recuperate the film scores from charges of "hackwork."[9] Michael Kennedy's early engagements with these compositions largely consisted of exploring the flow between movie theater and concert hall, and Richards's chapter on the wartime scores seeks to present "evidence for the close musical and philosophical interweaving of the film music with the rest of the composer's output."[10] By highlighting the cross-currents between film scores and concert music, the former could be pulled across the tricky divide between the technique of film music on the one hand and the process of composing concert music on the other, as if the two were mutually exclusive. During the time in which Vaughan Williams composed for cinema, critics posited a difference between those pieces that were worth publishing and performing in concert and those that disappeared with the films for which they were written. This twentieth-century dichotomy was mirrored in the development of several of Vaughan Williams's scores into suites. Even more controversial to the critics of the 1950s was the transfer of material and soundscapes from the score of *Scott of the Antarctic* into the *Sinfonia Antartica*. As Kennedy writes: "On the whole the critical verdict was favourable, although there was much debate whether or not it was a symphony."[11] Another approach can be seen in an essay by Daniel Goldmark, who explicitly criticized the comparative approach and instead sought to uncover through analysis the "narratological potency" in the film scores themselves, and their inter-action with photography and the filmic narrative.[12]

This essay will explore a selection of Vaughan Williams's eleven film scores through the lens of the composer's own project of turning film music into a "fine art." He set out this agenda in "Composing for the Films," written at the crossroads between his wartime scores and the grand fea-ture films of the postwar period. In his recipes for productive collaboration between composer, musical director, film director, and producer, and his ideas for effective scoring, he described ways that film music could fulfill "potentialities for the combination of all the arts such as Wagner never dreamt of."[13] His goal was not so much to pull his own film scores across an imagined art/craft divide, but to explore approaches that might create the truly unified *Gesamtkunstwerk* that Wagner had envisioned.

Vaughan Williams was supported and challenged in his quest by his principal collaborators, the musical directors Muir Mathieson and Ernest Irving. Their film-music aesthetics and collaborations with Vaughan Williams will be charted first. His work with Mathieson and Irving brought him into contact with the wider practical and aesthetic debates about the film music of his time.

Muir Mathieson and Ernest Irving

The phone call that began Vaughan Williams's film career resulted in his collaboration with Muir Mathieson on the British propaganda film *49th Parallel* (1940–41). Collaboration was (and remains) an essential part of film scoring, and Eric Saylor notes that Vaughan Williams had an "inter-est in artistic collaboration and his own personal creative growth" at an age when other composers might have steered clear of this fiendishly complex new genre of composition.[14] Ever fair-minded and curious, however, Vaughan Williams found that he "liked the people at the studio" when he first began work on *49th Parallel*.[15]

Few musical directors had greater influence than Muir Mathieson. He was the powerful and well-connected éminence grise of British film music, and he worked with several major British studios. Mathieson was a tireless pro-moter of music by British composers in the film industry.[16] Nicknamed the "supremo of British film music" by Elisabeth Lutyens, he conducted leading British symphony orchestras on countless soundtracks, including his own selection of the Rachmaninoff excerpts for David Lean's romantic feature *Brief Encounter* (1945).[17] A key part of the musical director's job was to manage film composers, nudging them to meet deadlines; discussing and sometimes implementing changes and cuts; mediating between directors, producers, and composers; advising on and managing recording practicalities; and frequently conducting the actual scores. Mathieson had studied piano, conducting, and orchestration as his main subjects at the Royal College of Music, and Ursula Vaughan Williams later identified him as Vaughan Williams's "ex-pupil," though it appears the two men only struck up a personal acquaintance when they met at Vaughan Williams's house in Dorking to discuss *49th Parallel*.[18] According to Mathieson's biographer S. J. Hetherington, Vaughan Williams's driving motive to work on the film was to support the war effort. The film's portrayal of multicultural and freedom-loving Canadians encountering the remnants of a desperate Nazi U-boat crew intent on cheating, stealing, and murdering their way into the then neutral United States provided a vehicle for this support. Despite the reflexive colonialism of the period, *49th Parallel* was remarkably diverse, including Inuits among the Canadian heroes.

The film was made by the Ministry of Information, whose musical director at the time was Mathieson. Themes of suffering and sacrifice as well as the resilience, decency, and hope of democratic peoples facing the Nazi threat reoccurred in Vaughan Williams's other scores for wartime films, *Coastal Command* (1942) and *The Flemish Farm* (1943). Mathieson worked with Vaughan Williams on these as well: he arranged suites from several of Vaughan Williams's film scores,[19] and he conducted the London Symphony Orchestra's recording of the scores for *49th Parallel*; the short documentary film about the National Trust, *The People's Land*; and *The Flemish Farm*. He also conducted the Royal Air Force Orchestra for *Coastal Command*.

Mathieson was dedicated to British film music, and this dedication struck a chord with Vaughan Williams. Mathieson wanted to make this music "valued as an entity in itself" and therefore to ensure that "film music [finds] its way into the contemporary repertoire." He further sought to increase the level of the general public's musical literacy through film music, declaring that "several of the leading composers in this country have each done a great deal to develop public taste, using the film as a medium."[20] Mathieson made himself the invisible initiator and curator of a self-proclaimed revolution of music appreciation in Britain. From his perspective, having Vaughan Williams create film scores was the best thing that could happen to British film music and, more broadly, to contemporary British music. It is not surprising that Mathieson declared himself "delighted" that Vaughan Williams had not only become a film music composer but that he was using his influence over the next generation of British composers in order to consider film music as "a fine art but it is applied art, and a specialised art at that."[21] Mathieson's desire to bring film music and art music together led him to mount a series of radio broadcasts featuring movie music in 1938 and to recruit musicians from the London Symphony Orchestra for recording sessions.[22]

During his career, Mathieson worked with a host of British film composers active at the time: from Walton to Lutyens, Bax, and Alwyn, and from Richard Rodney Bennett to Britten, whose *Young Person's Guide to the Orchestra* Mathieson oversaw and conducted.[23] For these composers, collaborating with the musical director was essential. This included responding to distinctly unmusical requests on short notice, discussing which scenes did, and did not, need music, and remaining flexible about the ways in which their music was used. Ursula Vaughan Williams remembered her husband saying that the same music could be used "for a landscape, a car crash, or a love scene."[24] Sometimes the composer wound up taking orders from the musical director. As film composer Doreen Carwithen remembered: "You always saw a film in a little theatre and had a look at it. Would you like to do it? Sometimes you would and sometimes you were told that you were going to do it!"[25] Even Vaughan Williams discovered somewhat to his dismay that once he had agreed to a film, notated music was required almost immediately. However, unlike most of his colleagues, he was given carte blanche for the size and composition of his film orchestras.[26]

Midcentury British film composers often worked on films with different directors and genres for the same studio and musical director. Although Mathieson was possibly the most powerful among them, figures like Ernest Irving at Ealing Studios also wielded considerable influence. Irving was only six years younger than Vaughan Williams, and he had composed and arranged theater music between the wars; he had joined Ealing Studios under its earliest director, Basil Dean. Irving had a fleeting acquaintance with Vaughan Williams from the Royal Philharmonic Society.[27] Like Mathieson, Irving was proud of his work for film, which included his scores for *Come on George!* (1939), *The Four Just Men* (1939), and *Turned Out Nice Again* (1941). He worked with some of Britain's best-known composers at Ealing and saw himself as a patron of the arts, declaring that one of his goals at Ealing was to ensure that "composers of good music should be able, if they wished, by spending three months on film music to write what they liked, however uncommercial, during the other nine."[28] Irving also sought to contribute to a public debate about the quality and aims of good British film scoring. He wrote a short-lived column on film music for *Tempo* and occasionally wrote on the topic for *Music & Letters* and the *Proceedings of the Royal Musical Association*. Irving was notorious for his critical wit, and he had criticized Vaughan Williams's scores for *49th Parallel* and *Coastal Command,* declaring that the latter was "perhaps not quite up to his best standard; neither was it particularly good film music."[29] Despite these initial misgivings, Irving worked with Vaughan Williams on the post–World War II feature films *The Loves of Joanna Godden* (1946), *Scott of the Antarctic* (1948), and *Bitter Springs* (1950). Vaughan Williams dedicated his *Sinfonia Antartica* to Irving. In 1953, he wrote an obituary for Irving in which the composer remembered that he sometimes received Irving's advice delivered in the form of light verse.[30]

Musical directors and composers often hotly debated two connected issues: first, the relationship between the soundtrack and moving image and, second, questions of ownership or control over what parts of the score actually made it into the finished film. Conflicts over the prominence of the music often occurred in the British film industry of this time. For instance, Vaughan Williams initially suggested that *Scott of the Antarctic* should be shot to accompany his music, because he had been so inspired by the tragic story of Scott and his doomed expedition that he wrote the score before he knew the exact timings for the film. This suggestion paralleled his argument in the essay "Composing for the Films." Vaughan Williams approached composition for cinema in an idiosyncratic fashion: "I usually think of most of the music directly I get the script. I do not wait for the photography. I know this is wrong, but I can't help it."[31] Ernest Irving responded to this argument in the starkest terms possible: "The music must always be subsidiary and ancillary and cannot be allowed to develop on formal lines for musical reasons only."[32] This debate continued for years after the release of *Scott of the Antarctic*. In the 1960s, the younger film composer Elisabeth Lutyens was overheard at a premiere party shouting at Mathieson, angry that he demanded musical "elastic" for his films rather than music. Mathieson replied that the musical director's role was akin to that of a dresser, ensuring that "the elastic on the knickers is tight enough, but not too tight, so that the whole thing . . . won't let you down!"[33]

Composers and musical directors often clashed over changes in how or when the already composed music was used in the film. This was particularly true because these modifications were often implemented for economic or technical rather than purely musical reasons. It seems to have been common to reappropriate music during this period; one of the most extreme is Alwyn's claim that music he had written for a film about butterflies appeared years later without his permission as music in a film about elephants.[34] Alwyn concluded that music was not capable of specific description in itself and that it was therefore only the "constant association with visual ideas" that enabled it to have an audiovisual or programmatic context.[35] Vaughan Williams concurred: "You must not be horrified to find that a passage which you intended to portray the villain's mad revenge has been used by the musical director to illustrate the cats being driven out of the dairy. The truth is that within limits any music can be made to fit any situation."[36]

Despite this seemingly philosophical outlook, Vaughan Williams tried to retain a level of control over how his music was used in films through the mediation of the musical director. Under ideal circumstances, the musical director acted as the composer's advocate, although the fraught exchange between Lutyens and Mathieson cited above shows that this ideal relationship was not always achievable. In an exchange of letters that took place between work on *The Loves of Joanna Godden* and *Scott of the Antarctic*, for instance, Vaughan Williams told Irving, the musical director of both films: "I want to make it quite clear that you have had my absolute permission to do what you like with my music, but this is not official."[37] A week earlier, he had stipulated to his film music agent that the official contract for the *Scott of the Antarctic* music should specify that no alterations could be made without the permission of both Vaughan Williams and Irving, because "if [Irving] retires I might not at all be in agreement with his successor."[38] As it happened, adapting Vaughan Williams's music for *Scott of the Antarctic* to the film footage involved omissions of cues, cuts to the music itself, and Irving's repositioning of scenes rather than changes to the score.

These two issues presented a challenge to Vaughan Williams as a film composer. He accepted these conditions in high spirits and referred to them as "a morning blush which has not yet paled into the light of common day."[39] If the "common day" is film composition as an art, experienced composers needed "to realize their responsibility in helping to take the film out of the realm of hackwork and make it a subject worthy of a real composer."[40]

War Films: Amassing Technique and Experience

Like most British film music of the time, Vaughan Williams's scores do not constitute continuous music, although they do cover large sections of the films.[41] The vast majority of the music is orchestral and non-diegetic "underscore."[42] In "Composing for the Films," Vaughan Williams established a general approach for this non-diegetic scoring, although he did not invariably follow his own practice. He stated that his usual procedure was to "ignore the details [of audiovisual synchronization points] and to intensify the spirit of the whole situation by a continuous stream of music. This stream can be modified (often at rehearsal!) by points of colour superimposed on the flow."[43]

This approach helped him to write at the required speed and allowed him to compose music that had "value outside its particular function," a quality he felt could not be achieved through a process by which the music reflects "every action, word, gesture, or incident."[44] The absence of this technique, colloquially known as "Mickey Mousing" by both film composers and scholars, made it easier to convert much of his film music into suites and other concert pieces.[45] This is not to say that diegetic music was of no interest to Vaughan Williams. In fact, nearly all of his scores contain intricate games with diegesis. For example, Anna and the Canadian Hutterites sing folksongs in *49th Parallel*, characterizing their German-language community's generosity and decency in the face of Nazis who are trying to convert them to their fascist convictions. In *The Flemish Farm*, a gramophone playing a jazz record evokes the memory of a fallen comrade and triggers the decision to rescue the Belgian Air Force's flag.

The earliest of these propaganda films, *49th Parallel*, shows the cruelty and futility of Nazi ideology in the face of a tolerant, democratic Canada, and it was designed to persuade Americans to join the Allied cause. The film's plot sought to demonstrate just how quickly the fascist threat could spread if even a small band of amoral Nazis roamed free on the continent. (By the time *49th Parallel* was released in the United States in 1942 under the title *The Invaders*, Americans needed no more convincing to join the war effort). *49th Parallel* was made by Ortus Films, and it premiered in London on 8 October 1941. It was produced and directed by Michael Powell from an original story by Jewish émigré Emeric Pressburger for which he won the 1942 Oscar for Best Story.[46] The score was recorded with Mathieson conducting the London Symphony Orchestra. The film opens with the best-known movement, an orchestral Prelude in G Major, which accompanies the dedication and title credits before a backdrop of the snow-covered Rocky Mountains. The Prelude's hymnic calm is retained through its climax and final plagal cadence. Here immediately was a "continuous stream of music," complete and rounded in itself, and possessing "value outside its particular function." This music was mined for a choral song, "The New Commonwealth" (1942, text by Harold Child). Michael Kennedy noticed that a more agitated passage from the film found its way into the Scherzo of Vaughan Williams's Second String Quartet of 1944.[47]

The Prelude is followed by a cinematic montage that casts doubt upon Vaughan Williams's supposedly laissez-faire approach to audiovisual synchronization. In this "Prologue," which includes a quotation from Canada's national anthem, "O Canada," a map of the North American continent and a voiceover that explains the role of the 49th Parallel as the peaceful border between two friendly nations (accompanied by

Figure 1. Nazi U-boat still from *49th Parallel*.

violin tremolos with clarinets) is followed by short vistas of fields (pastoral strings), city and mountain panoramas shot from the air (brass fanfares), and footage of the sea (string chords oscillating between E minor and G major under a clarinet solo). Just seconds later, the Nazi U-boat (Figure 1) breaks through the surface of the water to the accompaniment of a brass motif containing a distorted but clearly recognizable allusion to the opening of the Lutheran chorale "Ein' feste Burg ist unser Gott" ("A Mighty Fortress Is Our God"). (See Example 1.)

The rest of the chorale melody appears mockingly transformed, as the U-boat crew observes the damage to a Canadian tanker, but the chorale's main motif, a falling fourth, maintains its presence beyond this scene into the next, "Control Room Alert," alongside the hectic clacking of telegraph machines (lower strings) and a collage of the steps in the control room information chain. This precise approach to synchronizing sound, image and filmic narrative appears at crucial points throughout the score.[48]

In the music that follows, Vaughan Williams strengthens the atmosphere of each scene and smooths the cuts between new locations and cultures, as the desperate and dwindling Nazi submarine crew encounter the Canadian people. The Nazis are given an opportunity at each

Example 1. Vaughan Williams, *49th Parallel*, Prologue.

station of their unholy pilgrimage to change course or surrender, but each time they choose to cause further harm and grief. One by one they are either killed or captured. In the process they darken the lives of trappers living in harmony among a coastal Inuit community; a settlement of German-speaking Hutterites; a pageant of the First Nations peoples; and a solitary aesthete intent on sharing European culture with them in a lakeside camp. As the film proceeds, characteristic Canadian musical references are introduced and woven throughout both diegetically and non-diegetically, drawing together the landscape and its peoples. The French-Canadian children's song "Alouette," which appears at the trappers' station, for example, is first heard in the non-diegetic orchestra and then it is sung by Laurence Olivier's character in a bathtub. Later, the Hutterites are characterized by their hymn tunes and church bells, while drums and woodwinds mark the parade of the First Nations peoples. More unusual is the delineation of Leslie Howard's character, the reclusive author Philip Armstrong Scott, through an impressionist piano solo. Goldmark has argued that this unusual choice of instrument and style can be explained through the narrative: "Since neither the Nazis nor the audience know exactly what to think of or expect from this new personage, the composer fills in the blanks."[49]

Vaughan Williams's next venture, *Coastal Command* of 1942, was not a feature film but a propaganda docudrama, produced by Ian Dalrymple and directed by J. B. Holmes. Members of the Royal Air Force essentially play themselves; only a handful of professional actors appear in the film. Again, Muir Mathieson led members of the Royal Air Force Orchestra for this Crown Film Unit production.[50] The film provides exhilarating glimpses into the work of the RAF's Sunderland and Catalina flying boats. These large seaplanes were tasked with keeping Atlantic shipping lines open for supply convoys, and were also used for anti-submarine warfare and search and rescue missions. The survival rate of the crews who manned these unwieldy aircraft was very low; two members of the cast, Ernest Leslie "Johnny" Hyde and Charles Norman Lewis, were killed in action before *Coastal Command*'s premiere in London on 16 October 1942. The film succinctly presents the skill, determination, and camaraderie of the members of Coastal Command, from the highest commander in the Control Room to a young crewman on the Sunderland seaplane brewing tea mid-flight for his comrades. The film shows the diversity of the crew, as Jeffrey Richards observes:

> It is impossible not to notice the class difference between the strangulated upper-class drawl of the skipper, Lieutenant Campbell, and the unaffected regional accents of the crew— Hughie, Roy, Sean, Pam, Joe, Jammy, Henry, Izzy, Lew—who are Welsh, Irish, Northern, Southern, Jewish—but the film emphasizes the cross-class cooperation and genuine sympathy and affection between the crew and the shared qualities of dedication and good humour.[51]

The music has two main functions. The first is to provide atmosphere for the majestic views of the large seaplanes and the camaraderie of their crews surrounded by natural beauty but also threatened by Nazi fighter planes. Most of the underscore accompanies footage of the planes in mid-flight, views from the planes over the Atlantic or Icelandic mountains, and the battles between the Sunderland and a German U-boat and destroyer, with typical textures (brass for engines, fight, and triumph, violin tremolos for danger, a brass motif of rising tritones that would later be inserted into the Scherzo of Vaughan Williams's Sixth Symphony).[52] The music also helps viewers to distinguish between friend and foe in the air and sea battles shown in the film.[53]

The music's second function is to provide transitions between scenes. These could be changes of location and time (as when the Sunderland is moved to operate from a base in Iceland), or cuts between the Control Room and the Sunderland. In the latter instance, the underscore connects the commanders in the Control Room (who comment that the missing Sunderland has "got a good sting in her tail") with the work of the crew as they risk their lives to sink a German destroyer while losing fuel due to a hit on their tank. The music therefore added drama to the occasionally wooden delivery of lines by the amateur actors. As in *49th Parallel*, the portrayal of humanity exhibited by these crews and their superiors was due in no small degree to the underscore. Like the earlier film, Vaughan Williams's score included small infusions of diegetic music, such as a radio on the Sunderland that plays Ernest Bucalossi's uplifting "Grasshopper's Dance" as the crew repair their flying boat and hand around a self-made Hitler puppet they are planning to string up in the plane's galley as a mascot. The resulting juxtaposition of the crew's taste for tea and dance music on the one hand, and their heroic role battling for Britain's survival characterized by the orchestral underscore on the other, is mediated by occasional modal pastoral passages, such as at the officers' arrival for their daybreak briefing, or in the rural landscapes of their base in Iceland. According to Ken Cameron, the sound engineer on the set of *Coastal Command*, the studio staff were so impressed with the music that "on the rare occasions when the music was slightly too long or too short to match the existing picture, then it was the visual material which suffered the mutilation."[54] This came close to Vaughan Williams's ideal of assembling a film on the basis of its music in order to enable film music to be transformed into a finer art.

The Flemish Farm continues in this vein of sympathetic underscoring of human drama in combination with memorable and characteristic diegetic tunes. This film was made by Two Cities; the screenplay was written by Jeffrey Dell and his wife at the time, Jill Craigie. Dell directed as well, and it was produced by Filippo del Giudice; Vaughan Williams wrote the score immediately after *Coastal Command*, with Mathieson conducting the London Symphony Orchestra. Unlike *Costal Command*, which was a docudrama, *The Flemish Farm* is an entirely fictional narrative. The plot revolves around an attempt to retrieve a regimental flag, which was hidden at a farm in Flanders, the last post of the decimated Belgian Air Force before the arrival of the German Wehrmacht. Jean Duclos (played by Clifford Evans), one of the last survivors of a Belgian squadron, attempts to smuggle the flag through the occupied territories back to the Belgian government-in-exile in London. Spurred by his grief and guilt over the death of his comrade Fernand Matagne, who died in the Battle of Britain fighting with the RAF, Duclos seeks the help of Matagne's widow, Tresha, and the Belgian underground resistance in order to accomplish his dangerous mission.

Michael Kennedy sees the scores for *Coastal Command* and *The Flemish Farm* as precursors of Vaughan Williams's Sixth Symphony (1944–48, premiered 21 April 1948). Two omitted themes from *The Flemish Farm* appear in the second and fourth movements of the Sixth Symphony, and Kennedy further claims that the score of *The Flemish Farm* carries "pre-echoes of the symphony in harmony and orchestration."[55] He adds that *Coastal Command* contributed a symphonic scherzo that is a further anticipation of the Sixth Symphony along with a "beautiful melody" reminiscent of the Fifth (1938–43, premiered 24 June 1943).[56] Despite such connections, both film scores were conceived to work with the visual imagery projected on the screen. Due to the fast-paced narrative, there was less room for ruminative meditative music in *Costal Command* and *Flemish Farm* than in Vaughan Williams's other film scores. Even so, there are small pockets of well-synchronized pastoral music in *The Flemish Farm* through the glimpses of a landscape whose natural beauty interacts with human emotion.

The most important of these occurs during a scene of what appears to be a Belgian Air Force flag (later revealed to be an ordinary shirt) being sunk into the sea at night. The scene (No. 2 in the *Flemish Farm Suite*, "Night by the Sea, Farewell to the Flag") is framed by the tense chromatic $\frac{6}{4}$ single-file march of the Belgian airmen to the beach, where they attend what they believe to be the destruction of their flag in the sea by a single swimmer. The swimmer receives the wrapped parcel and instructions, upon which he turns sharply toward the sea, triggering a simple melody in flutes and trumpets over a B-minor seventh chord in strings and harp. This gesture accompanies the lapping waves glistening in the moonlight (Example 2a). The "sea music" underscores the first part of the Major's short address to his men standing at attention before switching back under the speech to the chromatic march, which in turn is overlaid by the diegetic trumpet signal as the false flag is pressed under the water by the swimmer. However, the melody itself, now in E major / C-sharp minor, carries across the cut from the beach back to the farm as

Example 2a. Vaughan Williams, *The Story of a Flemish Farm Suite*, No. 2, "Night by the Sea. Farewell to the Flag," B-minor melody.

Example 2b. Vaughan Williams, *The Story of a Flemish Farm Suite*, No. 2, "Night by the Sea. Farewell to the Flag," inflection to E-major / C-sharp minor.

Matagne is seen by Duclos wandering through the farm courtyard with a young woman (Example 2b).

For the audience, this transforms the motif from an evocation of the beauty of the moonlit sea into a romantic episode, and it thus prepares the stage for the following scene, the lovers at sunrise in the barn. There is even more to the scene: Duclos berates Matagne for missing the farewell to the flag for a fling with a farm girl, but it is later revealed that Matagne and the girl were already married and that they had buried the flag by secret order while the rest of the squadron was on the beach.[57] The motif's ability to create a connection between the natural (sea), the dramatic (flag), and romance (lovers) deepens the significance of all three. This musical material does not turn into a Hollywood-style leitmotif in the manner of Erich Wolfgang Korngold or Max Steiner, however—that is, it does not reappear at later points in the narrative.

In these three major wartime scores, Vaughan Williams paid careful attention to scoring not only action but also emotion and landscape.[58] In the process, he mastered the art and technique of writing music for film. His scores were written to match the projects for which they were created, but they were also able to be used as material for concert music. Both these aspects were to become more pronounced as he entered his second phase as a film composer after the end of the Second World War.

Postwar Films: Consolidation

It was by no means self-evident that Vaughan Williams would continue to compose for films after the war ended. The scores that he wrote up to and including *Stricken Peninsula* (1945), a Ministry of Information film about the effort to rebuild Southern Italy, were for explicit propaganda. This changed decisively with the highly successful *The Loves of Joanna Godden* (1947), directed by Charles Frend and produced by Michael Balcon of Ealing Studios. This film, characterized by its musical director Ernest Irving in his memoir as a "rustic romance,"[59] was the first of three important collaborations between Vaughan Williams and Ealing Studios. The music was recorded by Irving conducting the Philharmonia Orchestra. Irving described Vaughan Williams's contribution as "some grand music for sheep, cows, and the farmers" and wove in the anecdote of Vaughan Williams's struggle to depict through music foot-and-mouth disease for a scene in which the character Arthur, portrayed by John McCallum, loses his entire flock to the contagious disease.[60]

For *The Loves of Joanna Godden*, Vaughan Williams contributed much more than just music to accompany farm animals: the film required music for several montages that bridge the passing of the seasons on Romney Marsh, and for the passions of Joanna (the rising actress Googie Withers in her first starring role), the progressive but stubborn woman farmer at the center of the plot (see Figure 2). Joanna, who inherits a failing sheep farm from her father, decides to modernize both the farm and her life, to the chagrin of her neighbors, especially Arthur, whom her father had wished her to marry. Instead, Joanna plans to marry the sensitive Martin Trevor, who drowns at sea. While slowly acknowledging her attraction to Arthur, Joanna watches him fall for her spoiled sister Ellen, who leaves him when the disease strikes his farm and kills his sheep. Only in the final moments do Joanna and Arthur recognize their mutual love.

Figure 2. *The Loves of Joanna Godden*. The actors are (left to right): Jean Kent as Ellen Godden, Googie Withers (playing Joanna), and Henry Mollison as Harry Trevor.

As the plot moves its protagonists through the seasons and years to the accompaniment of a pastoral underscore, Vaughan Williams created music that intensified emotion at key points, such as the moment when Martin reveals to Joanna how to experience the romantic beauty of nature and, by contrast, the somber foot-and-mouth scene. Vaughan Williams did not write a cue for the actual disease; rather, the director portrays the grim preparations and beginning of the culling by alternating shots of Arthur's face as he attempts to maintain a stoic facade and the culling itself. Vaughan Williams provides a dominating motif, a rising minor third and semitone, followed by the same intervals in inversion, accompanied by brass "stinger" notes and string tremolos. This motif closely resembles that played by a clarinet during the film's title sequence over a shot of the bleak and isolated marsh.

Even more powerful is the portrayal of Joanna's terror at realizing that Martin has drowned while she slept on the beach. In this scene, threatening violin tremolos accompany her slow waking, jabbing "stinger" chords accentuate her frantic realization that Martin is missing, and a small wordless chorus of women depicts her growing anguish. This moment in the film enabled Vaughan Williams to prove to Irving that a form of vocal music could indeed be used under a character's speech—a feature they argued over during their following project, *Scott of the Antarctic*. Irving claimed that the very short wordless chorus in *Joanna Godden*, which depicts the danger just as she gazes around asking "Martin, where are you?" only worked because "there was no conversational dialogue" and warned against "using a singing voice in the distance at the same time as dialogue was going on in the picture."[61] Vaughan Williams and Irving would revisit this issue during the creation of the score for *Scott of the Antarctic*; this dispute was resolved in the composer's favor.

Vaughan Williams used *The Loves of Joanna Godden* as a musical and collaborative study for its successors, *Scott of the Antarctic* and *Bitter Springs*. Vaughan Williams and the team at Ealing, Irving in particular, had worked well together on *The Loves of Joanna Godden*; when Irving's letter arrived asking Vaughan Williams to score *Scott of the Antarctic*, the composer was keen to participate. He was also able to continue to experiment with elements that became central in *Scott of the Antarctic*, from the vocal non-diegetic interjection to the characterization of natural forces, most of which were far from benign.

The music for *Scott of the Antarctic* is widely regarded as Vaughan Williams's finest film score because of its portrayal of futile heroism in the face of the cruelly inhospitable Antarctic ice and because a substantial amount of material reappeared in the *Sinfonia Antartica*. After the success of *The Loves of Joanna Godden*, Vaughan Williams demanded exceptional freedom in the way he approached the score's composition.[62] *Scott of the Antarctic*, directed by Charles Frend, charts Robert Falcon Scott's ill-fated 1912 Antarctic expedition, which became a race against the competing party of the Norwegian explorer Roald Amundsen. Amundsen's party reached the pole first with dog sleds and skis, while Scott's belief in the superiority of a combination of motor sledges, ponies, dogs, and skis proved fatal. Scott and his party succumbed to the cold, hunger, and exhaustion in a tent merely a dozen miles away from their next fuel storage site (see Figure 3).

The orchestra Vaughan Williams employed for this grand project was larger than that for any of his prior film scores, and included women's chorus and solo soprano, organ, euphonium, and wind machine. From the beginning of the score, the composer appears at his most harmonically adventurous: the chord progressions of the highly chromatic "Heroism" theme foreshadow through their harmonic ambiguity that Scott's heroism will be disastrous (Example 3). The sudden jolt when E-flat minor moves to a brighter G major without any mediation, only to judder to an eerie A-flat minor and back to G major, is a curious way to portray heroism. The sliding between G major and A-flat minor in particular (which share their modal

Figure 3. John Mills as Commander Scott, in *Scott of the Antarctic*.

tones B/C♭) seems to question the quality of heroism itself.[63] On the surface, this progression seems to play with chromatic mediant-relationships,
but Daniel M. Grimley has identified the combined pitch-class content of
the central chords G major and A-flat minor as a pitch-class set with a strong
octatonic flavor (pitch-class set 5–22 [01478]), with consequences for later
sections of the film score and of the symphony.[64] However, when the surrounding chords are taken into account as well, a third possible reading
presents itself. The majority of chords in this theme are chromatic medi-
ants, whose interplay, or "transformation," can be captured particularly
well by neo-Riemannian theory.[65] Although the simplest and best known
of these transformations are the parallel—linking, for example, C major
and C minor, abbreviated P—and relative, linking, for example, C major and
A minor, abbreviated R, the most prominent and frequent ones in the
"Heroism" theme are so-called slides and hexatonic poles (H), which
describe the relation between a major triad and a minor triad, the latter
a major third below the former; for example, C major and A-flat minor.[66]
Richard Cohn connects the hexatonic pole with the early twentieth-
century fascination with the Freudian uncanny, centered around images
of "death, grotesquerie, disorientation, paradox, or the living dead."[67] The

Example 3. Vaughan Williams, *Scott of the Antarctic*, No. 1, Main Title, "Heroism" theme, mm. 1–12, reduction.

slide (S), as the name implies, is the relationship between a major triad and a minor triad a semitone above; for example, C major and C-sharp minor. It is serendipitous that the names of these two transformations invoke snowy worlds. What is unusual is Vaughan Williams's unwieldy voice leading, which induces countless parallels in the piano, strings, and harp as the chord progression trudges an octave upward through root position triads and accompanied by, firstly, a rising E-flat Lydian augmented scale and then a G-minor scale (melodic when rising, harmonic when falling) in oboe, English horn, trumpets, and trombone.

Whether this music is meant to evoke heroism, a depiction of the sliding of skis over the ice, or a party of unknowingly "living dead" in the face of an unyielding nature can be left open. This theme proved versatile both within and beyond the boundaries of the film project: it returns

when Scott's party climbs the Beardmore glacier onto the Antarctic plateau beyond and at various points during their arduous journey into
oblivion, and it is featured in the *Sinfonia Antartica*'s first movement as
well. Curiously, the theme does not reappear when Scott, who is portrayed by John Mills, and his party die.

The score for *Scott of the Antarctic* is characterized by a threefold contrast of which this theme is merely one aspect. First, there are themes like
heroism and others of its kind; second, the score includes some calculated
frivolity in the lighter music that appears before the expedition proper
gets underway—for example, the diegetic band at the ship's departure, a
gramophone record and player piano in the Antarctic base camp, or the
playful non-diegetic music of the penguins—and finally, the surprising
lack of music for some of the most emotional moments later in the film.
As nature begins to eradicate Scott's doomed party one by one, neither
the death of Edgar Evans (James Robertson Justice), nor his funeral, or
the decline of the ice's next victim, L. E. G. "Titus" Oates (Derek Bond),
are underscored. Even the flashbacks to happier days with Kathleen
Scott and Oriana Wilson and the writing of the men's last letters do not
have music.[68] Instead, the wordless women's chorus and solo soprano
now begin to hound and taunt the failing heroes. This keening, like that
heard in Vaughan Williams's one-act opera *Riders to the Sea* (1932), is
apprehended as if from outside as Oates tears open the tent and volun-
tarily goes to his death. The spectral disembodied voices reappear as the
men's ever slower skis struggle through the plunging temperatures. The
end of Scott's party is marked by raging nature without music. Music
returns only with the reappearance of human beings, as the search party
holds a memorial at Scott's collapsed tent months later in the film's last
scene.

It seems ironic that the now celebrated connections between *Scott of
the Antarctic* and the *Sinfonia Antartica* were the reason that, according to
Kennedy, "people were inclined to look down their noses at [the *Sinfonia
Antartica*] in 1953 because it originated in film music."[69] Although this
particular vector of material flow from film to concert music is the most
spectacular in Vaughan Williams's oeuvre, it is not the only such vector,
nor is it a one-way street. Another such vector connects the scores of *The
Loves of Joanna Godden* and the last feature containing music by Vaughan
Williams, the Australian adventure *Bitter Springs* (1950, directed by Ralph
Smart and produced by Michael Balcon of Ealing Studios and the Rank
Organisation). The tale of an Australian settler family, who move their
cattle and sheep across the Outback only to face embittered resistance
from Aboriginal Australians,[70] *Bitter Springs* belongs in the same category

as *The Loves of Joanna Godden*. Both chart the endurance and lives of non-conformist rural folk and their struggle with living conditions and other people, and both have a score that pays homage to their livestock: in the long trek portrayed in *Bitter Springs*, for instance, cows have a differently scored walking music than the short-legged sheep. Irving reused some of the sheep music from *Joanna Godden* for this film, musing that "after all, sheep are sheep, and a little change in orchestral colouring will soon flip them over to the Antipodes."[71] In fact, Vaughan Williams and Irving collaborated on the score of *Bitter Springs* with Irving assuming greater responsibility for the music than on the previous two Ealing Studio films. On 16 July 1950, Vaughan Williams wrote to the editor of *The Radio Times*: "One of the speakers on the 'Critics' section of your programme of July 16 . . . praised the 'Kangaroo' music in the film 'Bitter Springs.' This portion of the music was composed by my collaborator, Mr. Ernest Irving."[72]

Concert music influenced Vaughan Williams's film scores as well as vice versa, thus bringing the film music even closer to his ideal of art. This manifested itself in two of Vaughan Williams's later and shorter non-fiction scores: first, in the intimate relationship between the *Five Variants on "Dives and Lazarus"* and the short propaganda documentary *Dim Little Island* (1949); and, second, in the use of eight of the *Ten Blake Songs* for tenor and oboe in the documentary *The Vision of William Blake* (1958, Morse Films).[73]

Dim Little Island was a ten-minute documentary designed to restore the pluck of an exhausted, traumatized English population in the wake of the Second World War. Directed by Humphrey Jennings and produced by Wessex Film Productions, who were in turn sponsored by the Central Office of Information, it featured Vaughan Williams not only as the composer of the score, but also as one of four speakers whose role it was to laud the character, enterprising spirit, and culture of the British people.[74] Although its scoring of nature is central and the film belongs firmly in the postwar period, Richards rightly included it in his examination of wartime cinema because *Dim Little Island* explicitly addresses the fallout from a war that was morally necessary but economically disastrous.

By providing music for this documentary, Vaughan Williams returns to his cinematic origins in composing propaganda. Richards refers to *Dim Little Island* as "in essence a peacetime propaganda film."[75] In his voiceover, the composer can be heard at his most overtly nationalist, as he describes his concept of a pyramid of community, amateur, and professional music making, which fuels the renaissance of British music as a whole and whose crowning glory are the Proms and the wartime concerts. All the while, a montage of the title pages of Elgar's *Enigma* Variations, Vaughan

Williams's own *A London Symphony*, Bax's *Tintagel*, and Britten's *Peter Grimes* is shown. This short film did not have a formal musical director, but it bore Mathieson's stamp of approval. The twenty-four-year-old Doreen Carwithen, freshly graduated from her Arthur Rank film music apprenticeship, had taken on the uncredited role as music assistant to Vaughan Williams. Mathieson knew Carwithen from the apprenticeship (he had interviewed her for it) and sent her to Vaughan Williams to discuss the composition of a new title sequence and the use of some existing music for this film.[76] Although Vaughan Williams himself later disavowed the film (claiming that he could not remember ever having spoken or composed anything for it), Carwithen vividly remembered her first meeting with him in his home, including his curious behavior of feeding cake to his cat.[77]

Substantial parts of Vaughan Williams's *Five Variants on "Dives and Lazarus"* are excerpted to score *Dim Little Island*.[78] The *Variants* in their existing form offered just the right level of contrast as well as thematic and harmonic coherence to work as an atmospheric, folksong-derived underscore for this nationalist documentary. Three main elements were new, however: the Prelude (with a clarinet solo), which used the tunes of folksongs "Pretty Betty" and "The Pride of Kildare"; the reordering of materials drawn from the *Five Variants*; and finally, a vocal solo of the "Dives and Lazarus" tune itself.[79] Reusing this amount of material from the *Variants* was only possible because this film did not rely on precisely timed effects synchronized with the moving image. There was no need for diegetic music and large swathes of the underscore could be faded in and out as needed. Even the orchestration of strings and harp could be reused in its entirety, with the addition of a clarinet for the short new solo in the Prelude, and the voice to sing the "Dives and Lazarus" tune over the *Five Variants* theme.

The opening bars of film score are nothing but an intensification and transposition of the two opening bars of the *Five Variants*, and it contains a rhythmic augmentation of the four chords that set the scene through their "Aeolian" progression i–♭VII⁷–v⁷–i/I (in the *Variants*, this is in B minor; in the film in F minor, ending with a *tierce de picardie*). The additional use of violins, the lengthening of the double basses' notes, and not least the final cadence from Cmin⁷ to F major increase the film score's weight compared to the opening of the *Five Variants*. The *Variants* theme itself appears in the film score only after Variant II (or most of it—the film score short-circuits into the vocal statement of the theme ten measures before rehearsal number L of Variant II).[80] The theme itself is shortened as well, but the triumphant Variant V is played in full and extended by the return of the four opening chords.

Vaughan Williams was sought out by musical directors to lend gravitas to high-profile feature projects as well as shorter films with a nationalist flavor, such as the music he composed in 1955 for the British Transport Commission film, *The England of Elizabeth*.[81] He enjoyed special treatment by the studios in several ways, from visits to his home to discuss the projects over tea and cake, to the arrangement of several of his film scores into suites, to the size of his session orchestras. Through his initial engagement with film music, Vaughan Williams discovered a way to contribute to the war effort, "doing his bit." After the war, through work on the scores for *The Loves of Joanna Godden* and *Scott of the Antarctic*, he broadened his range of expression and his orchestral palette. The glittering timbres found in the score for *Scott*, for example, are echoed throughout late scores, such as the Christmas cantata *Hodie* (1953–54) and the Eighth Symphony (1953–55). Most important, by composing for films his music reached a large new audience. Although he respectfully bowed to the less attractive conventions of film scoring such as the required speed of composition and the potential loss of control over the role, placement, and the relevance of the music he composed for a film, he was able to choose his projects carefully within the industry. It is clear, however, that he never gave up on his high hopes for the future of this relatively new genre.

1. Ralph Vaughan Williams, "Composing for the Films," in *National Music and other Essays*, 2nd ed. (Oxford: Oxford University Press, 1963), 160–65, at 160.

2. [Vaughan Williams's masque, *The Bridal Day* (1939), was premiered over BBC television on 5 June 1953: see Michael Kennedy, *A Catalogue of the Works of Ralph Vaughan Williams*, 2nd ed. (Oxford: Oxford University Press, 1996), 164–65—Ed.]

3. Jeffrey Richards, "Vaughan Williams and British Wartime Cinema," *Vaughan Williams Studies*, ed. Alain Frogley (Cambridge: Cambridge University Press, 1996), 139–65 at 139–40.

4. Ibid., 141–42. [The GPO Film Unit was a subdivision of the United Kingdom General Post Office; in 1940, it became the Crown Film Unit under the aegis of the Ministry of Information—Ed.]

5. His film music scores were preserved. For recordings of many of the film scores or their suites, see *The Film Music of Ralph Vaughan Williams*, vols. 1–3 (CHAN 10007, 2002). Suite arrangements of *49th Parallel*, *The People's Land*, *Scott of the Antarctic*, *The Loves of Joanna Godden*, *Bitter Springs*, and *The England of Elizabeth* by Stephen Hogger (n.p., 2013); *The Dim Little Island* score partially reconstructed by Stephen Hogger, liner notes by Michael Kennedy. These arrangements and reconstructions drew scathing criticism: see Mark Doran, "*Vaughan Williams: The Film Music*, vol. 1, BBC Philharmonic Orchestra, cond. Rumon Gamba, W. Merrin Gamba (Sop.), John Scott (Organ), Sheffield Philharmonic Chorus, Chandos CHAN 10007," *Tempo* 58/227 (2004): 85–90.

6. [While patriotism played the dominant role in his initial desire to compose for films, Vaughan Williams's need for ready cash cannot be entirely discounted; during the war, he was supporting an ailing wife, a younger lover (Ursula Wood), and contributing money to Jewish relief organizations—Ed.] As he wrote to Hubert Foss in the early 1940s, "I thoroughly enjoyed my days at Denham—& am prepared to do another film, provided (1) I like the subject (2) I get good money (3) I have a say as to when & how the music should come in." See Vaughan Williams, *The Letters of Ralph Vaughan Williams 1895–1958*, ed. Hugh Cobbe (Oxford: Oxford University Press, 2008), 322–23.

7. William Walton, quoted in Mervyn Cooke, *A History of Film Music* (Cambridge: Cambridge University Press, 2008), 248, 249. For Walton's involvement in films during the 1940s, see Michael Kennedy, *Portrait of Walton* (Oxford: Oxford University Press, 1989), 108–26.

8. William Alwyn, "Film Music: Sound or Silence?," in *William Alwyn: Composing in Words*, ed. Andrew Palmer (London: Toccata Press, 2009), 274–89, at 276. See also Cooke, *A History of Film Music*, 237.

9. Vaughan Williams, "Composing for the Films," 162.

10. Richards, "Vaughan Williams and British Wartime Cinema," 165.

11. Michael Kennedy, *The Works of Ralph Vaughan Williams*, 2nd ed. (Oxford: Oxford University Press, 1980), 322.

12. Daniel Goldmark, "Music, Film and Vaughan Williams," in *Vaughan Williams Essays*, ed. Byron Adams and Robin Wells (Aldershot: Ashgate, 2003), 207.

13. Vaughan Williams, "Composing for the Films," 162.

14. Eric Saylor, "Music for Stage and Film," in *The Cambridge Companion to Vaughan Williams*, ed. Alain Frogley and Aidan J. Thomson (Cambridge: Cambridge University Press, 2013), 157–78 at 167.

15. Ursula Vaughan Williams, *R.V.W.: A Biography of Ralph Vaughan Williams* (London: Oxford University Press, 1964), 239.

16. S. J. Hetherington and Mark Brownrigg, *Muir Mathieson, 1911–1975: A Life in Film Music* (Dalkeith: Scottish Cultural Press, 2006).

17. Elisabeth Lutyens, *A Goldfish Bowl* (London: Cassell, 1972), 148.

18. Ursula Vaughan Williams, *R.V.W.*, 239. See also Hetherington, *Muir Mathieson*, 32, 84. According to Hetherington, Mathieson studied piano with Arthur Benjamin and conducting with Malcolm Sargent at the Royal College of Music.

19. Michael Kennedy, *A Catalogue of the Works of Ralph Vaughan Williams*, 2nd ed. (Oxford: Oxford University Press, 1996), 171, 226. See also Ralph Vaughan Williams, *Letters*, 407.

20. All from Muir Mathieson, "Aspects of Film Music," *Tempo* 9 (1944): 7–9 at 8.

21. Ralph Vaughan Williams, quoted in Mathieson, "Aspects of Film Music": 7.

22. Cooke, *A History of Film Music*, 230.

23. Hetherington, *Muir Mathieson*, 98–100.

24. Ursula Vaughan Williams, *R.V.W.*, 245.

25. Doreen Carwithen, quoted in Hetherington, *Muir Mathieson*, 121. Carwithen's career in film scoring was quite different from that of Vaughan Williams, having been awarded a place on the J. Arthur Rank Apprenticeship Scheme in 1947. Lewis Foreman, "Carwithen, Doreen," *Grove Music Online*, Oxford University Press.

26. Ursula Vaughan Williams, *R.V.W.*, 239.

27. Ernest Irving, *Cue for Music: An Autobiography by Ernest Irving* (London: Dennis Dobson, 1959), 174.

28. Ibid., 162.

29. Ernest Irving, "Music in Films," *Music & Letters* 24/4 (October 1943): 223–35, at 229.

30. Ralph Vaughan Williams, "Ernest Irving: 1878–1953," *Music & Letters* 35/1 (January 1954): 17–18, at 17. A bond between Vaughan Williams and Irving was that they both attended, at different times, the Charterhouse School in Godalming, Surrey.

31. Ralph Vaughan Williams, in Roger Manvell and John Huntley, *The Technique of Film Music: Revised and Enlarged by Richard Arnell and Peter Day* (London and New York: Focal Press, 1975), 223.

32. Irving, *Cue for Music*, 163.

33. Hetherington, *Muir Mathieson*, 110.

34. Alwyn, "Film Music," 277.

35. Ibid.

36. Vaughan Williams, "Composing for the Films," 162.

37. Ralph Vaughan Williams to Ernest Irving, 8 October 1947, VWL2325.

38. Ralph Vaughan Williams to R. W. Fenn, 1 October 1947, VWL2319.

39. Vaughan Williams, "Composing for the Films," 162.

40. Ibid.

41. British musical practice during the 1930s and '40s was quite different from the demands made on composers by American studios, where music was expected to be virtually continuous throughout the course of the moving picture. Steiner's score for *Gone with the Wind* of 1939 is a case in point.

42. "Diegetic" refers to music that belongs in the world of the narrative, and which can therefore usually be heard by the characters in the film; "non-diegetic" is the underscore, music whose source is not in the world of the film, and which may not be audible to the characters.

43. Vaughan Williams, "Composing for the Films," 161.

44. Ibid.

45. Interestingly, Vaughan Williams seems to have created only one suite himself, that of music drawn from *The Flemish Farm*. He conducted this suite at a Promenade Concert on 31 July 1945. See Kennedy, *Catalogue of the Works of Ralph Vaughan Williams*, 175. The other suites published by Oxford University Press during this period were compiled and arranged by Muir Mathieson.

46. The Academy of Motion Picture Arts and Sciences discontinued the category for "Best Story" in 1956 due to the decline of the studio system and the rise of independent screenwriters.

47. Michael Kennedy, "The Unknown Vaughan Williams," *Proceedings of the Royal Musical Association* 99 (1972–1973): 39.

48. Goldmark, "Music, Film, and Vaughan Williams": for example, see 215–16.

49. Ibid., 216, 218.

50. In addition to his wartime duties in the Crown Film Unit, Mathieson served as music director of the Army, Navy, and Air Force film units. See Hetherington and Brownrigg, *Muir Mathieson*, 87.

51. Jeffrey Richards, *Films and British National Identity: From Dickens to Dad's Army* (Manchester and New York: Manchester University Press, 1997), 296.

52. Byron Adams, "The Stages of Revision of Vaughan Williams's Sixth Symphony," *Vaughan Williams Essays*, 13, 16n21.

53. To save time, Vaughan Williams sent the score of *Coastal Command* to Roy Douglas (1907–2015) to be orchestrated; in addition, Douglas was tasked with "making the scores more readable." See Roy Douglas, *Working with Vaughan Williams: The Correspondence of Ralph Vaughan Williams and Roy Douglas* (London: The British Library, 1988), 3.

54. Ken Cameron, quoted in John Huntley, *The Story of British Film Music* (London: Skelton Robinson, 1947), 111. It seems odd that Ernest Irving should single out this score for his initial criticism of Vaughan Williams's competence as a film composer. However, as Vaughan Williams recalled in an obituary tribute, "Irving asked me to write some music for Ealing Studios and when, under his guidance, I made a success of this he literally went down on his knees and apologized for his former strictures." See Ralph Vaughan Williams, "Ernest Irving: 1878–1953," *Music & Letters* 35/1 (1954): 17.

55. Kennedy, liner notes for *The Film Music of Ralph Vaughan Williams*, vol. 3, Chandos CHAN 10368, 2006, 6.

56. Kennedy, liner notes for *The Film Music of Ralph Vaughan Williams*, vol. 1, Chandos CHAN 10007, 2002, 6–7.

57. As Michael Kennedy writes, "Vaughan Williams had enjoyed writing music for Jeffrey Dell's film *Flemish Farm* and had derived amusement from the exiled Belgian Government's protests over a love scene in a barn which had to be altered to make it clear that the couple were married." See Kennedy, *The Works of Ralph Vaughan Williams*, 286.

58. Further observations about Vaughan Williams's landscape scoring in Paul Mazey, *British Film Music: Musical Traditions in British Cinema, 1930s–1950s* (Cham: Palgrave Macmillan, 2020), esp. chap. 3, "Pastoral Music: Representations of Landscape," 49–82.

59. Irving, *Cue for Music*, 175.

60. Ibid.

61. Ernest Irving to Ralph Vaughan Williams, 22 January 1948, 22 January 1948, VWL2544. See also Vaughan Williams, "Ernest Irving: 1878–1953": 17.

62. Daniel M. Grimley, "Music, Ice, and the 'Geometry of Fear': The Landscapes of Vaughan Williams's *Sinfonia Antartica*," *The Musical Quarterly* 91/1–2, British Modernism issue (Spring–Summer 2008): 116–50.

63. Ursula Vaughan Williams recalled, "Ralph became more and more upset about the inefficiencies of [Scott's] organization; he despised heroism that risked lives unnecessarily." See Ursula Vaughan Williams, *R.V.W.*, 279.

64. Grimley, "Music, Ice, and the 'Geometry of Fear'": 129 et passim.

65. Richard Cohn, "An Introduction to Neo-Riemannian Theory: A Survey and Historical Perspective," *Journal of Music Theory* 42/2 (1998): 167–80.

66. Richard Cohn, "Maximally Smooth Cycles, Hexatonic Systems, and the Analysis of Late-Romantic Triadic Progressions," *Music Analysis* 15/1 (1996): 9–40; for hexatonic poles: 17. See also Cohn, "Uncanny Resemblances: Tonal Signification in the Freudian Age," *Journal of the American Musicological Society* 57/2 (2004): 285–324.

67. Cohn, "Uncanny Resemblances": 290.

68. Goldmark speculated that the lack of music for this last scene in particular might have stemmed from the omission of both women's musical themes and longer earlier scenes. See Goldmark, "Music, Film, and Vaughan Williams," 224.

69. Kennedy, "The Unknown Vaughan Williams": 40. See also Grimley, "Music, Ice, and the 'Geometry of Fear'": 125. Other articles and chapters on this score include Hugh Ottaway, "Scott and After: The Final Phase," *The Musical Times* 113/1556 (1972): 959, 961–62; Arne Stollberg, "Die Stimme der Eissphinx: Pastoralismus und Anti-Pastoralismus in Vaughan Williams' *Sinfonia Antartica* sowie der Filmmusik zu *Scott of the Antarctic*," in *Ralph Vaughan Williams,* ed. Ulrich Tadday (Munich: MusikKonzepte Sonderband, edition text + kritik, 2018), 186–205; Carolyn Philpott, Elizabeth Leane, and Douglas Quin, "Vaughan Williams and the Soundscapes of *Scott of the Antarctic*," *The Musical Quarterly* 103/1–2 (Spring–Summer 2020): 105–38.

70. The plot and Australian setting of *Bitter Springs* is reminiscent of *The Overlanders* (1946), an Ealing Studios film with a score by John Ireland.

71. Irving, *Cue for Music*, 175.

72. See Kennedy, *A Catalogue of the Works of Ralph Vaughan Williams*, 190.

73. Ibid., 237.

74. The other three were John Ormiston (industrialist), Osbert Lancaster (artist), and James Fisher (naturalist), cited in Kennedy, *A Catalogue of the Works of Ralph Vaughan Williams*, 188.

75. Richards, "Vaughan Williams and British Wartime Cinema," 161–64.

76. Adrian Wright, *The Innumerable Dance: The Life and Work of William Alwyn* (Woodbridge, Suffolk: Boydell Press, 2008), 108–9.

77. Ralph Vaughan Williams, "The Biter Bit," *The Musical Times* 97/1356 (February 1956): 89. See Kennedy, *A Catalogue of the Works of Ralph Vaughan Williams*, 189; see also Wright, *The Innumerable Dance*, 109. According to Kennedy, the film score may have been conducted by John Hollingsworth, Mathieson's assistant and later a successful musical director.

78. I do not disagree here with Richards, who mentioned in passing that the score resembles but does not exactly match Vaughan Williams's *Five Variants on "Dives and Lazarus."* Indeed, the addition of new materials and the reordering of the sections for the score blur the boundaries between resemblance and identity of the two pieces.

79. Kennedy, *A Catalogue of the Works of Ralph Vaughan Williams*, 188.

80. Ralph Vaughan Williams, *Five Variants on "Dives and Lazarus"* (Oxford: Oxford University Press, 1940).

81. Once again, Muir Mathieson adapted this film score for a concert work, *Three Portraits from "The England of Elizabeth."* See Kennedy, *A Catalogue of the Works of Ralph Vaughan Williams*, 226–27.

Pilgrim in a New-Found-Land:
Vaughan Williams in America

BYRON ADAMS

Come Muse migrate from Greece and Ionia,
Cross out please those immensely overpaid accounts,
That matter of Troy and Achilles' wrath, and Æneas', Odysseus' wanderings,
Placard "Removed" and "To Let" on the rocks of your snowy Parnassus
Repeat at Jerusalem, place the notice high on Jaffa's gate and on
*   Mount Moriah,*
The same on the walls of your German, French and Spanish castles
*   and Italian collections,*
For know a better, fresher, busier sphere, a wide untried domain awaits,
*   demands you.*

"For know a better, fresher, busier sphere, a wide, untried domain awaits, demands you."[1] Ralph Vaughan Williams so loved these lines from the American poet Walt Whitman's "Song of the Exposition" that he quoted them in print no less than three times. The full quotation first appears at the head of his controversial 1912 essay, "Who Wants the English Composer?,"[2] it shows up again in the first chapter of his volume *National Music* (1934); and makes a final appearance in the epilogue of his last book, *The Making of Music* (1954). *A Sea Symphony* (First Symphony, 1910) opens with another phrase from the same poem: "Behold, the sea itself."[3]

As his use of these quotations suggests, Vaughan Williams habitually used Whitman's poetry as a lens through which to view the United States and its people. The poet represented a vision of America that captivated Vaughan Williams even before he set foot on American soil. In her biography of her husband, Ursula Vaughan Williams notes that on his first visit to America, "Ralph had been excited by names familiar from the histories of the civil war and from Whitman's poems, as well as by the towers and chasms of New York."[4]

Whitman's poetry inspired choral-orchestral frescoes such as *Toward the Unknown Region* (1907) and *A Sea Symphony*, and in Vaughan Williams's mind it also represented the ideal of a dynamic, modern, and egalitarian society. The composer's own teacher, Hubert Parry, had exhorted him to "write choral music as befits an Englishman and a democrat."[5] Vaughan Williams's political convictions consistently tacked leftward, and he embraced them sincerely. Before and during the Second World War, he crisscrossed Britain giving lectures on behalf of the Federal Union, an organization that sought to end European warfare by instituting a federated Europe after the U.S. model.[6] His championing of the Federal Union reflected his admiration of the national community celebrated so exuberantly by Whitman. Whitman's vision of democratic freedom chimed so deeply with Vaughan Williams's own social and aesthetic convictions that he was ready to embrace America as enthusiastically as many Americans embraced his music.

The First Journey: "Manhattan with spires"
("When Lilacs Last in the Dooryard Bloomed")

The first of Vaughan Williams's three journeys to America was only a qualified success. At the invitation of the Norfolk Music Festival in Connecticut, Vaughan Williams traveled to the United States in 1922 accompanied by his first wife, Adeline. At this point, he was a fifty-year-old veteran of the First World War who was widely acknowledged as the leading British composer of his generation. His war experience cast a long shadow on Vaughan Williams's work and reputation during this time. He was engaged to conduct the first American performance of his symphonic "war requiem," *A Pastoral Symphony* (Third Symphony, 1921, premiered 26 January 1922), and the invitation to the Norfolk Festival came just as the composer was reinvigorating his interrupted career. The war may have even intensified his fondness for Walt Whitman's poetry. Vaughan Williams had carried a pocket edition of Whitman throughout his military service, and Whitman's time spent as a battlefield nurse in the Civil War may have recalled Vaughan Williams's recent service as a Wagon Orderly in the Royal Army Medical Corps.

By 1921, the Norfolk Festival was a prestigious event. Its founders and principal patrons were Carl Stoeckel (1858–1925) and his wife, Ellen Battel Stoeckel (1851–1939). Carl Stoeckel was the son of organist and Yale University faculty member Gustave Stoeckel, and Ellen was a member of the publishing dynasty that built Yale's Battel Chapel. In the late 1890s, they transformed a modest local festival sponsored by the Litchfield County Choral Union into an annual event of national and international renown. In 1906, the Stoeckels built an acoustically superb concert hall that they dubbed "The Music Shed." The festival hosted composers such as Jean Sibelius and Sergei Rachmaninoff. Samuel Coleridge-Taylor (1875–1912) was the first British composer to appear at the festival, and also became one of the first Black musicians to cross the "color line" in 1910 by conducting a white orchestra.[7] Four years later, Sibelius composed his tone poem *The Oceanides* (*Aallottaret*, Op. 73) especially for the festival and conducted its premiere in Norfolk on 4 June 1914.

Despite the Stoeckels' largesse, postwar economic forces eventually put an end to these elaborate events. In a 1925 obituary for Carl Stoeckel, Richard Aldrich (1863–1937), chief music critic of the *New York Times*, lamented, "Mr. Stoeckel was compelled to give them up in 1923 because of the exorbitant demands of the orchestral players, by direction of the Musical Union."[8] Indeed, by the penultimate festival in 1922, financial pressures had already taken a toll on the orchestra's quality. In a letter to Holst posted from Norfolk, Vaughan Williams complained, "Many of the players are v. good but the back desks of the fiddles are not v. good."[9]

Vaughan Williams's engagement at Norfolk may have resulted in part from a recommendation by his erstwhile teacher at the Royal College of Music, Charles Villiers Stanford (1852–1924). Stanford was a friend of the American composer Horatio Parker (1863–1919), who was dean of the music department at Yale and highly influential at the Norfolk Music Festival.[10] At Parker's suggestion, Stanford had been invited to the 1915 festival. Stanford had booked tickets on the HMS *Lusitania* for passage to New York in late May of that year, but a German U-boat torpedoed the liner on 7 May, causing the British government to advise British subjects against crossing the Atlantic. Stanford, disappointed, remained at home, although his Piano Concerto No. 2 in C Minor, Op. 126 (1911), was performed at the festival that year. Up until this time, all of Stanford's dealings with the Stoeckels had been through Parker.[11] If, after Parker's death, the Stoeckels invited Stanford again in the early 1920s, his fragile health would have precluded such a strenuous voyage, and he may well have proposed that Vaughan Williams appear in his stead.[12]

A Pastoral Symphony shared the program with the newly composed *Anniversary Overture* (1922) by George Whitefield Chadwick (1854–1931).[13] The symphony puzzled its first American audience. Adeline Vaughan Williams wrote to her sister Cordelia, "Ralph started the concert with his *Pastoral*—it went beautifully. . . . I don't know really what the audience made of the *Pastoral* but the feeling was as if they liked it."[14] When *A Pastoral Symphony* was first performed in New York on 24 November of the same year, Aldrich wrote in the *New York Times*:

At the concert of the Philharmonic Society yesterday afternoon Mr. Stransky had another new composition ready for
his program—R. Vaughan Williams's "Pastoral Symphony."
Mr. Williams [*sic*] has made his place as one of the heads of
the younger English composers. He is perhaps more than
any of them essentially English, and writes music that is
recognizably English from its foundation upon the basis of
English folksong. Mr. Williams has been an ardent student
and collector of that folksong; and this is evident, not in his
use of actual folk tunes themselves, for he has used none, but
in the saturation of his music with their essential spirit. . . .
First heard in London last January, it was played at the Music
Festival at Norfolk, Conn., in June of this year, when the
composer was brought over to conduct it himself, after
the princely fashion of Mr. and Mrs. Carl Stoeckel, whose gift
that festival is.[15]

By the end of 1922, Vaughan Williams's music was well known in New
York. The Russian-born British conductor Albert Coates (1882–1953) had
earlier presented the American premiere of Vaughan Williams's *A London
Symphony* (Second Symphony, 1914, revised 1920 and 1933–36) with
the New York Symphony Orchestra in Carnegie Hall on 30 December
1920. On that occasion, Aldrich was disconcerted by the score's alterna-
tion of modernist dissonance with the demotic music of London: "The
Symphony is not on the whole, pleasing . . . there are many passages,
including the imitative ones—the concertina, the old musician's fiddling
tune, the Coster girls' dance—that are singularly successful."[16] *A London
Symphony* fared better when it was conducted by Walter Damrosch with
the same orchestra in Aeolian Hall on 30 January 1921. Modifying his
earlier opinion, Aldrich declared that "to those who heard it a second time
it may have seemed even a more profoundly felt and original expression
than it did before."[17] During the same season, Damrosch conducted the
New York Symphony in the American premiere of Vaughan Williams's
Fantasia on a Theme of Thomas Tallis on 9 March 1922.[18] On 5 April 1922,
the Mendelssohn Choir of Toronto and the New York Philharmonic presented a successful performance of *A Sea Symphony* in Carnegie Hall. In
an uncredited review, the author (probably Aldrich) compared the score
to Elgar: "The sea music, indeed, stems from that of the storm in [Elgar's]
'The Apostles,'" and concluded by remarking that the "work made a more
profound, if not as varied, impression as his realistic 'London Symphony'
heard last year."[19]

At Norfolk, the Stoeckels' lavish hospitality made Vaughan Williams uncomfortable. In a letter dated 8 June 1922, Adeline Vaughan Williams wrote to her sister, "The Stoeckels are very dear people—only we have to do just what Mr. Stoeckel plans for us and Ralph feels a little restive from a surfeit of kindness!"[20] In a letter posted from New York seven days later, she noted, "Ralph is feeling restive and says he now knows how Mozart and his contemporaries felt living under a patron."[21] Writing to Holst, Vaughan Williams was forthright: "I never want a patron – it's too wearing."[22]

In contrast to his impatience with the comforts on offer at the Stoeckels' country house, Vaughan Williams adored New York as soon as he stepped off the boat. This visit was the beginning of a lifelong love affair with Whitman's "Mannahatta." (In 1922, more of Whitman's New York was still intact among the proliferating skyscrapers than exists in the twenty-first century.) For a composer so often described as a pastoralist, Vaughan Williams vastly preferred to live in cities while contemplating the countryside at a distance and venturing onto rural roads only at intervals (Figure 1). As he wrote to Holst:

> I have now seen (a) Niagara (b) the Woolworths [*sic*] Building and am most impressed by (b) – I've come to the conclusion that the Works of Man terrify me more than the Works of God – I told myself all the time that N'[ia]g[ar]a was the most wonderful thing in the world – & so it is – especially when you get right under it – but I did not once want to fall on my knees & confess my sins – whereas I can sit all day & look out my windows (16 floors up) at the sky scrapers.[23]

When Vaughan Williams visited America a decade later, he wrote to Maud Karpeles, "New York looks more classically & tragically beautiful than ever."[24] On his final trip to America in 1954, Vaughan Williams, by then in his eighties, insisted on ending his first day by watching the sunset from the observation platform of the Empire State Building. He told his second wife, Ursula, "I think this is the most beautiful city in the world."[25]

The Second Journey: "The great women's land!"
("Starting from Paumanok")

By the time of his second American journey in 1932, the sixty-year-old Vaughan Williams was a revered figure in both American concert halls and British musical life. Of his three visits to America, this second was the only one he undertook alone, as Adeline Vaughan Williams was virtually incapacitated by rheumatoid arthritis. Furthermore, this trip would

Figure 1. Woolworth Building, ca. 1920.

result in a volume that expounded at length upon his convictions concerning the nexus of music and nation.

In October, Vaughan Williams arrived at Bryn Mawr College near Philadelphia to give the Mary Flexner Lectures to an audience consisting primarily of intelligent young women. Each of the lectures included musical selections used as examples, and each was followed by an extended question and answer period. As he wrote in early November to Imogen Holst (1907–1984), "I have to stand up before a class the day after each lecture & be heckled by a crowd of young women – who ask me 'what I meant by' then refer to their note books – I've come off fairly unscathed up to the present."[26] In fact, the reactions to his lectures were more complicated than Vaughan Williams let on.

Alain Frogley has pointed out the paradox of these lectures, which were published in 1934 under the title *National Music*. They show Vaughan Williams distilling a culturally nationalistic ideology at the time when he was composing his Fourth Symphony (1932–34). The Fourth is a dissonant, abstract, and modernist score in which there are no overt allusions to either the substance or the style of folk music.[27] The timing was exact: the music paper upon which he wrote a draft of the scherzo was purchased from a Philadelphia music shop and bears the words "Bryn Mawr College / PA" in the composer's handwriting.[28] This paradox deepens when these Flexner Lectures are placed in the context of Bryn Mawr's invitation and that of the broader historical period.

If true irony consists of holding two opposing ideas simultaneously, Vaughan Williams found himself in an ironic position in 1932 as he made a conflicted return to an earlier cultural nationalism that coexisted with an impulse to transcend borders. Politically, this impulse was borne out through his vision of a "United States of the World," and musically it could be seen in the composer's adoption of a modernist aesthetic.[29] Vaughan Williams sought to make a connection with the women of Bryn Mawr by declaring, "I feel that the future of music in America has something in common with that in England."[30] Four years later, he reached out to America by using Whitman's poetry in his pro-peace cantata *Dona Nobis Pacem* (1936), which was completed two years after the 1934 premiere of the Fourth Symphony.

The students at Bryn Mawr were made aware of the tension between Vaughan Williams's nationalist musical ideology and his espousal of abstract modernism even before he gave his first lecture. In an incisive article announcing Vaughan Williams's lectures in Bryn Mawr's student newspaper, *The College News*, the anonymous author wrote, "He is an uncompromising Nationalist in music and his influence is among the most powerful forces in contemporary English music, with his large human outlook and disregard of all but the essential, the absence of every form of rhetorical address. His music is deeply tinged with the spirit of English folk-music, of English national character and of English musical tradition and ideals in particular." However, toward the end of the article, the author describes Vaughan Williams's modernism:

> In spite of the apparently great simplicity of his music he is actually a disciple of revolt. His chromatic flexibility points the way to an expansion of idiom other than that of the old scale system, the essentially modal character of his melodic writing, like that of Debussy, is responsible for a frequent parallelism of parts and his predilection for bare consecutive fourths and fifth[s].[31]

The College News covered each of Vaughan Williams's Flexner Lectures in detail: each column reads like a précis of the corresponding chapter in *National Music*. One telling paragraph, however, points to occasional pushback from those earnest students with their notebooks. The author reports that at the beginning of his third lecture, "Dr. Williams [*sic*] clarified his remarks of the previous week on the origin of music, and explained that he was not attempting to advance any theories on this difficult subject."[32] These accounts in *The College News* also contain lists of pieces that were performed in the course of the lectures. British folk songs unsurprisingly made up the bulk of the musical illustrations, but there was also music by J. S. Bach, the slow movement of a Haydn symphony played on the piano, and Tudor music, including Byrd's *The Carman's Whistle* and *Sellinger's Round*. Contemporary music was represented by the Sarabande from Debussy's *Pour le piano* (1902), the Minuet from Ravel's *Sonatine* (1906), and one of Satie's *Gymnopédies* (1888; the author does not identify which of the three was performed).[33] These more recent examples were selected to show the use of modal materials in modern music and reveal the influence of French music on Vaughan Williams's own style.

The reports that appeared in *The College News* do not touch upon what now constitutes one of the most controversial passages in *National Music*.[34] Writing of how the "folk-song movement" had prepared the way for the younger British composers in the postwar years such as Arthur Bliss, William Walton, and his own former student Constant Lambert, Vaughan Williams declared, "They may deny their birthright; but having once drunk deep of the living water no amount of Negroid emetics or 'Baroque' purgatives will enable them to expel [British folksong] from their system."[35] One hopes that the women of Bryn Mawr pulled out their notebooks the next day and heckled Vaughan Williams over "Negroid emetics" ("What, exactly, did you mean by that, Dr. Vaughan Williams?"). His point was certainly ill-expressed, especially since he did not seek to denigrate African Americans or jazz with his characterization. Rather, his scorn was aimed at British composers who neglected their own musical traditions in favor of expropriating others', whether imported jazz or Stravinskian Neoclassicism. As poorly as the quote has aged, the admonition to look to one's "native" cultural traditions sits at the heart of Vaughan Williams's musical aesthetics and practice.

Vaughan Williams saw jazz as a rich American musical vernacular. In his final lecture at Bryn Mawr, he remarked that jazz "does show that there is musical vitality in America which at any moment may manifest itself in some other form which has in it the elements of greatness." He continues in this vein for a couple of sentences before launching a diatribe against Europeans who attempt to add superficial elements of jazz to their work: "At all events jazz, whether you like it or not, is a purely indigenous art. No one but an American can write it or play it. Anyone who has listened to the helpless attempts of German or French bands to play jazz, or the pitiful efforts of some modern French or German composers to add a little sting to their failing inventiveness by adopting a few jazz rhythms, will realize this."[36]

The Mary Flexner Lectures thus articulate convictions to which Vaughan Williams returned throughout his career. Strangely, there has been little or no speculation about why he was asked to deliver these lectures in the first place. A definitive answer has proven to be elusive, but one might begin with the reasons for the creation of the series itself. In 1928, Bernard Flexner (1865–1945), a prominent New York lawyer, gave a princely sum to Bryn Mawr to establish a lectureship in honor of his sister, Mary Flexner (1873–1947).[37] She had graduated in the Bryn Mawr Class of 1895, and she periodically returned to her alma mater. According to the *New York Times*, the lectureship was to be "given to an American or foreign scholar distinguished in the fields of the humanities—that is, in literature, philosophy, art, archeology and history." Furthermore, the lecturer was "to be selected by the President of the college."[38]

It is unclear how much say the president of Bryn Mawr, Marion Edwards Park, or members of the faculty had over the selection of the lecturers during Mary Flexner's lifetime. A 1947 obituary published in the *New York Times* stated that since the lectureship was founded, "Miss Flexner had devoted much of her time to the selection of lecturers."[39] Flexner had completed a master's degree in history at Columbia University in 1906, and most of the lectures reflected her enthusiasms. The initial lecturer was the Egyptologist James Breasted and the last during her lifetime was historian Arnold Toynbee.[40]

Mary Flexner's health became precarious by the early 1930s, so she did not attend any of Vaughan Williams's lectures nor those given in 1937 by the art historian Erwin Panofsky.[41] During that period, however, she received regular reports about the lecturers from her niece Hortense Flexner, who taught in the English Department at Bryn Mawr from 1926 to 1940.[42] Nursing a heavy cold and utterly indifferent to music, Hortense Flexner was unimpressed by Vaughan Williams's first lecture:

> The Mary F. Lecturer had a grand start. A great big audi-ence, so big that I couldn't get a seat in the near section. . . . [Bryn Mawr's president] Miss Park gave a very hand-some introduction, describing the fund and its purpose "to do honor to his sister, Mary Flexner, an alumnae of the College." I am sure that you would have been pleased with that part of it, and Uncle Bengy [Bernard Flexner] too. The lecturer however was a bit dull. Only after he had wandered round the lot for an hour and a quarter did he confide in us that after all "You can't say anything about music." What he meant was that you either have to be very technical or very general—which latter he chose. However, he is a great lion. I hear on all sides how distinguished he is. . . . Everybody has been after him, and the students in music camp on his trail, so I am sure he will be voted a success.[43]

If Mary Flexner had indeed "devoted most of her time to the selection of lecturers," Hortense Flexner's objections might well have struck her aunt as tactless:

> But personally, I should think that in this time of the world's history, when funds such as he is receiving are darned rare, a college that is suffering from empty halls would look about a little before wishing such a lectureship on the department of music. Why not Keynes or Laski or anybody who knows about world affairs and could give us something thrilling and alive.[44]

In a letter sent to her aunt a few weeks later, Flexner's sardonic tone is still much in evidence:

> We're sorry however you're not coming over for one of the Mary Flexner lectures. . . . As for old Poppa Vaughan-Williams, he continues to be a great social lion, however his

audience may feel. He had lunch with Stokowski last week. .
. . For the rest, the music department seems to like Vaughan-
Williams and those who know him say nice things about how
sweet he is, and how shy and how modest. So I guess he will
rate as a success for the specialists.[45]

Mary Flexner's replies to her niece have not survived, so it is impossible to gauge how she reacted to such pointed observations. In a letter
posted from Hortense to Mary Flexner in early December, there may be a
hint of a remonstrance from her aunt: "It is certainly nice that the Oxford
Press is doing Vaughan-Williams['s] book, for doubtless by the time,
he gets it down to book-size, it will be full of interest." (This sentence
appears in a missive that continues with Hortense Flexner bemoaning
that Oxford University Press had rejected one of her plays.)[46] As Vaughan
Williams is thus far the sole composer ever to have held this lectureship,
Hortense Flexner's strenuous objections to her aunt concerning the waste
of money incurred by the frivolous selection of a composer may have had
a chilling effect on the choice of future lecturers.[47]

Indeed, Vaughan Williams might seem at first to have been an anomalous
choice among the more typical literary scholars, art historians, philosophers,
archaeologists, and historians featured on the series. He may not have been
chosen just for his reputation as a composer, since he did appear in the Flexner
Lectures as a humanist expounding upon British musical nationalism. There
is no evidence that either Bernard or Mary Flexner was particularly interested in music beyond their positions as cultured, wealthy New Yorkers, aside
from Bernard Flexner's subscription to the Friends of Music.[48]

During the 1920s and '30s, the New York Philharmonic-Symphony
and the Philadelphia Orchestra regularly programmed scores by Vaughan
Williams, but there is no evidence that the Flexners knew any of his music.
It is unlikely, however, that either of the Flexners escaped reading about
Vaughan Williams's music in the *New York Times* or the *New York Herald-Tribune*.
Times music critics Richard Aldrich and Olin Downes (1886–1955) regularly
reviewed works by Vaughan Williams. Aldrich, Downes, and Downes's assistant Harold Taubman (1907–1996) usually stressed Vaughan Williams's use
of modal scales, folksong, and nationalism.[49] Aldrich and Downes had a particular tendency to essentialize Vaughan Williams's "Englishness" in ways
that would later tarnish the composer's reputation in America. In a 1933
review of *A Pastoral Symphony*, Downes goes even further:

> For this is sheerest and purest music. Perhaps only Sibelius,
> among the contemporaries of Vaughan Williams, has felt

nature so deeply and purely and reflected its mystery with such originality in his scores. There is race in Vaughan Williams's music. . . . It is of the poetry that existed before there were town poets, and the sounds of the young world.[50]

Of course, Downes could not have known that Vaughan Williams used the title *A Pastoral Symphony* as a commentary on the human tragedy and ecological disaster in northern France during the First World War, rather than in an evocation of "lambkins frisking" in a placid English landscape.[51]

Downes's rhetoric about Vaughan Williams often slipped into frank eugenicism. Such characterizations were especially common among British music critics writing about Jean Sibelius, a composer whom Downes worshiped.[52] For example, Downes's descriptions of the music of both Sibelius and Vaughan Williams were replete with terms drawn from pseudoscientific schemes of racial hierarchy. Above all, Downes's repeated insistence on the "purity" he finds in *A Pastoral Symphony* or in Sibelius's Sixth and Seventh Symphonies—"the purest, the most absolute kind of symphonic music written today"—reveals his unquestioning acceptance of ethno-nationalist language.[53]

A second and perhaps equally unanswerable question arises: how much did Vaughan Williams know about the Flexners? Did Bryn Mawr supply him with any information? Did he hear about the Flexners from Una Lucas, a former student of Holst who matriculated at Bryn Mawr in 1932?[54] Did he know, for example, that the Flexners were the children of Jewish immigrants with an impressive portfolio of philanthropic projects in addition to the Mary Flexner Lectures? It is difficult to imagine that Vaughan Williams would have heard nothing of the brother and sister who had brought him to Bryn Mawr.

By 1932, the Flexner family was highly respected, both in New York and nationally. Mary Flexner's siblings included Abraham, co-founder of the Institute for Advanced Study at Princeton, and Simon, who was the first director of the Rockefeller Institute for Medical Research. While his brothers were indifferent to their Jewish heritage, Bernard was a secular Zionist who accompanied Justice Louis D. Brandeis to the 1920 World Zionist Congress in London.[55] He was one of the founders of the Palestine Economic Corporation in 1925 and its president until 1931.[56] While propinquity hardly ensures a shared ideology, there is some evidence that Mary Flexner was sympathetic to her brother's convictions. She worked as a "visiting teacher" at the Henry Street Settlement, a vocational school on Manhattan's Lower East Side. This institution was initially founded in 1892 to educate and provide health care for the daughters of impoverished Jewish immigrants, so Mary Flexner's involvement suggests that she, like her brother, was interested in the needs of the Jewish community at the time.[57]

Bernard Flexner and Vaughan Williams never met, but the rise of anti-Semitic fascism in Germany during the 1930s would alarm both of them. Working independently of one another, Flexner and Vaughan Williams sought to rescue and resettle Jewish refugees from Nazi Germany throughout the decade.[58] Just as the practical implementation of the Zionist cause became increasingly urgent for Flexner during this period, so the threat of German fascism paradoxically drove Vaughan Williams toward political internationalism.[59]

Vaughan Williams certainly did meet the pianist Harriet Cohen (1895–1967), a passionate Zionist who was concertizing in New York at the same time that Vaughan Williams was lecturing at Bryn Mawr (Figure 2). He composed several works for Cohen, including his angular, modernist Piano Concerto (1926–31). In her memoirs, Cohen describes her espousal of Zionism in terms reminiscent of religious conversion.[60] Furthermore, Cohen implies that Vaughan Williams viewed Zionism favorably. She quotes him as saying, "I think, or at least I hope, that I have a little Jewish blood: that would indeed make me proud," a statement that neatly sidesteps outright political endorsement while remaining sympathetic toward the Jewish people.[61] In marked contrast to his espousal of the Federal Union, Vaughan Williams never expressed overt public support for Zionism.

As Walt Whitman might say, the relationship between Cohen and Vaughan Williams was enlivened by the "subtle electric fire" of shared erotic attraction.[62] In November of 1931, Cohen had offered Vaughan Williams 10,000 kisses as an inducement to complete the Piano Concerto; he responded, "How can I say 'no' – when such a reward will be mine if I say 'yes'?" He goes on to declare, "I shall claim it to *the full*," and so he did, meticulously.[63] One letter that Vaughan Williams wrote to Cohen arranging for a meeting displays a curiously insistent tone: "Now look here – I am coming to N.Y. for the weekend on Nov 25 or 26 – can't we meet then – & don't give a tea party for me but just let me come to see you alone."[64]

Aside from his delight at the prospect of having tea *à deux* with Harriet Cohen, Vaughan Williams also made important contacts with American musicians. One such meeting was between Vaughan Williams and the young composer Samuel Barber (1910–1981). At that time, Barber was studying under the severe pedagogue Rosario Scalero at the Curtis Institute of Music in Philadelphia. Barber later recalled that he played and sang his setting of Matthew Arnold's "Dover Beach" for Vaughan Williams: "He liked it, and he encouraged me when no one believed in

Figure 2. Pianist Harriet Cohen.

my music."[65] Barber remained Vaughan Williams's favorite American composer, although he admired individual works by Roy Harris and Ross Lee Finney.[66] During the 1940s, Vaughan Williams wrote to Fritz Hart, "We've been hearing quite a lot of young American music here. Barber and Roy Harris seem to me to come out best." He then adds, "Copland in spite of his wrong notes seems to have something there though I cannot always get at it."[67]

Vaughan Williams's second sojourn further enhanced his fame in America. After taking him to a concert of the Boston Symphony, Harvard professor Archibald Davison (1883–1961) introduced Vaughan Williams to the orchestra's music director, Serge Koussevitzky. Ursula Vaughan Williams recorded that Koussevitzky asked her husband which of his scores he would like to have performed in Boston, to which the composer replied, "With that string section I would like to hear the *Tallis Fantasia*."[68] True to his word, Koussevitzky conducted the *Fantasia* in Symphony Hall on a pair of subscription concerts, the first of which took place on 2 December. Vaughan Williams had written to Maud Karpeles in November, "I start home on Dec 3rd," so he attended the performance of the *Tallis Fantasia* in Boston the day before he was scheduled to depart for Britain; earlier that week he had delivered an informal lecture for the music division at Harvard.[69] Ursula Vaughan Williams stated that "almost the entire orchestra stayed to listen to the rehearsals, instead of making their usual escape and leaving the string players to it."[70] Koussevitzky repeated the score six times during the 1932–33 season, and he conducted the *Fantasia* a dozen times from 1933 to 1942.[71] Repeated performances such as these by the Boston Symphony and other major orchestras testify to the popularity of Vaughan Williams's music in America from 1920 until the late 1950s.

The Third Journey: "Lo, body and soul—this land" ("When Lilacs Last in the Dooryard Bloomed")

The Fourth Symphony was not the only one of Vaughan Williams's symphonies to have been composed on American soil. He worked on his Eighth during his residency at Cornell University during the fall of 1954. The composer had recently married his second wife, Ursula, and they decided to go on a Whitmanesque pilgrimage across the length and breadth of the entire nation. Earlier that year, Ralph and Ursula Vaughan Williams had invited the distinguished British baritone Keith Faulkner (1900–1994), who had performed Vaughan Williams's music often throughout his career, to lunch.[72] During that meal, Vaughan Williams mentioned to Faulkner how much he yearned to see the Grand Canyon.

After learning of the composer's wish, Faulkner acted quickly. That afternoon he cabled the chair of the Cornell Department of Music, the musicologist Donald J. Grout (1902–1987). Acting with remarkable alacrity, Grout secured an appointment for Vaughan Williams as a distinguished visiting professor and arranged a coast-to-coast lecture tour. This tour included a stop at the Grand Canyon, of course, alongside appearances at Yale University, Harvard University, Toronto, the University of Michigan, and the University of California, Los Angeles.[73] Students from the Eastman School of Music traveled to Ithaca to hear Vaughan Williams's lectures at Cornell.

Published as *The Making of Music*, these 1954 Cornell lectures present a marked contrast to those he had delivered at Bryn Mawr twenty-two years earlier. The tone is far less pugnacious than the Flexner lectures, and, perhaps due to the composer's experience with refugees just before and during the Second World War, the Cornell lectures were far less concerned with cultural nationalism. Unlike *National Music*, which is a virtual transcript of the Flexner Lectures, *The Making of Music* is at times so terse as to be elliptical. An audio recording of his acceptance of the Henry Howland Prize in the Archive of Recorded Sound at Yale University reveals that Vaughan Williams spontaneously elaborated upon the spare published version of *The Making of Music*. In this recording, Vaughan Williams took excerpts from *The Making of Music* lectures and fleshed them out with spontaneous digressions and witty remarks.[74] Some of Vaughan Williams's exhortations from 1954 did in fact echo those that he had made in 1932 at Bryn Mawr. For example, he warned his audiences at Yale and Cornell—and presumably elsewhere—to avoid "watered down imitations of European models" and noted that "Even that American of all Americans, Walt Whitman, seemed to think that music, for him, consisted of nothing but Italian coloratura and cornets playing Verdi."[75] However, in *The Making of Music*, he revisits the commendation of demotic music that he made in his 1912 article "Who Needs the English Composer?": "We must not make the mistake of thinking lightly of the very characteristic art of Gershwin or, to go further back, the beautiful melodies of Stephen Foster."[76] In the epilogue to *The Making of Music* and in the Yale lecture on which it is based, Vaughan Williams pointedly qualifies his cultural nationalism:

> Now, the last thing that I want to do is to advocate a back-to-folk-song policy. Chaucer, Shakespeare and Milton have enriched the English language with cullings from France, Italy, Rome and Greece. In the same way we must, in America and England, enrich our music from foreign models, but it

must be an enrichment of our native impulse, not a swamping of it." [77]

While hardly a total repudiation of folk materials, this statement represents a significant modification of Vaughan Williams's earlier opinions on that subject, prompted, perhaps, by his firsthand experience of what George Steiner once referred to as the "venom" of untrammeled nationalism. Preceding the Second World War, Vaughan Williams's efforts at resettling Jewish refugees and his determined proselytizing for a united European government led him to soften his earlier convictions on the topic of the interaction of music and nationhood. If his first journey to the United States was about being in love with Whitman's expansive vision of America, and his second was about encouraging the young women of Bryn Mawr to explore American music (pointedly including jazz), then his pilgrimage to Cornell was made in order to exhort Americans to become citizens of the world, as they had just seen firsthand the horror and the price of extreme nationalism.

Anticipating Vaughan Williams's arrival by four months, Olin Downes wrote an enthusiastic article in the *New York Times* that hailed him as "the greatest living English composer" as well as a "precipitating force in contemporary music" second only to Downes's hero Sibelius.[78] Vaughan Williams conducted the Buffalo Philharmonic in concerts at Cornell and in Buffalo, and Downes reviewed the Cornell performance on 9 November, reporting that the *Fantasia on a Theme of Thomas Tallis* and *A London Symphony*, received "a prolonged standing ovation."[79]

Members of the Cornell music faculty were impressed by Vaughan Williams. The musicologist William W. Austin recalled that Vaughan Williams could play long passages from the last act of Debussy's *Pelléas et Mélisande* from memory.[80] As mentioned in Downes's review, John Kirkpatrick, a distinguished pianist and professor in the music department, painstakingly prepared and performed Vaughan Williams's *Fantasia (Quasi Variazione) on the "Old 104th" Psalm Tune* for piano, chorus, and orchestra (1949). In an insightful obituary tribute, Grout wrote that Vaughan Williams possessed a "startlingly original but none-the-less effective technique" at the piano and showed "greatness" in "a most unaffected modesty about himself."[81]

After the completion of his national tour, Ralph and Ursula spent some time in New York, shopping and enjoying luxuries that were difficult to obtain in Britain, where rationing was still in force. Before leaving America, Vaughan Williams renewed his friendship with the pianist James Friskin (1886–1967) and his wife, the composer Rebecca Clarke (1886–1979), both of whom had studied with Stanford at the Royal

College of Music in the first decade of the twentieth century. Another visitor was Samuel Barber, whom Ursula Vaughan Williams liked instantly.[82] As a fitting end to this third American visit, Vaughan Williams's Eighth Symphony, which he had sketched at Cornell, won the New York Critics Circle Award in 1956.

Epilogue

The writings of Sidney Finkelstein (1909–1974) articulate a compelling American response to Vaughan Williams. A Brooklyn native, Finkelstein was a Marxist sociologist and writer on music. He is best remembered today for his pioneering book *Jazz: A People's Music*.[83] In Vaughan Williams's music and writings, Finkelstein discovered a replacement for the ideology of Soviet Socialist Realism, with which Finkelstein had become disenchanted.[84] Indeed, several assertions made by Finkelstein in his 1960 volume *Composer and Nation: The Folk Heritage in Music* are virtual paraphrases of passages in *National Music*, from which Finkelstein also quotes directly. Finkelstein does not, however, merely parrot Vaughan Williams's views, he extends them into a pointed critique of the modernist elitism that he locates in the music of such composers as Stravinsky, Schoenberg, and Webern. Finkelstein judges these modernist composers in trenchant terms: "And while they have a flock of admirers and followers, it can be said that the future of their music is open to question. While their great musical gifts are unquestioned, their isolation in mind and heart from their people and nation has limited their development. . . . It has narrowed their human sympathies, and left them with little of significance to say to the people whose world they share."[85]

In contrast, Finkelstein lauds Vaughan Williams for eschewing the ivory tower and posits a reason for the relatively slow expansion of Vaughan Williams's reputation: "Vaughan Williams' music, like that of other social-minded humanists, failed to conform to the surface intellectual trends." Finkelstein then asserts, "To the 'modernists,' he offered no glittering novelties of technique, no sensational proclamations of having 'wiped out' the humanist past . . . to the academicians pretending to prize the humanist tradition, yet Tory-minded and cutting out its social and national heart, Vaughan Williams was equally disturbing." Finkelstein continues, "His music was too much of the twentieth century. It reminded listeners of the common people, and of the disturbing, discomforting moral problems in English life."[86]

Finkelstein concurs enthusiastically with Vaughan Williams's argument that composers must begin by addressing the parochial and only then reach out toward the universal. To illustrate this conviction, Finkelstein evokes *A Sea Symphony*. He locates points of contact between Vaughan Williams's "national democratic art" and Whitman's Transcendentalist universalism: "Using texts from Walt Whitman's 'Song of the Exposition,' 'Sea Drift,' and 'Passage to India,' it has a feeling of the brotherhood of humanity, calling to the sea, 'Thou unitest nations,' and singing 'a chant for the sailors of all nations.' The visionary indefiniteness of the closing measures carry out this mood, like a dream of the future, foreseeing, as Whitman does, 'the lands to be welded together.'"[87] In this quotation, Finkelstein echoes Vaughan Williams's own political convictions as found in the 1942 essay "Nationalism and Internationalism": "I believe, then, that political internationalism is not only compatible with cultural patriotism, but that one is an essential concomitant of the other."[88]

The author gratefully acknowledges the assistance of the following: Rosalba Varallo Recchia and the staff of the Seely G. Mudd Manuscript Library, Princeton University; Chris Scobie, Lead Curator, Music Manuscripts, Fiona McHenry, and the Rare Books and Music Reference Team at the British Library; Rama C. Bauer; Deborah Heckert; Julian Onderdonck; Elliott Schwartz; and Marcus Desmond Harmon.

This essay is dedicated to the memory of my father.

1. Walt Whitman, "Song of the Exposition," Section 2, in Walt Whitman, *Leaves of Grass: The "Deathbed" Edition* (New York: Modern Library Edition, 1993), 246.

2. Ralph Vaughan Williams, "Who Wants the English Composer?," *Royal College of Music Magazine* 9/1 (1912): 11–15.

3. For an extended discussion of Vaughan Williams's use of texts drawn from Whitman, see Byron Adams, "'No Armpits, Please, We're British': Whitman and English Music 1884–1936," in *Walt Whitman and Modern Music: War, Desire, and the Trials of Nationhood*, ed. Lawrence Kramer (New York: Garland Publishing, 2000), 25 passim.

4. Ursula Vaughan Williams, *R.V.W.: A Biography of Ralph Vaughan Williams* (Oxford: Oxford University Press, 1984), 144–45.

5. Ibid., 32.

6. Both Vaughan Williams and the conductor Adrian Boult were members of the Federal Union, which was founded in 1938. Shortly after the composer's death in 1958, Boult wrote a letter to the *Times* (London), declaring, "I have seen no word about Dr Ralph Vaughan Williams's support of movements for peace through world government. I think it should be put on record that he was a vice-president of Federal Union, and when giving the prizes at Petersfield Musical Festival some time before 1939, he spoke of his hope for the United States of Europe." See Nigel Simeone, *Ralph Vaughan Williams and Adrian Boult* (Woodbridge, Suffolk: The Boydell Press, 2022), 4–5.

7. Richard Aldrich, "Norfolk Festival a Choral Triumph," *New York Times*, 9 June 1912; "Coleridge-Taylor, Composer, Dead," *New York Times*, 2 September 1912. The American violin virtuoso Maud Powell (1867–1920) played the premiere of Coleridge-Taylor's concerto at Norfolk.

8. Richard Aldrich, "Mr. Stoeckel and His Music Festival," *New York Times*, 15 November 1925. After inviting Coleridge-Taylor twice, the Norfolk Festival forever marred its historical reputation in 1921 by programming the concert overture *In Old Virginia* by the white supremacist Virginian composer John Powell (1882–1963). This score was often programmed to provide a *cordon sanitaire* of whiteness when orchestras programmed music by Black composers. *In Old Virginia* opened the concert of the Chicago Symphony Orchestra, 15 June 1933, on which Frederick Stock conducted the Symphony in E Minor of the African American composer, Florence Price (1887–1953). For more on Powell's racism, see Stephanie Delane Doktor, "How a White Supremacist Became Famous for His Black Music: John Powell and *Rhapsodie nègre* (1918)," *American Music* 38/4 (Winter 2020): 395–427.

9. Ralph Vaughan Williams, *Letters of Ralph Vaughan Williams 1895–1958*, ed. Hugh Cobbe (Oxford: Oxford University Press, 2010), 133.

10. Jerrold Northrop Moore, *Edward Elgar: A Creative Life* (Oxford: Clarendon Press, 1998), 290, 462. Horatio Parker's cantata *Hora Novissima*, Op. 30 (1892) had been successfully performed at the Worcester Three Choirs Festival in 1899; he was a friend of both Stanford and Elgar. Glenda Dawn Goss notes that Parker recommended Sibelius to the Stoeckels; see Glenda Dawn Goss, "Jean Sibelius and His American Connections," in *Jean Sibelius and His World*, ed. Daniel M. Grimley (Princeton: Princeton University Press, 2011), 162.

11. Jeremy Dibble, *Charles Villiers Stanford: Man and Musician* (Oxford: Oxford University Press, 2002), 422–24.

12. Parker's role in Stanford's aborted engagement is an important reminder, however, that the Norfolk Festival habitually programmed the music of American composers. Two of Parker's choral scores were premiered at Norfolk: *King Gorm the Grim* in 1908 and *The Dream of Mary* in 1918. See Aldrich, "Mr. Stoeckel and His Music Festival."

13. Ibid. Chadwick was a favored composer at Norfolk.

14. Quoted in Ursula Vaughan Williams, *R.V.W.*, 144.

15. Richard Aldrich, "The Philharmonic Society," *New York Times*, 25 November 1925.

16. Richard Aldrich, "Mr. Albert Coates Conducts," *New York Times*, 31 December 1920. At this time there were two symphony orchestras vying for the attention of New Yorkers: the staid New York Philharmonic (sometimes confusingly referred to as the Philharmonic-Society) and the much more adventurous New York Symphony. The two orchestras merged in 1928 under the direction of Arturo Toscanini.

17. Richard Aldrich, "The New York Symphony Orchestra," *New York Times*, 31 January 1921. Aldrich opines that Aeolian Hall was a better venue for *A London Symphony*, and all but declares that he preferred Damrosch's interpretation. In his earlier review of the symphony's first New York performance, Aldrich declared, "The symphony is, for one thing, too long" and recommended that the composer "would do well to lay the blue pencil upon it again." Whatever the reason, Vaughan Williams cut the score several times. For a chronology of Vaughan Williams's extensive revisions of *A London Symphony*, see Michael Kennedy, *A Catalogue of the Works of Ralph Vaughan Williams*, 2nd ed. (Oxford: Oxford University Press, 1996), 67–72.

18. Richard Aldrich, "Music," *New York Times*, 10 March 1922. Aldrich gave the *Tallis Fantasia* a mixed review, declaring, "The listening ear is satiated with the gravity and severe decorum of the music." Undaunted, Damrosch continued to conduct this work for several seasons.

19. "'Sea Symphony' Given for First Time Here," *New York Times*, 6 April 1922.

20. Quoted in Ursula Vaughan Williams, *R.V.W.*, 144.

21. Ibid.

22. Vaughan Williams, *Letters*, 133. Vaughan Williams enjoyed encountering the exotic fauna of New England: in one of the letters to her sister posted from America, Adeline Vaughan Williams reported, "Ralph has seen a woodchuck." See Ursula Vaughan Williams, *R.V.W.*, 144.

23. Vaughan Williams, *Letters*, 132–33.

24. Ibid., 206. Maud Karpeles (1885–1976) was an accomplished folk dancer and folksong collector.

25. Ursula Vaughan Williams, *R.V.W.*, 348.

26. Vaughan Williams, *Letters*, 205–6. Hugh Cobbe dates this letter "about 1 November 1932." Vaughan Williams was put up in the College Inn at Bryn Mawr.

27. Alain Frogley, "Constructing Englishness in music: national character and the reception of Ralph Vaughan Williams," in *Vaughan Williams Studies*, ed. Alain Frogley (Cambridge: Cambridge University Press, 1996), 18.

28. See Anthony Barone, "Modernist Rifts in a Pastoral Landscape: Observations on the Manuscripts of Vaughan Williams's Fourth Symphony," *The Musical Quarterly* 91/1–2 (Spring/Summer 2008): 66. In a letter to Gustav Holst that Cobbe dates "on or about 21 October," Vaughan Williams alluded to purchasing this music paper: "I am fairly happy here and everyone is v. hospitable – I went to a music store in Phila:[delphia] yesterday and was introduced to the Manager – it was just like a chapter out of [Dickens's novel] Martin Chuzzlewit." See Vaughan Williams, *Letters*, 204.

29. Vaughan Williams, *National Music and Other Essays*, ed. Michael Kennedy, 2nd ed., (Oxford: Oxford University Press, 1986), 71.

30. Ibid., 62.

31. "Dr. Vaughan Williams to Lecture on Music," *The College News*, 19 October 1932. The lectures took place on 19 and 27 October; 3, 9, 16, and 21 November. The lectures were offered free of charge and open to the public. Musical illustrations were provided by Horace Alwyne (1891–1974), Director of the Department of Music, as well as the Bryn Mawr College Choir conducted by F. H. Ernest Willoughby (1895–1984). Both Alwyne, who was a noted concert pianist, and Willoughby were British-born.

32. "Folk Songs Grow From Communal Authorship," *The College News*, 9 November 1932.

33. "Dr. Vaughan Williams Gives Second Lecture," *The College News*, 2 November 1932.

34. Like the Charles Eliot Norton Lectures, the Flexner lectures are published by Harvard University Press. Bryn Mawr agreed to make an exception for Vaughan Williams so that *National Music* was published under the imprimatur of Oxford University Press.

35. Vaughan Williams, *National Music*, 47.

36. Ibid., 70-71. Clearly believing that "a foolish consistency is the hobgoblin of little minds," Vaughan Williams himself uses elements of jazz in the harrowing scherzo of his Sixth Symphony (1944–47, rev. 1950), a movement inspired by the bombing of the Café de Paris in London during the Blitz that resulted in the death of the popular saxophon-ist Ken "Snakehips" Johnson (1914–1941) and his jazz band. See Byron Adams, "The Stages of Revision of Vaughan Williams's Sixth Symphony," in *Vaughan Williams Essays*, ed. Byron Adams and Robin Wells (Aldershot: Ashgate Press, 2003), 12.

37. Bernard Flexner gave $10,000 in 1928, augmenting it annually until it reached $50,000.

38. "Bryn Mawr Gets $50,000," *New York Times*, 20 May 1928. By "art," Bernard Flexner seems to have meant "art history." The Mary Flexner Lectures are still being delivered at the time of this writing.

39. "Miss Mary Flexner, Sister of Educators," *New York Times*, 22 July 1947.

40. Ibid. See also Edith Pettit Borie, "Mary Flexner," *Bryn Mawr Alumnae Bulletin* 28/1 (November 1947): 15. In 1924, Flexner privately published two pamphlets consisting of her redactions from Breasted's scholarly writings, which were made with his permission. See Bernard Flexner Papers, 1917–1943, Seely G. Mudd Manuscript Library, Princeton University (henceforth Flexner Papers, 1917–1943).

41. In 1935, Erwin Panofsky (1892–1968), a refugee from Nazi Germany, joined the Institute for Advanced Study in Princeton, New Jersey, which had been founded by Abraham Flexner; this allowed Panofsky eventually to meet Abraham's younger siblings Mary and Bernard. There were no Flexner Lecturers appointed for the years 1934 and 1936.

42. Married to cartoonist Wyncie King (1884–1961), Hortense Flexner (1885–1973) published several books of poetry over the course of fifty years. In 1961, novelist Marguerite Yourcenar translated a selection of Flexner's poems into French.

43. *The College News* does not report Vaughan Williams saying anything remotely like "you can't say anything about music," nor is there such a statement in the first chapter of *National Music*. It is remotely possible that this was a throwaway line spontaneously interpolated by Vaughan Williams.

44. Hortense Flexner to Mary Flexner, postmarked 22 October Bryn Mawr PA, Flexner Papers, 1917–1943.

45. Hortense Flexner to Mary Flexner, postmarked 20 November 1932 Bryn Mawr PA, Flexner Papers, 1917–1943. Hortense Flexner's sarcasm was equally in evidence even when the Mary Flexner lecturer was someone of whom she approved, such as Panofsky—she praises him but has harsh words for Bryn Mawr president Park and others. See Hortense Flexner to Mary Flexner, postmarked 20 October 1937 Bryn Mawr PA, Flexner Papers, 1917–1943.

46. Hortense Flexner to Mary Flexner, postmarked 2 December 1932 Bryn Mawr PA, Flexner Papers, 1917–1943. Unfortunately, there are no letters from Mary Flexner preserved among her brother's papers, only letters to her from friends and family.

47. The only other Mary Flexner lecturer to take music as a topic was the Hungarian-American musicologist Paul Henry Lang (1901–1991) in 1959; Lang was not a composer, of course.

48. "Friends of Music Open Season Sunday," *New York Times*, 23 October 1931.

49. Downes succeeded Aldrich as chief critic of the *New York Times* in 1924. Harold Taubman joined the ranks of music critics at the *Times* in 1930; he was appointed chief critic upon Downes's death in 1955.

50. Downes, "Hans Lange Triumphs With Philharmonic," *New York Times*, 22 December 1933.

51. See Vaughan Williams, *Letters*, 265.

52. See, for example, Olin Downes, "Symphonic Prophet," *New York Times*, 8 December 1940.

53. Olin Downes, "Sibelius, the Solitary Dreamer of the North, Newly Revealed in a Koussevitzky Interpretation," *New York Times*, 9 April 1933. This ecstatic review of the Seventh Symphony is mild by Downes's standard of adulation; see Olin Downes, "Symphonic Prophet." In this essay, Downes uses the same vocabulary to describe Sibelius employed by British critics such as Cecil Gray, Constant Lambert, and Ernest Newman, chief critic of the *Sunday Times* (London); see Byron Adams, "'Thor's Hammer': Sibelius and British Music Critics 1905–1957," in *Jean Sibelius and His World*, 130–52. Not all music critics in New York were enamored of Sibelius or Vaughan Williams; see Allen W. Atlas, "Vaughan Williams in the New York Crossfire: Olin and Harold v. Virgil and Paul," *The Musical Times* 157/1936 (Autumn 2016): 75–88.

54. Vaughan Williams, *Letters*, 204.

55. See Thomas Neville Bonner, *Iconoclast: Abraham Flexner and a Life in Learning* (Baltimore: Johns Hopkins University Press, 2002). Bernard Flexner's father settled in Louisville, Kentucky. The Brandeis family, also Jewish immigrants, lived in that city at the same time. Woodrow Wilson nominated Brandeis to the Supreme Court in 1916; he was the first Jew to serve on the court.

56. "Bernard Flexner, Jewish Leader, 80," *New York Times*, 4 May 1945.

57. Edith Pettit Borie, "Mary Flexner," 15. See, for example, Mary Flexner, "A Plea for Vocational Training," in *The Survey: Social, Charitable, Civic: A Journal of Constructive Philanthropy* 22/19 (August 1909): 650–55.

58. Among the distinguished Jewish intellectuals that Bernard Flexner rescued was the art historian Ernst Kantorowitz (1895–1963); see Robert E. Lerner, *Ernst Kantorowitz: A Life* (Princeton: Princeton University Press, 2018), 216, 238, 341. For his part, Vaughan Williams petitioned for the release of composer Robert Müller-Hartmann (1884–1950), who had been interned with thousands of other Jewish refugees on the Isle of Man; see Vaughan Williams, *Letters*, 282 and Steven K. White, *Dear Müller-Hartmann: Letters from Ralph Vaughan Williams to Robert Müller-Hartmann* (privately published, 2009), 12–14. Vaughan Williams also assisted the architect and composer Richard Fuchs (1887–1947) and his family to leave Nazi Germany and immigrate to New Zealand; see Vaughan Williams, *Letters*, 272. It should be pointed out that both Flexner and Vaughan Williams did not restrict their aid to the prominent and accomplished; Vaughan Williams was chairman of a local organization in Dorking that assisted Jewish refugees settling in Britain. See Neil Wenborn, "'A desirable end': Vaughan Williams and the Refugee Relief Effort of the 1930s and 1940s," *Ralph Vaughan Williams Society Journal* 76 (October 2019): 9–11.

59. As Hugh Cobbe observes, "However, the genesis of the war had one telling effect on VW's political outlook: he became an ardent supporter of Federal Union, a movement which survives to the present day"; see Vaughan Williams, *Letters*, 282. Founded in

1938, this organization promotes a union of free peoples under a common government. Vaughan Williams's interest in a united Europe predated both the creation of the Federal Union and the outbreak of the Second World War. In the last of his Flexner Lectures, he declared, "When the United States of the World becomes, as I hope it will, an established fact, those will serve that universal State best who bring into the common fund something that they and they only can bring." Vaughan Williams, *National Music*, 71.

60. Harriet Cohen, *A Bundle of Time: The Memoirs of Harriet Cohen* (London: Faber and Faber, 1969), 286–88, 297.

61. Ibid., 292. While Cohen's memories cannot always be trusted, Ursula Vaughan Williams, the composer's second wife, once told me the same story in virtually the same words, but with this addition: "But at the end of the day, Ralph would shrug a bit and say, a little sadly, 'I guess that, like most English people, I am ultimately descended from John of Gaunt.'" Vaughan Williams's wry remark alludes to John of Gaunt, Duke of Lancaster (1340–1399), a son of King Edward III; Prince John was reputed to be a notorious seducer who engendered natural children over the length and breadth of England and Wales. Ursula Vaughan Williams, in conversation with the author, 24 June 1993.

62. Walt Whitman, "O You Whom I Often and Silently Come," *Leaves of Grass, The "Deathbed Edition,"* 169.

63. Vaughan Williams, *Letters*, 188.

64. Postmarked 15 November 1932; British Library MS. Mus. 1642, ff. 29–30. In both this letter and a later one postmarked 19 November, Vaughan Williams requests insistently that he meet Cohen alone: "P.P.S. Alone please! I don't want a party." See British Library MS. Mus. 1642, ff. 28, 31.

65. Ursula Vaughan Williams, *R.V.W.*, 357.

66. In the final week of his life, Vaughan Williams expressed his admiration of Barber's music to an American visitor, a young composer from the University of Michigan named Laurence Taylor. See "A Visit with Vaughan Williams," British Library MS. Mus. 1714/1/23, starting at f. 168.

67. Vaughan Williams, *Letters*, 421–22. Hugh Cobbe dates this letter to Hart as being posted in 1947, but it may have been sent earlier, as Barber's First Symphony and an overture by Roy Harris (1898–1979) were programmed on an Anglo-American Promenade Concert on 5 August 1941; Barber's Violin Concerto appeared on a Prom in 1944. These concerts were broadcast over the BBC. See Jenny Doctor, "The Parataxis of British Musical Modernism," *The Musical Quarterly* 91/1–2 (Spring–Summer 2008): 101–3. British-born composer Fritz Hart (1874–1949) had been a contemporary of Vaughan Williams at the Royal College of Music; after several decades in Australia, Hart was appointed the conductor of the Honolulu Symphony in 1931 and the first professor of music at the University of Hawaii.

68. Ursula Vaughan Williams, *R.V.W.*, 192.

69. C. W. D., "Symphony Hall, The Boston Symphony Orchestra," *Boston Globe*, 3 December 1932. This critic gives the *Tallis Fantasia* a glowing and detailed review, far more insightful than any that had yet appeared in the *New York Times*. The critic notes that Vaughan Williams was called to the stage by "hearty applause," and was obliged to bow twice more from his seat in the hall.

70. Ursula Vaughan Williams, *R.V.W.*, 192. The rest of that program included Mozart's "Gran Partita" for winds, K. 361, and Schubert's C-Major Symphony, the "Great." For the letter to Karpeles, see Vaughan Williams, *Letters*, 206.

71. *Fantasia on a Theme of Thomas Tallis* clearly found favor with Boston Symphony audiences, as Pierre Monteux conducted it eleven times with the orchestra from 1922 to 1923. In those days, a "novelty" was repeated only if the audience liked it or the conductor was determined to feature it.

72. Faulkner was on the faculty of Cornell University from 1950 to 1960, when he returned to Britain to become director of the Royal College of Music. By the time Faulkner left Cornell he had risen to the rank of full professor.

73. For a schedule of this tour, see Vaughan Williams, *Letters*, 547; for an eyewitness account, see Ursula Vaughan Williams, *R.V.W.*, 348–58. At the University of California, Santa Barbara, Vaughan Williams attended a student production of his opera *Riders to the Sea* (1932) conducted by Prof. Carl Zytowski (1921–2018).

74. For a transcription of Vaughan Williams's Henry Howland Memorial Prize Lecture held in the Yale University Archive of Recorded Sound, see Ralph Vaughan Williams, *Vaughan Williams on Music*, ed. David Manning (Oxford: Oxford University Press, 2008), 99–109. Vaughan Williams's propensity for verbal improvisation made his wife quite nervous, as she never knew what outrageous thing he might say. Ursula Vaughan Williams, in conversation with the author, 12 June 1986.

75. Ralph Vaughan Williams, *Vaughan Williams on Music*, 109; and Vaughan Williams, *National Music*, 242. Vaughan Williams was gratified to be awarded the Howland Prize, as Gustav Holst had received it in 1924 and Paul Hindemith in 1940. In the course of this lecture, he once again quotes his favorite passage from Whitman's "Song of the Exposition"; see Vaughan Williams, *Letters*, 548.

76. Vaughan Williams, *National Music*, 241.

77. Vaughan Williams, *Vaughan Williams on Music*, 109.

78. Olin Downes, "Vaughan Williams: Great English Composer Will Visit in the Fall," *New York Times*, 23 May 1954.

79. Olin Downes, "Vaughan Williams Hailed at Cornell," *New York Times*, 10 November 1954. That Downes made the long trip to Ithaca to review this concert testifies eloquently to his devotion to Vaughan Williams's music. As music director of the Buffalo Philharmonic from 1954 to 1963, Josef Krips (1902–1974) had previously performed Vaughan Williams's oratorio *Sancta Civitas* (1925, premiered 7 May 1926), translated into Latin by the composer, in Rome in 1949; see Ursula Vaughan Williams, *R.V.W.*, 292. In 1954, Krips repeated *Sancta Civitas* in Buffalo in 1954 with the composer present.

80. William W. Austin, in conversation with the author, 5 September 1985.

81. Donald Jay Grout, "Memorial Tribute," *The RCM Magazine* 40/1 (Easter Term 1959): 54.

82. Of this occasion, Ursula Vaughan Williams recalled, "William Schuman, then head of the Juilliard School, and his wife were guests . . . more musicians came to meet Ralph, among them his old pupil Peggy Glanville-Hicks." See Ursula Vaughan Williams, *R.V.W.*, 357.

83. Sidney Finkelstein, *Jazz: A People's Music* (New York: Citadel Press, 1948). Although subject to ridicule from certain scholars then and now, Finkelstein's use of a Marxist lens enabled him to see all too accurately the status of African Americans as an oppressed nation existing within the United States.

84. For the author's disenchantment with Socialist Realism, see Sidney Finkelstein, *Composer and Nation: The Folk Heritage in Music* (New York: International Publishers, 1960), 280–300. Alongside Finkelstein's quotations from *National Music* sit some drawn from the writings of Maxim Gorky and V. I. Lenin.

85. Ibid., 221.

86. Ibid., 229–30.

87. Finkelstein, *Composer and Nation*, 230, 232. Here Finkelstein, perhaps quoting from memory, compresses the following line from Whitman's poem "Song for All Seas, All Ships": "Thou sea that pickest and cullest the race in time, and unitest nations," which Vaughan Williams sets complete, but adds "the" before "nations."

88. Vaughan Williams, *National Music*, 155.

Vaughan Williams's Lecture on the
St. Matthew Passion (1938)

INTRODUCED AND ANNOTATED BY
ERIC SAYLOR

Vaughan Williams admired Johann Sebastian Bach above all other composers, and perhaps none of Bach's works meant more to him than the *St.
Matthew Passion*. Simona Pakenham said that he called it "the most wonderful story in the world," and he patterned his own nativity work *Hodie*
(1953–54) after the *Passion*'s alternating narrative and reflective passages.[1]
As a conductor, he treated the work not so much as an artistic presentation (much less as mere entertainment) but rather as a meditative exercise
worthy of deep consideration and reverence. Generations of Surrey musicians sweated, swore, and struggled along with Vaughan Williams as they
worked to unlock the magic and mystery of the piece under his guidance,
inspired by his devotion to the work, and its effective realization.

Vaughan Williams's fascination with the composition spanned decades.
William Harris, later the organist at Windsor Castle, remembered Vaughan
Williams and Gustav Holst "discussing Bach, Bach's choral writing and
instrumentation, and particularly some novel ideas of VW's regarding the
performance of the B Minor Mass and the St. Matthew Passion" during
the early 1900s when all three sang in the Bach Choir.[2] In March 1923,
about two years after Vaughan Williams accepted the directorship of that
ensemble, he led his first renditions of the *Passion* using Edward Elgar and
Ivor Atkins's English-language edition of the work. This obliged Vaughan
Williams to alter "a few notes of Bach's recitative, and in a few cases to sacrifice some of Bach's subtlety of phrasing," but he felt that "the only possible
language in which the Gospel history can be recited to an English audience
is that of the 'Authorized Version' of 1611; anything else would be an insult
both to Bach and to the Bible."[3] Other modifications were inspired partly
by his dissatisfaction with a performance he heard in Amsterdam the previous spring, but mostly by his own sense of the work's inherent drama.
For instance, he decided to employ a semi-chorus at more intimate points

in the story (such as those featuring the Apostles or Peter's questioners) in order to distinguish them both dramatically and musically from the larger *turba* passages. He also eliminated a few arias and *da capo* repetitions to improve the pacing or the aesthetic effect at the few points he felt did "not reach the high level of the rest" of the *Passion*.[4]

More controversial were some of his instrumental modifications, most notably replacing the original harpsichord continuo with a piano version of his own devising for the Dorking Halls during Leith Hill Festival performances (a modification he later applied in his edition of Bach's B Minor Mass). He also included clarinets and trombones in the ensemble, allowed violas occasionally to realize inner passages of the continuo, and sometimes doubled the sopranos with trumpets in order to strengthen the sound. Although such choices were controversial among purists, they were consistent with Vaughan Williams's belief that Bach would have willingly used better resources had they been available, so there was no reason why he should have to adhere to the same limitations as his predecessor.[5] Evidently none of these changes diminished the overall effect of the work, for Vally Lasker called the Bach Choir's rendition "the greatest spiritual & musical experience I have ever had in my life."[6]

Vaughan Williams's engagement with the *Passion* continued for the next thirty-five years, most significantly in conjunction with the choirs of the Leith Hill Musical Competition (later, the Leith Hill Musical Festival), though these performances took place in addition to the annual festival. That first production was mounted in 1931, thanks in part to the impetus of the composer's sister, Margaret "Meggie" Vaughan Williams, co-founder and Honorary Secretary of the LHMC from 1904 to 1914. In 1929, she proposed mounting a performance of the *Passion* to inaugurate the newly constructed Dorking Halls on Reigate Road (a statue of the composer now stands outside the Halls), a charge to which her brother, the LHMC Committee, and the participating choirs responded enthusiastically. Tragically, she died two months before the first performance on 24 March 1931, and so the concert was dedicated to her memory. It was a massive undertaking. Over eight hundred mostly amateur singers and instrumentalists underwent more than a year's worth of preparation, though professional vocalists and orchestral players were engaged for the solo arias and obbligato parts. Vaughan Williams also encouraged members of the audience to join the choirs in singing the chorales, a further demonstration of his belief in the communal dimension of music making, but insisted that those attending withhold their applause—and woe betide the unsuspecting patrons who failed to observe this convention (or even worse, arrived after the work had commenced). The close cooperation among amateurs and professionals impressed members of the national press in attendance, who responded with enthusiasm to the "powerful effect" the performance achieved.[7]

The critical acclaim the LHMC's *Passion* received led to subsequent annual performances in Dorking, though not initially under Vaughan Williams's direction. Between 1932 and 1937, William Cole led abridged performances—owing to the significant costs of mounting the work—at the local parish church of St. Martin's. Only in 1938 did Vaughan Williams retake the podium for a second rendition of the piece under the auspices of the LHMC. Although a smaller affair than the concert of 1931, involving slightly over half the number of participants as that earlier performance, Vaughan Williams personally trained both a dedicated semi-chorus and a ripieno choir composed of women and boys. Once again, the concert proved to be "a deeply moving occasion, the performance being lifted to great heights by the magnificence of the work itself, and through the inspiration of the conductor."[8] Vaughan Williams next led the LHMC in a rendition of the *Passion* in 1942, and then for every year thereafter until 1958, five months before his death. By good fortune, this performance—the composer's final appearance as a conductor—was recorded, preserving a unique historical document that was released on the Pearl label in 2000.[9]

Vaughan Williams spoke and wrote about Bach on numerous occasions, including the following lecture that he delivered before the *Passion* performance of March 1938. It touches on themes he addressed in other writings, including "Bach, the Great Bourgeois" and a program note on the *Passion* written for the Bach Choir in 1923, but is particularly notable for his focus on the work's historical and dramatic context, illustrating passages that he found particularly effective or moving, and revealing his conception of Bach as essentially a Romantic composer in spirit. The manuscript is largely written in the hand of his first wife, Adeline, with occasional emendations by Vaughan Williams himself, and it appears to have been dictated by him to her. In preparing this lecture for publication, I have added and modified punctuation for the sake of clarity (most typically, changing dashes to commas, semicolons, or periods), grouped standalone sentences into paragraphs, and moved passages to reflect changes that Vaughan Williams indicated in the manuscript. Endnotes are editorial. The score numbering has been updated to reflect the system employed in the *Neue Bach Ausgabe* rather than that of the Elgar/Atkins edition.

Bach *St. Matthew Passion*

It is true that the beauty of a work of art depends largely on its suitability to its purpose.[10] And it is equally true that that beauty remains when the original purpose is no longer there to be served. This is true of our castles, our cathedrals, our tithe barns and our windmills, and it is certainly true of Bach's musical setting of the Passion According to St. Matthew. That was originally a church service. It is now described in the *Times*, even when it is sung in church, as an entertainment. But its beauty remains and it has apparently still "entertainment value." But to appreciate it fully we must keep in mind that it was originally not a concert but an act of devotion.

If some of us find the narration of the story in recitativo secco (or "dry recitative" as it was called) a little *too* dry, if we find the reflective airs a little lengthy, or even if we were to find the unabridged version which lasted nearly three-and-a-half hours (not to speak of a sermon in the middle) too long for our modern restless spirits, we must remember that the recitation was not sung to amuse us, but to give us the whole history of the Passion, that the airs were there to stimulate our devotion, and that to sit in church for four hours was a spiritual exercise.

We must not imagine that Bach invented the Passion music form. When he arrived in Leipzig in 1723, he found the custom of reciting the Passion According to St. Matthew on Palm Sunday already established, and all he did was to substitute his own incomparable music for the probably rather tame efforts of his predecessors.

Bach wrote, in all, five Passions: that according to St. Luke, an early and immature work which some people indeed believe not to be his; one according to St. Mark and one to a poem by some local poetaster, both of which have disappeared; then the *St. John Passion*; and finally his crowning achievement, the *St. Matthew Passion*, first performed in the St. Thomas Church at Leipzig in 1729, and again in a revised form in 1740. For this setting, Bach used all the resources at his command: a double choir and a double orchestra corresponding to it, and in addition a third "Ripieno" choir, which sang the chorale in the opening chorus, and probably also joined in in all the chorales. There is also the organ, whose general purpose was to fill in when required, and the harpsichord, which accompanied the recitatives. It is usual in modern performances to substitute a pianoforte for the harpsichord. This I think is right; it avoids a feeling of sham antiquity. I cannot believe that Bach would not have preferred the tone of the modern pianoforte if it had been known in his day, just as he would have preferred the beautiful tone of the modern oboe to the coarse noise which I understand the instrument made in his day. To substitute the harpsichord for the pianoforte seems to me to be parallel to asking Mr. Goossens[11] to coarsen his tone or to ask our violinists to play with a flat bridge and a loose bow.

A great work of art seems to sum up all the tentative effort that has gone before it. This is certainly true of the St. Matthew Passion. We may describe it as the confluence of four distinct streams: (1) the liturgical chanting of the Passion of the Roman Church; (2) the Lutheran Service with its "Peoples hymns"; (3) the church cantata; (4) the popular mystery play.

It had been the custom from very early times in the Catholic Church (and still is the custom) to recite the gospel history of the Passion in church during Holy Week, chiefly in monotone or at most with certain plainsong inflections. This custom was taken over by the Lutheran Church with one or two additions. Firstly, the part for the turba, or crowd—namely the disciples, the multitude, et cetera—was sung chorally; then apparently the congregation demanded their part in the service, and at certain pauses in the narration they were allowed to sing some of their own popular hymns.

Then came the influence of the Italian cantata. The narration was no longer sung in monotone or plainsong, but was given dramatic significance by the inflexions of the voice, and in some of the emotional points a measured type of singing, or arioso as it was called, was added. Simultaneously with this, there was growing up a kind of sacred cantata in which the Bible's words were not used, but a versified setting of the story was set to music in a succession of recitatives and airs—again on the lines of the Italian cantata. One of the lost Passions of Bach was probably of this nature.

There is one more influence which, though not a musical one, must have strongly influenced Bach in his work: that is the popular Passion or Mystery Plays and Processions. There is fairly good evidence that Bach must have been familiar with these ceremonies where, after a church service, a procession to the Cross took place out of doors in which the various characters in the story, including a representative of Christ himself with his Cross, marched in traditional order chanting hymns. Surely a procession of this kind must have been in Bach's mind when he planned his great opening chorus in which two opposing choirs cry to each other ("See him—whom? The bridegroom"), and as the procession advances a third choir is heard singing the well-known hymn "O lamb of God most holy." Or to take another example, where two women softly lamenting the betrayal of Christ are interrupted by the fierce shouts "Leave him, loose him, bind him not."

Bach summed up all these influences in one great whole. The narration is given to a tenor voice while the part of Christ himself and the other characters are sung by a bass, and the utterances of the disciples and the multitude are given to the chorus. The main points in the narration are illustrated as they come in two ways: either by an air, usually for a solo voice, but occasionally with chorus reflecting on the situation (thus, after Christ has said, "Tarry ye here and watch with me" a tenor voice and chorus sing the well-known air "I would beside my Lord be watching"), or after the burial a bass voice sings the arioso "At evening hour of calm and peace."

I said before that in the early recitals of the Passion the people were allowed to join in with some of their well-known hymn tunes. Bach does not neglect this, and at certain points in the narrative introduces some of these then well-known tunes harmonized in four parts with all the wealth of his imagination. These, then, are the three main features of the Passion music: narration, reflective music, and popular hymn tune. Let us take the hymn tune or chorale first.

Bach evidently loved these tunes of his own Lutheran Church, and introduces them not only into his Passions but into almost all his choral and organ music. You are going to hear three examples of these this afternoon, and now is the opportunity to introduce to you those who are kindly going to allow you to hear what I can only speak about—indeed theirs is the most important part of this lecture. I need not introduce them by name—many of them are probably already well known to you.[12]

The first is No. 3, for those of you who have books, "O blessed Jesu." This is an adaptation of a melody by Crüger,[13] who flourished at the beginning of the seventeenth century, and is one of the best known of the writers of original tunes for the Lutheran Church. The second is a tune which I am glad to say is well known in England. It is closely connected with Passion services and is usually known as the Passion chorale. But few people know that it was originally a secular song either composed or arranged from a folksong by a German composer of the sixteenth century, Hassler.[14] Martin Luther—as you doubtless know—agreed with Wesley that he didn't see why the devil should have all the pretty tunes and adapted many of these secular tunes to the use of the Church, either writing new words or making what was known as a "spiritual parody" of the original text, rather as the Salvation Army does today. Later on this tune became associated with Gerhardt's poem "O Sacred head." Bach uses the tune five times in the course of the *St. Matthew Passion*. We are going to sing you two versions of it: one, No. 54, following from the words "and smote him on the head," and the other with subtly altered harmonies at the end of the crucifixion, No. 62.

Now I want to speak about one more chorale. When I was a boy we used to sing an extraordinarily bad hymn tune to the words "O Lord how happy should we be," which was said in the books to be by Bach. So I came to the conclusion that Bach must be a very bad composer. It was only years after that I discovered that the tune was not by Bach at all, but was a degradation of a very beautiful old German folksong, a farewell to Innsbruck.[15] It first appeared in print in a setting by a sixteenth-century German composer, Heinrich Isaak. [Play][16] This tune was also recruited into the service of the church, and is used here twice by Bach in his own incomparable way, as you will hear later.

Most of these hymn tune settings are harmonized simply in four parts, but in one or two cases Bach makes a more elaborate use of them. The outstanding example is No. 29, where Bach builds up an elaborate piece of music on the tune "O man thy grievous sin bemoan" as a climax to the first part of the Passion. He evidently thought well of this setting. It was originally composed as the opening chorus of the *St. John Passion*. It probably also was used in one of the lost settings, and found its final and most fitting place where it now stands.

We will now turn to the narrator's part. This is given to a tenor voice accompanied only by what is known as a figured bass: that is to say, bass notes with figures to indicate the appropriate harmonies. This was almost certainly played at performance by Bach himself, and it is the duty of the pianist or organist to realize as far as he can, humbly and reverently, the wonderful things which Bach probably did on the top of that bass. We can find out pretty clearly the sort of thing he did from the places where he wrote out the accompaniment in full. This opportunity is given us in this actual work where the words of Christ are accompanied in full harmony by a string orchestra, except in one instance—the words "Eli, Eli," where only the bass is given, and where I firmly believe only the bass with its sense of remote desolation is meant to be played.

The other characters in the story are given to appropriate voices. The words of the disciples, multitude, et cetera are sung by the chorus— sometimes a single shout as in "Barabbas," sometimes a tortuous fugal exposition as in "Let him be crucified." Once at the blasphemous climax of the mocking crowd, Bach sets the words "I am the Son of God" to all the voices in unison—a thing he very seldom did.

As I have told you, the Evangelist's words are given to the tenor solo, accompanied on the pianoforte. For the most part it follows the natural inflections of the voice, but occasionally a single word will set fire to Bach's imagination. The scene of Peter's denial gives us several examples of this, at its best in its famous melismatic passage at the words "wept bitterly," and at its worst in the naïve realism of the setting of "before the cock crow." In the same passage we find a more subtle example of Bach's art still. Peter sings "I know not the man" thus [No. 38c] then come the words "then immediately the cock crew" when Peter's musical phrase is repeated exactly, but in the highest part of the tenor voices' compass, as if in mocking derision. With regard to the cock crowing, which happens also in the *St. John Passion*, I should like to read you a passage from Spitta's life of Bach:

> We must admit that there is something rather startling in the mimicry of an animal's cry, and that the contrast it offers to the solemn gravity of the whole work threatens to fall into absurdity. But the direct connection with popular traditions of art gives the proceeding a deeper meaning, and even a certain justification, if we rightly comprehend the principles on which Bach bases his work. The crowing of the cock in the sacred plays formed a favourite crisis with the populace at any rate by reason of its simple naturalism, and it is no wonder that they objected to its omission even in the Passion music. . . . Bach's St. Matthew Passion as a whole is . . . in a remarkable degree a popular work; and this character does not rest solely on its connection with certain national aspects of thought, or in the faithful preservation of church traditions that had grown dear, but on the whole character of the music.[17]

I am now going to give you an example of an actual passage from the narration, Nos. 9a to 9e. The words are as follows: "Now the first day" to "Lord is it I." The tenor voice starts off, then the chorus sing quietly "Where wilt thou." The words "Lord is it I" are given to the chorus, who come in quietly one after the other with the question—whether by accident or design I do not know, Bach repeats the words "Lord is it I" eleven times.

So much for the narration. Now the people have their chance and they sing "Tis I, my sin doth bind thee" to the tune "Innsbruck." If any of you know the tune and would like to join in, please do so.

[Play.]

The other example I want you to hear is Nos. 36a to 37. The words are "And the high priest . . . smite thee." And as before, the people join in with their chorale "O Lord who dares to smite thee?" I will only call attention to Bach's use of a double chorus, suggesting so vividly the crowd pressing round Christ on all sides and saying "Prophecy unto us who smote thee."

We now come to the reflective songs. Some people think these very beautiful but rather long. Perhaps they are occasionally too long. As

Hubert Parry says, Bach seems to exhaust every possibility of his theme and then just writes da capo—"do it all again." In this he was a strong contrast to his great contemporary Handel, who was a practical realist and knew exactly when his audience was likely to have had enough. But Bach was not a man of the world: he was an idealist. Besides, he was not entertaining an audience: he was assisting the spiritual devotions of the congregation. We will give you two examples of these songs. No. 64, "At evening," comes immediately after the account of the burial, and is a characteristic example of the Romantic insistence of the poets of nature as actively sympathizing with human emotion. We do not find this aspect of nature in the great Classical period, but we do find it in Bach and again in the Romantic School of the nineteenth century.[18]

The *St. Matthew Passion* was not a success when first performed. It was probably very badly done, from what I know of the executive means at Bach's command. It continued to be sung for a few years after Bach's death, then it was apparently forgotten till it was revived by Mendelssohn in 1829. This period of neglect corresponds to the swing of the pendulum from Leipzig to Vienna and the growth of the great Classical school. Haydn, Mozart, and Beethoven knew little of Bach, though Mozart heard and admired one of Bach's motets when he went to Leipzig. But with the advent of the Romantic School and the swing of the pendulum back to Leipzig, Bach, the true precursor of the Romantics, came into his own again. Since this first performance under Mendelssohn, Bach's music generally and the *Passion* in particular has steadily grown in popularity.

The first performance in England took place under Sterndale Bennett—himself a pupil of Mendelssohn—in 1854, and we owe the steady growth of appreciation of this and the companion *St. John Passion* to two well-known church musicians. The modern organist does not always see eye to eye with the music of Stainer and Barnby,[19] but whether we think ill or well of their compositions, we must always be grateful to Stainer for having instituted the annual performance of the *St. Matthew Passion*, or rather a selection from it, at St. Paul's Cathedral more than fifty years ago, and to Barnby for doing the same service to the *St. John Passion* at St. Anne's Church Soho a few years later, both of which performances have gone on without lapse from that day to this.

You will remember that we performed the *St. Matthew Passion* here in 1932, and since then Mr. Cole has kept the torch burning by his annual performances in St. Martin's Parish Church. This year [1938] I believe he proposes not to do it, but I cannot believe that Dorking is too weak-spirited for two performances of this great work in one year. If you feel with me in this, please all write him postcards to tell him so.

May I remind you that the LHMF propose to perform the *Passion* on Tuesday March 22nd starting at 7:30 and finishing about 10:15. We shall make a few omissions: firstly in the narrative, because much as I hope this will approximate to a service it will actually be a performance, so I see no necessity to recite every word of the narrative. Secondly, some of the airs will be omitted. I think it very doubtful whether Bach meant them all to be sung at one performance, but I think rather that at successive performances he performed sometimes one and sometimes another. And thirdly, in those da capos to which I have already referred, I shall take the liberty of not repeating the whole da capo, but only the opening bars as indeed Bach does himself in No. 39 and No. 49.

Now I have told you all I know about the *St. Matthew Passion* and if you want any more you must sing it yourself.

1. Stephen Connock, ed., *Toward the Sun Rising: Ralph Vaughan Williams Remembered* (Tonbridge, Kent: Albion Music Ltd., 2018), 201, 236.

2. William Harris to Ursula Vaughan Williams, 29 July 1959, British Library, Gb-Lbl MS Mus 1714/1/2, f. 8.

3. See Vaughan Williams's program note for this concert, "Bach, St. Matthew Passion," in *Vaughan Williams on Music*, ed. David Manning (Oxford: Oxford University Press, 2008), 405–6.

4. Ibid., 406.

5. Vaughan Williams explained his thoughts on the subject at greater length in "Bach, the Great Bourgeois," in *National Music and Other Essays*, ed. Michael Kennedy, 2nd ed., (Oxford: Oxford University Press, 1987; Clarendon Press, 1996), 170–76.

6. Vally Lasker to Ralph Vaughan Williams, 8 March 1923, VWL1507.

7. "Leith Hill Festival: Bach's 'St. Matthew Passion,'" *Times* (London), 25 March 1931.

8. Margery Cullen, "The Passion According to St. Matthew," in *Leith Hill Musical Festival, 1905–1955*, ed. A. A. Gordon Clark (Epsom, Surrey: Pullingers Ltd., 1955), 72–73.

9. This recording of the 5 March 1958 Leith Hill Festival performance of the *St. Matthew Passion* conducted by Vaughan Williams (Pearl, GEMS 0079) features Eric Greene, tenor, as the Evangelist and bass-baritone Gordon Clinton singing the role of Christus; one of the original recording engineers was Christopher Finzi, eldest son of the composer Gerald Finzi.

10. The manuscript draft of this lecture is held at the British Library, GB-Lbl MS Mus 1714/1/32, ff.108–31.

11. Léon Goossens (1897–1988), distinguished British oboist.

12. The singers employed on this occasion are not known, but at a similar lecture given in 1931, both the Dorking Madrigal and Oriana Choirs provided musical illustrations; see Shirley Corke, *Music Won the Cause: 100 Years of the Leith Hill Musical Festival, 1905–2005* (Dorking, Surrey: Leith Hill Musical Festival, 2005), 54. The soloists in 1938 included Elsie Suddaby (soprano), Joyce Sutton (contralto), Jan van der Gucht (tenor), Arthur Cranmer (bass), Eric Greene (Evangelist), and Roy Henderson (Christus). It seems likely that some, if not all of them participated in this lecture, along with the select choirs previously noted.

13. Johannes Crüger (1598–1662), German composer and theorist. The tune to which Vaughan Williams refers is "Herzliebster Jesu, was hast du verbrochen," text by Johann Heerman.

14. Hans Leo Hassler (1564–1612). Hassler originally published the tune as "Mein G'müth ist mir verwirret" (1601). The upper part was subsequently troped to the text "Herzlich thut mich verlangen" in the *Harmoniae sacrae* of 1613, and then again to Paul Gerhardt's poem "O Haupt voll Blut und Wunden" by Crüger in his chorale collection *Praxis pietatis melica* (1647). This was the version Bach incorporated into both the *St. John* and *St. Matthew Passion*. See Walter Blankenburg and Vincent Panetta, "Hassler family, (2) Hans [Johann] Leo Hassler [Haslerus]," *Grove Music Online*, https://doi.org/10.1093/gmo /9781561592630.013.90000380199. Accessed 29 September 2022.

15. "Innsbruck, ich muss dich lassen," later troped as the hymn "O Welt, ich muss dich lassen." Isaak (or Isaac; various spellings of his name appear in the historical record) was a Flemish composer, born ca. 1450, and a contemporary of Josquin. He died on 26 March 1517.

16. At this point, Vaughan Williams presumably played "Innsbrück, ich muss dich lassen," but, alternatively, he may have had recourse to an assisting artist at the piano.

17. Philipp Spitta, *Johann Sebastian Bach: His Work and Influence on the Music of Germany,*

1685–1750, trans. Clara Bell and J. A. Fuller Maitland, vol. 2 (London: Novello & Co., 1899), 566–67.

18. No second example is present in the notes for the lecture, unless Vaughan Williams is also alluding to the bass aria that immediately follows: No. 65, "Make thee clean, my heart, from sin."

19. A close contemporary of John Stainer (1840–1901), Joseph Barnby was born in York on 12 August 1830 and died in London on 28 January 1896. He was precentor and director of music at Eton College, and later principal of the Guildhall School of Music.

Vaughan Williams's Common Ground

SARAH COLLINS AND DANIEL M. GRIMLEY

In an undated note of March 1943 to his future wife, Ursula Wood, Vaughan Williams wrote: "I am to see a private show of my Land for the People film at 5A Upper St Martin's Lane at 11.30 on Thursday—wd you like to come?"[1] The screening Vaughan Williams referred to was a short 10-minute documentary designed to convey the value of the preservation work undertaken by the National Trust. Properly titled *The People's Land*, the feature was distributed by Strand Films and "dicreted" (*sic*), according to the title card, by Ralph Keene. With a stirring voice-over by the familiar BBC announcer Freddie Grisewood (who had been commentator for the coronation of King George VI four years earlier), *The People's Land* was conceived and commissioned at the height of the Second World War, and its purpose was explicitly patriotic.[2] Vaughan Williams's score, as Jeffrey Richards has suggested, vividly amplified the film's projection of "an England of rural beauty, spiritual peace, open access, continuity, tradition, and folksong."[3]

Such patrician themes may seem little more than a casual rehearsal of the tropes that have so frequently shaped the popular reception of Vaughan Williams's music. Yet critical scrutiny of the key terms of reference that framed *The People's Land* can also serve a productive interpretive purpose. It can suggest that, although Vaughan Williams's work is regularly located as part of a longer history of landscape representation in British art and literature, it was also a means of expressive engagement with the politics of land management and land tax reform. As such, what has come to be understood as Vaughan Williams's pastoral tendencies, and particularly their commemorative affordances after the First World War, should be seen not merely as a reflection of a particular sensibility toward landscape, but rather as part of an ongoing attempt to sustain a progressivist view of history (and the reformist agenda it shaped) along the lines of the radical liberalism of Vaughan Williams's peers during his formative years. Vaughan Williams's work on patriotic projects such as *The People's Land* suggests a congruence between his position on preserving land for common use and his willingness to employ music in the actualization of a progressivist liberal vision.

Landscape representation, including pastoralism and anti-pastoral tendencies in British art and literature, served shifting cultural functions over time but have always signaled far more than rural nostalgia alone.[4] Vaughan Williams actively participated in the development of this discourse throughout his career with his use of pastoral themes and idioms, his folksong collecting, his advocacy for "national music," and his support of amateur music making. In the wake of the First World War, and in direct response to his frontline service in the ambulance corps, Vaughan Williams's engagement with landscape deepened and shifted register in works such as *A Pastoral Symphony* (Third Symphony, 1921), *The Shepherds of the Delectable Mountains* (1921), and *Flos campi* (1923).[5] In that sense, *The People's Land* reflects continued investment at a later moment of national crisis in ideas and materials that had already proven to be foundational for Vaughan Williams. But his film score also advances the no less urgent questions of on whose behalf *The People's Land* sought to speak, how, and to what end. Such questions reflect broader tensions that echoed throughout English public debate between the wars, and that formed part of a much longer-running argument which came to be known as the "Land Question."[6] Positioning Vaughan Williams's work within the wider aesthetic-political context of the Land Question can provide an alternative platform for thinking again about his creative relationship with notions of landscape, place, and the pastoral. This essay reassesses that relationship through a closer reading of his music for *The People's Land* and examines how it was shaped by Vaughan Williams's earlier immersion in the radical liberal circles at Trinity College, Cambridge, where he was a student. We then consider the collaboration with his neighbor and fellow member of the radical liberal generation, E. M. Forster, on two stage works, *The Abinger Pageant* (1934) and *England's Pleasant Land* (1938), written for local fund-raising events in the Surrey area, where they shared intertwined personal connections. The final part of the essay offers a brief commentary on one of his major interwar works, the oratorio *Sancta Civitas*, which draws out the tensions and ambiguities inherent within the Land Question in heightened and intensified form.

Tracking *The People's Land*: Usefulness, Value, and Place

The exact chronology of Vaughan Williams's engagement with *The People's Land* remains unclear, but the surviving evidence suggests that he must have been approached to write music for the film sometime in 1941, and that he worked on the soundtrack with characteristic speed and efficiency. An ink draft of the complete score in short 2-stave format includes detailed timings for individual sections alongside tempo markings and instrumental cues, implying that he was already composing with a scenario or storyboard in mind.[7] The fair copy in full score shows further signs of emendation, including erasures, crossings out, and rescored passages, indicating, as the composer's note to Ursula Wood suggested, that further work on the music was undertaken at the time of recording, relatively late in the production process.[8] The title page of the full score declares that the music was "founded on traditional melodies"; Jeffrey Richards has since identified some of the tunes employed, and a fuller scene-by-scene collation of musical cues and the film's spoken narrative and shooting locations signals the extent to which music, word, and image were carefully synchronized (see Table 1).[9]

The film's content is arranged in four broad sections or chapters, loosely assembled in the form of a scene-setting opening, with a fleeting reference to the industrial landscapes of the north, followed by a concise history of English settlement, invasion, and defense (at a time when the island nation felt under renewed threat of incursion); images of custodianship and good husbandry; footage of landscapes of leisure and recreation; and a stirring finale celebrating citizenship and common ownership. One of the passages excised at a late stage was a hymn-like five-measure prelude that survives at the head of the orchestral full score but was evidently omitted from the final cut (though it is included in Rumon Gamba's fine recording with the BBC Philharmonic).[10] Instead, the film commences with a sweepingly evocative panorama of the South Downs and the Sussex coast, from the Seven Sisters to Beachy Head (and not the White Cliffs of Dover, as Richards suggests, where filming during wartime would have been impractical), accompanied by a free variation on the Hampshire folk tune "The Banks of Sweet Primroses," played on the solo clarinet. After this affective introduction, the scene shifts inland to the Cuckmere Valley and the village of Alfriston, site of one of the National Trust's first properties (the Clergy House, purchased in 1896), as Vaughan Williams's score refers fleetingly to a phrase from the "Sussex Carol."[11] Later sequences are likewise focused on significant Trust holdings: Bodiam Castle, for example, appears alongside an arrangement of the "Agincourt Carol," a year before the tune's more bellicose use in William Walton's music for Laurence Olivier's acclaimed cinematic treatment of Shakespeare's *Henry V*; footage then dwells on West Wycombe village and the Ashridge estate in the Chilterns as well as on the sylvan surroundings of the Derbyshire Dales and the Lake District. A scherzo-like sequence throws together scraps of melodies including "Boys and Girls Come Out to Play," "Pop Goes the Weasel," and "John Barleycorn" to accompany a group of young cyclists, a scouting troop, and children tobogganing down a grassy slope:

Table 1. *The People's Land*: **Scenography**

Cue (Time)	Narration
Main titles (0.00–0.28)	
Introduction (0.28–0.59)	[No narration]
(1.00)	This is England; it's a small island but it has some of the loveliest country, some of the prettiest villages, and some of the largest, ugliest and most vigorous cities in the world.
Industrial interlude (1.15–1.21)	In many countries, the need to preserve natural beauty and noble surroundings has been recognized by the state.
(1.22–2.00)	In England, they've been saved by the people. In 1895, without assistance from the government, a number of private enthusiasts formed the National Trust, dedicated to this work. The fruits of their idealism are more than ever welcome today, when the cares of daily life lead more and more people to spend their leisure away from the cities in the peace of the countryside.
History sequence (2.00–2.35)	This great stone circle beneath mighty Helvellyn in the Lake District was set up in adoration of strange, forgotten gods. And magnificent Bodiam Castle was built in the fourteenth century by one of the Black Prince's knights as a comfortable residence which could yet house a community in time of siege.
(2.35–3.15)	Little Moreton Hall, a famous example of Cheshire black and white architecture, is still lived in by the family who built it in the days of Queen Elizabeth. Here in the mountains of Westmorland is a farm typical of the district. The Trust is an easy landlord to farmers and encourages good husbandry on its farmlands.
Custodianship (3.16–3.37)	West Wycombe in the Chilterns is one of several villages owned and protected in their entirety by the Trust.
(3.38–4.19)	Over a thousand places and over a hundred-and-fifty thousand acres of England are held in public trust for ever. There's every kind of country from high moorlands to rolling downs and every kind of homestead from splendid castles to humble cottages. Many estates were presented by their owners. Others were purchased by donations from many small contributors.
Recreation (4.20–5.23)	To the children, the open country holds a magic promise of adventure and in the fresh air and sunlight beyond the ancient lanes they can play in a world of their own.
(5.23–5.50)	Dovedale in the heart of England lies near mining towns and centers of the cotton and pottery industries whose people flock in their thousands every year to explore this lovely valley and its great pinnacles of limestone.
(5.51–6.15)	
(6.15–6.54)	Nine hundred years ago the Norman invaders found much of the East of England like this fenland at Wicken. Today, hardly changed, it is still bright with flowers, the haunt of birds, moths, and butterflies.
Summation (6.55–8.43)	Here is England's Lakeland, the countryside that Wordsworth loved. Small wonder that its islands and gleaming waters inspired some of the country's greatest national poetry. People come over these hills from far away, down the long slopes through Langdale, to the Pikes, past Friar's Crag, up birch-clad Borrowdale, up over the pass to Crummock Water.
Finale and End Credit (8.45–10.00)	The climbers, the children, and the fisherman, they come from the crowded cities to refresh their spirits. The land that welcomes them is administered by the Trust, but the people are its guardians, for the unspoiled beauty of this rich heritage of Britain, defended against every foe by the hearts and hands of their forebears, is still the responsibility of the people.

Musical reference	Geographical reference
"The Banks of Sweet Primroses" (clarinet solo)	[n/a]
"Sussex carol" fragment ("sea music"); "The Banks of Sweet Primroses" (reprise)	Seven Sisters, Sussex
"Sussex carol" fragment	Alfriston, Sussex, downland panorama
"Factory" music	2 panoramic shots of northern mill town (West Yorkshire)
Transition back to "The Banks of Sweet Primroses"; "Sine nomine" paraphrase	Dovedale, Bodiam Castle (Sussex), sign at Ashridge Estate (Hertfordshire); Viator's Bridge in Dovedale (Derbyshire); walkers approaching Bridgewater Monument, Ashridge
"Agincourt Carol"	Castlerigg circle, Keswick (Cumbria); Bodiam castle (Sussex)
"Love Will Find Out a Way"	Little Moreton Hall (Cheshire); Lake District hill farm in Westmorland
"Old Chairs To Mend"	Bus driving down main road in West Wycombe (Bucks); villagers in cottage gardens
"Sussex Carol" reprise	Haymaking above Dovedale (Derbyshire); heathland in New Forest; River Dove; view across Derwent Water to Borrowdale
"Halfe Hannikin"; "Pop Goes the Weasel"; "John Barleycorn"; "Boys and Girls"	Cyclists on country lane; ramblers in Lake District; crossing stepping stones at Dovedale; Scouts drawing stream water in Lake District; children tobogganing down grass slope
[Transition]	Panorama above Dovedale; flowing waters of River Dove
"The Rakish Highlandman"	Fly fisherman on River Dove
"The Springtime of the Year"	Entomologists at Wicken Fen (Cambridgeshire)
DOWN AMPNEY ("Come down, O love divine"); "Spurn Point"; LASST UNS ERFREUEN ("All creatures of our God and King")	Lakeland scenes: tracing Ullswater on map of Lake District; panorama across Tarn Hows toward Langdale; walkers descending in Langdale; Crummock Water; Lakeland beck; view of Grassmoor; Lakeland farm
DOWN AMPNEY peroration; LASST UNS ERFREUEN.	Lakeland farm; climbers above Langdale; panorama of Derwent Water; Ashridge estate; Seven Sisters (Sussex)

Example 1. Vaughan Williams, discarded draft for *The People's Land*.

a further passage, omitted at a late stage of the recording, dovetailed the popular jig "Halfe Hannikin" from John Playford's seventeenth-century collection *The Dancing Master* with an augmentation of "The Banks of Sweet Primroses" and a further counter-melody in the parallel minor (Example 1).[12] The final section of the film is devoted to a surging apotheosis, led by footage of climbers summiting a Lakeland crag, while the music assembles a strenuous concluding paragraph based on paraphrases of two melodies that Vaughan Williams harmonized for inclusion in *The English Hymnal* (1906): DOWN AMPNEY ("Come down, O love divine") and LASST UNS ERFREUEN ("All Creatures of Our God and King"). A radiant coda returns to the downs and the sea, as the narrator sonorously declaims that "the unspoilt beauty of this rich heritage of Britain, defended against every foe by the hearts and hands of their forebears, is still the responsibility of the people."

Vaughan Williams's commitment to such overtly national projects as *The People's Land* sits rather awkwardly in the context of recent critical attempts to stress his otherwise still underrepresented engagement with European modernism.[13] The same might be said of both his two interwar projects with Forster, *The Abinger Pageant* and *England's Pleasant Land*, as well as his wartime propaganda films in the 1940s.[14] (See Figure 1.) Such works seem supplementary to Vaughan Williams's wider artistic ambitions, serving merely to bolster his deeply felt sense of public duty, national pride, and a spiritual connection with landscape. But they were no less an expression of his desire to be "doing his bit," as he put it, both for the war effort and for preservation.[15] They were also an embodiment of his well-documented call for British composers to see themselves as servants of the people—to be useful to society, and to remain publicly minded rather than esoteric, elitist, or remote. Indeed, his musical involvement in historical pageants and propaganda films, together with his political thinking, point to a preoccupation with usefulness as a marker of value that might be viewed as a form of *Gebrauchsmusik*, music for practical everyday use, or "utility music." This was a category much derided during the interwar period by British musical modernists such as Constant Lambert, who lambasted the "mechanical" traits of Paul Hindemith's music from the 1920s and likened Hindemith's "metallic exactness" and "fatal efficiency" to Lytton Strachey's criticism of Thomas Babbington Macaulay's literary "hardness of outline and slightly hollow ring."[16] Lambert's analogy with Strachey's critique places the discussion squarely within the intellectual circles of Trinity College, Cambridge (discussed further in Julian Rushton's essay in this volume), where Strachey, Vaughan Williams, and his close friend George Macauley Trevelyan (T. B. Macaulay's great-nephew) had been students.[17] The college environment at Trinity was characterized by the close association between walking and mountaineering groups such as the Alpine Club and intellectual groups such as the Apostles, of which Strachey, Trevelyan, and Forster were members, whereas Vaughan Williams was an "embryo," the term used to describe undergraduate members of the university who were being considered for membership.[18] These groups combined intellectual high-mindedness and physical athleticism with a spiritual, aesthetic, and embodied relationship with a certain type of landscape—rugged and forbidding for Trevelyan, pleasant and undulating for Vaughan Williams—alongside an assurance in their future role in the nation's social and political advancement.

Although the notion of "utility" held quite different connotations in the British liberal tradition from that implied by the loose translation of the German term—"utility" for British writers was more about pleasure than usefulness[19]—the interwar discourse around *Gebrauchsmusik* illuminates Vaughan Williams's commitment to the concept in several ways. Four principles, approximately analogous to the fourfold organization of *The People's Land*, might be identified as underpinning this principle of musical utility:

1. a music of participation rather than consumption;
2. a music ready-to-hand like a vernacular language;

3. a music whose aesthetic component is inseparable from its social function;
4. a music thought to be of collective origin, even as it issues from the individual artist.[20]

Collectively, these themes illustrate the congruence between Vaughan Williams's wider musical aesthetics and his approach to writing for patriotic projects such as *The People's Land*. Calling for the preservation· of the English countryside for the purpose of productive human use, on the one hand, and putting music to use as the "maid-of-all-work" for the film narrative,[21] on the other, has the effect of valorizing usefulness as the prime marker of political and aesthetic value. It was a term that Vaughan Williams invoked explicitly in another wartime work, his eloquent *Household Music* (1940–41), based on Welsh hymn tunes and written for a pragmatically flexible ensemble of strings and wind instruments. Performing *Household Music* was the kind of domestic activity that might be undertaken by people "whiling away the waiting-hours of war," Vaughan Williams maintained in a radio broadcast, and offered a creative place "where sanity can again find a home."[22]

Trevelyan, likewise, wanted to write "useful" history, leading him to spend over twenty years of his professional life outside the academy. The moralistic and emotive language of Whig history, and its literary rather than "scientific" historical style, was predicated on the way in which a certain idea of the past can effect change in the present. For a Whig historian like Trevelyan, presenting a narrative of past progress was part of a cultural duty to help a progressivist political situation to come into being in the present. Whig histories were not simply progressivist tracts that bypassed objectivity in the service of a latent ideology of liberalism. They were a central part of liberalism's "need to impregnate politics with a morality derived not so much from dogma as from an atmosphere breathed by the past."[23] As later writers such as Raymond Williams observed, the mingling of pastoral conventions with communal production and consumption—namely the "organic community" attributed to pre-industrial English country life by early twentieth-century intellectuals, embodied in a collective spirit of labor and the breaking of bread together—occurred at precisely the time when these forms of social and economic life were first threatened by the rationalization of the agricultural economy—for example, through new forms of crop rotation, agricultural mechanization, and the wool trade. Referring to the transmutation of Arcadian elements into a particular image of society and the economy, Williams noted how "in a conventional association of Christian and classical myth, the provident land is seen as

Figure 1. Forster, Vaughan Williams, and the bandleader during preparations for *England's Pleasant Land*.

Eden. This country in which all things come naturally to man, for his *use and enjoyment* and without his effort, is that Paradise."[24]

The vision of the contemplative shepherd, timeless and non-aspiring, inheritor of the land, could thereby be transmuted into a manorial setting and contrasted with the active tiller of the land, just as the shepherd Abel was favored over the doomed farmer Cain in the Book of Genesis.[25] In this reading, the sanctity of land ownership emerged as a moral order to stabilize the new economic modes and their associated social shifts. It was an image that would find a powerful symbolic and expressive parallel in much of Vaughan Williams's music, but which would ultimately prove agonistic and far from stable.

The "liberal love of the countryside"

Vaughan Williams's interwar commitments can be understood generationally as a legacy of his political status as a radical liberal, whose sense of the world was forged in 1890s Cambridge among other members of the so-called intellectual aristocracy—that is, late-Victorian radical liberals who saw themselves charged with a public responsibility to continue a tradition of incremental democratic reform set in motion by their forebears. Vaughan Williams's struggles were shared by Trevelyan, who likewise turned to preservation activism after the First World War, but who became more closely aligned with Stanley Baldwin's Conservatives than with Labour, at least for a time. Forster later described himself (with his tongue partly in his cheek) as belonging to the "fag-end of Victorian liberalism," which practiced "benevolence and philanthropy, was humane and intellectually curious, upheld free speech, had little colour-prejudice, believed that individuals are and should be different, and entertained a sincere faith in the progress of society," but which did not acknowledge the basis of economic inequality that made these values possible: "In came the nice dividends, up rose the lofty thoughts."[26]

Despite Hubert Foss claiming that Vaughan Williams had "no aristocratic muse: the goddess breathes her inspired words through him without any Cambridge accent,"[27] the composer was deeply imbedded in the intellectual aristocracy in both familial and intellectual terms. The ways in which this shaped his thinking on subjects such as history and international politics have been the topic of much discussion.[28] What is less often remarked is the meanings that landscape and English rural life held for these figures. It was a combination of what David Cannadine has referred to as the "liberal love of the countryside," comprising an aesthetically oriented tradition of walking, cycling, and hiking as a form of spiritual communion—an idealization of pre-industrial times, and a political engagement with land use reform.[29] These investments in landscape drew from Romantic poets such as Wordsworth, socialist aesthetes such as William Morris, and novelists who critiqued industry and the conditions of the working poor such as Dickens, George Eliot, and Thomas Hardy; but it also drew from Victorian liberal thinkers such as John Stuart Mill, who thought deeply about the democratic implications of laws related to land ownership, and was overtly hostile toward the ruling classes.[30]

For Trevelyan, the landscape held a personal connection, especially his home at Wallington and its surrounding Northumbrian moors, as well as national and literary associations. Alistair MacLachlan notes how for Trevelyan this area was a "storied landscape," and that country houses "provided tangible moorings for elite Victorian families like the Trevelyans, enshrining family archives, memories and emotions . . . they were palimpsests of local and national history."[31] Long-haul walking and cycling through the countryside were prominent leisure activities of this social group. "Whether I am alone or with one fit companion, then most is the quiet soul awake," Trevelyan wrote in 1913, "for then the body, drugged with health, is felt only as a part of the physical nature that surrounds it and to which it is indeed akin, while the mind's sole function is to be conscious of calm delight."[32]

Leslie Stephen (Vaughan Williams's first wife Adeline's uncle by marriage) established the Alpine Club which undertook Sunday walks, and Trevelyan reignited these, following a tradition of poetic and intellectual walkers stretching back through Wordsworth, Carlyle, Coleridge, Keats, Arnold, and Meredith—another resident of the Surrey downs above Dorking, and the author of the ecstatic lyric "The Lark Ascending," which provided the inspiration for one of Vaughan Williams's best-loved pre-1914 works.[33]

For Vaughan Williams, the associations with his childhood home at Leith Hill Place and the surrounding region provided enduring points of meaning and connection, stretching back through his mother's childhood (included the oft-told story of her uncle Charles Darwin asking for measurements from their garden to ascertain earthworm activity), and stretching forward also, through Vaughan Williams's advocacy for the area's preservation. Following the death of his brother Hervey in 1944, the composer donated Leith Hill Place to the National Trust in lieu of death taxes: an arrangement promoted by the passing of the National Trust Act in 1937, which encouraged such benefactions under the terms of the Country Houses scheme. In a letter dated 1 August 1944 to his neighbor Elizabeth Trevelyan, wife of the poet Robert Calverly Trevelyan (G. M. Trevelyan's brother), who had been another member of the Cambridge Apostles, Vaughan Williams wrote: "I shall certainly stipulate—if and when the National Trust accept Leith Hill Place—that the public shall have rights of access to the woods & some of the fields. Anyhow you & Bob and your friends must feel yourselves free to walk in the woods as you have always done," citing the "great tradition" of community relations established by his grandfather, mother, and recently deceased brother.[34] Vaughan Williams maintained a keen interest in the property and its surroundings for the remainder of his life, writing to Ralph Wedgwood on 24 March 1950 to express concern about tree-felling and clearance on the estate and noting that, in the terms of his gift agreement with the Trust, "there is a stipulation that no trees should be cut except to improve the amenities and in the interests of good forestry."[35]

In other words, for these radical liberals—professionals, not the ruling class—born in the 1870s, the land was "storied" not only with national and historical and spiritual connections of the kind lauded in *The People's Land*, but also as a matter of personal connection, and ultimately, personal responsibility. They were well aware of the arguments for increasing housing availability and affordability, and of the need to create satellite towns to accommodate a growing urban population, especially in the crowded southeast of the country. They were also aware that their preservationist commitments were not shared by either the political elite or the population at large, and that initiatives like the National Trust and arguments for countryside preservation were considered anachronistic and elitist by the majority when not explicitly for the purpose of facilitating countryside tourism and recreation.[36] Yet they felt a divided loyalty toward their progressive values, on the one hand, and their desire to preserve the idiosyncratic individualism that they associated with rural life, on the other. These same tensions were also sensed by Forster, who explored them creatively throughout much of his writing career. One of the recurrent themes in his epochal 1910 novel *Howard's End*, for example, is the image of tides and waves of red housing and gray tracts of countryside, soon to be given over to new building. At the muted climax of the final chapter, Helen Schlegel and her sister Margaret look out over the meadowland at the rear of the house toward a "red rust" of encroaching development. "You see that in Surrey and even Hampshire now," Helen maintains; "I can see it from the Purbeck downs. And London is only part of something else, I'm afraid. Life's going to be melted down, all over the world."[37]

A Passage to the Country:
The Abinger Pageant and *England's Pleasant Land*

Forster had moved back to the Surrey countryside with his mother in 1924, where they rented a house at West Hackhurst, five miles west of Dorking, on the estate owned by the Farrers of Abinger Hall. Forster's mother, Laura, was a friend of Katherine Euphemia ("Effie") Wedgwood, the second wife of the first Lord Farrer (who had died in 1899) and first cousin of Margaret Wedgwood, Vaughan Williams's mother. Evangeline Farrer, the second wife of the second Baron, would later become one of the principal patrons of the Leith Hill Musical Festival, and Lord Farrer himself was a member of the National Trust's Board of Trustees. Forster purchased a four-acre parcel of woodland called Piney Copse, which he bequeathed to the National Trust in 1935, partly as a way of trying to ensure his long-term tenure on the lease at West Hackhurst (a strategy that ultimately proved unsuccessful). Aside from the growing tensions between tenant and landlord, Forster was also moved by the pressure on rural space created by the demands of London's ever-increasing urban population. As Forster reflected in 1946:

> "Well," says the voice of planning and progress, "why this sentimentality? People must have houses." They must, and I think of working-class friends in north London who have to bring up four children in two rooms, and many are even worse off than that. But I cannot equate the problem. It is a collision of loyalties. I cannot free myself from the conviction

that something irreplaceable has been destroyed, and that a little piece of England has died as surely as if a bomb had hit it. I wonder what compensation there is in the world of the spirit for the destruction of the life here, the life of tradition.[38]

Though Forster sensed that the doctrine of laissez-faire promulgated by his peers at the turn of the twentieth century was no longer an economic model capable of sustaining the material demands of the subsequent decades, he sought to preserve a laissez-faire of the "spirit." For Forster, suburban sprawl created a spiritual loss that could not be compensated in monetary terms, a suspicion bolstered by the fact that government planning and intervention in private lives had not been adequately rolled back after the First World War.[39]

Both apparent failures of compensation echo what Forster, Vaughan Williams, Trevelyan, and others took to be the origin of the problems with modern Britain's approach to land: namely, the system of parliamentary enclosure and the loss of the open-field system, in which the seasonal rhythms and routines of the fabled yeoman farmer, with his idiosyncratic and forgetful ways, gave way to those of the tenant farmer who was beholden to a landlord.[40] In other words, they mourned not only the death of a particular rural lifestyle and landscape, but also of a particular type of person—one they imagined to be individual and self-reliant. The notion that countryside and the rural lifestyle it represented had embodied the free individualism that was thought to be the bedrock of the English temperament (with this conflation of nature and nation being threatened by the planned and standardized lives of the masses) is symbolized by the image of the tree in Forster's *Abinger Pageant*. The Prologue begins with a Woodman narrator offering a paean to the trees of the area:

> Before there were men in Abinger, there were trees. Thousands of years before the Britons came, the ash grew at High Ashes and the holly at Holmwood and the oak at Blindoak Gate; there were yew and juniper and box on the downs before ever the Pilgrims came along the Pilgrim's Way. . . . Do not expect [stories of] great deeds and grand people here . . . they will pass like the leaves in autumn but the trees remain.[41]

Forster's emphasis on the diversity of trees is significant, given that both he and Vaughan Williams were concerned not only with the enclosure of the countryside, but about the effect of the rhetoric of productivity on interwar forestry policy (as Vaughan Williams's letter to Ralph Wedgwood would later suggest). Wartime restrictions on imports had made the extent of Britain's reliance on externally sourced timber—approximately 90 percent of demand was met by imports before the war—into a national security concern.[42] After 1918, a state-sponsored system of reafforestation was established in order to create a local source of timber, overseen by the newly established Forestry Commission, which was given powers to manage royal forests and local council woods, in addition to incentivising private landowners to plant their land. This led to a reduction in "semi-natural broadleaved woodlands; some [of which] had existed for hundreds of years," now replaced by homogenous plantations of Douglas fir and Sitka spruce: "even-aged, non-native and fast-growing conifer species, planted in geometrical blocks on open ground."[43] Trevelyan was vocal in the agitation against this homogenization, and a similar concern can be seen in the way Forster equates the loss of tree diversity in old England with the loss of individualism in the modern English temperament. In an entry in his commonplace book dated 8 March 1928, he wrote, following a stroll around the grounds at West Hackhurst, of the countryside as both a site of ecological particularity and of lost knowledge, portending his own subsequent departure from the estate:

> I take a longer walk to Honeysuckle Bottom. The path is blocked by trees that had fallen in the snow. Wild, wild, wilder than the genuine forests that survive in the south of Sweden. I excite myself by learning the names of the woods on the Ordnance Map, by hearing a wryneck and by seeing a swallow and a bat— all three phenomena early. Think I will learn the names of all the fields in the parish, although the lease of the house expires in a few years' time. Wish I had talked to old men.[44]

Ten years later, in *The Abinger Pageant*, it becomes clear that the tree symbolizes not only nature but also nation: "King John is evil; he will fall like a rotten branch, but the tree of the Kingdom of England remains."[45] Here, trees represent the eternal essence of both nature and nation—an idea that has a temporal component that is latent in Whig history as well: "You can make a town, you can make a desert, you can even make a garden; but you can never, never make the country, because it was made by Time."[46]

Vaughan Williams employs these same temporal implications of the arboreal metaphor to argue for the importance of tradition in musical development: "Let the tree develop flowers and leaves undreamt of before, but if you pull it up by its roots it will die."[47] This aesthetic position reflects a liberal commitment to incremental change—reform rather than revolution—in broader political discussions. For liberals of Vaughan Williams

Figure 2. Woodman narrator: "Before there were men in Abinger, there were trees." Scene from *Abinger Pageant*, 1934.

and Trevelyan's generation, the countryside exhibited what they held to be natural processes of development, namely incremental change underpinned by eternal laws. This view conditioned their understanding of the process of historical development, political development, and the realm of aesthetics, namely gradual change with reference to supposedly eternal values of "beauty."[48] But as the interwar period progressed, the faith in such eternal values came to seem increasingly contingent, hard-won, and difficult to sustain.

The tensions inherent in these interwar iterations of the Land Question left an indelible mark on Vaughan Williams and Forster's pageant *England's Pleasant Land*. In the opening scene of the pageant's first act, "Squire George's Difficulty—A.D. 1760," titled "The Enclosures," the characters Jeremiah and Mr. Bumble describe to the city ladies what an enclosure is, namely, taking away the fields from the villagers and the common land, enclosing it with palings and hedges for private use— "of course in a strictly legal way."[49] Jeremiah, the capitalist, adjures the Squire George to agitate for a parliamentary bill to allow him to enclose, in order to "Put an end to profligacy and idleness, and promote the development of agriculture."[50] After the Squire refuses, on the basis of tradition, Jeremiah outmaneuvers him to make it a matter of national duty and efficiency in production:

> Jeremiah: Have it as you will! But I thought you had your country's interests more to heart.
>
> Squire George: My country's interests? Of course I have them to heart! What do you mean, sir?
>
> Jeremiah: You seem to forget that England is at war with France. She needs more food, more corn—and you and your foolish peasants do not supply enough, because of your wrong method of agriculture. . . . Your villages are lazy, half their time they dance and sing. And you—well, I do not wish to give offence, but you spend not *half* your time but nearly all of it in hunting, fishing and the bottle . . . my life is as useful as yours, I warrant, although I do work for money! Wake up, neighbour! You are half asleep. And waken up your worthless village! Take the land, enclose it, and work it properly, to grow corn and make England strong. It is your *duty* to enclose.[51]

After the villagers' revolt, the Squire's son tries to broker a deal to enable them to work together toward a shared future, but his efforts are thwarted by death taxes which force him to sell his father's estate on the free market.[52] This is initially cast as a good thing for the villagers, as they can recover their land, but it is quickly shown to be a mere replacement of the aristocracy for the capitalist landowner, embodied in the character of "Jerry" (presumably a pun on the pejorative phrase "Jerry builder"), who buys up the land, prosecutes the villagers for trespassing, and begins to imagine a future of the land filled with motor cars and bungalows, paper and empty tins and "masses of adverts." Jerry chants mechanically about the merits of law, money, and the land market:

> Ripe for development. Ripe for development,
> Ripe, ripe, ripe for development,
> Ripe, ripe for development
> Is England's Pleasant Land.

And Mr. Bumble echoes his robotic style:

> Strictly legal, strictly legal
> To break up the big estates.
> Ripe, ripe for development,
> And very good for the rates![53]

Figure 3. The ghost of the old Squire's ancestors pass by as he dies in *England's Pleasant Land*.

The pageant concludes with a "Pageant of Horrors" showing England's possible future, and the sage words of the Recorder, who calls for the audience to help "save the country . . . through good laws rightly applied, though Parliament."[54]

Alongside the realities of shifting agricultural fortunes and practices, and the expansion of middle-class rural life, there was undoubtedly a popular sense, during the interwar period, that rural England was in decline—namely that traditional crafts, rural community, and smallholder farming, were on the edge of extinction. Literary works such as A. G. Street's *Farmer's Glory* (1932), Flora Thompson's *Lark Rise* (1939), and George Sturt's *The Wheelwright's Shop* (1923) were typical, the last of which was taken up by F. R. Leavis and D. Thompson in *Culture and Environments: The Training of Critical Awareness* (1933), as were topographic studies such as H. J. Massingham's *The English Downland* (1936) with its valorization of organic community and village life. It was the same narrative of imminent social and artistic loss that had motivated and underpinned much of the preservationist work of the first folksong revival, under the aegis of Cecil Sharp, Lucy Broadwood, Vaughan Williams, and others who sought to gather and collate what was understood as an essentially rural vernacular musical tradition as a form of national cultural capital. Yet the specter of the "death of rural England" was only partially true. As Alun Howkins has pointed out, there were drastic declines in agricultural workers after the war, while at the same time there was an increase of middle-class white-collar workers moving to semi-rural areas and commuting into the cities, especially in the southern areas of England such as Sussex, Surrey and Middlesex.[55] The narrative of decline, in other words, was more properly one of rapidly shifting social-geographic mobilities. With the electrification of the railway network in the home counties and the provision of fast and frequent service into the capital, the red tide of housing, which Helen and Margaret Schlegel had spoken of in *Howard's End*, seemed to be advancing with increasing speed.

The Country and the City: *Sancta Civitas*

Vaughan Williams was clearly interested in the everyday practicalities of the question of how to manage the competing demands of a rapidly growing urban population and the desire to preserve open space and the character of rural districts. In August 1940, he received an official notice from the Dorking Urban District Council thanking him for "lending land for allotments."[56] And in a 1940s letter to Edward Newill, Anglican Archdeacon of Dorking, Vaughan Williams wrote:

> I understand that you are interested in preserving the belt of trees at the corner of Sandy Lane and Westcott Road which are threatened by the Soundes Place building operations. I saw Mr. Smith the other day who now owns the property and he suggested that those who are interested should buy a strip of land which would at all events preserve enough trees to screen the buildings. This seems the only way of preserving them— I believe that Mr. Smith might consider an offer of £200 for a strip of land 35ft wide extending from the new fence in Sandy Land as far as his proposed new entrance to Westcott Road. This would be about 1/3 acre and would include about 3 rows of trees and it would of course be possible to plant more.
>
> I suppose that if we consider this project we ought to add another £150 and others have offered to help with unspecified amounts. If you are interested would you care to join in the scheme?[57]

It is entirely characteristic that at a time of such extreme national pressure, Vaughan Williams's attentions should have been focused on essentially parochial matters of this kind. But such pragmatic local action was not in fact so distant from his more "serious" art works of the mid-1920s, when he was reengaging with notions of landscape and the pastoral with renewed intensity and depth. One of the recurrent themes in those earlier works— which would remain a central thread in his later scores—was the image of the Celestial City: the heavenly space or realm to which the mortal soul journeyed on their departure from earthly life. In a sustained series of compositions, especially those inspired by Bunyan, the pathway to the Celestial City became a pilgrimage or sacred journey that traversed landscapes of hazard and temptation as well as carefully tended pastures marked by patterns of cultivation, good husbandry, and care. Elsewhere, images of desolation and loss give way to the radiant light, sometimes only distantly perceived, of the divine. Symbolically, works such as one-act opera *The Shepherds of the Delectable Mountains* and oratorio *Sancta Civitas* have been read in the light of Vaughan Williams's wartime experience, and in the wider context of postwar English pastoralism.[58] *Sancta Civitas* was commissioned by Hugh Allen and premiered at a Bach Choir concert to mark the 300th anniversary of the Heather Chair of Music at Oxford on 7 May 1926, and was preceded by a staging of *Shepherds*. Though the performance took place during the vicissitudes of the General Strike, called by the Trades Union Congress to protest against working conditions at collieries across the United Kingdom, *Sancta Civitas*'s apocalyptic text, drawn from the Book of Revelation (especially its vivid account of the fall of Babylon), must inevitably have led thoughts back to the cataclysm of the previous decade. But a revealing comment by Ursula Vaughan Williams, drawing upon the Greek quotation printed at the head of the score, suggests another way of approaching the music:

> The images of the river and the tree come from many mythologies: the holy city is not only the new Jerusalem "whose gardens and whose gallant walks continually are green," which Ralph always saw as the landscape of Van Eyck's *Adoration of the Lamb*, but also the dream in which Plato believed man must trust to give sense and reason, proportion and truth to daily life.[59]

The painting to which Ursula Vaughan Williams referred, which forms the central panel of the Ghent altarpiece, depicts an idealized landscape of towers and spires set amid a sunlit scene of rolling hills, trees, and lush meadows. Van Eyck's vision offers the utopian glimpse of a heavenly paradise on earth, the imaginary product of an idealized mode of guardianship in which countryside, city, and community are brought harmoniously together. But the composer's allusion to Platonic principles of sense, reason, rationality, and truth point to a more particular mid-twentieth-century preoccupation: the challenge of effective land management and urban planning. With its soft verdure, carefully spaced buildings and tree-lined prospects, Van Eyck's landscape might be reinterpreted as a template for the garden city, the theory and practice of ecologically sustainable urban development first advanced by Ebenezer Howard at the close of the nineteenth century and later adopted widely by architects and planners across Britain and continental Europe in the interwar period.[60] Raymond Unwin's designs for the first modern English garden city at Letchworth were laid out in precisely that same portion of the Hertfordshire countryside that formed the setting for Forster's *Howard's End*, and the legacy of the garden city movement led to the introduction of formal green belt planning legislation in 1938 and the passing of the postwar New Towns Act in 1947. Modernist architectural designs within an urban setting could now be conceived, theoretically at least, with greater heed and sensitivity to the particularities of a specific landscape and place. The garden city seemingly promised a new way of modern living in England's "green and pleasant land," an optimal configuration of utility and aesthetic beauty, and a means of mediating the long-standing tensions of class, property, and access that lay at the heart of the Land Question.

Locating Vaughan Williams's evocation of the Celestial City alongside the leftist, Fabian-inspired foundations of the garden city movement provides a new way of hearing the hymnic strains that accompany the start of the third section of *Sancta Civitas*: "And I saw a new heav'n and a new earth." The passage opens in a radiant E major—one of the oratorio's key points of tonal reference, but fully actualized here for the first time—and with a familiar pastoral signifier: a slow, rising, rhapsodic violin solo, which gradually unfolds in a seemingly organic "tree-like" fashion until it becomes a more sustained choral paragraph. It also provides a means of contextualizing the oratorio's concern with notions of community: the conjunction of the sacred and the civic captured in the work's title, which becomes less prominent when rendered in its English translation, "The Holy City." Charles Edward McGuire suggests that, whereas Edward Elgar's music had often been motivated by its concern with a series of "flawed but extremely human individuals, from Gerontius to Falstaff," Vaughan Williams's individuals were "symbols of the community within a frame of nationalism," an observation that emphasizes the extent to which the liberal reference to "nationalism" should be understood in the context of an international league of nation-communities rather than in its narrower, more insular and exclusionary sense. "Vaughan Williams's approach in *Sancta Civitas* is much more cooperative," McGuire suggests, "avoiding character as it does for a smaller amalgamation of sacred texts presented by the community for the community."[61] It is this same sense of the cooperative that shapes *Sancta Civitas*'s relationship with landscape, and which supports a more genuinely democratic vision of shared ownership and common ground as opposed to the older, more feudal or paternalistic model of the open field system—a space of liberty and social freedom in which no temples to elite privilege remain. But at the same time, *Sancta*

Civitas highlights Vaughan Williams's keen awareness of the contingency and impermanence of that vision. Despite McGuire's suggestion that "there can be no doubt of the final outcome," and that the music offers little more than a "limited presentation of tribulation," Vaughan Williams's evocation of the Celestial City appears far from permanent or assured, either in *Sancta Civitas* or indeed elsewhere.[62] Rather, the oratorio feels marked by a much deeper, more agonistic sense of its own ambivalence. The text of the work's final section, drawing on the Sanctus from the *Book of Common Prayer*, may indeed have been associated with "tradition, stability, and the church community," as McGuire suggests. But the music's attempts to consolidate and reaffirm the celebratory E major with which the third section begins are frustrated and ultimately undermined by the persistence of the work's underlying tonal argument: the dissonant interaction of two related third cycles, both centered on E and based on alternating major and minor third intervals (Figure 4).

This tonal schema is in fact a form of pitch-class set (01478), in Allen Forte's nomenclature "5-22," one of the primary motivic devices in much of Vaughan Williams's later work and the musical figure that both concludes the desolate final bars of the Sixth Symphony and initiates the opening of its successor, the *Sinfonia Antartica*.[63] In *Sancta Civitas*, it renders the chorus's repeated appeals to the divine as increasingly strained and urgent, with attempts to stabilize E major at the 1925 edition's rehearsal number 58 consistently thwarted by modal instability through the presence of C naturals (suggesting E *minor*) in the bass (Example 2). The oratorio hence concludes not with the glowing outcome seemingly promised by the E-major music of the third section, but with the more umbrous shades of its opening. The prospect of a "new heav'n and a new earth" is ultimately offered as merely a distant light on the horizon, a sense of what *might* come to pass, rather than as a preordained or certain future.

For a radical liberal of Vaughan Williams's generation, greater value lay in the solidarity and solace of companionship and community than in the hoped-for goal of individual salvation. Little wonder, then, that the landscapes to which Vaughan Williams's later works increasingly turned were the ice-scoured existential wastes of the Antarctic plateau or the bleak unenclosed heights of Salisbury Plain, as much as the more homely and domesticated environs of *The Abinger Pageant* and *The People's Land*.[64] Forster evidently shared a similar sense of belatedness, of things slipping past and falling apart, though with a lingering beauty still discernible in the wild woodlands clinging to the scarp slope of the Downs and in those parts of the countryside not yet fully rationalized: edgelands, scrub, and flood-plain. In a letter to the music historian Edward J. Dent, sent from his post in Alexandria during the First World War, Forster wrote that "the ground has broken off sheer, yet it's as if

Example 2. Vaughan Williams, *Sancta Civitas*, J. Curwen and Sons 1925 edition, rehearsal nos. 56–58.

Example 2, continued.

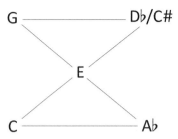

Figure 4. Vaughan Williams, *Sancta Civitas*, tonal schematic.

the beautiful flowers and creepers that grow there wave for a little over the precipice and hide the first few feet of the descent."[65] Forster conceded in an entry titled "Fallen Elms" in his commonplace book, written sometime during the 1930s, that "age and death are more distinct than they used to be, owing to the war." Contemplating the mutability of land, liberty, and human mortality as he walked the field paths around West Hackhurst, the fallen trees remained part of the Land Question's complex and unresolved dialectic.

Conclusion

Though the Land Question seemingly receded from public view after 1918, it remained a preoccupation for the generation of radical liberals of the 1890s, for whom landscape held a range of emotional, affective, and social meanings. The liberals' preservationist activities were explicitly aimed at safeguarding a national heritage of diverse forms and media (whether through folk traditions, land management, or social custom), and were shaped by a common set of emotional investments and liberal values of character, high-mindedness, public duty, and sincerity. Postwar pastoralism was not only concerned with linking land to mourning and commemoration, or to a form of romantic nationalism, or to imperial contraction and cultural recuperation of the center, as suggested by the extant literature, but was part of longer-standing debates over land use riven by political reformists, whose progressive politics were increasingly confronted by unintended consequences and effects—namely suburbanization and the specter of property "cursed by a public footpath," as Forster wrote.[66] Many of Vaughan Williams's views—on folk music and amateur music making, the development of language, and the public role of the artist—were shaped by similar ideas about usefulness.

But what of the usefulness (or otherwise) of music in this landscape? In his essay "Why Do We Make Music?" Vaughan Williams wrote explicitly that "one thing we can be certain of: we do not compose, sing, or play music for any useful purpose."[67] Yet he also saw his composition for films as a practice of business-like self-discipline and, ultimately, of humility to the collective ends of the production.[68] And in his writings on the role of the British composer he clearly saw a purpose or function to music—namely, to be the expression of the people, and to support that expression in some way, voicing the spirit of the nation. A similar tension is evident in Forster's thinking. In an address at the American Academy of the National Institute of Arts and Letters in New York in 1949, Forster declared his unfashionable belief in "art for art's sake," though he went on to distance himself from the "peacock-feather aspect" of this maligned phrase, and defined this belief in terms of a formal property of art that gives it an internal order, allowing it to persist as societies rise and fall, much like the attribute he ascribed to trees in *The Abinger Pageant*.[69]

Landscape hence served as the locus for a series of unresolved debates about class, property, social mobility, and aesthetics in the first half of the twentieth century. For the radical liberals of Vaughan Williams's generation, the patrician concern with the Land Question was motivated by a deeply felt sense of public duty and sincerity, albeit from a position of social privilege and economic advantage. They sought to preserve the countryside, principally for communal use, but their attitude to landscape as both personal and national history was intimately bound up with leisure activities that were characteristic of the "intellectual aristocracy"—namely cycling and walking as opposed to the blood sports of the older aristocracy and *nouveau riche* alike. But this is not, of course, the sum total nor the final value of their involvement with landscape. Despite the radiant image of the Celestial City glimpsed all too fleetingly in the pages of *Sancta Civitas*, Vaughan Williams's own powerfully intense interaction with landscape was agnostic and spiritually nondenominational, distancing him from the evangelical tendencies of his Cambridge peers, and of late nineteenth-century Gladstonian liberalism more generally. Yet his ongoing commitment to notions of community and participation, to preservation and to producing useful music, was predicated on the same moral vision of a shared social and economic life that came under increasing strain in the early decades of the twentieth century. For Vaughan Williams, this vision remained a vital creative resource and a continued point of connection with both his aging liberal contemporaries and his wider artistic environment, even as its boundaries felt stretched to breaking point. As his music for *The People's Land* attested, no less than his symphonies and choral works, landscape was where Vaughan Williams perennially sought his common ground.

Sarah Collins's research was supported by a visiting fellowship at the Humanities Research Centre, Australian National University.

1. Although the letter is undated, the first public screening of *The People's Land* took place on 17 March 1943, so it is likely that the note was written slightly earlier that month. *The Letters of Ralph Vaughan Williams*, VWL1839.

2. Frederick Grisewood was not the original narrator of the film, but he was commissioned to re-record the narration after the British Council became dissatisfied with the original, unknown narrator. The film is available at https://film.britishcouncil.org/resources/film-archive/the-peoples-land.

3. Jeffrey Richards, "Vaughan Williams and British Wartime Cinema," in *Vaughan Williams Studies*, ed. Alain Frogley (Cambridge: Cambridge University Press, 1996), 139–65, esp. 156–58.

4. Elizabeth K. Helsinger, *Rural Scenes and National Representation: Britain, 1815–1850* (Princeton: Princeton University Press, 1997), addresses specifically how the presentation of loss of values and lifestyles associated with a life on the land and pastoralism's latent nostalgia allowed it to become a shared symbol of a new collectivity (that is, the nation) in the nineteenth century.

5. Daniel M. Grimley, "Landscape and Distance: Vaughan Williams, Modernism and the Symphonic Pastoral," in *British Music and Modernism, 1895–1960*, ed. Matthew Riley (London: Routledge, 2010),147–74. See also J. P. E. Harper-Scott, "Vaughan Williams's Antic Symphony," *British Music and Modernism*, 175–95.

6. For an excellent historical overview, see *The Land Question in Britain, 1750–1950*, ed. Matthew Cragoe and Paul Readman (Basingstoke, Hampshire: Palgrave Macmillan, 2010); and on its ramifications for understanding twentieth-century English culture, see David Matless, *Landscape and Englishness*, 2nd ed. (London: Reaktion, 2016 [1998]).

7. The short-stave ink draft is contained in two volumes now held in the British Library, shelfmark GB-Lbl add MS 50427A and B, consisting of a pair of A4 music booklets, MC. 142, no. 21 (the inside front leaf contains a printed advertisement for Susan Forde's "Modern Pianoforte Album for Beginners"). The first volume also contains a 17-measure pencil sketch for music for the film *The Flemish Farm* (f. 2v), alongside an ink draft for three verses of *The First Nowell* (f. 8v, sketched again on f. 9v).

8. GB-Lbl add MS 50428. The source is written on 28-stave ms, ii + 20ff (numbered pp. 1–35), and is mostly in Vaughan Williams's hand in black ink, with pencil and crayon annotations—it was clearly used as a fair working score for recording and copying.

9. Richards, "Vaughan Williams and British Wartime Cinema," 157–58.

10. *The Film Music of Vaughan Williams*, vol. 1, CD Chandos CHAN 1007 (2001).

11. The "Sussex Carol" was included as "Second Tune," no. 24, in *The Oxford Book of Carols*, ed. Percy Dearmer, R. Vaughan Williams, and Martin Shaw (Oxford: Oxford University Press, 1964 [1928]), in Vaughan Williams's arrangement. As Vaughan Williams noted, the tune had been first printed in the *Journal of the Folk Song Society* 2/7 (1905): 126, credited to James Culwick in Dublin.

12. The passage appears in the second short-stave draft, GB-Lbl add ms. 50427B, f.3r.

13. See, for example, *The Musical Quarterly*'s special issue on "British Modernism," ed. Byron Adams, 91/1–2 (2008).

14. Vaughan Williams was also involved in three other pageants over the course of his career: *English Church Pageant* (1909), *Pageant of London* (1911), and *Music for the People* (1939), the latter written for the Republican effort in Spain in support of the Popular Front. For a fuller account of Vaughan Williams's involvement with historical pageantry

see Paul Readman and Alexander Hutton, "Pageantry," in *Vaughan Williams in Context*, ed. Ceri Owen and Julian Onderdonk (Cambridge: Cambridge University Press, forthcoming 2023). Vaughan Williams's engagement with pageantry is also discussed in Eric Saylor, *English Pastoral Music: From Arcadia to Utopia, 1900–1955* (Champaign: University of Illinois Press, 2017), and his chapter "Music for Stage and Film" in *The Cambridge Companion to Vaughan Williams*, ed. Alain Frogley and Aiden J. Thomson (Cambridge: Cambridge University Press, 2013), 157–78; in Deborah Heckert, *Composing History: National Identities and the English Masque Revival, 1860–1920* (Woodbridge: Boydell Press, 2018); and by Roger Savage, *Masques, Mayings and Music-Dramas: Vaughan Williams and the Early Twentieth-Century Stage* (Woodbridge: Boydell Press, 2014). Vaughan Williams did compose some new music for these pageants, but his contribution was mostly in the form of harmonizing folk tunes and hymns that are incorporated into the drama, such as when the villagers sing the Surrey folksong "The Sweet Nightingale"—"which has been sung in these parts for generations"—in Episode 5 of *Abinger Pageant*. The interwar fad for pageants is often associated with conservative political agendas, but in fact they ran across the whole political spectrum. See *Restaging the Past: Historical Pageants, Culture and Society in Modern Britain*, ed. Angela Bartie et al. (London: University College London Press, 2020). For more on the renewed literary preoccupation with pageants in the 1930s, including the extraordinary treatment of the pageant in Virginia Woolf's final novel *Between the Acts* (published posthumously in 1941), see Jed Esty, *A Shrinking Island: Modernism and National Culture in England* (Princeton: Princeton University Press, 2003), 76–85.

15. Muir Mathieson described Vaughan Williams's view of his film work during the 1940s in just this way. See John Huntley, *British Film Music* (London: Skelton Robinson, 1948), 57; and Jaclyn Howerton, "'Doing His Bit': Ralph Vaughan Williams's Music for British Wartime Propaganda Films" (PhD diss., University of California, Riverside, 2019), 73. See also Annika Forkert's discussion in this volume.

16. Constant Lambert, *Music Ho!: A Study of Music in Decline* (Harmondsworth, Middlesex: Penguin, 1948 [1934]), 179.

17. Wade Davis, *Into the Silence: The Great War, Mallory, and the Conquest of Everest* (New York and Toronto: Alfred A. Knopf, 2011), 4–5. Davis gives a nuanced account of how these elements of prewar Cambridge and Oxford played out for this generation after World War I, linking their sense of elite public duty before the war, their personal suffering and loss during the war years, the promise of the Everest expeditions in the 1920s as a feat of human survival, and the importance of an affective and spiritual connection with landscape throughout.

18. W. C. Lubenow, *The Cambridge Apostles 1820–1914: Liberalism, Imagination and Friendship in British Intellectual and Professional Life* (Cambridge: Cambridge University Press, 1998), 31.

19. Sarah Collins, "Utility and the Pleasures of Musical Formalism: Edmund Gurney, Liberal Individualism and Musical Beauty as 'Ultimate Value,'" *Music & Letters* 100/2 (2019): 335–54. In other ways, Vaughan Williams's approach comes close to that of the French notion of *utilité publique*. For a comprehensive discussion of the French context, see Jann Pasler, *Composing the Citizen: Music as Public Utility in Third Republic France* (Berkeley: University of California Press, 2009).

20. See Stephen Hinton, *The Idea of Gebrauchsmusik: A Study of Musical Aesthetics in the Weimar Republic (1919–1933), with Particular Reference to the Works of Paul Hindemith* (New York: Garland, 1989). For an alternative view that highlights the specifically auditory aspect of this notion—namely, viewing certain music as not merely functional but as enabling a phenomenological practice of "hearing without hearing," see Benjamin Steege, *An Unnatural Attitude: Phenomenology in Weimar Musical Thought* (Chicago: University of Chicago Press, 2021), 133–34.

21. Ralph Vaughan Williams, "Film Music," *RCM Magazine* 41/1 (February 1944): 5–9, reprinted as "Composing for the Films," in *National Music and Other Essays*, ed. Michael Kennedy (London: Oxford University Press, 1963), 160–65, 164.

22. Vaughan Williams, "The Composer in Wartime," *The Listener* 23/592 (1940): 989, reprinted in *Vaughan Williams on Music*, ed. David Manning (Oxford and New York: Oxford University Press, 2008), 83–86, at 84.

23. Victor Feske, *From Belloc to Churchill: Private Scholars, Public Culture, and the Crisis of British Liberalism, 1900–1939* (Chapel Hill and London: University of North Carolina Press, 1996), 3.

24. Raymond Williams, *The Country and the City* (Oxford and New York: Oxford University Press, 1973), 31. Emphasis added. In another film for which Vaughan Williams wrote the music, *49th Parallel* (1941), this anachronistic association of rural life with Christian values of collective production and consumption seems to block the progress of the stranded Nazi officers as they make their way across Canada toward the border of the United States, trying to avoid detection. They come across a commune of the descendants of Hutterite German migrants to Canada, who present just the form of "loving relations between men expressed as a community of consumption" that Williams refers to, clearly offering an alternative vision of German community against the Nazi ideology of domination. The episode links the communal with the rural, and the religious symbolism is further concretized when one of the officers slips out during the night to bake bread with the other commune members—an act that is punished by his superior. There are various visions of pastoral idealization in the film that adhere to others identified by Williams, including an episode when the final remaining Nazi officer stumbles across a gentleman in a canoe in a secluded part of the landscape, served by first nation communities and unaware of and unconcerned about the war, seemingly at peace with his surroundings and an embedded part of the natural order. This mirrors the way in which the plenty delivered by nature and community came to be the plenty delivered by the Lord of the Manor, in the moralization of the pastoral.

25. On the significance of the Cain and Abel story for early modern English writers such as Francis Bacon, Philip Sidney and John Milton, at the start of the Land Question, see Peter Lindenbaum, *Changing Landscapes: Anti-Pastoral Sentiment in the English Renaissance* (Athens and London: University of Georgia Press, 1986), 53–90. This binary has also, incidentally, been applied to Trevelyan (the active) versus George Moore (the contemplative). See Virginia Woolf's "George or George or Both?," quoted in Feske, *From Belloc to Churchill*, 143.

26. E. M. Forster, "The Challenge of Our Time," reprinted in *Two Cheers for Democracy* (London: Edward Arnold, 1972 [1951]), 54–55. This was a talk broadcast on the BBC Home Service on 7 April 1936. *The Challenge of Our Time* was the name of the series; this was the fourth installment, with Forster being invited to give "The Point of View of the Creative Artist" on this theme. See B. J. Kirkpatrick, "E. M. Forster's Broadcast Talks," *Twentieth-Century Literature* 31/2–3 (1985): 329–41, 339.

27. Hubert Foss, *Ralph Vaughan Williams: A Study* (London: George G. Harrap, 1950), 47.

28. For a discussion of where Vaughan Williams is positioned within this group see Julian Onderdonk, "The Composer, and Society: Family, Politics, Nation," in *The Cambridge Companion to Vaughan Williams*, 9–28; and Sarah Collins, "Vaughan Williams and the 'Intellectual Aristocracy,'" in *Vaughan Williams in Context*. For non-musical treatments of Vaughan Williams's involvement in the group, see David Cannadine, *G. M. Trevelyan: A Life in History* (London: HarperCollins, 1992); and Paul Levy, *Moore: G. E. Moore and the Cambridge Apostles* (London: Weidenfeld and Nicolson, 1979).

29. Leonard Woolf famously called Trevelyan a "muscular agnostic" due to his obsession with long walks and his involvement with establishing the athletic "Man Hunt" and

similar initiatives that involved vigorous physical exercise in the countryside. See *G. M. Trevelyan: A Life in History*, 145–46.

30. See David Martin, *John Stuart Mill and the Land Question* (Hull: University of Hull Publications, 1981).

31. Alastair MacLachlan, "Becoming National? G. M. Trevelyan: The Dilemmas of a Liberal (Inter)Nationalist, 1900–1945," *Humanities Research* 19/1 (2013): 23–43.

32. G. M. Trevelyan, "Walking," in *Clio: A Muse* (1913, reprinted 1931), quoted in Matless, *Landscape and Englishness*, 128.

33. Trevelyan later wrote a book titled simply *Walking* (Hartford, CT: Edwin Valentine Mitchell, 1928); see also Leslie Stephen's essay "In Praise of Walking" (1902) and Arthur Sidgwick's *Walking Essays* (1912).

34. Vaughan Williams to Elizabeth Trevelyan, 1 August 1944, VWL1924. The Trust formally accepted the offer of the house in a letter dated 15 November 1944, with an accompanying endowment of £4,000. The property was subsequently let to Vaughan Williams's cousin, Ralph Wedgwood, so that the family connection was maintained.

35. Vaughan Williams to Ralph Wedgwood, 24 May 1950, VWL1997.

36. Peter Mandler, "Against 'Englishness': English Culture and the Limits to Rural Nostalgia, 1850–1940," *Transactions of the Royal Historical Society* 7 (1997): 155–75, at 173.

37. E. M. Forster, *Howard's End* (London: Penguin, 2012 [1910]), 358.

38. Forster, "The Challenge of Our Time," 57. Only a few years later Foss picked up on this trope, writing that "we may talk of 'planning,' but we are in fact men of action first and consideration after. Of intellectual and artistic planning we are particularly suspicious, as the way we treat our artists shows. 'Art for art's sake,' said Vaughan Williams in *National Music*, 'has never flourished among the English-speaking nations.'" See Foss, *Vaughan Williams: A Study*, 57.

39. This sentiment was expressed in Forster's view, for example, that George Orwell's novel *1984* (1949), was not being taken seriously enough in postwar Britain. See E. M. Forster, "George Orwell" (1950), reprinted in *Two Cheers for Democracy*, 59–61. In this essay he drew upon an argument that had roots in post–First World War criticism of the interventionist policies of New Liberalism, which saw social reform measures as a slippery slope to totalitarianism. For more on this discourse, see "Modernism, Democracy, and the Politics of Lateness," in Sarah Collins, *Lateness and Modernism: Untimely Ideas About Music, Literature, and Politics in Interwar Britain* (Cambridge: Cambridge University Press, 2019), 85–122.

40. Foss described Vaughan Williams as dressing "like a forgetful farmer" (*Vaughan Williams: A Study*, 52), and indeed the character of Squire George in Forster and Vaughan Williams's *England's Pleasant Land* is another iteration of this symbolic image.

41. E. M. Forster, "The Abinger Pageant," reprinted in *Abinger Harvest and England's Pleasant Land*, ed. Elizabeth Heine (London: Andre Deutsch, 1996), 333–49, at 337.

42. Susanne Raum, "Land-Use Legacies of Twentieth-Century Forestry in the UK: A Perspective," *Landscape Ecology* 35 (2020): 2713–22.

43. Ibid., 2716. See also Charles Watkins, "The First World War and British Forestry," in *Trees, Woods and Forests: A Social and Cultural History* (London: Reaktion, 2014), 219–23. It is poignant to note how the native broadleaf species named by Forster have more recently been subject to attack by invasive species such as ash dieback and acute oak decline, most likely under the influence of Anthropocene climate change.

44. E. M. Forster, *Commonplace Book*, ed. Philip Gardner (Stanford: Stanford University Press, 1985), 67–68.

45. Forster, "Abinger Pageant," Episode 1: From Briton to Norman, 339.

46. Ibid., Epilogue, 349.

47. Ralph Vaughan Williams, "Tradition," in *National Music and Other Essays*, 59–60, at 59.

48. See Matthew Riley, "Liberal Critics and Modern Music in the Post-Victorian Age" in *British Music and Modernism, 1895–1960* (London: Routledge, 2010), 13–30. This

collection of associations once again plays into Foss's depiction of Vaughan Williams. Describing the English temperament he saw Vaughan Williams as embodying, Foss wrote: "The Englishman is suspicious of sudden changes. He likes that which grows naturally aided by skilful gardening and apt grafting: his roots are in the past, and he reveres the past with all his loyalty, longing for it to blossom naturally into the present, as he wants his own landscape to be natural in growth. . . . Vaughan Williams's music can be called arboreal, essentially tree-like. Each work is a tree, a separate growth, different according to the circumstances of the soil . . . allowed to grow to its own shape and size by the natural process of development, only influenced by the skilful forester's hand. His is no formal garden, but an open landscape." See Foss, *Vaughan Williams: A Study*, 53–54.

49. Forster, "England's Pleasant Land": Act 1, "The Enclosures," scene 1, "Squire George's Difficulty—A.D. 1760," 365.

50. Ibid., 366.

51. Forster, "England's Pleasant Land", 368–69. Emphasis in original.

52. The lawyer Bumble notes that these death duties are to the "advantage of the Lower Orders: They're going to break up the big estates, and then you villagers and small folk'll come into their own again. . . . Can't you see—you're going to get back the little bits of land what this family stole from you nigh a hundred years ago." Act 2, scene 2, "The End of the Old Order," 395.

53. Ibid., 399.

54. Forster, "England's Pleasant Land," Epilogue, 400.

55. Alun Howkins, "The Discovery of Rural England," in *Englishness: Politics and Culture 1880–1920*, ed. Robert Colls and Philip Dodd (London: Croom Helm, 1986).

56. Vaughan Williams to Ursula Wood, ca. August 1940, VWL1494. The provision for allotments (community gardens) was enshrined in United Kingdom legislation by the Small Holdings and Allotments Act of 1908, and later by the Allotments Act of 1922 (modified again in 1950). The importance of such plots for small-scale domestic cultivation became especially pronounced both in the wake of the First and Second World Wars, when food supply chains were severely disrupted, and given the increasing pressure on land for urban development and the concomitant loss of public access to open space.

57. Vaughan Williams to Edward Newill, 16 November [1940s], VWL4572.

58. Byron Adams, "Scripture, Church and culture: biblical texts in the works of Ralph Vaughan Williams," in *Vaughan Williams Studies*, 99–117, esp. 112–13.

59. Ursula Vaughan Williams, *R.V.W.: A Biography of Ralph Vaughan Williams* (Oxford: Oxford University Press, 1984), 163. In this passage, Ursula Vaughan Williams cites *Adoration of the Lamb*, the central panel of the Ghent Altarpiece, which was started in the 1420s by Hubert van Eyck and was completed by his brother Jan in 1432.

60. For a formative account of the origins and political context of the movement, see Standish Meacham, *Regaining Paradise: Englishness and the Early Garden City Movement* (New Haven: Yale University Press, 1999). Its legacy is discussed in Dennis Hardy, *From Garden Cities to New Towns* (London: Routledge, 2011 [1991]), and Rosemary Wakeham, *Practicing Utopia: The Intellectual History of the New Town Movement* (Chicago: University of Chicago Press, 2016).

61. Charles Edward McGuire, "From *The Apostles* to *Sancta Civitas*: The Oratorios of Elgar and Vaughan Williams," in *A Special Flame: The Music of Elgar and Vaughan Williams*, ed. John Norris and Andrew Neill (Rickmansworth: Elgar Editions, 2004), 99–115, at 99 and 114.

62. Ibid., 115.

63. This pitch-class set later motivates the harmonic argument of much of the nativity cantata *Hodie* and the Ninth Symphony. See Alain Frogley, *Vaughan Williams's Ninth Symphony* (Oxford: Oxford University Press, 2001), 291–92.

64. On the symbolism and meaning for Vaughan Williams of the references to Salisbury Plain and Thomas Hardy's novel *Tess of the d'Urbervilles*, see Frogley, *Vaughan Williams's Ninth Symphony*, esp. 263–74. On the Seventh Symphony, see Daniel M. Grimley, "Music, Ice, and the 'Geometry of Fear': The Landscapes of Vaughan Williams's *Sinfonia Antartica*," *The Musical Quarterly* 91/1–2 (Spring 2008): 116–50, at 129.

65. E. M. Forster to Edward J. Dent, 10 June 1916, Cambridge University Library, shelfmark GB-Cu, add. MS 7973/F/12.

66. E. M. Forster, "My Wood," reprinted in *The Abinger Harvest*, 23–26, at 23.

67. Vaughan Williams, *National Music and Other Essays*, 205.

68. Vaughan Williams, "Composing for Films (1945)," in *National Music and Other Essays*, 160–65.

69. E. M. Forster, "Art for Art's Sake" (1949), in *Two Cheers for Democracy*, 87–93.

Tracing a Biography: Michael Kennedy's Correspondence Concerning
The Works of Ralph Vaughan Williams

INTRODUCED AND ANNOTATED BY
DANIEL M. GRIMLEY AND BYRON ADAMS

Following Ralph Vaughan Williams's death from a heart attack on 26 August 1958, his widow, Ursula, in accordance with instructions in the composer's will, undertook the task of gathering and organizing his papers in connection with two independent but closely interrelated biographical projects. The first, Ursula Vaughan Williams's own biography of her husband, appeared alongside a comprehensive survey of his musical output written by a young critic and close friend of the couple, Michael Kennedy. Both volumes were published in 1964 by Oxford University Press, which had long been associated with Vaughan Williams's music.[1] Despite strategic obfuscations on Ursula's part, both volumes have had a profound and lasting impact upon the appreciation of Vaughan Williams's life and work, and of his wider significance within twentieth-century musical culture.

Kennedy was born in Chorlton-cum-Hardy, a suburb south of Manchester, on 19 February 1926, and first joined the staff of the *Daily Telegraph* in the paper's Northern Office as a fifteen-year-old copy boy, returning to the *Telegraph* as assistant to the Night Editor after serving in the Royal Navy.[2] It was during his naval service that he first wrote to Vaughan Williams directly, expressing his enthusiasm for the Fifth Symphony (1943), an exchange that led to an increasingly close friendship between the two after the war. Kennedy later became the *Telegraph*'s northern editor and from 1986 was the paper's chief music critic, before becoming chief music critic at the *Telegraph*'s sister publication, the *Sunday Telegraph*, in 1989, a position he held until 2005. Kennedy's career as a young journalist was also inspired by meeting Neville Cardus (1888–1975), one of the most influential writers on music in England and for many years chief music critic and cricket correspondent at the *Manchester Guardian*.[3] Kennedy shared Cardus's keen interest in both contemporary English music and late nineteenth- and early twentieth-century composers such as Gustav Mahler. Alongside his study of Vaughan Williams's work, Kennedy published well-received books on Elgar (1968, 1970, and 2004), Richard Strauss (1976, 1984, and 1999), Benjamin Britten (1981), and William Walton (1989), as well as volumes on the conductors John Barbirolli (1971) and Adrian Boult (1987), and a history of the Manchester-based Hallé Orchestra (1982).

Like Vaughan Williams, Kennedy was married twice; his first wife, Eslyn (née Durdle), suffered from a severe debilitating illness. Kennedy remarried after her death, having acted as her primary caregiver for many years. After Kennedy's own death, at the age of eighty-eight on 31 December 2014, his second wife, Joyce (née Bourne), who was a senior partner in a medical practice as well as a writer on music, donated his papers and correspondence to the John Rylands Library at the University of Manchester. The Michael Kennedy Papers consist of five series of material gathered in a dozen folders comprising 174 individual items, and includes letters, notes, reviews, manuscripts, and typescripts, relating to many aspects of Kennedy's musical research. The materials connected with his Vaughan Williams study reveal his painstaking attention to historical detail—as a professional journalist, Kennedy sought wherever possible to identify two independent sources to corroborate a date or quotation—as well as his meticulous concern with tracing the genesis and reception of Vaughan Williams's work, particularly his film scores. Indeed, Kennedy was one of the first writers to devote sustained attention to this significant but frequently neglected area of the composer's output. A part of the archive consists of his correspondence with Ursula Vaughan Williams, who would respond to Kennedy's regular inquiries about major performances and premieres or the whereabouts of certain manuscripts and musical materials on her characteristic handwritten blue postcards. Kennedy would in turn pass relevant documents to Ursula to assist her own biographical study, and comment on or review drafts of material and corroborate dates and other facts as appropriate. In addition to the phone calls and personal visits that evidently took place, the correspondence underlines how close the collaborative work on their companion volumes became.

The materials in the Kennedy Papers offer more than merely documentary evidence of his research method. They also reveal his deep immersion in the musical culture and wider artistic climate of Vaughan Williams's time. Letters from some of Vaughan Williams's colleagues and contemporaries, such as Britten and the philosopher Bertrand Russell (a contemporary of the composer's at Trinity College, Cambridge) were quoted verbatim in Kennedy's study. Other sources, however, did not appear directly, and were either referenced in footnotes as "letter to author" or paraphrased or used indirectly to support details of the chronological narrative or musical commentary. Inevitably, the materials also indicate some of the boundaries and limitations of Kennedy's study. Though admirably comprehensive in its coverage, Kennedy's interest tended more strongly toward works from the latter half of Vaughan Williams's career. The discussion of earlier works, especially from before the 1920s, was at times somewhat more schematic, presumably because of limited access to relevant primary source materials (not all of which would have been in Ursula Vaughan Williams's possession), although Kennedy made strenuous attempts to trace the details of early performances of key works such as *The Lark Ascending* and the *Fantasia on a Theme of Thomas Tallis*. Equally notable is the relative lack of emphasis on Vaughan Williams's folksong-collecting activities. Although a major chapter is devoted to this aspect of Vaughan Williams's work in Kennedy's book, his correspondence with Maud Karpeles (reproduced below) indicates he felt that this was an area where he lacked sufficient professional expertise (or potential interest). Similarly, Kennedy's book arguably downplays Vaughan Williams's lifelong radical-liberal political sympathies—very different from the Conservative Party affiliation of the *Daily Telegraph*. It is perhaps for this reason that Kennedy wrote comparably little about Vaughan Williams's commitment to music making in the community, such as the Leith Hill Musical Festival, in favor of his work in more elite musical genres—his pioneering interest in film scores notwithstanding. At the same time, Kennedy also devoted little attention to the wider issue of Vaughan Williams's relationship with musical modernism, beyond noting in passing the influence of figures such as Bartók and Hindemith and his lack of enthusiasm for Schoenberg's work. Kennedy's preference was invariably to place emphasis instead on Vaughan Williams's individuality and the development of his independent musical style, underestimating, for example, the impact of Ravel on his work. Such reservations aside, the overriding impression when working through the papers is of Kennedy's enormous energy and professionalism, and of his profound knowledge of and enduring love for Vaughan Williams's music.

The Selected Correspondence

There is no systematic basis for the selection of documents reproduced here. Rather, the choices are intended to provide an overview of the correspondence Kennedy gathered as he worked on his study. The earliest document is a letter to Vaughan Williams from the Dutch pianist-composer Julius Röntgen (1855–1932), formerly one of the closest friends of Edvard Grieg, detailing Röntgen's response to the score of *A Pastoral Symphony*. Kennedy translated the letter from German, but it does not appear in either his study nor in Ursula Vaughan Williams's biography, though it is a valuable record of an early continental European response to one of Vaughan Williams's most original and characteristic works. The correspondence with Imogen Holst (1907–1984) is fascinating as an indication of her keen interest in Vaughan Williams's legacy, inspired no doubt by his intimate friendship with her father, Gustav; her experience as one of his composition students at the Royal College of Music; and certainly for her detailed methodological description of how Kennedy's project might proceed. At the time of their correspondence, Holst was already working as musical assistant to Benjamin Britten in Aldeburgh, and for many years she was joint director of the Aldeburgh Festival. Though Kennedy did not undertake any formal academic musicological training, it is clear he adopted many (if not quite all) of Holst's recommendations as he prepared his work list and chronology. A fully comprehensive *Werkverzeichnis* of the kind imagined by Holst has yet to be undertaken.

Following Bertrand Russell's short note, reproduced because it is such a significant indicator of the intellectual and political circles in which Vaughan Williams moved during his student years in Cambridge, are a series of letters from the tenor Steuart Wilson (1889–1964), one of the most celebrated oratorio singers of his day who was particularly praised for his performances in Elgar's *Dream of Gerontius* and Bach's *St. Matthew Passion*. A distant relative of Peter Pears, Wilson attended "public" school at Winchester College and matriculated at King's College, Cambridge, during which time he met Vaughan Williams and Edward J. Dent. Vaughan Williams composed his *Four Hymns* specifically for Wilson to perform at the 1914 Three Choirs Festival at Worcester (an event cancelled following the outbreak of war), and Wilson later became the leading proponent of Vaughan Williams's luminous Housman cycle *On Wenlock Edge*. Injuries sustained during active service in the First World War may have curtailed Wilson's professional performing career.[4] He later taught briefly at Bedales School and then at the Curtis Institute in Philadelphia. In 1943, he was appointed overseas music director at the BBC. In later years, however, he became virulently homophobic, initiating a campaign in 1955 directed against "homosexuality in British music."[5] His correspondence with Kennedy is often of a scurrilous, sensationalist kind, and needs to be read with caution, but his testimony as a performer who worked closely with Vaughan Williams earlier in his career is nonetheless of considerable value. In her touching obituary for the *International Folk Music Journal*, Ursula Vaughan Williams described Steuart Wilson as an "enthusiastic, wise, turbulent and knowledgeable musician . . . a splendid human being."[6]

One of the principal points of tension in Wilson's administrative career at the BBC was his fraught relationship with the conductor Adrian Boult (1889–1983). Wilson's first wife, Ann (née Bowles), divorced him in 1931, and subsequently married Boult, who had provided a refuge during the breakdown of her marriage. In what Kennedy and others considered retaliation, Wilson subsequently oversaw Boult's forced departure from the BBC in 1948.[7] One of the most distinguished British conductors of the time, Boult studied at Christ Church, Oxford, and at the Leipzig Conservatory, before returning to England where, on 29 September 1918, he gave the premiere of Gustav Holst's *The Planets*, Op. 32. He was a committed champion of Vaughan Williams's music, and a lifelong advocate for British music more widely.[8] His correspondence with Kennedy, in characteristically clipped fashion, includes his impressions of directing a significant performance of *A Pastoral Symphony* by the Czech Philharmonic on Sunday, 17 May, 1925 at the International Society for Contemporary Music festival in Prague—which took place barely a few months after Vaughan Williams received Julius Röntgen's letter about the symphony. Boult also supplied Kennedy with an unvarnished report of the less than ideal conditions at the Carnegie Hall premiere of the *Five Variants on "Dives and Lazarus"* in June 1939. Kennedy's other queries concerned recordings of the ballet score *Job*—which Vaughan Williams dedicated in gratitude to Boult—and of the Violin Concerto in D Minor.

Among Kennedy's senior colleagues, Frank Howes (1891–1974) was a particularly astute and sensitive writer on twentieth-century English music. Howes studied at St. John's College, Oxford, and was later editor of the *Journal of the English Folk Song and Dance Society*, before taking up the position of chief music critic at the *Times* in 1943. A particularly valuable detail from Howes's correspondence concerns the premiere of Vaughan Williams's oratorio *Sancta Civitas*, which took place during the upheaval caused by the General Strike of 1926. Howes published his own study of the composer, *The Music of Ralph Vaughan Williams*, in 1954. His correspondence with Kennedy is characterized by a sense of nostalgia for a passing generation: Howes refers to himself as the "oldest inhabitant." Howes is interred in the hilltop churchyard at Combe, above the Evenlode Valley looking toward Oxford, Blenheim Park, and the Cumnor Hills, the landscape that inspired Matthew Arnold's poem "The Scholar Gypsy" and provided the text for Vaughan Williams's *An Oxford Elegy* (1949), for which Steuart Wilson was narrator at the premiere.

Histories of the first folksong revival have stubbornly focused on the work of a small group of male collectors and musicians—preeminently Cecil Sharp, Percy Grainger, and Ralph Vaughan Williams. The essential contribution of female collectors, from Lucy Broadwood to Ella Mary Leather, both of whom collaborated with Vaughan Williams, remains underacknowledged. Maud Karpeles belongs to this remarkable generation of women musicians who collected folksongs and dances. Born in 1885, the daughter of German-Jewish parents, she met Sharp at the Shakespeare Festival in Stratford-upon-Avon in May 1909 and later worked as his amanuensis, accompanying him on his collecting trips in the remote and mountainous region of southern Appalachia. After Sharp's death in 1924, Karpeles continued her collecting work and was elected to the Board of Artistic Control of the English Folk Song and Dance Society in 1932, later working closely with refugee groups during the Second World War; she died in 1976. The key element of Karpeles's correspondence with Kennedy is her critical commentary on a draft of the second chapter of Kennedy's book, "Folk Song and Nationalism" (23–40), which he sent to her in 1963 before submitting his final text for publication. The draft that formed the basis for Karpeles's review does not survive, but it is possible to track her comments alongside Kennedy's final text, which reveals how closely he followed her advice, including, at times, virtually quoting her revisions verbatim.

Two short pieces of correspondence follow: Vaughan Williams's publisher at Oxford University Press, Alan Frank (1910–1994), husband of the composer Phyllis Tate (1911–1987), was himself a composer and clarinetist. Frank became head of the music department at the press in 1954. It is interesting to speculate what Vaughan Williams may have been seeking in Mahler's music and the "wrong-note school"—Schoenberg, Berg, and Webern—as he worked on his film score for *Scott of the Antarctic*. It may have been the spare, "icy" handling of register and instrumental timbre in Webern's work that seemed especially relevant, summoning up images of the desolate wind-blown plateau. Percy Hull (1878–1968) was held as a prisoner-of-war at Ruhleben Internment Camp in Berlin, and was later organist at Hereford Cathedral from the end of the First World War to 1949. During his tenure in Hereford, he was one of the leading lights behind the Three Choirs Festival and was a friend of both Elgar and Vaughan Williams. His correspondence with Kennedy concerns two works: the Two Hymn-Tune Preludes for orchestra, and the one-act opera *The Shepherds of the Delectable Mountains*, based on John Bunyan's seventeenth-century Puritan allegory *The Pilgrim's Progress*, engagement with which was a recurrent point of reference throughout Vaughan Williams's career. Though rarely performed today, *The Shepherds of the Delectable Mountains* is one of the key works that Vaughan Williams composed in the aftermath of the First World War, alongside the Mass in G Minor and *A Pastoral*

Symphony, and he reused much of the music in his 1951 "morality" opera *The Pilgrim's Progress*.

Vaughan Williams's attitude to opera in England, and to the politics of domestic opera production, is the concern of Jani Strasser's correspondence. Strasser was born in Hungary in 1900 and joined the staff of the Glyndebourne Festival Opera at its inauguration in 1934, working alongside Fritz Busch and coaching many of the festival's singers. George Christie described him in the *Times* as "one of the more flavoured, and therefore more important, ingredients in the Glyndebourne concoction before the war."[9] He died in Ringmer, Sussex, in October 1978. Britten's short note follows—a document that Kennedy quoted directly in his book.

The final letter in the selection is from Kennedy himself, written to the borough clerk in Dorking, concerning plans to demolish Vaughan Williams's house, called "White Gates," which was suffering from dry rot. Vaughan Williams had vacated "White Gates" following Adeline's death and moved to Hanover Terrace overlooking Regent's Park in central London in 1953, and so the immediate biographical connection with the property had been broken. But it is nonetheless a curious irony that just as one physical link to the composer's life and work was to disappear, victim to the dictates of local town-planning regulations, Kennedy's own tribute was about to be published, initiating the next phase of Vaughan Williams's critical reception.

Selections from the Kennedy Files

Julius Röntgen to Ralph Vaughan Williams, 14 March 1925[10]

J.R.

Bilthoven (Holland), 14 March 1925

Dear Sir,

At last the moment has come that I can manage to say to you something about your works; you have given me great pleasure by sending them to me. I have been so busy during the recent months with my own works that I didn't have the possibility to study your scores. I hope you can understand this!

Now I have started with your Pastoral Symphony, and I would very much like to tell you something of my impression—as far as it is possible for me to judge the work without having heard it.

My impression is that you have created a work of genius, and that one finds in it the genuine "Naturton." It is primitive art in the best sense of the word. The symphony must be beautiful to listen to, and I admire greatly your art of instrumentation and the often very strange sounds and colours which you have used.

But just because of all this I ought to hear the work—perhaps I would lose then the puzzled feeling I have in a number of places while reading the score.

For instance, the harmonic combination:

hurts me when I read it (the same happens in bar 2 after A)—and the ear might be better able to understand it than the eye. The many consecutive fifths will no doubt sound very well—it is H[ucbald]?[11] redivivus—they are so characteristic of the modern English music, and to be found also— and they are very effective!—in Gustav Holst.

As regards the work as a whole I have the feeling that the two first movements are not sufficiently contrasted. The contrast doesn't come until the più mosso E in the 3rd movement, and it makes a very lively impression. I find all this section particularly good and truly symphonic—it is rewarding to find that here the definite form has replaced the "free improvisation," and that it even remains at 3/4 time for a while (don't laugh!)—The same applies to the Presto after S., which is also particularly interesting contrapuntally. The ending after that is splendid and witty! The last movement is of course again entirely "improvisation"—the beginning and the end will no doubt sound most poetic and strange.

Of course these are but superficial remarks, but you can gather from them how thrilled I was by your score. I do hope I shall soon hear the symphony, and I shall give the score to the conductor of the Utrecht and the Haag orchestra with the particular advice to perform it. About your Mass I shall write to you soon, if you want it. Do come soon again to Holland—in which case your visit in our "pastoral" surroundings is hoped for by your obedient servant.

Best regards from my wife!
Julius Röntgen.

Imogen Holst to Michael Kennedy, 20 April 1960

20 High Street, Aldeburgh, Suffolk
20 April 1960

Dear Michael Kennedy,

When I was staying with Ursula a little while ago, helping her edit some of Ralph's unpublished folk song MSS., we spoke of the books that are going to be written about him and his music, both now and in years to come, and I said how passionately I hoped there would be a chance of bringing out an official thematic catalogue of all his works, on the lines of Köchel.[12] Ursula doesn't know Köchel, so I said I would write to you, and put my request to you myself.

I think Köchel and the Deutsch Schubert[13] and the other important thematic catalogues that have recently been published, or are about to be published (including Zimmerman's Purcell) are *by far* the most valuable reference books ever written. Over and over again one consults them to find out the reliable facts.

It would be MARVELLOUS if you could give the world an R.V.W. Köchel. Not only would it be of practical help to all future performers of his works, but also it would be the foundation of all future books that may be written about him.

You are, I know, thinking in terms of a critical and discursive book about his music, which will be one of the many books that will be written about him during this and the next century (or centuries). But there surely is room for this as well as for a separate thematic catalogue—and the thematic catalogue would be unique, and authoritative for all time.

The Köchel pattern is, I think, much the best, though there are several details, including *duration*, which are missing, and are important. The main essentials, though not necessarily in this order of course, are:

> Title
> Author of libretto, if any
> List of Instruments and/or voices
> Thematic opening bars of movements, or each solo or chorus,
>   with the remaining number of bars in brackets, as in Köchel
> Duration (with a note to say where it is the composer's *own*
>   timing, as in the B.B.C. card index)
> Where the original MS. is

By whom published

Whether full score can be bought (i.e. in miniature score) or whether only on hire

Any published arrangements (i.e. vocal score, excerpts, etc.)

Dedication

Place and date of first performance

If first performance was provincial, add details of first London performance. (This was Ralph's own advice to me, when I was writing the biography of my father.)

Details of conductor, chief soloist, orchestra or choir at first performance

Additional information—any references to the work in Ralph's own words, either from his letters or his books and articles.

There will be others, but these are the main points. Forgive me for pouring it out to you like this, but it is because I feel so strongly that there is an *overwhelming* need for such a book.

With all possible good wishes,
Yours sincerely,
Imogen Holst

Michael Kennedy to Imogen Holst, 4 November 1962

4 November 1962.

Michael Kennedy, Esq.,
3 Moorwood Drive,
The Avenue, Sale, Cheshire.

Dear Miss Holst,

It is a long time since you were kind enough to send me your views on how I ought to tackle my side of the RVW biography, and I feel I owe it to you to say that I have largely followed your advice as to lay-out and detail (slightly modified in regard to the number of bars etc.). I have done chapters in decades, more or less. The main chapter carries the narrative and sets Ralph against the musical scene of the times, with first critical reactions, etc., and after each chapter is an enormous chronological order-of-works appendix giving all the factual details, followed by a personal "commentary" on the music. In this way I feel the book will have permanent use and appeal, and yet not be too formidably tome-like. Ursula and I dovetailed material very neatly we think. There will be overlappings, but they are not many and are seen from two angles and will not matter. The tracing of first performances is a wonderful game and I have unearthed some surprises. Also, what charming oddities one discovers. I have always been tickled by the idea of Monteux's conducting Egdon Heath—as a companion to it, I have found that Reznicek conducted one of Ralph's early performances![14]

May I trouble you for some information?

1. Was your father appointed to a professorship at R.C.M.? Or only to the teaching staff?

2. Can you give me the date of the first performance of the Mass by its *dedicatees*, the Whitsuntide Singers?[15]

3. You quote a letter from your father about the Mass in which he says (Gustav Holst p. 93), "I've heard—perform it . . . " etc. Ne[e]d the blank remain a secret now? Was it Terry or Joseph Lewis?[16]

4. A similar tantalising blank is in Ralph's letter about the *Choral Fantasia* (*Heirs and Rebels*, p. 77)—"I just want to tell the press (and especially + + +)" etc. Who was the critic? Just to see if I have guessed right, not necessarily for publication![17]

5. The first London performance of *Ode to Death* is always given as Dec 19, 1923. But your father's diary, of which Ursula has given me a copy, has the following tantalising entry for April 23, 1923 "O. to D. Q. H." ???? (I can of course look that up in the *Times*)

I am sorry if these are irritating questions. The pursuit of accuracy is utterly fascinating and often surprising. Which reminds me of two places in *Heirs and Rebels* which you may like to correct whenever it is reprinted:

p. 2. "I think H. J. (Wood) must have gone abroad by now." Not Wood, surely, but Howard Jones, the pianist. He went to study in Berlin at this time and was much closer to R. and G. at this period than Wood. You will notice that when referring to Wood in later letters they said Henry J.[18]

p. 62 footnote. The *Concerto Accademico*[19] had its first performance on November 6 1925 at the Aeolian Hall. *Flos* was first played at Queen's Hall on Oct 19, 1925. The date of Oct 10 for *Flos*, given in several books, stems loke [*sic*] numerous errors of a similar kind from misprint in Grove 3rd edition. As I go along I find that on nearly every count Grove is the most slipshod reference book in the world!

I do hope we meet one day. I should so much like to talk to you about Gustav Holst.

Yours sincerely,
[signed] Michael Kennedy

Imogen Holst to Michael Kennedy, 7 November 1962

9 Church Walk, Aldeburgh
Nov 7 1962

Dear Dr Kennedy,

Thank you so much for your letter. I'm *MOST* grateful for the information about Howard Jones: *OF COURSE* this is right!

Answers to your questions:

1. I'm afraid I don't know if it was a professorship at the RCM—would you ask them?
2. Date of Mass—I'm afraid I have no records *here* of which year it was—it would be the Whit Sunday of the year when it was completed. Could Ursula help?
3. The name of the choir who sang it badly: I *don't* want this disclosed, because it would cause personal distress.
4. Ditto the name of the critic—a close relation is still living and is a friend of mine (who I was in touch with day after day for many years.)
5. 1st perf (London) of *Ode to Death*—As I told Ursula some months ago, I think this was a private performance or run-through—possibly connected with Oxford and Sir Hugh Allen.[20]

All possible good wishes,
Imogen Holst

Bertrand Russell to Michael Kennedy, 25 November 1961[21]

PLAS PENRHYN
PENRHYNDEUDRAETH
MERIONED
TEL: PENRHYNDEUDRAETH 240

25 November, 1961.

Dear Mr Kennedy,

Thank you for your letter of November 23. I knew Ralph Vaughan Williams well when he was an undergraduate, though not as well as I knew his cousin Ralph Wedgwood. I was very fond of Ralph Vaughan Williams who was in those days a most determined atheist and was noted for having walked into Hall one evening saying in a loud voice, "Who believes in God now-a-days, I should like to know?" I hardly ever saw him in later years, though I retained an affectionate admiration for him. I am sorry that I have not more to tell you.

Yours sincerely,
[signed] Russell

Steuart Wilson to Michael Kennedy, 26 July 1962

Fenn's, Reservoir Lane, Petersfield
26 July 1962

Dear Michael,

I am glad to be able to fill in a few blanks in the Book.

1. The Four Hymns. I have looked up my "Ledger." The first performance was in Cardiff 16 May 1920. A strange character called Jenkins who was a "starving composer" earlier in life, was a shipping clerk in Cardiff who in the first war bought a tenth share of a tug & made a fortune & floated a Company & for a time was an inflation million-aire. He hired the LSO and Elgar to conduct for a tour in Wales. He went out later to Australia having I think gone bankrupt and had a chequered career as an adjudicator of festivals having styled himself "Doctor Jenkins." This is quite a story in itself.[23] Julius Harrison conducted[24]—we had no rehearsal as the instruments of the LSO failed to turn up until 30 mins before the concert *began*! The violist then was the LSO leader—I *think* it was Hobday.[25]

2. Francis Harford I first knew in about 1905 or 6 singing at the local choral festival at Moreton in Marsh. I think he was in some way connected with Reading University.[26] Foxton Ferguson[27] was the brother of the one-time H.M. of Radley. He was at the [T]emple Church & founded a mixed group of singers 5 & 6[28] – not the famous Templar male voice quartet. I remember his group singing at Cambridge in about 1909.

3. I first met Ralph over rehearsal for *Wasps* in 1909. I was in the chorus. The next year I think I sang *Wenlock Edge* at the Club and repeated it at the 500th & 1000th anniversary concerts![29]

4. I have got a proof only of the 4 hymns with a note in by RVW commemorating the run-through at the piano in July 1914!

W. Steuart

Steuart Wilson to Michael Kennedy, 28 August 1962

Fenn's, Reservoir Lane, Petersfield
28 Aug 1962

Dear Michael,

There is a good deal of scandal which I will tell you one day about Cyril J. and his ultimate—and perhaps current—career in Australia.

Rupert Brooke[30] was in no way *musical* though he was very music-*minded*!

I think that Charles Wood[31] conducted all the performances of the *Wasps*, I'm sure that V.W. did not conduct *any* himself. Miles Malleson was certainly the man.[32] I never heard of the early performance of "Is my team," was it in its original shape for strings and piano, or for piano only[?]

This is a foul summer and I am still *cold*!

W. Steuart

Steuart Wilson to Michael Kennedy, 19 January 1963

Fenn's, Reservoir Lane, Petersfield
19 Jan 1963

My dear Michael,

Your queries of Jan 14.

1. 'Merciless Beauty' is the printed title: the *text* is in Chaucerian spelling. The trio was very amateur as to 1st Dorothy Longman,[33] viola Kitty Farrer,[34] cello young prof. Valentine Orde.[35] Dorothy was a v. old friend of V.W.s who married Bobby Longman who was likewise an old V.W. fan. Kitty Farrer now Lady Bridges was one of the Leith Hill "nymphs." V. Orde now lives in Northumberland. I think it was still in MS. then.

2. *Oxford Elegy. Date* 19 June 1952. *Place* The Queen's College Oxford. Bernard Rose, org.[36] of Queen's College. Chorus & Orchestra of the College Music Society which had a special name which I have not taken a note of.[37]

The Chaucer rounds were also performed by me at the I.S.C.M. festival of Venice Sep 1925 along with *Wenlock Edge*.[38]

I hope I shall be able to answer the next lot!

W. Steuart

CORRESPONDENCE WITH ADRIAN BOULT[39]

Adrian Boult to Michael Kennedy, 23 November 1962

53 Welbeck Street
London
W1
November 23rd 1962

Dear Michael,

Many thanks for your letter. We ran through the work[40] several times on Fridays before the first performance, which was as you know on which I imagine was a Thursday as that was the Philharmonic's day at that time. I do not know why I should have pin-pointed it as a single occasion because there were several weeks, I am sure, but I remember Gustav [Holst] was there the very first time and was the first person to accept it as a masterpiece in my hearing.

After the first performance or two I went to Birmingham and was off the map, but I did the work several times up there. I did not meet RVW over it until the 1925 Festival in Prague,[41] at one of the rehearsals at which he said everything I was doing was too fast. I reminded him that at the first rehearsals I had tried to do it all slower and he would not let me. His reply was something like this "Yes, but I have conducted it a good deal myself in these years and I know that people are not so bored with it as I thought they would be, so I think it will go all right at the slower pace."

"Job": I do not think I have ever done a concert performance of anything but the full work, and I certainly have never done John Barbirolli's abominable version which leaves out some splendid stuff.[42]

I hope you flourish; all greetings

[postscript in ink:] I enclose a list of my early dates which may amuse you. I suspect the RCM Fridays began 2 or 3 weeks before 26 June 1922.

Yours ever,
ACB

Adrian Boult to Michael Kennedy, 28 November 1962

53 Welbeck Street
London
W1
November 28th 1962

Dear Michael,

Many thanks for your letter. That is a sad story about "Job" in Manchester. If they ever invite me again I must really do it there.

I have never had anything to do with Constant Lambert's[43] abbreviated version which does, I think, include every bar of the music and is an extremely clever re-orchestration, I believe, but it just does not happen to have come my way. The few ballet performances I have done of it have all been with full orchestra.

Yours ever,
Adrian

Adrian Boult to Michael Kennedy, 3 April 1963

April 3rd 1963

Dear Michael,

The first performance of "Dives" I have discovered in programme diary to be June 10th 1939. It took place at Carnegie Hall because the concert hall at the World's Fair was (rather at the eleventh hour) discovered to be extremely porous to outside noises. There was no air-conditioning in Carnegie Hall, and the poor fat Leader had the greatest difficulty in keeping his fiddle under his chin at all. The whole audience fanned itself continuously with its programmes, and I believe the thermometer stood at 89°, but I am not sure. It was, of course, the Philharmonic Symphony, and I think the Leader's name was Piastro.[44]

I have a date for the Violin Concerto with Pougnet on July 27th 1934,[45] and with Menuhin on February 28th 1952.[46] The first was in the Concert Hall, Broadcasting House, with Section C of the B.B.C. Symphony Orchestra, and the second was a recording for H.M.V. in Abbey Road. I rather think David Bicknell[47] was in charge, so the Columbia people would have a record of this.

Many thanks for your good wishes in relation to the anniversary.

I hope you both flourish, and I do not intend to read Dickinson's effusion;[48] I prefer to wait for yours.

Yours ever,
ACB

Frank Howes to Michael Kennedy, 15 November 1962

Newbridge Mill, Standlake, Oxon.
Nov 15/62.

Dear Michael,

Last things first—I must defer reply to the rest of your first letter till I have time to collect the material.

The trouble about the Heather Festival of 1926 was that it occurred during the General Strike. I represented the *Times* down in Oxford, where my home was, but the paper could take nothing as it wasn't being printed & all I could find in my cutting book is a summary of events on May 21 of what happened between Nov 3 & 8, so I can't give you the soloists, I fear, but after all these years & so many events . . . ! The tenor may well have been Steuart [Wilson]. It was an Oxford Bach Choir performance in the Sheldonian with [Hugh] Allen & his orchestra. Cranmer[50] is extremely probable.

It was at an earlier event of the same sort that my "O Rest in the Lord" episode occurred. Did I relate it to you, for I can't find it (mercifully!) in my own book? The speaker was William Harris, then organist of New College, who was sitting next to me.[51] I shared his opinion & only changed it when I heard it later at Aberystwyth & a little later still Westminster Abbey. The Sheldonian has a very dry acoustic which would not help that particular kind of choral writing. But I don't think you'd better betray us!

I begin to find myself in the role of the oldest inhabitant & quite pleased to exploit it!

Yours Frank

p.s. I'll tell you what . . . though—I'll dig out the actual programme, I have a tea chest full of my past!

Frank Howes to Michael Kennedy, 30 November 1962

Newbridge Mill, Standlake, Oxon.
Nov 30/62

My dear Michael,

I have an idea that I owed you a letter with answers to queries, but I can only trace one outstanding, namely the *Sancta Civitas* programme. For your August letter I surely answered—denying my authorship of a sleeve note to the *London Symphony*. After a few searches in the many envelopes of my past, where incidentally I found the programme of the G minor Mass June 17, 1923, solo quartet, Vivienne Chatterton, Constance Taylor, Trefor Jones & Keith Faulkner, I took up the point in your letter that it was at a Heather Festival. So I proceed at once on the programme book which gives the answer. It says First performance (Fri[day] May 7, 1926), Tenor: Trefor Jones. Baritone: Keith Faulkner crossed out & Arthur Cranmer substituted. Oxford Bach Choir, Oxford Orchestral Society, H.P.A. So there we are.

Frank Pownall story is new to me. Tell me if I've mislaid another letter from you & still owe you some queries.[52]

Yours ever
Frank

Maud Karpeles to Michael Kennedy, 6 May 1963[53]

INTERNATIONAL FOLK MUSIC COUNCIL
35 Princess Court, Queensway, London W.2.
Tel: BAYswater 6501

6th May, 1963

Dear Michael,

Here is your script and my illegible pencil notes. I think the chapter will be of great interest, particularly when read in conjunction with the rest of the book. I am also sending you a copy of the definition concerning folk music, about which I spoke.

I hope that I have not been too presumptuous. You will realise that most of my comments are intended merely as suggestions.

Good luck and love to you both.

Yours

Maud K.

p. 3 a) note corrections. Are you sure about your figure of songs from Somerset, I have not checked.[54]

b) [Wld. not] "adulterations" be better[?] Harmony hardly applies.

c) I suggest you are less definite about date. Substitute "in 2nd half of 19th cent."

p. 4 a) This is too strong. Folk singing was not extinct by 1914. This passage needs modifying. I should feel inclined to omit all between square brackets. [As a matter of fact] add something like this: "there are still a few traditional singers living even at the present day, but the situation both as regards quantity & quality of songs has greatly deteriorated in the last 50 years."[55]

p. 7 a) I feel this business of national song is all rather ancient history & it is treated at too great length. I doubt if national song was ever popular. I think you shld introduce a word abt. popular song as we understand the term.[56]

p. 10 variants do not merely enhance or detract from a tune. They may do either, but they are an indispensable factor in the evolution of f[olk] s[ong][57] You shld refer to the definition of f.s. adopted by IFMC at 1954.[58] Quotation from RVW at foot of page is good. It illustrates its point.

p. 11 Sharp believed it could thus not be condemned.

p. 12. Quotation. This is misleading. I suggest omitting 1ˢᵗ sentence &
substituting some of this sort: V.W. believed that we had reached a
stage when the evolution of f.s. by oral transmission was no longer
possible.[59]

p. 13. Suggest omitting. You have already referred to this.

p. 15. Modes. I am not sure that it is correct to talk of "Greek" modes.
Wld "medieval modes" be better? This is altogether unsatisfactory.
The Ionian mode is to all intents and purposes the major scale. I
think you shld mention that a good percentage of Eng. F. tunes are
in dorian, aeolian & mixolydian modes.[60]

p. 14 a) I think you might amplify this. ~~The use of modes in~~ the greater
melodic possibilities in modal music & VW's use of modes in his
own music, but perhaps that comes later.

p. 21–22 Shorten v. much. Not interesting.

p. 26 John Wesley etc.[61] Omit. Such an old chestnut & it has been alluded
to by so many people.

p. 28. Omit "pastoral." Too much stress on this aspect of f.s.

p. 29–35. Might be condensed. The subject matter is so well known.

p. 34 a) Not clear what this means

p. 35. Omit portion between brackets. Enough has been said.

p.p. 51–2. ~~It might be worth adding if it does not appear elsewhere that
he often said that one moment of inspiration meant had to be followed by hours of manual labour.~~[62]

See p. xii of introduction by M.K. [Maud Karpeles] in some conclusions
if this is quoted. I think from the body of the book, but I cannot at
the moment trace it.

Alan Frank to Michael Kennedy, 3 April 1963[63]

OXFORD UNIVERSITY PRESS
MUSIC DEPARTMENT

44 Conduit Street
London W.1
3 April 1963

Dear Michael,

We will work through your list of queries, though it may take a little while.

I have just seen Dickinson's book but haven't opened it. I am not in the least bit surprised at your comments.

About the Mahler business, I still can't find the original letter but am sure that I can quote the relevant sentences exactly as he wrote it. The letter had asked me to buy for him a selection of scores of the "wrong note school"—that was his phrase, and he wanted these for study in connection with the film score of "Scott."[64] Then he wrote "P.S. Will you please also buy for me a score of Mahler's Resurrection Symphony—not for its wrong notes, his all sound painfully right to me."[65]

Yours,
Alan

Vaga House,
64 Lynch Road,
Farnham,
Surrey,
14/6/63

Dear Mr Kennedy,

My apology for this delayed reply to your letter of May 31ˢᵗ, due to absence abroad until last night. Here are the answers to questions: Exact title—Two Hymn Tune Preludes (for Orchestra)

1. "Eventide[,]" Monk. 2. "Dominus Regit Me," Dykes. (Specially composed for Hereford Three Choirs Festival 1936)

    a. First performance Sept. 8[,] 1936.

    b. London Symphony Orchestra (leader, W. H. Reed)[67]

    c. Conductor. R. Vaughan Williams.

    d. (Place) Hereford Cathedral.

It may be of interest to you that in 1926, I heard a performance of "The Shepherds of the Delectable Mountains" staged in Bristol, and I returned to Hereford convinced that it was most suitable for the Cathedral. I wrote to "V.W." that I proposed to perform it there the following year and asked whether he would conduct "the first performance otherwise than on the Stage?" A somewhat furious letter arrived *by return*, refusing to have anything to do with it!! He said it would be entirely out of place, most unsuitable and would most certainly get me into trouble! My answer was "Right, then I'll do it without you." A week or so before the Festival, another letter came asking the time of the final rehearsal of soloists & orchestra in London & whether I still wanted him to conduct? My reply was "*do as you like*"! He turned up at the R.C.M. & went through the work & asked whether he should do it at the Festival!! (the following week) Of course I consented, but "not if it went against the grain"!!! He afterwards confessed that his judgment as to the suitability of the work in the cathedral etc. was entirely wrong and that he really enjoyed the performance. (There was no chance at that late hour to announce that it would be conducted by the composer).

I put the work in the Hereford programme again in 1933, and this gave him great pleasure & he again completely revised his judgment re suitability in the cathedral, etc.

Please forgive this poor typing, my machine has been out of action for some considerable time. Needless to say my wife & I much look forward to your official biography of the "really great V.W."

Yours sincerely,
Percy Hull

Jani Strasser to Michael Kennedy, 23 August 1963[68]

Glyndebourne Festival Opera
GLYNDEBOURNE, LEWES, SUSSEX
Telephone Ringmer 321   *Box Office* Ringmer 234

23rd August, 1963.

Dear Mr Kennedy,

Thank you very much for your letter of August 16th and the enclosed copy which I herewith return, and which helped me to remember some details of this exchange.

During the repeated visits of Dr Vaughan Williams we somehow came to discussing singing in general and the difference between English and other ways of singing in particular. It was but one logical step towards arguing the suitability of the English type of singing for opera. It was soon discovered that there was a fundamental divergence of outlook between us two, as V.W. insisted that opera and operatic tradition in England must develop from the existing English spirit of *music*, whereas I vainly tried to convince him that opera, although to a major extent a musical activity, is not simply music but an independent, if hybrid, form of art which has its own conventions and exigencies. Therefore one must first of all create a foundation, a point of departure for opera, a knowledgeable audience with appropriate demands which will automatically create a race of suitable singers, and ultimately of operas by English composers.

Accordingly Glyndebourne supplied this point of departure, which, I maintained, had more future than that represented by performances of existing English operas. V.W's letter was[,] I think, one of the links in this discussion. I am sure, that had he lived longer, he would have acknowledged that developments have proved my thesis to be the right one.

Yours sincerely,
Jani Strasser

Benjamin Britten to Michael Kennedy, 7 September 1963[69]

THE RED HOUSE, ALDEBURGH, SUFFOLK

7th September, 1963

Dear Mr. Kennedy,

Please forgive the delay in answering your letter, but I have been away and very busy. Of course you can quote my letter to Ursula on Dr. Vaughan Williams' death; it was certainly a private letter, but I have no wish to retract from what I said then.

Thank you for your kind words about War Requiem.

With best wishes.
Yours sincerely,
[signed] Benjamin Britten

3 Moorwood Drive,
The Avenue, Sale,
Cheshire.

February 5th, 1964.

F. G. Sutherland, Esq.
Clerk to Dorking Urban District Council,
Council Offices, Fippbrook,
Dorking, Surrey.

Dear Sir,

I have heard with regret that there is a proposal to demolish "The White Gates," the former home in Dorking of the late Dr Ralph Vaughan Williams O.M. I should like, as a writer on music, as Northern Editor of The Daily Telegraph and as one who had the privilege of the composer's friendship, to make my protest against this proposal and to implore your council to refuse to allow such a thing to be done.

I do not think anyone who knows "The White Gates" would pretend that it should be preserved as of architectural interest, but on the grounds of historic interest there is surely the strongest case. Under its roof were written four of the nine symphonies (including those which some regard as the three greatest of them), the morality "The Pilgrim's Progress," the two great choral works "Dona Nobis Pacem" and "Five Tudor Portraits" as well as a host of smaller works. There, within its walls, the Leith Hill Festival performances of the Bach Passions were planned, and there some of the most famous musicians of the century gathered to talk and sometimes to play.

It might be said that the works themselves are what matter and not the house in which they were composed. That, surely, is to take too mundane a view of things. Who is there who loves the novels and poetry of Hardy who does not feel some extra indefinable understanding of them through visiting Max [G]ate?[71] Why do hundreds visit historic places associated with the great if there is no special ~~image~~ magic attached to the fact that there they once lived and worked.

Not, of course, that I would wish "The White Gates" to become that thing a museum. If such a proposal was put forward, I should be writing to you to oppose it, and I know the composer himself would have deplored such a thing. When he left it, a musician took it over, and I feel sure there must be other musicians who would be glad to make the house their home, with the knowledge of its part as an inspiration. For this, I submit, is the real heart of the matter. If Vaughan Williams's life and example meant anything, it meant that an artist should live among his fellows and take part in their everyday life. Today we see too many artistic people—writers, poets, musicians, painters—settling in ivory towers, living secluded and detached lives. Their work reflects it. Vaughan Williams was a great and extraordinary composer, but he was an ordinary man and for 25 years he lived in your town, took part in its life in many aspects, and lived, accessibly and modestly, there just off the Westcott Road. Surely that fact alone is the justification for retaining "The White Gates"—that future generations should know that a great man worked and lived in your town in that house.

We today have vivid memories of him—we do not need houses and busts to remind us of his presence. But when the time comes that no one remembers him, will there not be Dorking dwellers who would wish that "The White Gates" was still there so that they could point to it and say "One of England's greatest men and composers lived there"? I think your Council must consider those future generations rather than take a short-sighted view of the present.

Yours faithfully
[unsigned]

1. Ursula Vaughan Williams, *R.V.W.: A Biography of Ralph Vaughan Williams* (London: Oxford University Press, 1964); Michael Kennedy, *The Works of Ralph Vaughan Williams* (Oxford: Oxford University Press, 1964; 2nd ed., 1980).

2. Simon Heffer, "(George) Michael Sinclair Kennedy," *Oxford Dictionary of National Biography,* https://doi-org.ezproxy-prd.bodleian.ox.ac.uk/10.1093/odnb/9780198614128.013.108217

3. Michael Kennedy obituary, *Daily Telegraph*, 31 December 2014, https://www.telegraph.co.uk/news/obituaries/11319299/Michael-Kennedy-obituary.html.

4. In his obituary in the *Times* (19 December 1966), Frank Howes suggests that damage to Wilson's lungs during the war seriously impaired his breath control and that his voice suffered as a result.

5. *The People*, 24 July 1955, quoted in Donald Mitchell, Philip Reed, and Mervyn Cooke, eds., *Letters from a Life: The Selected Letters of Benjamin Britten 1913–1976*, vol. 3: *1946–1951* (London: Faber and Faber, 2004), 7.

6. Ursula Vaughan Williams, "Steuart Wilson," *International Folk Music Journal* 19 (1967): 115–16, at 116.

7. See Michael Kennedy, *Adrian Boult* (London: Hamish Hamilton, 1987), 224–25, at 215.

8. Nigel Simeone, *Ralph Vaughan Williams and Adrian Boult* (Woodbridge: Boydell Press, 2022). Simeone devotes a whole chapter to Boult's interpretations of *Job* (55–70).

9. George Christie, "Jani Strasser," *Times*, Tuesday, 24 November 1970.

10. Ink letter on A5 paper. Kennedy's unsigned translation, reproduced here, is written with a ballpoint pen—known in Britian as a "biro"—on an A4 sheet. Kennedy Papers, John Rylands Library, University of Manchester, shelf mark GB Mr KEN/3/1/1-6.

11. Hucbald of St. Amand (ca. 850–20 June 930) was a Benedictine monk, poet, composer, and one of the most important theorists of the Carolingian period, whose treatise, *De Musica*, is a comprehensive manual on the performance of psalmody. On the comparison with Vaughan Williams, see Deborah Heckert, "Hucbald's Fifths and Vaughan Williams's Mass: The New Medieval in Britain Between the Wars," in *The Oxford Handbook of Music and Medievalism,* Stephen C. Meyer and Kirsten Yri, eds., (New York: Oxford, 2020), 327–39. Hucbald had been cited by H. C. Colles in his review of the Birmingham premiere of the G Minor Mass in December 1922: "Dr. Vaughan Williams's Mass," *The Musical Times* 64/959 (January 1923): 36–37, which had presumably placed Hucbald in Röntgen's mind. Kennedy was unable to decipher his name in Röntgen's original text, though he later referred disparagingly to the reference in *The Works of Ralph Vaughan Williams*, 160.

12. The model Imogen Holst proposes here follows Ludwig von Köchel, *Chronologisch-thematisches Verzeichnis sämmtlicher Tonwerke W. A. Mozarts* (Leipzig: Breitkopf & Härtel, 1862).

13. Otto Erich Deutsch, *Schubert: Thematic Catalogue of All His Works in Chronological Order* (London: J. M. Dent & Sons, 1951).

14. Pierre Monteux (1875–1964) was a French conductor who directed the premiere of Stravinsky's *Le sacre du printemps* with the Ballet Russes in 1913. Emil von Reznicek (1860–1945) was an Austrian composer-conductor and friend and colleague of Richard Strauss.

15. This date remains unclear, although the Singers performed an early version of the Kyrie in 1920 at the Whitsun Festival in Dulwich College Chapel. See Harvey Grace, "Gustav Holst: Teacher," *The Musical Times* 75/1098 (August 1934): 689–96, at 694. An undated letter of May 1922 from Holst to Vaughan Williams expresses his thanks for the dedication but does not give any concrete plans for performance (VWL3959). The first full concert performance was instead given by the City of Birmingham Choir on 6 December 1922, directed by Joseph Lewis (1878–1954).

16. Richard Runciman Terry (1865–1938) directed the first liturgical performance of the G Minor Mass in Westminster Cathedral on 12 March 1923. The reference is to Imogen Holst, *Gustav Holst* (London: Oxford University Press, 1938), which carried a tribute by Vaughan Williams (vii–ix).

17. Letter to Gustav Holst of September 1931, VWL1167. Vaughan Williams's full text reads: "I played through the fantasia again yesterday & it is most beautiful – I know you don't care, but I just want to tell the press (and especially Foxy) that they are misbegotten abortions." The critic (unnamed in *Heirs and Rebels*) was A. H. Fox Strangways, founding editor of *Music & Letters*.

18. Pianist Evlyn Howard-Jones (1877–1951) was a student at the Royal College of Music and a contemporary of Vaughan Williams. He later studied with D'Albert and Jedlicka at the Stern Conservatory in Berlin.

19. The Violin Concerto in D Minor (1925) was initially titled *Concerto Accademico*.

20. The first public performance of the *Ode to Death* was at the Leeds Festival on 6 October 1922. The London premiere was given by the Bach Choir, directed by Vaughan Williams, and did indeed take place at the Queen's Hall on 19 December 1923; no evidence survives of a private run-through, nor of the identity of "D Q H."

21. Typescript on headed A5 notepaper. The letter is quoted in Kennedy, *The Works of Ralph Vaughan Williams*, 42. KEN/3/1/6.

22. Ink on headed notepaper. KEN/3/1/14/1-3.

23. David Cyril Jenkins (1885–1978), born in Swansea and later Director of Music for London City Council and a judge at the National Eisteddfod. He emigrated to Australia in 1929.

24. Julius Harrison (1885–1963), composer and conductor, born in Stourport in Worcestershire. He was assistant to Arthur Nikisch and Felix Weingartner in Paris. He joined the British National Opera Company before taking up a position as Professor of Music at the Royal Academy of Music in 1924.

25. Alfred Charles Hobday (1870–1942), born in Faversham, Kent, and studied at the Royal College of Music. He also took part in the premieres of Frank Bridge's Phantasy for Piano Quartet and Vaughan Williams's Quintet in C Minor. He was lead violist of the London Symphony Orchestra from 1904 until 1930.

26. Jack Francis Harford (1864–1948) was a bass-baritone and the dedicatee of Vaughan Williams's "Tears, Idle Tears." He gave the premiere of the song at the St. James Hall in 1903. See Sophie Fuller, "The Songs and Shorter Secular Choral Works," in *The Cambridge Companion to Vaughan Williams*, ed. Alain Frogley and Aidan J. Thomson (Cambridge: Cambridge University Press, 2013), 106–20, at 114.

27. Arthur Foxton Ferguson (1866–1920) was born in Leeds and was founder of the Folk-Song Quartet. He was a commoner at New College, Oxford, and an academic clerk at Magdalen College, before studying in Leipzig. He later taught at Eton. His brother, William Harold Ferguson, mentioned by Wilson, was also a singer and was Warden at Radley College (1925–37).

28. The Temple Church is a heavily restored Romanesque church located in central London, between Fleet Street and the River Thames embankment. It has had a fine singing tradition since the mid-nineteenth century. Wilson's letter refers to an ensemble of five or six singers (with male and female voices), as opposed to the professional male voice quartet who took their name from the church. John Barbirolli's famous 1962 recording of Vaughan Williams's *Fantasia on a Theme by Thomas Tallis* was recorded at the Temple Church.

29. Wilson refers to the Cambridge University Music Club, founded in 1889. The 500th concert took place in 1912 (Kennedy, *The Works of Ralph Vaughan Williams*, 105).

30. The poet, who was born in 1887 and died of septicaemia on Skyros in 1915. Brooke was a member of the Cambridge Apostles, a decade after Vaughan Williams matriculated there.

31. Charles Wood (1866–1926) was an Irish composer and conductor who taught Vaughan Williams in Cambridge. In 1924, he briefly succeeded Charles Villiers Stanford as professor of music.

32. William Miles Malleson (1888–1969), born in Croydon, was an actor and dramatist. He played the slave Sosias in the 1909 Cambridge production of Aristophanes's *The Wasps*, for which Vaughan Williams wrote music. His cinematic credits included roles in *The Thief of Bagdad* (1940), *Kind Hearts and Coronets* (1949), and *The Importance of Being Earnest* (1952).

33. Dorothy Marriott Longman, née Fletcher (1875–1944), wife of the publisher Robert Guy Longman, one of Vaughan Williams's contemporaries at Trinity College, Cambridge. Dorothy Longman was for many years the leader of the Leith Hill Festival Orchestra.

34. Katherine ("Kitty") Dianthe Farrer (1896–1986), daughter of Thomas Farrer, Second Baron Farrer of Abinger, married Edward Ettingdene Bridge, son of the poet laureate Robert Bridges, in 1922.

35. Valentine Orde (1889–1984) studied cello at the Royal Academy of Music and later with Emanuel Feuermann. She taught throughout her career and was involved with the founding of the Northern Sinfonia in 1958.

36. Bernard Rose (1916–1996) was educated at Salisbury Cathedral School and the Royal College of Music, and was organ scholar at St. Catharine's College, Cambridge, before being appointed organist at Queen's College, Oxford, where he taught Kenneth Leighton (1929–1988). He was later director of music (Informator Choristorum) at Magdalen College, Oxford.

37. The Eglesfield Musical Society.

38. The concert took place at Teatro La Fenice on Monday, 7 September; the program also included the world premiere of Artur Schnabel's Piano Sonata, and a performance of Schoenberg's Serenade, Op. 24. *On Wenlock Edge* does not, in fact, appear on the program that evening, so Wilson was presumably mistaken. It did, however, appear on the ISCM program the previous year, on 7 August 1924, in Zurich.

39. The letters are all in typescript on A5 notepaper, signed in ink. KEN/3/1/15/2-6.

40. *A Pastoral Symphony* (1921–22).

41. The concert also included Paul A. Pisk's Partita, Rudolph Réti's Concertino No. 2, and Bohuslav Martinů's *Poločas*.

42. John Barbirolli was an English cellist and conductor, born on 2 December 1899, died 28 July 1970. He was permanent conductor of the Hallé Orchestra in Manchester between 1943 and 1958, having previously been Toscanini's successor at the New York Philharmonic, and thereafter the Hallé's Principal Conductor (and named Laureate for life in 1968). Vaughan Williams referred to him as "glorious John." He directed the premiere of the *Sinfonia Antartica* with the Hallé in Manchester on 14 January 1953.

43. Constant Lambert (1905–1951) was a gifted composer, conductor, and pianist as well as an acerbic writer on music. He was one of the founding members of the Royal Ballet, and a former student of Vaughan Williams at the Royal College of Music. Though Boult never conducted *Job* in Manchester, he performed it frequently elsewhere and recorded it several times. It was also on the program for his last appearance at the BBC Promenade concerts on 17 August 1977. As Simeone notes (*Ralph Vaughan Williams and Adrian Boult*, 274–75), Boult did later conduct Lambert's version of *Job* at least once, on 16 March 1973.

44. Michel Piastro (1891–1970), Russian-American violinist, concertmaster of the New York Philharmonic between 1931 and 1943.

45. Jean Pougnet (1907–1968) was born in Mauritius and studied at the Royal Academy of Music in London. Primarily a soloist and chamber music player, he led the London Philharmonic from 1942 until the end of the Second World War.

46. New York–born Yehudi Menuhin (1916–1999) was a child prodigy and later one of the century's most celebrated virtuosos, who had earlier recorded Elgar's Violin Concerto, Op. 61, with the composer conducting, in 1932.

47. David Bicknell (1906–1988), formerly Fred Gaisberg's assistant at HMV, and later Manager of International Artists at EMI.

48. A. E. F. Dickinson, *Vaughan Williams* (London: Faber & Faber, 1963). Several writers in the correspondence compare Dickinson's volume (unfavorably) with Kennedy's, which was published a year later.

49. Blue ink on embossed A5 letter paper. KEN/3/1/16/3-4.

50. Baritone Arthur Cranmer (1885–1954) was born in Birmingham and began his professional career at the Repertory Theatre before appearing in Rutland Boughton's *The Immortal Hour*, conducted by Appleby Matthews. He sang at the coronations of George VI and Elizabeth II.

51. Recalling his first hearing of Vaughan Williams's modal Mass in G Minor, Howes mentioned that an "eminent musician . . . said to me when it was over, in distressed tones: "O play me [Mendelssohn's] 'O Rest in the Lord': play it as a cornet solo; play it anyhow; but play me 'O Rest in the Lord' after that!" Quoted in Kennedy, *The Works of Ralph Vaughan Williams*, 176. In this letter, Howes reveals that the "eminent musician" was William Henry Harris, who was appointed organist of New College, Oxford, in 1919 and was later appointed organist of St. George's Chapel, Windsor.

52. Concerning the premiere of Vaughan Williams's early orchestral work *Heroic Elegy and Triumphal Epilogue* (1901, rev. 1902), Kennedy writes: "Dr. W. H. Harris recalled that Frank Pownall, registrar of the R.C.M., said to Parry during the performance, 'Fine strong stuff, Hubert.' 'Yes,' Parry replied, 'there's no shadow of doubt about *him*.'" See Kennedy, *The Works of Ralph Vaughan Williams*, 78.

53. The covering note is typed and signed in ink on A5 paper. The notes that follow are written in pencil on loose-leaf lined A4 sheets. Crossings-out and emendations are reproduced here exactly as they appear in Karpeles's text. KEN/3/1/18/4.

54. KEN/3/1/18/4, 2.

55. Kennedy, *The Works of Ralph Vaughan Williams*, 25.

56. KEN/3/1/18/4, 3.

57. Kennedy, *The Works of Ralph Vaughan Williams*, 27.

58. Karpeles referenced the definition in her article "The International Folk Music Council," *Journal of the Folklore Institute* 2/3 (December 1965): 308–13, at 312. The text, agreed upon at the IFMC meeting in São Paulo in 1954, begins: "Folk music is the product of a musical tradition that has evolved through the process of oral transmission. The factors that shape the tradition are as follows: (i) the continuity which links the present with the past; (ii) variation which springs from the creative impulse of the individual or the group; and (iii) selection by the community, which determines the form or forms in which the music survives."

59. Kennedy, *The Works of Ralph Vaughan Williams*, 28.

60. Ibid.

61. Ibid., 33.

62. Ibid., 39.

63. Typed letter on A5 paper, signed in ink. KEN/3/1/25/7.

64. The "wrong note school" refers to the music of Schoenberg, Berg, and Webern. The "Scott" film was the 1948 Ealing Studios feature *Scott of the Antarctic*, produced by Michael Balcon and directed by Charles Frend, starring John Mills. Vaughan Williams later reworked much of the film score as the basis for the *Sinfonia Antartica* (1952).

65. Kennedy reproduces this quotation exactly in *The Works of Ralph Vaughan Williams*, 376.

66. Ink handwritten letter on A5 paper. KEN/3/1/67.

67. William ("Billy") Henry Reed (1876–1942) was an English violinist who studied at the Royal Academy of Music under Emile Sauret and later became leader of the London Symphony Orchestra. He was a close friend of Elgar and gave the premieres of his three late chamber works: Violin Sonata, Op. 82, String Quartet, Op. 83, and Piano Quintet, Op. 84.

68. Typed letter on A5 paper, signed in ink. KEN/3/1/80/2.

69. Typed on A5 sheet in landscape format. Kennedy quotes the letter verbatim in *The Works of Ralph Vaughan Williams*, 346. KEN/3/1/81.

70. Typed draft letter on A5 sheet. KEN/3/1/101.

71. Max Gate is the house which the novelist Thomas Hardy designed and built for himself on the outskirts of Dorchester in southern England, and where he lived until his death in 1928. Like Leith Hill Place, it is now in the care of the National Trust.

"His own idiom": Vaughan Williams's Violin Sonata and the Development of His Melodic Style

O. W. NEIGHBOUR

The following text is based on a digital typescript of musicologist O. W. Neighbour's draft, which remained incomplete at the time of his death in January 2015. The current essay follows the original document closely, with a substantial portion of the early part of the text, which Neighbour had marked "deleted," newly reinstated so as to provide a fuller sense of the underlying argument and its musical context. Other editorial changes are minor. Though Neighbour would surely have elaborated some of his remarks in greater detail if he had been able to oversee a final draft, the editors firmly believe that the value and insight of his commentary more than justify posthumous publication in the present volume. The essay is published with the kind permission of Neighbour's estate.

It need not be the cause of much surprise that the great violinist Joseph Szigeti, who gave the first public performance of Vaughan Williams's Violin Sonata in 1955, should have written to the wife of his piano partner Joseph Levine: "Naturally I want to 'exploit' this valuable 'property' before the work will be printed and on sale, and before the rush will start on this really wonderful Sonata."[1] Years later, in a letter to the composer and publisher Mervyn Horder, Szigeti asked him to tell Ursula Vaughan Williams that he had been unable to locate a tape of one of his "dozen or so performances of the V. W. Violin Sonata at universities in USA around 1959," and commented that "no younger violin 'star' seems to have taken up this fine and challenging work."[2] But why a violin sonata in the first place? That was not a question likely to be asked when the work made its unobtrusive first appearance in a broadcast on Vaughan Williams's eighty-second birthday in October 1954, the year before Szigeti gave its public premiere. The composer's admirers have tended to see the sonata as simply one more example of his continuing vitality in unexpected contexts, while others may have thought it beneath notice. Between them it faded to some extent from view, as Szigeti foresaw, and it has rarely attracted much attention since. Nevertheless, it is probably his finest chamber work, and it is of some interest to ask what prompted its composition. Vaughan Williams liked to write music that he thought might be useful in a particular context and would sometimes provide smaller pieces on request, but, with the exception of his film scores, he seldom accepted commissions. He preferred to write the pieces that he wanted to write and only then dedicate them to friends or performers whom he admired, in the present case to the Canadian-born violinist Frederick Grinke (1911–1987), who gave the first performance with pianist and composer Michael Mullinar (1895–1973). Since there was no obvious call for him to produce such a work, he presumably had reasons of his own for doing so.

It is hard to think of another major work of Vaughan Williams for which a texture of composition or technical procedure appears to have provided the primary impetus. Perhaps the sonata's nearest relative in this respect, however distant in every other, is the Mass in G Minor, a modal study in which unaccented passing notes are the only dissonances permitted. This belongs, with the *Pastoral Symphony* and *The Shepherds of the Delectable Mountains*, to a group of works written immediately after the First World War which, as has long been recognized, occupy a special place in the composer's stylistic development. Vaughan Williams himself was seemingly aware of this shift: in an essay of 1920, he remarked that "idiom is a part of the inspiration."[3] A composer must "discover his vocabulary" to provide the necessary means of expression for what he has to say; "every true composer makes his own idiom." He might have added that, at least by that time, no true composer's idiom could stand still, for he obviously knew that too. Vaughan Williams is unlikely to have had a consistent technical program in mind as he embarked on what would become in some respects the most adventurous and fruitful period of his career. Each more ambitious project made its own demands, so that the vocabulary discovered for one could be developed in another only if the new context required it. But viewed more broadly, the increasing chromaticism from the *Pastoral Symphony*, through *Sancta Civitas*, *Flos campi*, *Riders to the Sea*, *Job*, and the Piano Concerto to the Fourth Symphony, though not a step-by-step progression, is striking. It tends to dominate accounts of Vaughan Williams's output in these years. However, alongside the chromatic exploration there is a diatonic counterpart more easily overlooked. Apart from the exaggerated importance often accorded to chromaticism as somehow forward-looking and progressive, a reason may lie in Vaughan Williams's considerably wider use of diatonic means.

At the risk of some oversimplification, Vaughan Williams may be thought of as having cultivated diatonic modal language in two types of pieces. In one, idiom is as clearly part of the inspiration, and the techniques as various, as in his more chromatic music; each case is special. Some examples, such as the opening scene and the dream in *Job*, build in their own way on elements present in the *Pastoral Symphony*, though not through chromatic bimodality so much as the quieter opposition between lines of parallel triads or intervals. In others, the parts may be single lines, but as in the last section of *Flos campi* the influence of parallelism affects both their relation to one another and their vertical coincidence (in the Hymn Tune Prelude on Gibbons's Song 13, a study in four-part counterpoint, where there are consecutives at every interval from thirds to ninths except the octave). Such a texture allows the musical pulse to weaken or fluctuate. In *Flos campi* itself, the contrapuntal imitations keep their hold on meter, but elsewhere, for example intermittently in "Jane Scroop," the fourth movement of *Five Tudor Portraits*, cross-accentuation between the parts subtly undermines it. The same principle governs the choral setting of prose in the introductory (E-flat) section of "Nation shall not lift up" at the end of *Dona nobis pacem*.

During the 1920s Vaughan Williams established at the same time a kind of general-purpose diatonic manner familiar from many of his works. Dissonant to the extent that most chords or aggregates in the part-writing consist of four or more different notes, usually (though not necessarily) containing a triadic element, the style supports the composer's fertile melodic gift in music that is often eloquent and memorable. This was the style appropriate to three of the no fewer than four operas across four different genres begun between 1924 and 1927 (the exception being *Riders to the Sea*). In opera he wished to provide works that could be enjoyed by all kinds of people. He came nearest to success in his comic opera *Sir John in Love*; with a less impossible libretto his operetta *The Poisoned Kiss* might have run it a close second. But the project by which he set the greatest store, *The Pilgrim's Progress*, did not prosper. After twelve years of intermittent work it ground to a halt in 1936, with at most only the first two of the four acts in first draft. He found himself up against a compositional block. Internal evidence suggests that technique was at the root of it.

Up to the First World War and beyond, Bunyan's by turns moralizing allegory and humorous depiction of everyday characters in the England of his time was familiar to people in all walks of life; many a soldier's kit contained a copy. To Vaughan Williams, with his life-long commitment to social cohesion and belief in the importance of spiritual aspiration, it must have seemed uniquely capable of bringing together his most cherished ideals in a work of the widest appeal. However, it presented considerable practical difficulties. The book's picaresque construction could not easily be converted into stage action, and the frequent ceremonial scenes in which the pilgrim receives all manner of instruction, advice, tokens, armor, and ointments for his safety are by their nature undramatic. That might not have mattered if the promise of eternal life had been matched with more elevated musical expression. But the hymn tune–like vocal style, skilfully devised for the work and no doubt intended through its simplicity to reach a broad popular audience, set limits. The idiom could not be stretched in the service of inspiration.

Vaughan Williams must have seen well enough that the work had taken a direction that did not allow him to achieve what he had hoped: namely, that he could not retain the common touch while reaching for the stars. He abandoned it, as he thought at the time probably for good, and set about embodying the vision that had eluded operatic form in a symphony, his Fifth. In this score, idiom and inspiration could nourish each other freely, whether in the larger structure or in the vocabulary on which it relied.[4] The concluding passacaglia serves to illustrate the point: the music at the beginning, though distinctive, may not at first suggest any new departure. The pervasive mild dissonance in the refined part-writing does not imply any regular metrical pattern, the clear triple meter being supplied by the passacaglia theme and the countersubject with its important overlapping second phrase. Up to the emphatic central turn from major to minor (ten measures after rehearsal number 8), this meter is ever more forcefully stressed (Example 1).

Thereafter the music is notated in common time, although that is initially scarcely perceptible because the accompaniment is static. Rhythm is very fluid; only gradually does the highest note in the passacaglia theme (previously unaccented except where the basic $\frac{3}{4}$ is coupled with implied $\frac{6}{4}$) move to the strong beat. At the climax (rehearsal number 13) which precipitates the return of the first movement material, the theme in severely reduced form lays bare the metrical conflict; it is then reduced still further to emphasize the long-term conflict between the tonal poles C and D. When D major, in doubt since the first bars of the work, quietly but unforgettably makes its definitive return at the beginning of the coda, metrical ambiguity returns with it. The coda is based on three statements of the passacaglia's countersubject, not the theme itself.[5] Both phrases now contain inserted beats to make them compatible with common time. Yet after the first notes of the first statement, the change to D major brings about a harmonic hiatus above the D pedal after which it is almost impossible not

Example 1. Vaughan Williams, Fifth Symphony, fourth movement, ten measures after rehearsal number 8, four measures before rehearsal number 9.

to hear the continuation in the triple time associated with it in the earlier part of the movement. Exactly the same situation arises at the second statement of the countersubject (rehearsal number 16 in the score), even though the harmony is different and the new D pedal enters a crotchet beat (quarter note) earlier. There are times when the counterpoint leaves the scansion open; it is only toward the end that off-beat stretto entries over the last D pedal establish duple time unequivocally, only to lose their hold as contrary motion drifts slowly toward the final D-major harmony. If the coda is felt to transcend in some sense all that precedes it, one reason must lie in the special use of the idiom to loosen metrical ties.[6]

The Fourth and Fifth symphonies mark a watershed in Vaughan Williams's output. They are the culminating points in the respective chromatic and diatonic explorations that had occupied him since the First World War. Now, it seems, both veins had been worked out, in so far as their vocabularies no longer inspired new developments. Technical stimulus remained as important as ever, but now less closely bound up with the detail of the idiom. In the Second Quartet, motivic density became the guiding principle; in the Sixth Symphony, the challenge was to incorporate the broader effects of the film music which had absorbed so much of his time since the early phase of the Second World War, in a structure as cogent as that which he had achieved in its two intermediate predecessors. True, he found a new idiom for his *Antarctic* film music and symphony; it involved a great leap of the imagination but was difficult to integrate with his more usual habits of thought and remained largely a thing apart. In particular, it was calculated to freeze out rather than encourage any melodic expansion. While at work on the Sixth and Seventh symphonies the composer pushed on with *The Pilgrim's Progress*, apparently hoping against hope that something of his original conception could be salvaged; his bitter disappointment at its poor reception was surely due in part to a fear that his earlier doubts had been justified. However that may be, the special style of the work did not favor lengthy melodic continuations, just as the *Antarctic* idiom had proven by its very nature inimical to them. The scene was set for a change in the melodic sphere.

It was this expansion of melodic scale and range that was ushered in by the Violin Sonata in 1953–54. The previous two years had seen the completion of two large-scale undertakings, but relatively little that was new. A great deal of 1951 was taken up with worries over the first production of *The Pilgrim's Progress* and with its subsequent revision, and the year was overshadowed by the illness and death in April of the composer's first wife, Adeline. Labors on the *Sinfonia Antartica* dragged on through most of 1952. However, with the return of a more ordered existence after his marriage to Ursula Wood early in 1953 he was ready for fresh projects. Much of the work on the Tuba Concerto, the Violin Sonata, and the nativity cantata *Hodie* was undertaken in 1953, although they were not completed and performed till the following year. In addition, he began thinking about the Eighth Symphony and took up sketches that he had made some ten years before for a Cello Concerto and then abandoned. It was not unusual for him to be occupied with several works at the same time, often as disparate as these. But it seems that on this occasion he also had in mind a technical challenge which left none of them untouched, to which the sonata holds the key.

What must be the very first sketch for the first movement is found in a sketchbook that seems to have been reserved for preliminary jottings rather than more continuous drafts.[7] Although brief, it reveals that the idea of setting the main melody against its diminution (and the inversion of this) was present from the start. The interplay of related strands dominates the movement and gives rise to an outpouring of unfettered melody owing little to the symmetries and points of articulation, founded ultimately in loosened stanzaic patterns, such as had usually supported Vaughan Williams's longer melodic paragraphs; a few motivic recurrent shapes suffice to ensure continuity of character. Similar melodic principles govern the second and third movements of the work.

These rather surprisingly take earlier pieces as their starting point. The *furioso* scherzo is based on music for *49th Parallel* (1940), the first film for which Vaughan Williams provided the score. The action starts with the appearance of a German submarine in Canadian waters and its destruction; the rest of the film depicts the long trek of a few Nazi survivors across Canada in their ultimately unsuccessful attempt to reach the safety of the at that time still neutral United States.[8] Like Debussy in the second of his wartime scores *En blanc et noir* (1915), Vaughan Williams uses the Lutheran chorale "Ein' feste Burg" to represent the German enemy, but subjects it to far greater fragmentation and distortion, suggesting the Nazis' perversion of their national heritage. Deformed versions of phrases from the chorale accompany the first sighting of the submarine and symbolize the Nazi threat at later points of the score. Toward the end of the film, for example, a cue for "Nazis on the run" originally comprised a fast toccata-like movement driven by shifting accents and employing motifs derived from the chorale, especially the first and fifth lines. For Vaughan Williams, remembering Thomas Carlyle's translation adopted in many hymnals (including those edited by himself), these lines would have carried the words "the ancient prince of hell hath risen with purpose fell." Although it is a movement over which Vaughan Williams evidently took much trouble, different music was eventually substituted for the running Nazis and the original piece was moved forward to the "Control room alert" scene when the submarine is first spotted; here, it mainly accompanies a Morse-code operator and passes almost without notice. Yet

Example 2. Vaughan Williams, Quintet in C Minor (1903), third movement, Fantasia (quasi variazione), main theme.

Example 3. Vaughan Williams, Sonata in A Minor, third movement, Tema con variazione, main theme.

Vaughan Williams attached special importance to the sequence, and after it had lost its place in the concert suite drawn from the film score, which he withdrew, he entirely refashioned it to form the sonata scherzo, which takes its own course with the addition of one or two new figures and hurtles on for over twice the length of the orchestral version. It now barely hints at the characteristic four-note motif from the beginning of the chorale-tune, and although the ancient prince of hell and his closer or more distant progeny are ubiquitous, they are made almost unrecognizable for those who are unaware of the source. What remains is a more generalized but no less powerful evocation of danger essential to the trajectory of the sonata, which echoes that of a much earlier and very different work.

This is overtly referred to in the concluding variations, the theme of which is taken from that of the similarly placed set in the posthumously published Piano Quintet in C minor of 1903, with each of its long constituent phrases further lengthened and its accompanying harmony replaced (Examples 2 and 3).

The variations in both works are very free but have scarcely anything else in common. In his last years Vaughan Williams borrowed several ideas from unpublished early works,[9] but he may have had more than one reason for his choice in the present case. In the Quintet the first phrase of the variation theme, with its distinctive rhythm, irrupts *fortissimo* in the development of the first movement, and less violently but still *minacciando* in the second. Any unsettling effect it may have had is then smoothed away as the same rhythm takes its place in the even course of the slow variation theme. In the Violin Sonata the theme has not been anticipated in the earlier movements but performs the same office, introducing calm after the whirlwind counterpoint of a scherzo originating in a much greater though now unspecified Nazi menace. Naturally, Vaughan Williams did not need to go back fifty years to create this dramatic contrast. The theme had additional potential, for its long, leisurely lines could be treated in free imitation or canon, often by inversion, and so balance without replicating the procedures used in the first movement. The composer's development of constantly evolving melody unites the three movements in a compelling whole.

The chronology of the pieces begun in 1953 is very uncertain; the Tuba Concerto, with its melodically expansive slow movement, may have been completed before the Violin Sonata. However, it is in the latter work that the conscious adoption of new technical means is unmistakable. Perhaps the composer's reconsideration of the Cello Concerto sketches provided the impetus.[10] These date from about the time of the Second Quartet, with which they share a motivic economy that proved less well suited to an appropriately concertante style. They also seem to strive for the kind of free melodic flow later achieved in the sonata. If the sonata was intended to find solutions to the concerto's ills, it may merely have confirmed a diagnosis rather than supplying a cure. In any case, the composer clearly remained dissatisfied with the concerto: he would surely have found time to finish it had he thought it possible to do so.

At the same time, however, he continued to exploit the rich melodic vein that he had opened up in the sonata in all his major works from then on. This is obvious enough in the finely worked songs, whether in stanza form or through-composed, in *Hodie* and in the Cavatina of the Eighth Symphony.[11] But it is in the Ninth Symphony that he draws the most far-reaching consequences from his preoccupation with linear prolongation. As in the sonata, lines invariably develop in lengthy passages of imitative or contrasted counterpoint, though naturally the orchestral texture allows for much greater complexity than the chamber work. The result is a new kind of symphonic thinking quite distinct from that of the earlier symphonies, particularly in the first movement and the second half of the finale. In the former, it is the vehicle for an opening sonata structure recognizably related to others by the composer; in the latter, the almost continuous polyphony itself plays a part in shaping the music's course right through to the impressive close, while the pervasive turbulent character of both is intensified by the frequent jostling of lines in duple and triple meter against one another. These troubled movements are among the most powerful things in Vaughan Williams's entire output. To have found the language for them, or to have imagined a conception that required it, was an extraordinary final achievement.

1. Letter of 8 July 1955, part of Lot 382 in Sotheby's sale of 21 May 1998. [The Sonata was premiered via BBC broadcast on 12 October 1954, and then received its first public performance at the Rochester Civic Music Association in Rochester, New York, on 14 November 1955. —Ed.].

2. Letter of 29 November 1972, no. 773 in May & May's catalogue no. 201 of May 1992. The loss of Szigeti's interpretation is unfortunate, but there is at least one excellent recording, by Hugh Bean and David Parkhouse. The following is a no doubt incomplete list of errors remaining in the corrected issue (1968) of the printed score; corrections are from the autograph. P. 1, vln, last bar, 1st note: C not A; p. 5, system 1, bar 3, RH, beat 3: top note B♭, not D♭; p. 15, system 2, bar 3, RH, eighth note 2: should be eighth note c, not c- and b♮-sixteenth notes; p. 17, system 4, bar 1, RH, beat 2: top A should be A♯; p. 26, system 2, bar 1, RH, 3rd chord: bottom note F not G♭; next bar, LH, 2nd chord: 2nd note from top should surely be F♯, though autograph has G; same page, system 4, bar 1, LH, 1st chord: top note A not B♭; p. 27, system 3, bar 4, RH, 1st eighth note: D should be D♭; p. 40, vln cadenza, 5th group of thirty-second notes (AGAC) should be sixteenth notes.

3. Ralph Vaughan Williams, "Gustav Holst," *Music & Letters* 1 (1920): 181–90, 305–17, at 311. Reprinted in Ralph Vaughan Williams, *Some thoughts on Beethoven's Choral Symphony, with writings on other musical subjects* (London: Oxford University Press, 1953), 64–93, at 86.

4. See especially Arnold Whittall, "'Symphony in D Major': Models and Mutations," in *Vaughan Williams Studies*, ed. Alain Frogley (Cambridge: Cambridge University Press, 1996), 187–212.

5. To be exact, phrases 1 and 2, the same again with the addition of a second (slightly lengthened) statement of phrase 2, and phrase 1 accompanying the only recurrence in the coda of the passacaglia theme.

6. Both phrases of the countersubject end in a stepwise descent to the tonic, versions of which close the very first and last vocal phrases in the opera (both sung by Bunyan) and many of the hymn-like tunes in between; they contribute to the work's musical identity. It is worth noting that although the stretto at the end of the symphony employs such a phrase the sense of closure typical of the opera is avoided.

7. The manuscript source in the British Library, GB-Lbl Add. Ms 50482 B, contains very vague sketches under the heading "Symphony," in which only a short phrase from the Cavatina of the Symphony No. 8 can be recognized, soon overtaken by ideas for the Tuba Concerto. These are followed by sketches for the Violin Sonata, another for a viola or cello concerto containing only a non-thematic single-line gesture, an appendix to *The Pilgrim's Progress* no doubt in anticipation of the Cambridge production of February 1954, and sketches for *Hodie* interspersed with carols not belonging to it and headed "Christmas Oratorio" (when published, the word "cantata" was inappropriately substituted, reversing the case of *Sancta Civitas*, surely more cantata than oratorio).

8. For more detailed accounts of the film and its music, see Annika Forkert's discussion in the present volume; Jeffrey Richards, "Vaughan Williams and British Wartime Cinema" in *Vaughan Williams Studies*, 139–65; and Daniel Goldmark, "Music, Film and Vaughan Williams," in *Vaughan Williams Essays*, ed. Byron Adams and Robin Wells (Aldershot: Ashgate, 2003), 207–33.

9. Other examples include a tune from *The Solent* (1902–3) which ended up in the Ninth Symphony after a couple of stops on the way. See Michael Kennedy, *A Catalogue of the Works of Ralph Vaughan Williams*, 2nd ed. (Oxford: Oxford University Press, 1980), 20; and the theme of the Variations for Brass Band, which is taken from the *Heroic Elegy and Triumphal Epilogue* (1900–1901).

10. GB-Lbl Add Ms 57292 contains an unbroken three-stave draft of the Cello Concerto's opening Rhapsody, reaching a convincing conclusion. It is marked "fair copy," but Vaughan Williams habitually marked new drafts in that way, often meaning only that it was fairer than the last one; he is very unlikely to have regarded this version as final. The other two movements break off much earlier.

11. Some free-wheeling speculation may be offered here in an attempt to explain the puzzling claim in his dedication of *Hodie* to Herbert Howells that he had cribbed a phrase in it from the latter's *Hymnus Paradisi*. When asked about it, Vaughan Williams said that he could not remember what it was; nor could Howells identify it. However, the prelude to the sixth section of the Howells work is based on the motif that opens Vaughan Williams's Eighth Symphony. I have argued elsewhere ("The Place of the Eighth Among Vaughan Williams's Symphonies," in Frogley, *Vaughan Williams Studies*, 213–33, at 231–32) that this motif derives from Holst, which for both musical and contextual reasons seems much more likely. But if it was the Howells that reminded him of the Holst in the first place, it would have been typical of Vaughan Williams to feel guilty about not acknowledging his debt. Since the real debt was to Holst he thrust the matter to the back of his mind, though without managing to lay it entirely to rest. In the end, by an odd psychological twist he made an acknowledgement that was very vague, and attached it to the wrong work.

Critical Reception: Early Performances of the Symphony No. 9 in E Minor

INTRODUCED AND ANNOTATED BY
ALAIN FROGLEY

"Vaughan Williams, 85 and deaf, scores a hit." Thus proclaimed the headline of Arthur Jacobs's *Sunday Dispatch* review of the premiere of the composer's Ninth Symphony on 2 April 1958.[1] As a window onto the initial reception of this symphony and of Vaughan Williams's late music in general, the breezy tabloid tone of the Jacobs headline perhaps reveals more than its staid counterparts in the broadsheet press. While a poignant reminder that popular papers such as the *Dispatch* still regularly covered "serious" music (not just controversies surrounding the Last Night of the Proms), by 1958 the term "hit" was more likely to evoke for its readers the new world of pop music, especially imported American rock 'n' roll, and by implication a postwar Britain in the throes of rapid social and cultural upheaval. While the Sixties were not yet swinging, deference was in decline, and the Angry Young Men of the Fifties were already taking an ax to hallowed British assumptions and institutions.[2] By 1958, Vaughan Williams had become one such institution; as remarkable as scoring a "hit," one may surmise, is that he was composing at all at "85 and deaf."

This is to read much—perhaps too much—into an eight-word headline. I have lingered on it, however, because both the headline and the review that follows encapsulate several key themes expressed more decorously but nevertheless pointedly in many other reviews of the symphony's premiere. Although skillfully tailored to engage a middlebrow audience, Jacobs's review (reproduced in full below) is serious and sympathetic in its response to the symphony. But in attempting to tackle head-on the issue of originality, about which he found "some music-lovers tut-tutting," even Jacobs finds that the work does not break significantly new ground, except in expanding the orchestral palette to include three saxophones and a flugelhorn (though in Vaughan Williams's defense he rebuts the idea that a composer must demonstrate an "advance" from one work in a genre to the next). For some other reviewers, the issue went deeper, suggesting not just a lack of progress, but a kind of regress: the symphony seemed to recycle ideas presented more compellingly in the composer's earlier works, the Sixth Symphony (also in E minor) in particular. Even those who were markedly more positive did not apparently hear much that seemed distinctively new (though there was much talk of the saxophones and flugelhorn, both for and against). Indeed, while the symphony may have been "a hit" with the packed Royal Festival Hall audience at its premiere, the critical response was lukewarm overall, and in some cases outright patronizing. As Ursula Vaughan Williams comments in her biography of the composer, "It was what he had meant, but for some reason it was one of the most difficult of his works to get hold of."[3] It is hard to escape the impression that even among his supporters, Vaughan Williams had become a prisoner of preconceptions around what he had achieved and what he represented: most listeners were not open to hearing new directions in his work. This sealed the fate of the Ninth Symphony for several decades thereafter. It received few performances after Vaughan Williams's death, and only in recent years has it begun to enjoy something of a revival.

One may nevertheless sympathize to some degree with the critics. Vaughan Williams is almost unique among composers in having produced a whole string of major works, including five of his nine symphonies, after his seventieth birthday, and this creative arc challenged well-established tropes of a coherent career narrative. By the end of the Second World War, and after a Fifth Symphony (premiered in 1943) in which many heard serene valediction, it had seemed safe to assume that Vaughan Williams would wind down gently. Although the premiere of the Sixth Symphony in 1948 initially came as a violent shock, retrospectively it could be assimilated by analogy with the similarly turbulent Fourth. But the last three symphonies, written essentially back-to-back and appearing between 1953 and 1958, presented a different kind of challenge—or challenges. The imposing, programmatic *Sinfonia Antartica*, based on the composer's score for the film *Scott of the Antarctic* (1948), was followed by the relatively light and subtle (and untitled) Eighth Symphony, which was then itself countered in turn by the largely somber Ninth. Despite their outward contrasts, however, the three works are not as sharply differentiated in relation to one another as the composer's preceding trio of symphonies. For the most part they eschew both unbridled violence and unclouded diatonicism, sharing instead a new synthesis in which expressive emphasis shifts rapidly, sometimes from measure to measure or chord to chord. An important agent of synthesis (or at least combination) is the brusque juxtaposition of contrasted ideas, a technique common in the composer's late works in general and likely shaped in part by Vaughan Williams's intensive involvement with film music during the 1940s. Composing music to enliven a rapid succession of cinematic images may also have encouraged a newly experimental approach to timbre in the late symphonies, manifested most directly in an expanded orchestral palette, particularly in terms of percussion, and in the Ninth by the inclusion of the flugelhorn and saxophones.

Whereas recent commentators have focused increasingly on what is new, for some even radical, in Vaughan Williams's late music,[4] it is perhaps hardly surprising that this element eluded most of his contemporaries—at least in the last two symphonies—the *Sinfonia Antartica*, even if not universally embraced, wore its novelties more conspicuously. At a time when major newspapers no doubt kept on file a draft of his obituary in readiness for the sorry day, and when a critical establishment still struggling with the mature Benjamin Britten had to deal with the incursions of a youthful postwar avant-garde, it was easier to understand Vaughan Williams in terms of the past than the present. Among younger critics, a backlash against Vaughan Williams had already begun. In 1955, a year before the premiere of the Eighth Symphony, Donald Mitchell had thoughtfully but trenchantly presented the case for the prosecution—at least as it appeared to one of Britten's closest and most articulate supporters.[5] For Mitchell, Vaughan Williams was a victim of his own nationalist revolution and a prisoner of his mannerisms, with a compositional technique not fit for purpose; posterity would likely view him as a brave pioneer, but ultimately no more than a "major minor" composer. It was an unfortunate—if in the circumstances perhaps inevitable—aspect of the rise of Britten that he and his circle manifested an almost Oedipal drive to topple Vaughan Williams from his pedestal in national musical life.

In this increasingly challenging environment, Vaughan Williams may himself have raised a further obstacle to a full appreciation of the Ninth Symphony. Programmatic ideas had played a crucial role in the genesis of the work, but the composer kept private all details of this background. Sketches and other evidence make possible the reconstruction of a dense network of allusions, centered on a theme of pilgrimage and innocent sacrifice, that refers, in approximate order of appearance by movement, to Bach's *St. Matthew Passion* (I), Stonehenge and Hardy's *Tess of the d'Urbervilles* (II), the story of a ghostly drummer haunting Salisbury Plain (II and III), and, finally, Salisbury Cathedral (IV). Although the composer eventually decided to keep this program largely to himself, I have argued elsewhere that it was integral to the conception and composition of the symphony.[6] All that Vaughan Williams offered his listeners, in the notes he provided to the work, was a teasing acknowledgment that the second movement "started off with a programme, but it got lost on the journey—so now, oh no, now we never mention it—and the music must be left to speak for itself—whatever that may mean."[7] It is indeed in this movement, based on the final tragic events of Hardy's *Tess*, that the narrative seems to have been worked out in most detail; and it is also here that one may be most inclined to question the composer's decision to withhold this information: despite tight underlying motivic and tonal organization, the episodic surface of the movement can be difficult to grasp, and a number of early reviewers were evidently perplexed by it. More broadly, many seem to have struggled to find an interpretative key to the symphony as a whole. This may account for the disproportionate amount of space allotted in many reviews to the work's novel instrumentation, its echoes of the composer's earlier works, and his frequently flippant program notes.

Another factor that may have weighed on the symphony's initial reception was that the circumstances surrounding the first performance were less than ideal. The premiere was given by the Royal Philharmonic Orchestra under Malcolm Sargent (the work is dedicated to the Royal Philharmonic Society). Although Sargent admired Vaughan Williams and was familiar with his music, he was not a trusted interpreter of the caliber of Adrian Boult or John Barbirolli, who had between them launched the composer's three preceding symphonies (Boult the Sixth, Barbirolli the *Sinfonia Antartica* and the Eighth). At least two of those closest to the composer at the time had grave reservations about the performance. Future biographer Michael Kennedy felt that it "did not do the work full justice"; the composer's amanuensis Roy Douglas went much further, proffering in his memoir of working with Vaughan Williams a scathing denunciation of Sargent's whole approach to the symphony.[8] Matters were surely not helped by the shortage of rehearsal time allotted—Vaughan Williams himself had to pay for the first, and main, orchestral rehearsal on 21 March.[9] The dense orchestration employed in many parts of the symphony requires careful balance, and its fragmented formal processes depend on sensitive performance to cohere and retain momentum. That said, the critics were almost entirely complimentary about Sargent and the orchestra's account of the work. Of course, with a new and unfamiliar work, and a first performance that is at least efficient, it can be difficult to discern deeper interpretative weaknesses until a more extensive performance history has accumulated.

The selection of reviews chosen here is representative but not comprehensive. I have omitted a number of shorter newspaper reviews, and some longer accounts that appeared outside the main daily press and journal literature and do not significantly add to the range of opinion expressed here. The symphony was performed on two additional occasions between the April premiere and the composer's death on 26 August, at a BBC Proms concert on 5 August, with Sargent conducting the BBC Symphony Orchestra, and at the Vancouver Festival in Canada on 10 August, with William Steinberg conducting the Vancouver International Festival Orchestra. Barely a month after Vaughan Williams's death, Leopold Stokowski and the Philadelphia Orchestra gave the American premiere of the Ninth Symphony at Carnegie Hall. I have included two reviews of the Proms performance, and one reporting on the American premiere. The consistently laudatory tenor of the American review contrasts with much of the British reception, and is an example of the stature that Vaughan Williams enjoyed in the United States, where his reputation had grown steadily since the 1920s and attained an extraordinary peak in the 1950s.

As for the critics themselves, they include a number of the leading figures of the day, and represent several different generations and perspectives. These ranged from the "establishment" voice of Frank Howes (1891–1974) at the *Times* (an admirer who had written a book about Vaughan Williams) to younger and often more skeptical critics such as Felix Aprahamian (1914–2005) and Colin Mason (1924–1971).[10] Mason published what was in some aspects the harshest review of the Ninth, though he had been impressed by the *Sinfonia Antartica*. Perhaps the most surprising review, and one of the most discerning, came from an older critic and giant of British journalism, the maverick music and cricket enthusiast Neville Cardus (1888–1975). This was a critic whom Vaughan Williams had considered "allergic" to his music;[11] yet Cardus's review of the August Prom performance boldly argued that the Ninth Symphony, rather than rehashing the past, represented an important new step forward in the development of the composer's musical language. Nevertheless, in one respect the strongest endorsement was left to Harold C. Schonberg (1915–2003), the influential critic of the *New York Times*: he was the only writer to dub the score unequivocally "a masterpiece." It would be decades before such an assessment would once again become a serious strand in the critical discourse surrounding the work. The Ninth Symphony may well continue to divide opinion to some extent—indeed, at one level equivocation is woven deeply into its fabric—but we are certainly now better able than ever to appreciate its unique expressive qualities, and its place within Vaughan Williams's extraordinary creative oeuvre.

Philharmonic Concert
Vaughan Williams's
New Symphony
The Times, Thursday, 3 April 1958, 3

This review included no byline, but was undoubtedly written by Frank Howes, then chief music critic at the Times.

The first performance of Vaughan Williams's new symphony, No. 9 in E Minor, dedicated like another Ninth Symphony to the Royal Philharmonic Society, made last night's Philharmonic concert at the Festival Hall a great occasion. It was flanked in the programme by two other notable works which are not often to be heard, Kodaly's Concerto for Orchestra and Berlioz's *Harold in Italy*. Sir Malcolm Sargent, conducting the Royal Philharmonic Orchestra, was a brilliant advocate for all three works.

Vaughan Williams's new symphony is in the line of No. 4 and No. 6. It deals with strife and the world's evil. The first two movements are alike in outlook though there is menace, acknowledged as such, in the second, which is the slow, though not very slow, movement of the symphony. In the scherzo, as in other of his scherzos, the sinister elements are externalized. One of its themes had been already heard at the organ recital which preceded the concert, when M. André Marchal extemporized on it in such a way as to show that he had some acquaintance with Vaughan Williams's hobgoblins and foul fiends. The finale does not end in triumph, for this is a stoic symphony. It does conclude with the survival of the human spirit—the last cadence of all in E major is suffused with a gentleness that signifies so much. There is no abatement of vigour or originality in our octogenarian symphonist, nor can one really think that at his age he has any illusions to lose, but the general mood of the symphony is dark. The new element in No. 8, tone colour for the fun of it, survives in No. 9 in the use of a flugel horn, three saxophones (which in V. W. are not the demented cats of his own irreverent programme note but the wily hypocrites of *Job*) and a gong. The only substantial novelty of form is the double structure of the finale, which is not immediately self-revealing. As so often before, the prophetic quality of Vaughan Williams's mind reveals aspects of the world in which we live.

[*The final paragraph of the review, which deals with the Kodály and Berlioz works, is omitted here.*]

Vaughan Williams's Ninth Symphony
Dedicated to Royal Philharmonic Society

by Colin Mason

The Manchester Guardian, Thursday, 3 April 1958, 5

London, Wednesday.

The new symphony by Vaughan Williams, his ninth, is dedicated to the Royal Philharmonic Society. It was given its first performance by Sir Malcolm Sargent and the Royal Philharmonic Orchestra at the Society's concert in the Royal Festival Hall to-night. The key is E minor, the same as that of the sixth, and the composer has followed the precedent he set with that work of introducing his symphonies with a facetious analytical programme note of his own, in which he tilts at the professional analysers of musical forms. Many of his targets are Aunt Sallies.[12] Even in Vaughan Williams's youth there can hardly have been anybody left who thought the second subject of a symphony in E minor should necessarily be in G major, and though there may still be a few academicians at the Royal College of Music who would be perturbed by the return to the home key without the principal subject, in the living world of music these bogeys have been laid these 50 years.

Other strange notions nod in this composer's head. There is a march theme in the slow movement described by him as "barbaric." Later in the movement there is a "menacing" stroke of the gong, introducing a "sinister" recapitulation of an earlier theme. This is no more sinister than that harmless olde-modal mixolydian theme in the last movement of the Eighth Symphony, for which the composer proposed the same adjective. The gong stroke makes no effect at all, and the supposedly barbaric march theme, in the pseudo-Chinese vein of the Eighth Symphony, is the silliest and poorest music in the work. The composer also makes much to do about the lack of apparent thematic logic in this movement, which we are expected to scratch our dunderheads over. It is of a perfectly sound, not at all revolutionary, and not at all puzzling construction. Mixed with the march music it has some of the most attractive material in the work. The gentle opening melody (unusually scored for flugel horn, an instrument scarcely known in England outside the brass band) and the extended lyrical middle section, with a new flowing tune, leave a pleasurable impression in spite of the frivolous interruptions.

This is the second movement of the four. The first opens with a strong and splendid ascending theme said by the composer to have been suggested by something in the opening of Bach's St. Matthew Passion. It bears a strong resemblance, in both shape and character, to the theme of "aspiration" in the Sinfonia Antartica. As in the Eighth Symphony, this is the finest and most serious movement of four, with very few lapses into routine or aimless meandering. The form is of a similar originality and subtlety, and every stage in the development of the theme adds something to the breadth and interest of the movement. The most prominent secondary theme seems to unwind from the opening of the first, as is true of various themes throughout the work. After the slow movement comes an interesting scherzo of fairly extended design, less original but more ambitious than the scherzo of no. 8. In the competition between the witty and the commonplace, wit wins by a few lengths. There is a good deal of excellent counterpoint here too, of more compositional weight than its jocular spirit might at first suggest, as well as a chorale played by three saxophones, which have a fairly prominent part in the score.

The last movement returns to the serious mood of the first. Unlike the last movements of the Sixth, Seventh, and Eighth symphonies, which are respectively an epilogue, a flash-back, and what Elgar would have called a "jape," this is a summing-up. It is dominated by the opening theme from the first movement, and its other material consists largely of transformations of earlier themes in the symphony, worked into a form of a strength and coherence more readily perceived than defined. It is in this movement and the first that the main weight of the work is concentrated, and the first impression of them promises a lasting musical satisfaction likely to outweigh objection to the various weaknesses of the middle movements.

9th Vaughan Williams Symphony
Jocose Vitality
by Martin Cooper
The Daily Telegraph, Thursday, 3 April 1958, 10

Martin du Pré Cooper (1910–1986) was a British musicologist best known for his 1951 volume French Music.

It can safely be presumed that a composer who writes a symphony at the age of 85 does so for his own satisfaction and no other reason.

Now if ever he can afford to pull a long nose at the so-called rules, even if he obeys many of them from second nature.

It was in this spirit, to judge from his own jocose programme notes, that Dr. Vaughan Williams wrote his ninth symphony which had its first performance at the Festival Hall last night.

This is a bigger, generally more serious work than No. 8 and shows at least occasional affinities with two of the composer's finest creations—the sixth symphony (whose key of E minor it shares) and "Job."

Note of fantasy

There is a very personal note of fantasy in the orchestration, including a flugelhorn, whose mellifluous tone dominates much of the slow movement, and a choir of saxophones.

In the Scherzo—perhaps the most successful of the four movements—these announce a theme whose rhythm and shape recall "The Teddy Bears' Picnic" rather than Job's comforters, though honour is saved by their eventually uniting in a mock chorale.

Formally the music coheres by association and contrast (or is it sometimes the fashionable technique of "alienation"?) rather than according to the textbook rules of symphonic development and its easy yet original sequence of thought and feeling must convince all but the pedant.

Prophetic glimpses

There is certainly evidence of abounding vitality in each of the very different movements and both the first and last contain glimpses of the old prophetic manner. These are nonetheless impressive for being interspersed with excursions into a world of humour from which all sardonic feeling is absent.

Under Sir Malcolm Sargent the Royal Philharmonic Orchestra gave a lively and eloquent account of the new work. The programme also included Berlioz's "Harold in Italy" in which Frederick Riddle was the admirable soloist, and Kodaly's seldom-heard concerto for orchestra.

Vaughan Williams, 85 and Deaf, Scores a Hit

by Arthur Jacobs

The Sunday Dispatch, 6 April 1958, 3

At 85 you are lucky to be living, doubly lucky to be active. As for composing a symphony at that age—well, just let us say that Vaughan Williams's Ninth Symphony, first heard last Wednesday at the Festival Hall, is almost without parallel in the history of music.

Vaughan Williams has become very deaf. But, despite what counts as a major affliction for a musician (Beethoven had it, too), he has kept up an interest in new sounds.

Big success

Into the orchestra of the Ninth Symphony he has brought a flugelhorn (a brass band instrument, with a tone somewhere between a cornet and an orchestral horn) and three saxophones.

Ten years ago, a mere stripling of 75, Vaughan Williams scored a major success with his Sixth Symphony. Sir Malcolm Sargent and the Royal Philharmonic Orchestra showed the new symphony to be out of the same stable.

It is sometimes harsh, sometimes questioning, sometimes beautifully meditative. It sometimes bursts into galumphing tunes, which sound like an elephant's sports day.

But just because it brings reminders of Vaughan Williams's older compositions—I could tick off half a dozen—I found some music-lovers tut-tutting about it. "Not original," they said.

Salute it

Well, really! When Haydn came to London in the 1790s with 12 symphonies specially written for the occasion, did people demand that No. 104 should show some sort of advance on No. 93? Of course not.

I salute the new symphony. And I salute a composer who can poke fun at the composers and musical commentators by writing such a facetious programme-note as he provided for listeners at the premiere. *Sample:* "When the tune is finished, the side drum goes on by itself and quietly taps itself to death."

Another Ninth

by Felix Aprahamian

The Sunday Times, 6 April 1958, 9

Vaughan Williams's ninth symphony received its first performance at Festival Hall on Wednesday from the R.P.O. under Sir Malcolm Sargent. Like another Ninth associated with the Royal Philharmonic Society, it proved unconventional, but there the resemblance ends.

Senior composers have licence to indulge their fancies; the later Strauss simplified his harmony and revelled in being an old fogey while cocking a snook at certain stylistic textbook conventions. Vaughan Williams's *materia musica* remain fundamentally unaltered since the days of "Job," but his particular foible now is orchestral colour. In the eighth symphony he rediscovered instruments that could be hit—although that is the least significant feature of a delightful work. In his ninth, he adds to a normal score some that are blown—a flügelhorn and a trio of saxophones—but their participation is not intrusive.

At first hearing, only the opening *allegro*[13] seems sure of itself. Sturdily built, it calls for no explanatory key. The other three sections are more discursive. They consist of a slow movement that juggles with several disparate elements—including a tune for the flügelhorn which would sound equally well on a more common orchestral instrument—a scherzo as grotesque as any, and an extended finale rather like a long fresco which retains the interest of the viewer's eye while he scans it but which leaves him questioning its unity. The composer's own bantering analysis of the work leaves the listener guessing at the programmatic basis it would appear to have. Nevertheless, the contrapuntal second half of this last movement is R. V. W. at his truest.

Vaughan Williams's Ninth Symphony
by Harold F. Rutland
"Opera, Ballet and Concert Notices: London," *The Musical Times*
99/1383 (May 1958): 272

Harold F. Rutland (1900–1977) was a music critic, composer, editor, and pianist.

The whole of musical London, as well as many distinguished visitors from elsewhere, seemed to have gathered in the Festival Hall for the Royal Philharmonic Society's concert on 2 April, when Sir Malcolm Sargent conducted the Royal Philharmonic Orchestra in the first performance of Vaughan Williams's Symphony No. 9 in E minor. This, like Beethoven's Ninth Symphony, is dedicated to the Society. It was completed last November and it reveals, as did its predecessor, No. 8, an interest in unusual sonorities, since to the normal symphony orchestra are added three saxophones (which are not expected, in the composer's words, 'to behave like demented cats') and a flugelhorn (which is also 'obliged to sit up and play straight'). In a programme note for whose flippancy any other writer would have been severely reprimanded, and with the aid of no fewer than twenty-four music examples, the composer described the four movements of his Symphony, from its fugal-like opening on the brass, through a slow movement with a "barbaric march theme," a grotesque, Dukas-like scherzo, to a finale in two sections, with an expansive close.

To have written a large-scale work of such interest and vitality at the age of eighty-four or so is an astonishing, almost unprecedented feat: Verdi, after all, was a mere eighty when *Falstaff* was produced. However, admirer of Vaughan Williams though I am, I cannot pretend that at a first hearing the new Symphony made a strong appeal to me: its basic material struck me as derivative and undistinguished, its structure as wanting in firmness. But it may be that on further acquaintance the echoes of earlier works, such as *Job* and the Sixth Symphony, will seem less obtrusive. It is plain that Vaughan Williams enjoyed writing it; it was equally plain that the audience enjoyed listening to it. The performance appeared to meet with the full approval of the composer, and after the orchestra had taken its bow at the bidding of Sir Malcolm Sargent, he disappeared from the platform, to reappear in a flash in the ceremonial box, where he joined hands with the composer while receiving the further acclamations of the audience. The Symphony was preceded by Kodály's attractive Concerto for Orchestra, and followed by Berlioz's *Harold in Italy*, in which Frederick Riddle gave a splendid account of the part for solo viola.

Composer at the Proms:
Vaughan Williams Hears Symphony
The Times, 6 August 1958, 4

*There is no byline, but the review was probably written by William Mann (1924–
1989), then assistant music critic on the paper.*

Dr. Vaughan Williams himself was in last night's large Prom audience to hear
Sir Malcolm Sargent and the B.B.C. Symphony Orchestra give the first performance at these concerts of his ninth symphony; in years to come many a
young Promenader may recall the occasion with pride and pleasure.

In this symphony Vaughan Williams maintains his search for new sonorities (he augments the orchestra with three saxophones and a flugelhorn) but
not necessarily for new things to say. In fact nearly all the themes serve to
remind us of the things we have known longest and loved most in this composer's musical personality through the years, and even if here they return
with less compulsion than of old in the two central movements, the *Andante
Sostenuto* and the *Allegro pesante* (this is the least worthy movement of the
four), the opening and closing movements carry enough strength and nobility of purpose in themselves to give the work true symphonic stature.

[*The last part of the review, which reports on the performances of Peter Racine
Fricker's* Dance Scene *and Beethoven's "Emperor" Piano Concerto that made up
the remainder of concert, is omitted here.*]

Musical Satisfaction at the Promenade Concerts
by Neville Cardus
The Manchester Guardian, 7 August 1958, 3

[*The first part of the review, which reports on several other performances from the preceding week of Proms concerts, is omitted here.*]

Tuesday's concert also included the Ninth Symphony of Vaughan Williams, an astonishing production from a composer in his eighty-sixth year. Much of the technical formulas are familiar: his music is much an art of cadence, with blocks of harmony the supporting pillars. But this Ninth Symphony is not repetitive of the content of the immediately preceding ones. The changes go deeper than the externals of instrumentation—saxophones and flugelhorn, and so on. The texture of musical brainwork is different and more direct, subtle yet simple.

In an entirely different way, psychological and musical, Vaughan Williams in his latest period puts me in mind of Bruckner—allowing for differences religious and racial. But both make great use of simple melodic and harmonic material, both have the faith in sequences that move symphonic mountains. Both are noble without a single self-conscious attitude. And both are occasionally clumsy and hardly "professional." Bruckner was, of course, a less inhibited melodist than Vaughan Williams: but that is because in a romantic tradition he was free to indulge his senses without fear of corruption and hell-fire.

Vaughan Williams's great achievement has been to dispense with the current musical coin of the period of his basic culture and maturity, and to modulate to the contemporary tone and language without obvious iconoclasms. He is of our period, and yet he is full of harvest—which means to say that he is a master. At the end of a strong, convincing interpretation of the Ninth Symphony by the B.B.C. Orchestra and Sir Malcolm, the composer walked down a high stairway, bent precariously on his stick, as he made his way to the platform to acknowledge tumultuous applause—applause led by young people standing in the arena. It was a very moving sight: and somehow it epitomized all that we had just been hearing from the symphony.

Music: A Vaughan Williams Premiere

Stokowski Leads Ninth Symphony in U.S. Bow
Conductor Honored by President and Mayor

by Harold C. Schonberg

The New York Times, 26 September 1958, 22

Quite a number of new works appeared on last night's Carnegie Hall program of the Contemporary Music Society, but the evening was Leopold
Stokowski's. He conducted the music, received congratulatory messages
from President Eisenhower and Mayor Wagner, made a speech and
indulged in repartee with the Mayor.[14]

Almost lost in the shuffle was the fact that the late Ralph Vaughan
Williams' Symphony No. 9 in E minor was receiving its American première.
The score completed late in 1957 and received its first performance
in England last April 2. Vaughan Williams died about six months later, on
Aug. 26, at the age of 85.

The Ninth Symphony is a big score and a complicated one. Its instrumentation includes, beyond the normal complement of a large orchestra,
such unusual additions as a fluegelhorn in B flat and three saxophones.
A fluegelhorn is a sort of keyed bugle.

Vaughan Williams always was fond of the saxophone. He had used
it to good advantage in such previous works as "Job." In this score the
three saxophones are not used in a solo role, but as part of the wind choir,
underpinning it and lending an unusual timbre.

The symphony is packed with melody, strong, personal melody, from
beginning to end. And the idiom is largely diatonic. There are none of the
taut discords of the Fourth or Sixth Symphonies. A mellow glow suffuses
the work, as it does the work of many veteran composers who seem to gaze
retrospectively over their careers. Brahms, Richard Strauss, and Bartók
come to mind, their music, too, became calm and resigned toward the end.

•

Curiously there is in the symphony, especially in the third movement,
a touch of Sibelius. It is well known that Vaughan Williams considered
Sibelius the greatest contemporary symphonist. Could he have been honoring the Finnish composer's memory with suggestions of the Caliban
episodes in "The Tempest"?[15]

In any case, the Ninth Symphony is a masterpiece. There is a theme
in the first movement that is haunting in its simple beauty. This theme, in
one form or another, plays a prominent part in the symphony, appearing

and reappearing in transfigured forms. The last movement is an andante tranquillo, with pronounced polyphonic lines, and it ends on a triple pianissimo. The last word in the score is "niente"—nothing. Those who read symbols into music can find much here.

[*The remainder of the review, which reports on the first half of the concert—works by Wallingford Riegger, Juan Orrego-Salas, Paul Creston, and Alan Hovhaness— and the celebratory speeches, has been omitted here. It is curious that Schonberg does not comment on the many echoes of Vaughan Williams, especially the* Fantasia on a Theme by Thomas Tallis, *in the Hovhaness work, his Symphony No. 2, "Mysterious Mountain."*]

1. *The Sunday Dispatch*, 6 April 1958, 3. Arthur Jacobs (1922–1996), a critic and prolific author of wide musical interests, had been writing for a number of London newspapers since the late 1940s; he is best known today for his pioneering work on Arthur Sullivan.

2. It should be noted that playwright John Osborne, the original Angry Young Man, greatly admired Vaughan Williams's music and made sympathetic reference to it in *Look Back in Anger* (1956). But for Osborne's similarly disillusioned and rebellious counterparts among young British composers, Vaughan Williams, at least in his perceived role as the progenitor of a meandering musical pastoralism, was an obvious target. The contrast between Osborne's views and those of his musician peers speaks tellingly to a larger rift in Vaughan Williams's reception, particularly from the 1950s onward, between the attitudes of the musical elite and those of a wider public.

3. Ursula Vaughan Williams, *R.V.W.: A Biography of Ralph Vaughan Williams* (London: Oxford University Press, 1964), 390.

4. See in particular Daniel M. Grimley, "Music, Ice, and the Geometry of Fear: Vaughan Williams's *Sinfonia Antartica*," *The Musical Quarterly* 91 (2008): 116–50; and Julian Horton, "The Later Symphonies," in *The Cambridge Companion to Vaughan Williams*, ed. Alain Frogley and Aidan J. Thomson (Cambridge: Cambridge University Press, 2013), 199–228.

5. See Donald Mitchell, "Contemporary Chronicle: Reevaluations: Vaughan Williams," *Musical Opinion* 78 (1955): 409–11, 471. Donald Mitchell (1925–2017) wrote books on Britten and Mahler.

6. See Alain Frogley, *Vaughan Williams's Ninth Symphony*, Studies in Musical Genesis and Structure (Oxford: Oxford University Press, 2001). The compositional process of the Ninth Symphony is the most comprehensively documented of any major Vaughan Williams work, at least in terms of surviving sources; though the composer normally destroyed most of his sketches and drafts, on this occasion he made a deliberate decision to retain them.

7. The composer's note for the first performance is reprinted in Michael Kennedy, *A Catalogue of the Works of Ralph Vaughan Williams*, 2nd ed. (Oxford: Oxford University Press, 1996), 231–36, quote at 233. A version differing from the concert program in a few insignificant details appeared as "The Music of My New Ninth Symphony: An Analysis of this Month's Premiere," *Music and Musicians* 6 (1957–58): 12–13.

8. See Michael Kennedy, *The Works of Ralph Vaughan Williams*, 2nd ed. (London: Oxford University Press, 1980), 342; and Roy Douglas, *Working with Vaughan Williams: The Correspondence of Ralph Vaughan Williams and Roy Douglas* (London: The British Library, 1988), 96.

9. The background to the three-hour run-through on 21 March, the only rehearsal before that on the morning of the concert, is discussed in Kennedy, *Catalogue*, 342. A recording of the premiere was released on CD in 2010 (Pristine Classical, PASC234). Though this confirms many of Douglas's criticisms, in fairness to Sargent it should be noted that he received the final score only in mid-March, and so had very little time to prepare. This was in stark contrast to the Eighth Symphony, to which John Barbirolli and the Hallé Orchestra had been able to devote nine hours of initial rehearsals, held almost three months before the premiere. See Douglas, *Working with Vaughan Williams*, 86.

10. Felix Aprahamian was deputy music critic of the *Times* for forty-one years; Secretary of the Organ Music Society; and, in 1994, the first music critic to be made an Honorary Member of the Royal Philharmonic Society. Colin Mason was known for his determined advocacy of Bartók's music; he served as editor of the musical journal *Tempo* from 1964 to 1971.

11. See Michael Kennedy, *The Works of Ralph Vaughan Williams*, 345.

12. An "Aunt Sally" is the equivalent of a "straw man": a figure set up to be easily refuted in argument.

13. The first movement is in fact marked "Moderato maestoso."

14. The concert marked the fiftieth anniversary of Stokowski's debut as a conductor.

15. The reference is to one of the movements from Sibelius's incidental music for a Danish production of *The Tempest*, Op. 109, of 1925, which he later gathered into two orchestral suites.

Goodness and Beauty: Philosophy, History, and Ralph Vaughan Williams

LEON BOTSTEIN

The state of "classical" music today is very different from that of 1958, the year in which Ralph Vaughan Williams died at the age of eighty-five. At the time of his death, high modernism, particularly the strand claiming its origins in the music of Schoenberg, Berg, and Webern, had entered a sustained period of prestige among critics, composers, and even performers. Modernism dominated, particularly within universities in continental Europe and North America. This *succès d'estime* would last until the closing years of the Cold War.

In the 1950s, music that explicitly foregrounded its character as "modern" drew inspiration from a historical imperative that mostly went unquestioned. Composers should break with the past so that new music might be in step with the radical and novel innovations of contemporary life, which were understood in terms set earlier in the century by Busoni, Schoenberg, and Adorno, and the subsequent polemical exchanges they inspired. This required abandoning inherited compositional practices, including tonality, rhythmic transparency, evident continuities (including the use of repetition), standard expressive and narrative ambitions, and formal models handed down from the nineteenth century.

Although concert life after World War II was never really dominated by modernism, this aesthetic commanded the political and moral high ground that it had earned during the interwar era. Modernism openly rejected the norms of art and culture held to be complicit with the senseless and brutal conflict of the Great War. In the 1930s and early 1940s, the aesthetic ideologies of Nazism and Soviet Communism under Stalin derided it variously as "degenerate" and subversive. Modernism therefore found itself allied with the struggle against fascism, autocracy, and tyranny.

Immediately after World War II, in the shadow of Auschwitz and Hiroshima, modernism retained its ethical pre-eminence; it was understood as the only viable way to make new art. In its postwar incarnation, modernism became a symbol of artistic freedom and individuality. After the student unrests of 1968, the historical trajectory that justified modernism weakened. It gained, nonetheless, a brief second wind as a presumed barrier to the spread of cultural decline, seemingly evident in the character of mass culture and the success of capitalist commerce in music achieved through the dominance, stunning creativity, and wide range of popular music.

Not surprisingly, a revolt against this ideological orthodoxy among contemporary composers began in the 1970s, including many who had started out as modernists. An eclectic reversal was in the making, embracing a return to tonality and clear rhythmic profiles, and above all, the cultivation of explicit expressiveness, immediate comprehensibility, and accessibility. George Rochberg, Steve Reich, David del Tredici, Louis Andriessen, Lou Harrison, John Adams, John Corigliano, Jennifer Higdon, Joan Tower, and John Tavener are just a few examples.

The decline of modernist ideologies made way for the emergence of new music with overt spiritual and expressive ambitions, evident links to popular cultural forms, and free of a lingering distaste for nineteenth-century Romanticism. This shift has motivated musicians, scholars, and the public to take a fresh look at twentieth-century music. One consequence of this "postmodern" reevaluation is renewed enthusiasm and high praise for the music of Ralph Vaughan Williams. Indeed, Vaughan Williams's own aesthetic and ambitions for music align remarkably closely with the direction taken by contemporary music in the twenty-first century.

Classical music composed for the concert stage and musical theater faces an uncertain future in the wake of the worldwide COVID-19 pandemic. How inherited patterns of musical culture will survive is uncertain, particularly the frequency and format of large-scale live instrumental concerts. Active amateurism is on the decline, as are the scale and size of the audience. The overwhelming presence of computational technology has altered our access to sound reproduction and the priority of live acoustic performance in real time. Novel habits of listening are emerging. Vaughan Williams faced comparable historical changes. He charted a path along which inherited musical practices might reinvent themselves successfully, thereby finding a continuing place in an altered technological, social, political, and economic environment. Vaughan Williams succeeded in doing so in the early twentieth century; his example therefore merits emulation in the twenty-first.

After the Great War, Vaughan Williams secured his place in modern British musical life as the dominant figure after Edward Elgar. Between his death in 1958 and the early 1990s, however, the trajectory of his posthumous critical reputation seemed unpromising. Even during the composer's intensely productive final years in the 1950s—achievements included the Eighth and Ninth symphonies—doubts were expressed whether, apart from a few relatively early works, such as the *Fantasia on a Theme of Thomas Tallis* and *The Lark Ascending*, Vaughan Williams's music would remain in the repertory outside Britain.

At the end of the twentieth century, a sharp reaction against the perceived elitism of musical modernism and its attendant dismissal of genres of commercial and popular music brought a return to the concert stage, frequent recording, and repeated broadcasts over "classical" radio of Vaughan Williams's orchestral music, once trivialized as "conservative." In recent decades, Vaughan Williams's symphonies and larger-scale instrumental works have earned him a place alongside Sibelius and Shostakovich as a representative voice of the twentieth century.

The doubts once routinely expressed about Vaughan Williams's stature as composer revolved around the long-term consequences of the explicitly "English" character of his music. His allegiance to national traditions, however authentic, doomed his music to being deemed by some as dull. In this narrative, Vaughan Williams failed to escape the ultimately insular character of the historical materials upon which he relied. Writing in July 1953, Ronald Taylor argued that the national element—the "English" sources in the music—would prevent Vaughan Williams from being regarded as one of "the few great, the few significant composers of the twentieth century." The particular evocation of traditional English sensibilities and materials limited the compositional horizon and imagination.[1] "To future generations," Taylor wrote, "Vaughan Williams will probably appear as a serene kindly character" who "cloistered himself in his own place of refuge—a haven in the English countryside, a quiet, parochial retreat." Vaughan Williams remained too content, for the most part, to stick fast to the "melancholy beauty of his own remote kingdom."[2]

Vaughan Williams's construct of the national seemed to Taylor too retrospective and colored by nostalgia; the composer was reluctant to grapple with the central characteristic of the twentieth century—its brutality, novelty, and violence. Taylor acknowledged a few major forays designed to confront the "real world of strident assertion and compromise"; but, in the end, the "outside world . . . the world of cruel reality" was "alien" to him. The attempts Vaughan Williams made—Taylor cites the Fourth and Sixth symphonies, but one should also include the Second, *A London Symphony*, with its startling mix of rumination, anxiety, and pessimism—were noble failures and destined to remain so. Taylor contrasted Vaughan Williams with the one twentieth-century composer who had succeeded in using national sources to create an original and universally inspiring body of new music: Béla Bartók.

Taylor's skepticism was hardly novel. As early as 1934 John Foulds, the underappreciated, idiosyncratic composer and a contemporary, compared Vaughan Williams unfavorably to his Continental contemporaries (including Manuel de Falla), many of whom also worked with folksong and dance. Foulds described Vaughan Williams as a pronounced "nationalist" in music, citing his modal excursions and free use of counterpoint. Although Foulds found Vaughan Williams's musical language "novel" and occasionally "arresting," his self-conscious English "mystical tinge and natural religious instinct" failed to transport his "Englishness" much beyond an "effete sacerdotalism."[3]

The line of argument pursued by Taylor and Foulds did not go uncontested. In December 1954, eighteenth months after Ronald Taylor had his say, Eric Taylor (no relation), in a short essay titled "Vaughan Williams and the English Tradition," took the opposite view.[4] Vaughan Williams, Eric Taylor argued, had used English sources with brilliance and originality. The result was a unique and lasting aesthetic and spiritual achievement comparable to Bartók's, one that had its roots precisely in Vaughan Williams's distinctive modern musical transformations of the English traditions that Ronald Taylor had derided. In Vaughan Williams's music Eric Taylor located a "vital comprehensiveness" and "creative universality." There was "a rapturous beauty in so much of Vaughan Williams's writing which analysis cannot comprehend, a profound mystical quality which words are powerless to express. For as with Bach or Beethoven, Vaughan Williams is not just a composer, a maker of musical tunes, but a great living soul giving expression in sound. If St. Thomas More had lived in the twentieth century and had written music, it would have been like this."[5]

Eric Taylor's image of Vaughan Williams as a twentieth-century Thomas More and his characterization of the beauty in his music as reaching beyond linguistic description and analysis may capture not only the qualities that now make his music strikingly compelling to twenty-first-century listeners and performers, but also the essence of what might be regarded as "English" about his music. Furthermore, Taylor's claims about Vaughan Williams's cultivation of "beauty" in a "mystical" manner while also projecting a normative ideal of beauty pointed to a particular quality of Englishness beyond the composer's attachment to English musical sources. It will be argued here that the composer was persuaded of a fundamental connection between beauty and goodness, a claim that was debated by contemporary English philosophers, particularly G. E. Moore.[6]

Furthermore, Vaughan Williams's location of a fundamental ethical quality in beauty was evidence of what Foulds identified as Vaughan Williams's "natural religious instinct." That instinct was supported by new philosophical arguments. Breakthroughs in philosophy deepened Vaughan Williams's determination to confront, throughout his career, the harsh realities of modernity by offering music that provided respite, hope, and an antidote to, and not a mirror of, modernity. The "melancholy beauty" Ronald Taylor derided was in fact Eric Taylor's "rapturous beauty": music as a direct spiritual challenge to modernity, not a retreat.

Foulds and the two Taylors all concurred on the specific English musical sources Vaughan Williams had deployed, as well as their compositional consequences. Vaughan Williams's attraction to modal harmonies, transparency in form and sound, and folksong stood out. There was little mystery about this, since the composer himself was an articulate and enthusiastic proponent of the utility of the historically "national" for contemporary music, albeit in a manner that was explicitly not exclusive or chauvinist. Along with Cecil Sharp, Vaughan Williams pioneered the research of "folk" traditions in song and dance specific to the British past. He believed in the indispensable link between local traditions of music making and the mission of contemporary composition. He had little regard for new music not connected to the daily life of a particular community, considering it abstract cosmopolitanism. As he wrote in 1939, "I believe that it is better to be vitally parochial than to be an emasculate cosmopolitan."[7]

Precisely on account of the discontinuities with the past it appeared to cause—the radical transformation of the landscape, particularly the acceleration of individual alienation and suffering in the economic and social life of the population associated with urban life, a concern he shared with E. M. Forster—modernity demanded that contemporary music, in part through its evocation of a shared past, play a key role in advancing and sustaining a sense of community. This required not just serious new music for the professional concert stage and opera house but also music that could be made, by active participation, with amateurs, in churches, schools, the home, and public venues. Against all odds, musical culture and practices could reaffirm a common ground of shared values. Contemporary life required that renewed connections among the citizenry be forged. Using local, regional, and national traditions that bridged class and status, new music could contribute to nurturing a humane and generous cultural consciousness of patriotism that resisted the unprecedented spread of intolerance and violence Vaughan Williams himself had witnessed during his lifetime: Ronald Taylor's "world of cruel reality."

Like Bartók, who, alongside Vaughan Williams's teacher Ravel, was one of the contemporary European composers that he admired most, Vaughan Williams focused primarily on the musical inheritance from a pre-industrial and rural national past, one presumed authentic due to oral transmission.

The survival of that inheritance was endangered by the demographic and social consequences of urban growth. Vaughan Williams, again like Bartók, saw in the aesthetics of pre-industrial, pre-nineteenth-century rural and urban musical culture a source for contemporary instrumental, choral, and operatic music that would capture the attention and imagination of local audiences as well as the wider international musical community of composers, performers, amateurs, and listeners.

In one respect Vaughan Williams went further than Bartók. Unlike his Hungarian contemporary, he took an intense interest in the place of music in the religious life of his country. Despite his own agnosticism, he sought to emancipate Anglican Church music from the cloying sentimentality of Victorian Romanticism. The musical aesthetics of the mid-nineteenth century had managed to distort the ethical virtues in the sacred and secular musical practices Vaughan Williams believed he had uncovered in the more distant English past. These historic virtues were simplicity, sincerity, immediacy, and transparency; they were communicated by the musical beauty of form and sound that prevailed before the nineteenth century. That music, in turn, suggested normative spiritual ideals of moral goodness. Vaughan Williams's intuition was that the character of the "good" in ethical behavior might be revealed and strengthened in contemporary life not with language, or by ritual, prayer, and preaching, but through the experience of a collective encounter with beauty through newly created music. The opening section of *A London Symphony* of 1913 is a case in point.[8]

Vaughan Williams should be compared not only to Bartók but to other contemporaries such as Leoš Janáček, Aaron Copland, Karol Szymanowski, Manuel de Falla, Carl Nielsen, and George Enescu, each of whom shared in the project of creating modern evocations of national styles. But he was influenced primarily in this respect by his teachers C. Hubert Parry and Max Bruch (the latter drawing his source material from cultures other than his own German-speaking Europe) and inspired by predecessors such as Antonín Dvořák. However, what truly differentiated Vaughan Williams as an "English" composer was the exceptional impact that specifically English cultural currents had on his approach to composition and his attachment to English musical sources. Vaughan Williams's political and philosophical beliefs aligned with the way he sought to shape a contemporary national musical character, particularly one that would be at least as universal as it was English. Unusual for a composer, Vaughan Williams revealed a debt to extra-musical currents, especially in philosophy—Moore in ethics and epistemology—and in the writing of English history by friends and contemporaries, particularly George M. Trevelyan and H. A. L. Fisher.

Vaughan Williams and His Generation

The manner in which music history continues to be written and understood is tied to a tradition of biography in which a self-referential, auto-poetic logic prevails. An artificial perimeter has been erected around the dynamics of influence in the evolution of musical style. Music is too often understood as a hermetically sealed cultural practice. In Vaughan Williams's case, however, his remarkable and original transformations of English material, and their reception—including the critical skepticism and the surprising return to prominence in recent years—point to roots and influences outside of musical discourse.

Vaughan Williams's contemporaries, both skeptics and supporters alike, had too restricted an understanding of his music. They heard his works as narrowly derived from the strikingly "English." On the occasion of the composer's seventy-fifth birthday in 1947, Adrian Boult, a champion of Vaughan Williams's music, observed that "it is probable that there are a number of his works which no one could expect a foreigner to understand." Among them was *A Pastoral Symphony*, long an object of derision. Boult considered it a "most elusive" score, and "a very difficult work for a non-English audience to comprehend."[9]

Indeed, all the pianist Artur Schnabel heard in *A Pastoral Symphony*, as conducted by Boult in Prague in 1925, was something "oriental" and "primitive Keltic" that Schnabel assumed had been inspired by Mendelssohn's "Scottish" Symphony. The result may have been "poetical," Schnabel conceded, but "rather *vieux-jeu* nowadays!" Edward J. Dent defended Vaughan Williams to Schnabel. With his incisive critical faculties, Dent was one of few who grasped in Vaughan Williams's work the significance of influences not strictly of a musical character. After seeing *The Pilgrim's Progress* in 1951, he wrote to the composer that he found himself able to surrender "completely" to the work owing to his own "deep-rooted inherited Quakerism (although I have never been able to live up to it!)." Dent doubted, however, that "most of my friends would think it possible."[10]

Dent's speculation about the reasons for his own susceptibility to Vaughan Williams's aesthetic was not wide of the mark. Vaughan Williams's conception of music and the obligations of a composer in the modern world were influenced by the distinct ethos of his generation. Bertrand Russell, Vaughan Williams's exact contemporary and a Cambridge acquaintance, put the "change in mental climate" between the 1890s and the mid-1920s in terms of an ironic contrast between his and Vaughan Williams's generation and previous generations, as well as differences with contemporaries born some ten years later, notably Lytton Strachey and John Maynard Keynes. Those younger men of the 1880s, Russell observed, were Edwardians, while he and his exact contemporaries were "still Victorians"; they "believed in ordered progress by means of politics and free discussion." They sought to be "leaders of the multitude" but did not wish to "be divorced from it." As Russell put it, unlike the Edwardians, who "aimed rather at a life of retirement among fine shades and nice feelings, and conceived of the good as consisting in the passionate mutual admiration of a clique of the elite," his own contemporaries, like Vaughan Williams, sought to "preserve" a "kinship with the Philistine."[11]

The peculiarities of Vaughan Williams's biography confirm Russell's insight. Vaughan Williams was not destined for a career in music. He was not a child prodigy in the mold of Felix Mendelssohn, Camille Saint-Saëns, or Erich Wolfgang Korngold. His musical talent, even as an instrumentalist, seemed circumscribed. Although in 1898 he passed all the required examinations on the organ to become a Fellow of the Royal College of Organists—no small feat—he never distinguished himself as a virtuoso on any instrument. His choice of vocation was not evinced as a child and adolescent through a display of extraordinary talent.[12]

Vaughan Williams's mother's distinguished and affluent family was hardly enthusiastic about a career in music. His father had been an Anglican clergyman who died when the composer was a small child. This event left a lifelong residue in Vaughan Williams's conception of the ideal of a healthy national musical culture. The young Ralph Vaughan Williams exhibited a fine intelligence and wide curiosity sufficient to qualify him for career paths outside music that befitted his social status as a member of the intellectual gentry. Personal convictions regarding religion formed in adolescence ruled out ordination in the clergy. The fact that Vaughan Williams did not become a composer as a consequence of precocity did spare him, however, from a child prodigy's often troubled transition to the status of mature professional. He escaped the psychological burden early accomplishment can create (as in the cases of Mendelssohn and Korngold), though his awareness that he lacked a history of brilliant musicality in childhood made mustering self-confidence as a professional a lifelong struggle.

Vaughan Williams's ambition as a composer drew strength from civic idealism and secular cultural manifestations of values traditionally associated with religion. At stake was not musical originality or virtuosity in musical skills. Vaughan Williams's attitude toward religion may have wavered between atheism and agnosticism, but he nonetheless was persuaded that churches and religious faith in the nation were salutary. The social function of churches—the ethics they promoted, the communities they sustained, particularly through active lay participation in Anglican liturgical music—was central to Britain's distinct character.

Vaughan Williams believed that modern church music had the potential to become a powerful secular formal means to sustain and advance mores historically, dependent only on faith. Vaughan Williams's friend and classmate, the historian George M. Trevelyan, who was four years younger but exerted a decisive influence on the composer, shared similar convictions. Even the "Agnostics" of the age, Trevelyan observed, "were Puritan in feeling and outlook." Trevelyan approvingly endorsed the view that the rage for literature in late nineteenth-century England, particularly for the novels of George Eliot, was a "quasi-religious" movement that promoted restatements of "the moral law and process of soul making" once the sole province of religion, in a manner acceptable to the rationalist agnostic conscience."[13]

Music could advance the same goals. Becoming a musician gave Vaughan Williams the opportunity to continue the spiritual care of souls that had been his father's calling without forcing him to sign on to a specific theology. His agreement to work on hymns to be sung collectively in church signaled his support of church membership as a social custom. By influencing communal worship through music, he could reach the widest range of social groupings in England at a time of massive economic and social pressure on traditional patterns of daily life. Music offered a means that could be novel and persuasively egalitarian as well as protective of an orderly and peaceful continuity with the culture of the past. Once late nineteenth-century Anglicanism, particularly the revival of High Church and Anglo-Catholic liturgical practice had weakened the legacy of puritanism in Anglicanism, the preservation of a broad range of admirable values in British life through music seemed eminently possible.[14]

The supposition that Vaughan Williams's reasons for becoming a musician were not reasons from solely within music is further substantiated by the fact that he read modern history at Trinity College, Cambridge, although he did so while studying, writing, and performing music. The extra-musical ambitions behind his choice of vocation helps explain his regard for and affinity to C. Hubert Parry, his teacher and mentor. Parry himself had come to music indirectly, having trained and studied law and modern history at Oxford.[15]

Vaughan Williams shared Parry's inclination toward political and social reform. He knew Parry had also abandoned religious belief. Yet Parry believed that music could be a key component of England's national strength and character. Parry taught music, Vaughan Williams observed in 1918, "as a part of life."[16] Vaughan Williams emulated Parry's example and never tried "to divorce art from life; [Parry] once said to me 'Write choral music as befits an Englishman and a democrat.'"[17] Although Parry acknowledged a debt to German musical culture (at the outbreak of World War I, he described himself as "a pro-Teuton" for a "quarter of a century and more"), Parry began to emancipate English music from its nineteenth-century dependency on German practice, a task Vaughan Williams continued during his own career.

Parry's concept of the composer's duty powerfully attracted Vaughan Williams. Parry's book, *Studies of Great Composers*, contained an elegant articulation of the purpose and impact of music, and therefore, of the obligations demanded by the vocation of a professional composer. In the final lines of *Studies*, Parry wrote:

> The greatest composers are not those who merely entertain us and make us for a while forget boredom and worry in trivial distraction; but such as sound the deepest chords in our nature and lift us above ourselves; who purify and brace us in times of gladness, and strike no jarring note in the time of our deepest sorrow.[18]

Vaughan Williams became a composer in Parry's image: an artist determined to advance the role of music in assisting others to cope with the existential challenges of life. Parry's influence was reinforced by Vaughan Williams's contemporaries at Trinity College, the most significant of whom were Trevelyan and Moore. Although Vaughan Williams wrote eloquently about music, he developed few pretenses of competing with the high-minded intellectualism of either friend. By going on long walking tours with Trevelyan and Moore, and, more important, finding himself regularly in their company, Vaughan Williams listened to and participated enough in the stream of intense conversation to realize he was not their equal. Nonetheless, their ideas became familiar to him, first through conversation and later through their writings. Vaughan Williams's conception, not surprisingly, reveals the impact of Moore's pathbreaking thoughts on language, truth, and ethics, while his views on English politics and society mirror the perspectives of Trevelyan's pioneering popular writings on the history of England.

Moore on Ethics, Realism, and Common Sense

If Parry and Vaughan Williams were determined to establish a modern English tradition of music that marked a break from nineteenth-century German models, Moore and his Trinity philosopher friend Bertrand Russell were equally intent on breaking the dominance exerted by

German philosophy, particularly Kant and Hegel. Just as Vaughan Williams, following Elgar's achievements of the late 1890s, was instrumental in establishing a distinct English tradition within twentieth-century composition, Moore, Russell, and, subsequently, Ludwig Wittgenstein spearheaded the development of analytic philosophy and the philosophy of language in opposition not only to German Idealism but also to the English legacy of Utilitarianism, the tradition of Jeremy Bentham and John Stuart Mill. Revealing these modern "English" philosophical underpinnings helps refute the charge of provincialism that has been aimed at Vaughan Williams's music.

The strategies and arguments in philosophy pursued by Moore in particular reveal family resemblances to Vaughan Williams's ideas of what distinguished music of great beauty and what communicative qualities music ought to exhibit in order to flourish in a community and the life of a nation. Moore's influence on Vaughan Williams developed in the context of a personal relationship. Among Vaughan Williams's Trinity classmates not destined to become professional musicians, Moore was the most musically inclined.

In his autobiographical sketch from 1942, Moore credits the head of the music department at Dulwich College for playing a decisive role in his intellectual development. Moore had dropped piano lessons with his father, but in school he was encouraged to take private lessons in singing, where he encountered for the first time "the best of Schubert's songs."[19] Moore proceeded to study the organ and harmony. His love of music cemented his friendship with Vaughan Williams, and he recounted with delight how he and Vaughan Williams played four-hand arrangements of Schubert's "Unfinished" Symphony and part of "The Great" C-Major Symphony for their circle of friends. Moore, who genuinely liked and admired Vaughan Williams, presented a wedding gift to Ralph and Adeline Vaughan Williams and corresponded with the composer during his trip to Germany in 1897. Although their lives subsequently took them in vastly different directions, Vaughan Williams remained in contact with Moore, visiting him in 1953 and 1954. Both received the Order of Merit, and both died in 1958.

Their friendship was not just defined by music. Like Vaughan Williams, Moore had drifted from a childhood attachment to religion, moving from an "intense religious phase" to "complete" agnosticism. His "religious beliefs gradually fell away," just as Vaughan Williams would eventually profess agnosticism.[20] Yet both held on to traditional ethical principles of social responsibility and kept their distance from the fashionable rejection of middle-class mores widespread among their contemporaries. Vaughan

Williams was not elected to the Apostles, the celebrated intellectual society at Cambridge, but he shared an allegiance to the secularized Christian values of kindness, generosity, duty, and obligation to others. Unlike many of their contemporaries—notably Moore's fellow Apostles—both Vaughan Williams and Moore were less reluctant to embrace these residues from religion as ethical maxims.[21]

Evidence of this shared bond was Moore and Vaughan Williams's enduring fondness for the Salvation Army and its straightforward Protestant devotion to duty. To both men, the Salvation Army showed that if one took the tenets of Christian ethics set forth in the Gospels seriously, connecting directly with a genuine commitment to act specifically in a Christ-like manner, kindness and benevolence might flourish in everyday life. What they saw in the ethos of the Salvation Army was similar to John Bunyan's ideal of a Christian community as well as to the contemporary example of Tolstoy's influential late radical Christianity. Both were distillations of Christian beliefs that exposed the smugness of Victorian Anglicanism.[22]

Moore launched his career in 1903 with two publications, the landmark paper, "The Refutation of Idealism," and, more significantly, his book *Principia Ethica*. Moore's debut was sensational, as suggested by the enthusiastic response from academic colleagues in philosophy and writers such as Strachey, Virginia Woolf, and W. B. Yeats. Strachey wrote to Moore, "I think your book [the *Principia*] has not only wrecked and shattered all writers on Ethics from Aristotle to Herbert Spencer . . . it has laid the true foundations of Ethics . . . it has not only left all modern philosophy *bafouée* [scorned] . . . the truth, there can be no doubt, is really now upon the march. I date from Oct. 1903 the beginning of the Age of Reason."[23] Russell doubted whether admirers of Moore's book properly understood his argument. He thought that those who praised Moore, like Keynes and Strachey, trivialized his notion of the "good" as "a series of isolated passionate moments," justifying "fine shades and nice feelings" without recognizing Moore's emphasis on morality's character as a rational ideal and his "doctrine of organic unities."[24] Vaughan Williams did not fall into that trap, but found the book—Moore had sent it to him when it came out—"difficult but wonderful."[25]

When *Principia Ethica* appeared, Vaughan Williams had started to work on his first symphony, *A Sea Symphony* (1910), based on the poetry of Walt Whitman. Although Edward Elgar was fifteen years older than Vaughan Williams, his international breakthrough with the *Enigma* Variations (1899) and his oratorio *The Dream of Gerontius* (1900), had occurred just a decade earlier. Yet, for all its striking originality, power, and markedly "English" character, Elgar's music remained indebted to the late Romanticism that flourished on the Continent, best exemplified by the work of Richard Strauss. In his First Symphony and its successor, *A London Symphony*, Vaughan Williams certainly exhibited links to Elgar's aesthetic. The Second betrays traces of influence from Wagner's *Die Meistersinger*, a score that Vaughan Williams admired. Not only was it the one "comic" work in Wagner's output, but it centered on the nature of beauty in music and the vital role music plays in the formation and preservation of community and nation.[26] Nonetheless, both symphonies were widely understood as sharp departures from convention and something distinctly new in harmony, texture, and sensibility. The novelty of these first two Vaughan Williams symphonies mirrors Moore's mix of a debt to the past and a break with the philosophical discourse of the nineteenth century.[27]

In Moore's case, Henry Sidgwick (1838–1900) played a role analogous to Elgar in relation to Vaughan Williams. And the impact J. M. E. McTaggart (1866–1925) had on Moore's thought matched the importance of Parry's influence on Vaughan Williams. Just as Vaughan Williams came to reject Parry's reliance on German models, so Moore admired McTaggart while opposing his commitment to Idealism. Both Sidgwick and McTaggart taught Moore, but while he found Sidgwick a less appealing figure than McTaggart, it was Sidgwick's area of philosophy—ethics—in which Moore made his greatest mark. Sidgwick's *The Methods of Ethics*, a massive and comprehensive work, appeared in 1874.[28]

Sidgwick's project was to provide a detailed account of how individuals ought to arrive at rational judgments about the right thing to do. He argued that there were three basic routes to ethical action: (1) intuition; (2) egoism guided by reason, "ethical egoism"; and (3) an "ethical altruism" that aimed to justify the validity of Utilitarianism. Sidgwick's "altruistic egoism," or "universalistic hedonism," represents the most highly developed moral motivation, for it shows how the deepest human feelings of pleasure, or the highest degrees of "agreeable consciousness," have become tied, rationally, to a concern for the greatest happiness for the greatest number of human beings.

An ethical egoist is further motivated by a rational determination of moral obligations, but the actions that cause pleasure, and not pain, are those connected merely to the greatest happiness for oneself alone; the calculation is for the individual actor. Since the ethical altruist or universal hedonist is someone who construes personal happiness and pleasure in terms of the greatest well-being and happiness of others, for Sidgwick the task is to lead the egoistic hedonist into becoming a deliberate agent of reasoned altruism. Sidgwick's goal was to strengthen the truth of Utilitarianism by philosophically articulating the evolution of ethical action. First there were mere intuitions. These could then become the basis for judgments that link personal happiness, narrowly defined in terms of oneself, to pleasure. In the case of the "ethical altruist," our ethical reaction to wrongdoing would carry the sensation of pain based on the awareness of the greatest unhappiness of the greatest number.[29]

Sidgwick's novel strategy was to rescue Utilitarianism by linking both ethical egoism and universal hedonism to human intuition, which he loosely connected to common sense.[30] According to Sidgwick, humans experience three types of intuition. First, there is an affective, unexamined perceptual intuition. This is a mere feeling about the seemingly self-evident character of what is moral or "good" and occurs through our perceptions. The second form of intuition is our capacity to infer from perceptions general rules of conduct. Third, and finally, we can intuit guiding principles that inform rules. Intuition, in Sidgwick's scheme, provides the bridge in human nature to the higher forms of moral reasoning and conduct. These higher forms are a deliberate, reasoned ethical egoism and the more enlightened universal hedonism.[31]

Moore posited that the problem was Sidgwick's mistaken reliance on a "natural" basis for ethics. Judgments and actions, however rational, were nonetheless still contingent on human feelings, responses, and attitudes caused by the character of behavior and the consequences of action, either for the individual or for humanity in general. Moore opposed Sidgwick's "natural" defense of Utilitarianism and argued on behalf of an "ethical neutralism." This demanded that ethics be rooted not in human nature, empirical observations, or experience. Moore challenged Sidgwick's claim that "the Intuitional method rigorously applied yields in its final result the doctrine of pure Universal Hedonism—which it is convenient to denote by the single word Utilitarianism."[32]

Moore disputed the notion that advancing a faculty of intuition could redeem Utilitarianism as a moral doctrine. Moore insisted that ethical principles needed to be inferred not from inarticulate subjective preferences, intuitions, or a chain of reasonings based on them, but from the conscious recognition of an "intrinsic value" of the "good," something not found in nature. A reasoned recognition—not any sensations of pleasure or pain—of the inherent objective quality of what we mean when we judge something to be "good" in action and thought was required to justify moral obligations. The naturalistic fallacy relied on subjective criteria for goodness based in nature and experience. Pleasure and happiness, no matter how transformed from narrow self-interest into a universal altruism, could not be a sufficient basis for the answer to what is good or right.[33]

In his *Principia*, Moore, guided in part by Kant, abandoned any reliance on arguments around human self-interest—either egoistic or altruistic. Likewise, he walked away from the argument that the rightness or wrongness of an action derives from either its individual or social consequences, including sensations of pleasure and pain. Intuitions did not suffice; only rational recognition of a shared quality of goodness in action was required. Moore's opposition to what he termed "the naturalistic fallacy" in Sidgwick's ethics had an oddly Platonic metaphysical quality. Unlike Plato, however, Moore did not posit a metaphysical realm in which ideal entities existed that things in the real world somehow reflected or exemplified. Rather, the "good" as an intrinsic value existed in the real world, even though its essence was not material or "natural."

Moore's "the good" existed as a consistent and singular "intrinsic" value of a unique kind. It could not be defined by language or be found in anything in nature. To say that something is "good" is to reference only its intrinsic quality. The good is an "organic whole" that is not subject to logical proof. It is a matter of fact in that it refers to something that can be found in the world as a non-material quality. As an intrinsic value, the good is non-divisible. In other words, its whole is greater than any sum of its parts.

Moore insisted that not only the ends of actions but their means must be "good," just as any part of any action must be considered in relation to the whole of any "good." We should therefore act individually and collectively to promote as much intrinsic good in the world as possible. But the "good" remains simple and not dependent on our response to it. The claim that an action is "intrinsically good" is proved by locating the unique character of goodness. The "good" is the highest of all intrinsic values, and true. Since it is a complete coherent organic "whole," it includes no other properties. Ethical action is therefore a process of calculating the "greatest possible balance of intrinsic value which is always our duty to produce."[34]

"Good" as an intrinsic value must be understood therefore by reason. It cannot be thoughtless. Only through reason should we justify our obligation to act.

Moore defended his arguments by using an analogy to "beauty," a parallel "intrinsic" value. This move locates the connection with Vaughan Williams. Moore chose to describe ethical judgments by comparing them to the way we make aesthetic judgments: "Beauty," like "the good," was an intrinsic value and an organic consistent and coherent whole. Therefore, beauty could not be determined on a relative or subjective basis, neither on the basis of any "natural" responses of pleasure, nor an appeal to taste, however cultivated by reason. Moore summed up his fundamental rejection of naturalism in the language of ethical discourse by citing how we make aesthetic judgments. In the sequel to the *Principia*, his 1912 book *Ethics*, Moore wrote:

> It involves our saying that, even if the total quantity of pleasure in each was exactly equal, yet the fact that all the beings in the one possessed in addition knowledge of many different kinds and a full appreciation of all that was beautiful or worthy of love in their world, whereas *none* of the beings in the other possessed any of these things, would give us no reason whatever for preferring the former to the latter. It involves our saying that, for instance, the state of mind of a drunkard, when he is intensely pleased with breaking crockery, is just as valuable, in itself—just as well worth having, as that of a man who is fully realizing all that is exquisite in the tragedy of King Lear, provided only the mere quantity of pleasure in both cases is the same.[35]

In the last section of the *Principia*, titled "The Ideal," Moore considered the sense in which judgments about the highest intrinsic value, the "good," can be considered universal.[36] Moore again resorted to a resemblance to aesthetic judgments of beauty. What justified this strategy was Moore's contention that the two intrinsic values were both "neutral" organic wholes not derived from nature. Therefore, the "beautiful" was understood as sharing characteristics of the "good." Aesthetic values may be subordinate to ethics, but true beauty was nonetheless inherently good, and therefore possessed an ethical quality and ethical meaning. As Moore claimed, "To say that a thing is beautiful is to say, not indeed that it is *itself* good, but that it is a necessary element in something which is: to prove that a thing is truly beautiful is to prove that a whole, to which it bears a particular relation as a part, is truly good."[37] The "good" and "beauty" each become an "unanalyzable predicate of value." Both are simple, indivisible, not subject to definition, not found in nature, but organic wholes. The recognition of these predicates of value is not intuitive, but a consequence of the use of reason in judgment and action. As Moore concluded:

> To assert that a thing is beautiful is to assert that the cognition of it is an essential element in one of the intrinsically valuable wholes we have been discussing; so that the question,

whether it is *truly* beautiful or not, depends upon the *objective* question whether the whole in question is or is not truly good, and does not depend upon the question whether it would or would not excite particular feelings in particular persons. This definition has the double recommendation that it accounts both for the apparent connection between goodness and beauty and for the no less apparent difference between these two conceptions. It appears, at first sight, to be a strange coincidence, that there should be two *different* objective predicates of value, "good" and "beautiful," which are nevertheless so related to one another that whatever is beautiful is also good.[38]

Vaughan Williams was surely influenced by Moore's rejection of a metaphysical reality in favor of some manner of realism. Beauty and goodness—and indeed a sense of certainty and truth—were real and did not require some special gift to see (or hear) and understand them. In contrast to Plato, Moore's arguments made ethics and aesthetics part of an external everyday world, and therefore accessible to the many, not the few.

Moore's attack on Idealism as a philosophy of knowledge was directed at McTaggart, whose primary allegiance was to Hegel. As Moore put it, "I think it can fairly be said that what McTaggart was mainly engaged in was trying to find a precise meaning for Hegel's obscure utterances."[39] McTaggart held that reality is not fundamentally material but spiritual and anchored in ideas. Only through the study of ideas can truth in the world be determined and understood. An "absolute reality," a single dynamic spiritual essence, is that in which everything participates, including all relations between appearances and beliefs. All is spiritual in nature. The "bath of German Idealism"—as Russell described the set of ideas by which both he and Moore were initially entranced—was characterized by McTaggart's conviction that the things we believe in by experience draw their shape, meaning, and significance from a framework of a total encompassing and final ideational reality, "the absolute."[40]

Such an "absolute" identified a metaphysical source for certainty and truth. Grasping the metaphysical "absolute" was restricted, as in Plato and Hegel, to the very few who could come to terms with the existence of an overarching, counterintuitive hidden reality that was non-material. Idealism undercut what and how most humans learn in everyday life— empirically through experience—and how they use language on a daily basis to express what they believe they know. Moore sought to demolish the idea that the truth is expressed by and accessible only to an elite.

In his 1903 "The Refutation of Idealism," published in the journal *Mind*, Moore did not contest the belief that all reality is spiritual in nature—and that only ideas are "real." Everyone has the right to some sort of belief. Moore's concern was the attempt by philosophers to justify a mere belief with arguments that sought to prove the proposition that reality was ultimately spiritual, or that an all-encompassing "absolute" existed. There was no harm in a belief in Idealism, but there was possible harm in defending as true that belief through reasoned argument.

Idealism, ironically, owed a fundamental debt to Bishop George Berkeley, the eighteenth-century Anglo-Irish philosopher. Moore's attack on Idealism as anything more than a superstition began with Berkeley's legendary dictum that "to be is to be perceived" (*esse is percipere*). Moore's conclusion is that there are no valid arguments to conclude that things in the world that correspond to our experience and our sensations—the external world and material objects—do not exist independent of our perception. The arguments that determine they do exist, or do not exist at all, demand evidence that ends up being our "sensations." If one does not concede the existence of matter, the belief in the reality of the spirit becomes itself a "baseless superstition."

In order to support McTaggart's Idealism, one would have to prove "that our experience does not exist either." Such radical skepticism would deny the existence of both the material and the spiritual, resulting in the conclusion that nothing exists at all. Such absurdity can be avoided only by the rational conclusion that both spirit and matter exist without making the material contingent on the spiritual.

In 1908 McTaggart published a legendary paradoxical claim that pushed Moore further toward arguing on behalf of various forms of realism and, ultimately, common sense. McTaggart made the startling assertion that time was not real. Only the "absolute" was real and it was timeless. Moore was shocked by the idea that time, as ordinarily understood and experienced, was not real. McTaggart's assertion fundamentally denied the actual and "concrete" context of human action. All action (including music, of course) takes place, and is understood, in time. Stripping human action of being in the framework of time, understood as real, renders ethical judgment moot. Rejecting the reality of time even trivializes the idea that everything in the world is part of an "absolute." Moore thought McTaggart's notion "monstrous."[41]

The decisive link between Moore's forays into epistemology and Vaughan Williams's ideas about music, particularly as a dimension of life in the human community, can be found in the conclusion to Moore's celebrated 1925 article in *Contemporary British Philosophy*, "A Defence of

Common Sense."[42] Here Moore takes on philosophical arguments that all-too-frequently use arcane reasoning to counter the experiences and conclusions expressed in the way human beings are accustomed to speak. He defends the experiences and conclusions ordinary people accumulate and develop in their daily conduct of life. There was no reason to challenge the certainty and plausibility, if not truth, of many of our basic beliefs concerning what is real in the world:

> To speak with contempt of those "Common Sense beliefs" which I have mentioned is quite certainly the height of absurdity. And there are, of course, enormous numbers of other features in "the Common Sense view of the world" which, if these are true, are quite certainly true too: e.g. that there have lived upon the surface of the earth not only human beings, but also many different species of plants and animals, etc. etc.[43]

In this essay, Moore challenged the tradition of philosophic doubt—radical skepticism—of common-sense assumptions based on humanity's shared, repetitive, continuous experience in the world. Moore noted, with irony, that he differed from philosophers who held that "there is a good reason to suppose that all material things were created by God," and those who held that "there is good reason to suppose that there is a God at all, whether or not they have held it likely that he created all material things," and certainly those who claimed that human beings "shall continue to exist and to be conscious after the death of our bodies."[44] His point was that the alternative to some sort of realism—Idealism—requires a much more dramatic counterintuitive leap. There was far greater reason to trust common sense and the empirically based belief in the external world than to posit a metaphysical ideal like McTaggart's "the absolute."

Moore's purpose was to show that the common-sense beliefs in external realities (the existence of one's hands, for example) are a legitimate foundation for establishing criteria of knowledge and the truth. To Moore, McTaggart's view that time was unreal raised the need to consider ideas about truth and being from the vantage point of how one comes to believe that one knows things and how one uses language to establish knowledge. Moore's "A Defence of Common Sense" suggested the need to examine what we say, how we say it, and how we investigate the nature of facts and propositions. Refuting Berkeley, Moore concluded that "there is no good reason to suppose that *every* physical fact is *causally* dependent on some mental fact."[45]

Moore ended "Defence" by paying close attention to the ways in which we explain common-sense beliefs, such as the concept of sense-data, and the logic of the language we use to assert what we sense and believe. For Moore, "the assertion of the existence of many human beings" leads to a "proposition about *human knowledge* in general."[46] In his refutation of radical skepticism and Idealism Moore takes a decidedly egalitarian turn, to which Vaughan Williams was sympathetic, and gave epistemological credence to the existential predicament and continuity shared by the human community, including its experiences, habits, and language.

By the early 1940s, the consequences of Moore's 1925 essay became clear. Moore pursued the distinction between facts and propositions, and turned his attention to propositions. In his legendary contribution to philosophy, known as "Moore's paradox," there is the sentence "I don't believe it's raining, but as a matter of fact it is" (or, "Though I don't believe it's raining, yet as a matter of fact it really is raining"). What it appears to say is, as Moore put it, "perfectly absurd or nonsensical." At the same time, there is "nothing nonsensical about *merely saying these words*." Speech and the everyday use of language by ordinary people became the object of philosophical scrutiny. Keys to understanding the world and ourselves were locked in ordinary usage, particularly the English language as practiced continuously not by literary elites but everyday citizens. If there is nothing "nonsensical" about uttering a paradoxical sentence asserting a state of affairs that seems bizarre, self-contradictory, and incomprehensible on its surface, then the task of the philosopher is to discover why. The privileging of everyday language was a democratic turn against the prestige of specialized languages, of jargon, in the history of philosophy and the traditions of theology that implicitly showed contempt for everyday speech and underestimated what language might teach us about the world and human nature. Nothing could have been more encouraging to Vaughan Williams's embrace of folk traditions, hymn writing, his mixed amateur and professional performances of Bach, and, later in his career, film music than the direction Moore took in his thinking.

Moore's 1903 argument against Utilitarianism in the *Principia* already suggested that he paid close attention to the way we talk about making ethical judgments. The notion of intrinsic value, the existence of organic wholes, things in the world we identify as "good" or "beautiful" that cannot be taken apart and are more than the sum of their parts, do not exist in nature or depend for validity on how we react, and remain ultimately indefinable in other terms than the use of the words "good" and "beautiful," point to Moore's having paid acute attention to how common folk speak in contrast to professional philosophers.

Similarly, Vaughan Williams believed that the music made by the ordinary person, past and present, deserved respect and contained the timeless qualities of beauty. Folksong, hymns, and the simple dance tune contain clues to a normative aesthetic of musical beauty; they also carry ethical merit, markers of the "good." Moore's refutation of natural ethics justified the composer's belief in the rational character of the indivisible quality of beauty as an intrinsic value, one not rooted in nature yet true, and one that ought to be present in every work of music, of any kind. Beauty did not require or privilege any style or form and could be located throughout the history of music.

Moore's early work contributed decisively to the thinking of Ludwig Wittgenstein, who was deeply versed in music as well as art, architecture, and aesthetics. Wittgenstein arrived in England in 1908 and worked first in the field of engineering, only to shift his interests toward philosophy. He went to Cambridge to work with Russell at Trinity College in 1911, and there met Moore. Wittgenstein was elected to the Apostles, in which he was never particularly active. Like Vaughan Williams, he served in World War I, and its impact on him was as decisive as it was for the composer.

Wittgenstein returned to Cambridge in 1929, submitted the 1921 *Tractatus Logico-Philosophicus* as his thesis, and ultimately succeeded Moore as professor of philosophy. The *Tractatus* reflects, among other things, the consequence of how Moore sought to grapple with the elusive character of the fundamental issues of ethics and epistemology. The limitations in Moore's ideas of intrinsic value and organic wholes and of the non-natural character of the "good" and the "beautiful" led Wittgenstein to put forward three claims:

> It is clear that ethics cannot be put into words.
> Ethics is transcendental.
> (Ethics and aesthetics are one and the same.)
>
> And so it is impossible for there to be propositions of ethics.
> Propositions can express nothing of what is higher.
>
> There are, indeed, things that cannot be put into words.
> They *make themselves manifest.* They are what is mystical.[47]

Wittgenstein asserted that beauty and the good make themselves manifest outside language. They were mystic truths dealing with realms out of the reach of language, thereby eluding argument and verbal description.

Nonetheless, in aesthetics, as in ethics, there is an imperative: the pursuit of beauty that also has the ethical quality of the good. The ideal of beauty is not relative or subjective. Nor is it abstract, since, as Wittgenstein put it (more forcefully than Moore), aesthetics and ethics are "one and the same." They are real. Beauty in music, for example, must make its presence known within the fabric of a community, as a matter not only of art but also of ethics. Beauty in music must possess its own peculiar self-evident "grammar," as Wittgenstein once argued, and a quality that resists translation into words.

These formulations are consonant with Vaughan Williams's deepest convictions. Wittgenstein's suggestion that music belongs to a class of things that are mystical and cannot be expressed in language echoes the "mystic tinge" Foulds heard in Vaughan Williams's music. The overriding quality of music for Vaughan Williams was beauty, a word he used over and over again and understood in ethical as well as aesthetic terms.

In connecting ethics and aesthetics, Moore and Vaughan Williams carried forward an eighteenth-century tradition of thought, eloquently distilled in Shelley's Preface to *Prometheus Unbound* from 1820, verses from which Vaughan Williams set to music in his 1940 *Six Choral Songs To Be Sung in Time of War*. "My purpose," Shelley wrote, "has hitherto been simply to familiarize . . . poetical readers with beautiful idealisms of moral excellence; aware that until the mind can love, and admire, and trust, and hope, and endure, reasoned principles of moral conduct are seeds cast upon the highway of life which the unconscious passenger tramples into dust, although they would bare the harvest of his happiness."[48] Moore and Vaughan Williams endorsed Shelley's expectation that "moral excellence" ought to be "beautiful," and that the capacity for aesthetic judgment—"to love," "to admire," as well as an intuitive resilience in life—is a necessary precondition for understanding and acting on "reasoned principles of moral conduct."

Early in his career, in 1902, Vaughan Williams published three essays. In the first, "Palestrina and Beethoven," Palestrina was described as being "possessed by an intense and self-conscious love of beauty, and nothing else. Beethoven on the other hand, seems to have throughout much more of strength of expression than of beauty of the sounds he was inventing. His music was the outcome of his life and thoughts. He wrote, not because he wanted to do something beautiful, but because his mind could only find relief in musical expression."[49] For Palestrina, beauty was the explicit goal. He sought what Vaughan Williams called a "purely aesthetic" response through his music.[50] This meant that the emotion engendered by music is "purely that of pleasure in the perception of beauty." That placed a marked obligation on the listener.

Vaughan Williams was skeptical about reading music silently from a score as if reading literature: for him, music had to sound in real time and space. Consequently, he never ceased to build audiences that were capable of active listening. But for the thirty-year-old Vaughan Williams, since "the function of music is to be beautiful and nothing else—it cannot be more."[51] Beethoven, who lived in a historical era in which the subjective expression of emotions through music prevailed alongside a growing attachment to music as narrative, demonstrated how a personal impetus to write music could, in the end, result in music possessing more beauty than Palestrina's. This was possible not because of Beethoven's subjective attachment to music as expressive of emotions, or Beethoven's comparative modernity, but "simply and solely insofar as he is more beautiful." Beauty was a normative constant. True appreciation of music from any age could only be measured, so Vaughan Williams concluded, by "a pure delight in beauty."[52]

In the essay on Bach and Schumann, Vaughan Williams defined "'absolute' music"—the nineteenth-century's ideal notion of music as forms generated through self-referential sounding elements—as uniquely capable of communicating "beauty for its own sake."[53] In a 1920 program note for *A London Symphony*, he underscored that, despite his work's title, the music of the symphony "must stand or fall as 'absolute' music."[54] Music that succeeded as "absolute" was a "united whole," a claim reminiscent of Moore's insistence that the beautiful and the good were organic wholes greater than the sum of their parts.[55]

In the third 1902 article, an essay on Wagner, Vaughan Williams articulated a claim that bears an uncanny resemblance to the thinking of both Moore and Wittgenstein. "The nature of music," he argued, is that it "cannot touch reason and fact."[56] Insofar as music is capable of truly expressing "sentiment and emotion," that capacity is exclusive to music since sentiment and emotion can merely be "indicated" by words and not actually realized or communicated.[57] When characterizing Brahms in the context of Wagner, Vaughan Williams used beauty as the criterion to argue that Brahms was more than merely a conservative craftsman. Unlike most composers, he realized in his music the difference between great and average craftsmanship by making "beautiful music out of his counterpoint."[58]

Vaughan Williams's philosophically framed notion of beauty in music as normative and not contingent on history or human responses, and therefore as having intrinsic value, required the "right approaches to forms of composition." In the 1906 Preface to *The English Hymnal*, he explicitly referenced the ethical dimension of such "right" approaches: "The only correct music is that which is beautiful and noble."[59] The young Vaughan Williams here appropriated the attributes of clarity and coherence that his contemporary philosophers had applied to the notion of the organic completeness of normative beauty.

Vaughan Williams's belief in the resistance of music to translation to the visual or the linguistic, and therefore in its unique essence and in the resultant inability to construct a persuasive theory of correspondence between music and the external world, echoed Moore's and Wittgenstein's understanding of the aesthetic as distinct from the linguistic. Claims of correspondence can be made on behalf of realism in painting or realist prose; they benefit from the illusion of realism in art. Music, however, cannot enhance our ability to understand the external world. When Vaughan Williams wrote, in 1903, about a major tone poem by the finest living master of musical realism, Richard Strauss's *Ein Heldenleben*, he doomed Strauss's project to failure: "Music is not a symbol of anything else, it has no 'meaning'"; as a matter of fact, "it is the external world which is the symbol of the music." It is subordinate to, and actually symbolizes, music. To Vaughan Williams, music can never be "the symbol of the external event."[60]

Music in any age lacked ordinary, historically contingent meaning. As part of history, so wrote Vaughan Williams in 1957 at the end of his career, music was "but an expression of a vision through magic casements of the eternal verities."[61] That vision needed to be grounded in norms revealed through tradition and result from developing "something even more beautiful and vital out of the tradition which has been handed down."[62]

The philosophical underpinnings behind Vaughan Williams's repeated assertions that the purpose of writing music was to create "a true art which has beauty and vitality now in the twentieth century" became more visible after World War I.[63] In his 1920 essay "The Letter and the Spirit," Vaughan Williams stressed that the "object of an art," and therefore music, is "to obtain a partial revelation of that which is beyond human senses and human faculties."[64]

Vaughan Williams decried the "fear of beauty" among contemporaries. It flourished under the guise of a self-conscious and overt musical modernism that demanded a break, after the Great War, from the prewar culture held culpable for the pointless catastrophe. Yet the fear of beauty contradicted the true nature of music. Such fear of beauty could result in works unable to realize the promise of music for the community, particularly in times of suffering and fear. Vaughan Williams asked, "in our imperfect existence what means have we of reaching out to that which is beyond the senses?"[65] Like Moore, he understood art as a spiritual, non-natural but objective phenomenon that does not lead or refer to "other visible and audible things," but only to "what lies beyond sense and knowledge."[66]

In his 1950 "A Musical Autobiography," Vaughan Williams challenged the prestige of originality as a criterion of judgment of music, particularly new music. Since "the object of art is to stretch out to the ultimate realities through the medium of beauty," the "duty of the composer" is to express "the right thing to say," even if the music ends up sounding as if it had been heard a thousand times before.[67] Using the language of ethical reasoning, Vaughan Williams described the vocation and obligations of the composer as the "duty" to do the "right" thing. The cultivation and elevation of the sensibilities of a community to experience ultimate ideals constitute a moral obligation derived from the "good" within beauty. At the end of his career, Vaughan Williams's notion of the aesthetic continued to resemble Moore's "ideal" from the *Principia*. Vaughan Williams cast the structural similarities among the historical models of beauty across history in moral terms: the "right thing to say" at any "right moment." The beautiful remains constant, but the sounding result may change due to the historical circumstances at the moment the composer begins to create.[68]

In Vaughan Williams's case, the historical circumstances that most severely tested the validity of his philosophical claims on behalf of music were the two world wars. First came the years after the 1918 Armistice, with the difficulty of coming to terms with the experience of World War I and simultaneously the imperative to return to a productive civilian life. Second was maintaining courage in the face of fear during the mid-1930s, coupled with the resilience required to survive World War II. The idea of beauty as an autonomous, non-natural value that implied ethical and moral imperatives seemed vindicated in both instances. Confronted with violence and inhumanity during the years of the First World War, in which he saw active military service, and then with the threat of tyranny and autocracy during the 1930s, expressing and communicating beauty through music seemed essential in the darkest of times.

As Vaughan Williams well understood, music was not "useful" in the ordinary sense. That was among its virtues. Indeed, the moral significance of Vaughan Williams's so-called pastoral music and of the civic choral music from the interwar years lies not in its capacity to evoke nostalgia, but in its ability to inspire hope in the face of danger, terror, and loss. Vaughan Williams used evocations of the past to suggest a different future. Michael Tippett, writing in the 1990s, noted "with hindsight perception" that in the case of Vaughan Williams's *A Pastoral Symphony*, "the pastoral idyll can now be seen as an essential psychological counterbalance to the horrors of the trenches, replacing them with an imagined Arcadian ideal."[69]

Vaughan Williams's motivation, however, was less retrospective than suggested by the word "Arcadian." The contradictions and sufferings specific to his own times required the recognition of the present moment, as *Job* and the Fourth Symphony (both from the 1930s) exemplify. Beauty is present, yes, but in a new incarnation. Eric Saylor, the composer's most recent biographer, eloquently observed that the Third Symphony, the *Pastoral*, long an object of critical skepticism, represents Vaughan Williams's ability "to imagine beauty under such conditions, and to express that beauty so that others too might find hope within the wreckage." That, Saylor concluded, "is the mark of the true artist and the challenge Vaughan Williams took up throughout his career."[70] The ambition "to view tragedy through a lens of beauty" was forged both by philosophical conviction and the ravages of war.[71] Since music was "purely of the spirit" and had "no place in the world of alarms and excursions," given the brutality of modern life, Vaughan Williams wrote, "would it not indeed be better for music to keep out of the struggle and reserve for us a place where sanity can again find a home when she returns to her own?"[72]

Philosophy, as pursued by Moore, shaped the composer's views on music's social function, how it should communicate and for whom it ought to be written. Moore's argument on behalf of common sense and the epistemological reliability of ordinary language bolstered Vaughan Williams's notion that the appeal of music should "in the long run" always be as broad as possible, even "universal." But "like charity," he wrote in 1912, "it should begin at home. If it is to be of any value it must grow out of the very life of himself, the community in which he lives, the nation to which he belongs."[73] One had to "break down the distinction between 'classical' and 'popular'—all music should be classical and all music should be popular."[74] These prewar convictions became linked in the interwar period to a political agenda in which music, as a participatory and public art, could contribute to the renewal of the nation; that meant foregrounding the local, the people with whom one lived and whose language and history one shared. As Vaughan Williams wrote in 1931:

> A few years ago, someone invented the very foolish phrase, "A good European." The best European is the most convinced nationalist, not the chauvinist but he who believes that all countries should be different and friendly rather than all alike at enmity.[75]

Vaughan Williams was never content to write for an elite, or for his fellow musicians, let alone for critics. His work on *The English Hymnal* and collecting and arranging folksongs revealed a respect for, if not an idealization of, the "common" folk: the poor, both rural and urban laborers, and outsiders such as Jews and "Gypsies" (as the Roma were called during his lifetime).[76] Music, whether folksong or symphony, must be "an art which grows straight out of the needs of a people."[77] Vaughan Williams was determined not to let "the amateur side of music" atrophy.[78] He feared that the "passive" habits of listening engendered by modern sound reproduction (despite its many virtues) might overwhelm lay participation in public music making.[79] In the concluding chapter of *National Music*, a distillation of his 1932 Bryn Mawr lectures, Vaughan Williams validated "common sense" as a foundation in a nation's cultural life:

> The art of music above all the other arts is the expression of
> the soul of a nation, and by a nation I mean not necessarily
> aggregations of people, artificially divided from each other
> by political frontiers or economic barriers. What I mean is
> any community of people who are spiritually bound together
> by language, environment, history, and common ideals and,
> above all, a continuity with the past.[80]

Vaughan Williams's analogue to Moore's advocacy of common sense was the radical conception of the community as a source of musical beauty. He believed that if one could advance the aesthetic sensibilities of one's fellow human beings, utilizing their musical heritage, one could advance beauty through newly composed music and, indirectly, through aesthetic merit, the moral betterment of humanity.[81]

England, Its History and Future

Owing in part to his work with folksongs and hymns, Vaughan Williams was an avid reader of history and lived through a period of new research and writing about England's past. The historian who helped shape his framing of national identity, pride, and the past and present, was George Macaulay Trevelyan, a closer personal friend of the composer than Moore.[82] Owing to his membership in the Apostles, Trevelyan was friendly with Moore as well. Vaughan Williams cited Trevelyan with approval more than once in his writings; in 1931, the composer observed wryly, "for a self-styled Philistine, [he] has an extraordinary quantity of pregnant things to say about the arts."[83] The essay "Making Your Own Music" concludes with a long quote from Trevelyan.[84]

Moore's philosophical turn turned out to be congruent with Trevelyan's views on England's national history, its contemporary circumstances, and its future. Moore's realist views eliminated the anti-democratic bias implicit in earlier arguments on behalf of normative metaphysical entities, most apparent in Plato. In most arguments about the existence of spiritual substances, the highest form of knowledge—at the top of the "divided line" described in *The Republic*—is accessible only to a tiny class of human beings. Consequently, genuine aesthetic discernment and moral judgment are reserved for an elite. As noted above, in Moore's account, the beautiful and the "good" are "neutral" wholes not subject to rational analysis or dissection; they are, consequently, independent of differentials in the human capacity to reason and in levels of formal education. Recognizing and responding to beauty and goodness in the world cease to be a potential held by the privileged. For Vaughan Williams, recognizing the good and the beautiful is an aspiration shared by many. Moore's pursuit of common sense and the claims of realism gave philosophical legitimacy to Trevelyan's notions about a peaceful and civilized democratization in English history.

Vaughan Williams's affinity with Trevelyan's valorization of England's historical and political uniqueness as well as the imperative of further democratization is evident early in his career. Apart from his enthusiasm for Moore's epistemological egalitarianism, Vaughan Williams also developed an early fascination with the poetry of Walt Whitman, whose vision of a democratic culture, for all its swaggering celebration of America, was popular at the turn of the century with British readers. Since music, as an art, could assume a role in history on behalf of moral progress it could also advance a fundamental equality within the vision of national cohesion. Through his love of Whitman's poetry, and by endorsing Trevelyan's account of history, Vaughan Williams located a justification for such aspirations. Vaughan Williams went far beyond commonplace ideas concerning English exceptionalism. He embraced aspects of socialism, and supported ideas for a "United States of Europe." As his opera *Hugh the Drover* suggests, the common man was not only an ideal source of the good and the beautiful, but the beneficiary of the trajectory of history.

Vaughan Williams's egalitarian instincts were not just rooted in Whitman, but were reinforced by his oft-cited enthusiasm for George Borrow's picaresque novel *Lavengro* (1851). This now-obscure novel concerns the power of language, the virtues of cultural difference, and their capacity to foster a sense of common humanity. Its "scenes of action lie in the British Islands."[85] It was "a dream, or drama" about a "scholar, a Gypsy, and a Priest." It was harshly critical of religion, notably High Anglicanism and Roman Catholicism. But its primary "quarrel" was "with the aristocracy."[86]

Language was a common possession, and in its many types, it transcended class and ethnicity. Borrow asserts the dominance of a common origin among all peoples and seeks to shatter the illusion of the natural homogeneity and legitimacy of class divisions. The novel ranges through theology, philosophy, and comparative linguistics; it is an ethnographic *Bildungsroman* with Whitman-like commitments to democracy and egalitarianism. Borrow defines England less by its reigning cultural, ethnic, and linguistic habits than by the injuries inflicted by an allegiance to privilege, as well as the tragic, but sometimes also comic, aspirations of outsiders to high social status. Borrow seeks to defend individuality, minorities—particularly "Gypsies" and Jews[87]—and all those who are rendered marginal by the conceits of a ruling class; he feared that the hugely admirable simple folk with different cultures and mores in England might be seduced to abandon what differentiates them by the allure of "being accepted and absorbed by the genteel majority." The novel challenged equally the pieties of both Tory and Whig politics.[88]

Borrow's mix of radicalism and idealism fit Vaughan Williams's conception, shaped initially by the views within his immediate family, of what distinguished England, its character, and its history from other nations. Vaughan Williams came of age in the shadow of the Whig interpretation of history. From 1868, after the passage of the Second Reform Bill, to 1901, the ideas of two key figures from the midcentury, J. S. Mill and Thomas Babington Macaulay, maintained a position of importance. Of course, Whig ideas encountered challenges from subsequent generations. Although Mill pushed Utilitarianism beyond economic behavior as a basis for the extension of democracy and freedom of speech, and thought, as noted above, Moore, Vaughan Williams, and their contemporaries weighed Utilitarianism in the balance and found it wanting.

Macaulay's version of history required reevaluation as well. His five-volume *History of England* (published between 1849 and 1861) put forward the Whig interpretation of why England's history did not follow that of Continental Europe's nations. He believed that England's history revealed the possibility of progress without revolutionary violence, the centrality of reason in the deliberations of politics, the superiority of constitutional and parliamentary government, and the need to spread the use of reason through education in order that the government could further humanitarian ideals. For Macaulay, reason encompassed both morality and science. He argued that England was distinctive in that it had benefited from the 1688 Revolution, a revolution that had been the "least violent" and most "beneficent." For that reason, it would be England's "last revolution."[89]

Vaughan Williams absorbed Macaulay's premise that progress in England would not be the result of armies or politicians. Macaulay believed that "events" (e.g., treaties) do not influence the happiness or the shaping of a nation. Happiness was achieved by "noiseless revolutions":

> The changes of manners and morals, the transition of communities from poverty to wealth, from knowledge to ignorance, from ferocity to humanity . . . are carried on in every school, in every church, behind ten thousand counters, at ten thousand firesides. The upper current of society present no certain criterion by which we can judge of the direction in which the under current flows. . . . But we must remember how small a proportion the good or evil affected by a single statesman can bear to the good or evil of a great social system.[90]

Culture—especially music—had a role to play. However, historians in the last quarter of the nineteenth century challenged Macaulay's sanguine view of British history. A dramatic social transformation marked by an ever more rapid exodus from rural regions and the striking expansion of cities was well underway. Writing in 1944, Trevelyan had this to say about changes in daily life and the drift away from religion that flourished during his and Vaughan Williams's youth:

> The gradual modification of the "English Sunday" has had effects both good and bad. In this transition period, between the over-great strictness of the past and the entire laxity of the present day, there was much good in the practice of many families who still insisted on "Sunday reading" of serious though not necessarily religious books. For one day in the week, novels and magazines were laid aside, and great classical literature like the Bible, *Pilgrim's Progress* and *Paradise Lost*, besides more secular poetry and history, had a chance of perusal which they no longer enjoy.[91]

During the final decades of the Victorian era, modern technology, the product of the growth of science and industry, challenged this idyllic "transition." As Trevelyan argued in two separate essays from 1901, contemporary England demonstrated that "man's power over nature outstripped his moral and mental development."

Neither he nor Vaughan Williams could shed a sense of disquiet and pessimism about such innovations. The upheavals of modernity undercut

Macaulay's blithe assumption of an alliance between reason and material progress, on the one hand, and moral and aesthetic advancement on the other. Trevelyan concluded that modern currents in economic and social life bred "vulgarity" and threatened to turn England, once "beautiful and instructive," into an "ugly and trivial" place. "The sudden destruction of rural life," Trevelyan wrote, "which never was more prosperous than it was fifty years ago, the substitution of life in 'great cities' for life in large towns, the rapid diffusion of the vulgarity bred in those great cities into every corner of our island by locomotion and the cheap press, has destroyed all that was characteristic of Old England."[92] By 1944, Trevelyan's critical assessment of the late nineteenth century had deepened:

> More generally speaking it has produced a vast population able to read but unable to distinguish what is worth reading, an easy prey to sensations and cheap appeals. Consequently, both literature and journalism have been to a large extent debased since 1870, because they now cater for millions of half-educated and quarter-educated people, whose forebears, not being able to read at all, were not the patrons of newspapers or of books. The small highly educated class no longer sets the standard to the extent that it used to do, and tends to adopt the standards of the majority. Whether in the twentieth or twenty-first centuries the lower forms of literature and journalism will completely devour the higher has yet to be seen. If they do not, it will be due to improved secondary and higher education forming a sufficiently large class to perpetuate a demand for things really worth reading.[93]

Trevelyan's image of "Old England" had been influenced by his glorification of the moral influence of nature. Wordsworth was his touchstone. Nature was the countryside, and the open spaces, fields, and forests defined beauty and secured essential moral values. He was, as David Cannadine put it, a "rural elegist." No doubt, Vaughan Williams shared Trevelyan's love of the outdoors, of small towns and the rural landscape, but despite the composer's reputation for a "pastoral" aesthetic and a romance with premodern England, he did not entirely share Trevelyan's despair. He seconded Trevelyan's lament that "under the new conditions England bade fair to become one huge unplanned suburb."[94] But Vaughan Williams saw in music a chance to compensate for these modern developments and sustain inherited values by integrating them into the new realities of contemporary life. Vaughan Williams's affinity for

Moore's notion that neither the good nor the beautiful were derivative or contingent on nature bolstered his own ambition to write music that "would voice the ideals" of "his fellow men," new music for the Britain of the present. Music was "above all things the art of the common man," even in modern times.[95]

If it was not Vaughan Williams's ambition to give nostalgia musical shape and sound, "building on the past" certainly was an objective. The past must be preserved so that it could provide a foundation for further evolution. Vaughan Williams was committed to the modern: he relished writing for the relatively new medium of film. He had little patience with the rise of what is known today as the "performance practice" of Baroque music, notably Bach, that sought an ersatz re-creation of the past. His concern with the gramophone was not with its potential but with the ease of its use, which threatened active participation in music making by ordinary people. Ravel's teaching and influence tempered his criticism of modernisms. He was not "cloistered" in a "refuge" defined by a nostalgia for the English past or a premodern world, as Ronald Taylor had claimed.

What Vaughan Williams drew from Trevelyan, his doubts notwithstanding, was an updated allegiance to the Whig account of the exceptional political history of England and the peculiar mores of his nation fostered by history. In this regard, Trevelyan, as a historian and writer (he did not wish to be regarded as a professional historian in the academic sense), saw himself within the tradition of English historical writing established by Macaulay, a great prose stylist with a wide audience. Macaulay, who considered Thucydides (rather than Herodotus) a model historian, did not believe in "distorting narrative into a conformity with theory," as he put it in his 1828 essay "The Task of the Modern Historian."[96] Trevelyan followed the path of his namesake. Despite his degree from Cambridge in modern history, Vaughan Williams never aspired to be a historian. Rather, he sought to influence the "great social system" of England through the culture of its peoples in order to redeem the aspirations embedded in the Whig interpretation. Rather than writing history, Vaughan Williams composed music that sought to redeem Macaulay's optimistic vision of a rational, free, humanitarian nation.

The influence of H. A. L. Fisher—Vaughan Williams had married Fisher's sister Adeline in 1897—supplemented the composer's allegiance to Trevelyan's views. Fisher was a distinguished historian, primarily of Europe, who sought to move beyond Macaulay. Fisher and Trevelyan, and indeed Winston Churchill, all emulated Macaulay in pursuing parallel careers as writers and political actors. Fisher particularly admired the great legal historian Frederick William Maitland for his ambition as a reformer and his "natural proclivity of mind."[97] He recognized the decisive impact of imperialism on late nineteenth-century Britain. Not the so-called Glorious Revolution but rather the Empire defined modern England. Fisher expressed the growing discontent of his and Vaughan Williams's generation with the impact of Empire, but somewhat reluctantly recognized that patriotic sentiment was centered around the monarchical institutions that had kept the Empire intact.[98] Like Trevelyan, Fisher addressed how new technologies of communication and travel changed politics. Politics had become too dependent on innovative ways to manufacture popularity, thereby strengthening the hand of political leaders—and even the aristocracy—in an era of expanded literacy and social mobility. This was the result of "the planing down" of social and intellectual inequalities.[99] In a series of 1911 lectures delivered at Harvard University, Fisher declared that in the modern age, England had taken an unexpected and unusual turn that favored the influence and authority of the monarchy:

> Yet no one can have lived in England through the last twenty years without acknowledging that a great change has been silently and insensibly accomplished by the joint influence of Queen Victoria and King Edward. The monarchy is stronger and more respected; its place in the scheme of a democratic polity is more comfortably settled, and a sphere of unchallenged utility has been discovered for the king and the royal family.[100]

The view that England had achieved a stable "democratic polity" and unity was one Trevelyan, Fisher, and Vaughan Williams shared; but they questioned its future. England had flourished through a balance of aristocratic leadership, parliamentary system of debate, and commitment to social and political reform framed by an allegiance to king, country, and Empire. Fisher's optimistic pre–World War I view of the stability of progress and modern politics ended up not being shattered by internal revolution, as Macaulay had predicted. Rather, it was upended by the failure of diplomacy that led to the cataclysm of the Great War.

The momentous change sparked by World War I led to a less optimistic outlook for Vaughan Williams, a darker view of the future that Trevelyan articulated in the early 1920s. The present had been transformed into "a more mechanical and a more democratic world, the world of the great city instead of the country village, a world expressing itself more through science and journalism, and less through religion, poetry and literature." In 1926, Trevelyan lamented that while England still contained "God's plenty of all manner of beautiful birds and beasts . . . the vast wealth of trees and flowers," these were "treasures, which modern man, careless of his best inheritance, has abolished, and is still abolishing, as fast as new tools and methods of destruction can be invented." In a letter to his brother he confessed, "I don't understand the age we live in, and what I do understand I don't like."[101] Vaughan Williams, committed to bringing the past into the present, never quite shared his friend's somber reaction to the immediate postwar years, but hoped that the arts and culture could counteract the ravages of the present.

By the 1930s, however, with the worldwide Depression and the rise of fascism in England and on the Continent triggering increased fear and uncertainty, Trevelyan was inspired in 1938 to reassert the Whig interpretation of England's past. He did so in order that the British public would not waver from its special history and keep a distance from European politics. He defended England's imperialism by asserting that it shared in the virtues of the history of English politics: "The [1688] Revolution gave to England an ordered and legal freedom, and through that it gave her power. She often abused her power as in the matters of Ireland and of the Slave Trade, till she reversed the engines; but on the whole mankind would have breathed a harsher air if England had not grown strong."[102]

Yet during the "gathering storm," England needed to be reminded that "engrained habits of toleration and respect for law sank deep into the English mind during the hundred years that followed the [Glorious] Revolution, and had their effect when the stresses of a new era began—with the democratic movement, the French Revolution and the social problems of the great industrial change."[103]

For Trevelyan, England must not deviate in the face of danger. Democracy in England faced the striking success of tyranny in Nazi Germany, in Soviet Russia under Stalin, in Italy under Mussolini, in Franco's Spain, and under Austro-fascism in Austria (eclipsed by the Anschluss in the year Trevelyan published his book), as well as other examples of dictatorship in smaller post-1918 Continental nations. England needed to understand that "the system of government by discussion has its disadvantages, under which in new forms we are labouring to-day, in face of absolutist governments of a new and more formidable type than those of Europe of the *ancien* régime. But if, on the balance, we prefer the path on which our feet are planted, we must commend the choice that was made once for all at the English Revolution."[104]

Trevelyan believed that "the victims of the Industrial Revolution at the beginning of the nineteenth century sought a remedy for their ills by demanding the franchise and Parliamentary Reform instead of general overturn; this happy choice was due in part to our national character but largely also to our national institutions, in which the oppressed saw a way of escape. The English Revolution had the ultimate effect of saving the Crown and much else besides."[105] Britain had managed to triumph because it proceeded as a nation "on lines laid down by the eighteenth-century pioneers of thought and mercy. This great humanitarian movement, to whose sphere of operation there is no limit, was a new birth of time."[106] Contrary to common wisdom, Trevelyan maintained that "our island people were, in some respects, the least insular of all mankind. To Europeans we appeared insular, because we were not continental. But our experiences and opportunities were greater than those of the folk of other lands."[107]

Before the Second World War, Vaughan Williams mostly shared Trevelyan's views, in part because they were reinforced by Fisher during the 1930s. Fisher, who published a history of Europe in 1936, observed with regret: "I begin this book with Neolithic man and conclude with Stalin and Mustapha Kemal, Mussolini and Hitler. . . . The fact of progress is written plain and large on the page of history; but progress is not a law of nature. The ground gained by one generation may be lost by the next. The thoughts of men may flow into the channels which lead to disaster and barbarism."[108]

He went on to articulate the sense among his contemporaries, including Vaughan Williams:

> And if I speak of Liberty in this wider sense as experimental, it is not because I wish to disparage Freedom (for I would as soon disparage Virtue herself), but merely to indicate that after gaining ground through the nineteenth century, the tides of liberty have now suddenly receded over wide tracts of Europe. Yet how can the spread of servitude, by whatever benefits it may have been accompanied, be a matter for congratulation? A healthy man needs no narcotics. Only when the moral spine of a people is broken may plaster of Paris become a necessary evil.[109]

Fisher closed his massive survey with a description of the challenge facing the core beliefs of English liberalism, and the English self-image of its history and character shared by Vaughan Williams and Trevelyan:

> Europe, then, has now reached a point at which it would seem, as never so clearly in past history, that two alternative and

sharply contrasted destinies await her. She may travel down the road to a new war or, overcoming passion, prejudice, and hysteria, work for a permanent organization of peace. In either case the human spirit is armed with material power. The developing miracle of science is at our disposal to use or abuse, to make or to mar. With science we may lay civilization in ruins or enter into a period of plenty and well-being the like of which has never been experienced by mankind . . . the war has left us an evil legacy. The moral unity of Europe is for the time being broken. Nordic paganism assails Christianity. An insane racialism threatens to rupture the seamless garment of civilization. May future generations close the rents, heal the wounds, and replace our squandered treasure of humanity, toleration, and good sense.[110]

Epilogue: A New Elizabethan Age?
Tolkien, Lewis, and Vaughan Williams

In 1956, three years after the death of George VI, Trevelyan attempted to frame the decline of England and the loss of Empire in a manner that now seems an indefensible apologia for colonialism. He attempted to redeem the Whig interpretation that had left such a lasting imprint on him and his contemporaries:

> Our countrymen no longer rule India. But we shall always take a just pride in the great story of how we once controlled that vast subcontinent; how we established the Pax Britannica in place of a chaos of violence and war; how for a century and a half the first thought of the governors was the interest of the governed, and how when the time was ripe the Indians, because of what we had done, were able to undertake the task of self-government.[111]

Perhaps because he showed little or no interest in the Empire, Vaughan Williams did not succumb to Trevelyan's laconic pessimism. (In addition, Vaughan Williams was an active member of the Federal Union, an organization dedicated to the creation of a federated Europe that included Britain.) As his post–World War II music exemplifies, he sought to extend the spiritual quality of the good and the beautiful by fashioning music that addressed contemporary life in the West, not just those circumstances specific to England. The last three symphonies and the

completed *Pilgrim's Progress* illustrate a turn from the local social obligation of the composer and his own personal sense of purpose to the more
fundamental links between music and the human condition.[112]

To do so, Vaughan Williams picked up the thread that had been
articulated by Moore's pre–World War I writings. After World War II,
the existential predicament of the Atomic Age rendered the boundaries
established by nation-states less and less significant, including the pro-
tection offered by England's insularity and exceptional history. Modern
technology, including film and television, made the capacity for music to
communicate, universally, the spiritual character of goodness and beauty
ever more crucial. The limits of national history as a framework had been
exposed in the context of the threat of nuclear war. A discontinuity with
the past, far greater than had been experienced by Vaughan Williams
as a young man, now faced all of humanity. In the conduct of life, the
ethics of human contact and the formation of community—questions of
ultimate meaning—were now commonsense grounds for promoting solidarity beyond borders. For Vaughan Williams, philosophy, in the end,
took priority over history as a guide to the creation of new music in his
last period, a new and unprecedented age.

Vaughan Williams's twin convictions—that beauty is a whole and unified attribute, accessible to all of humanity, normative and constant in
history, and that beauty is intrinsically linked to moral goodness—suggest, in light of the return to accessibility and spirituality evident in music
written in the twenty-first century, that his career and achievement can
be placed alongside those of two Oxford-based younger contemporaries
and fellow veterans of the First World War, whose fame and reputation
have blossomed over the past years: C. S. Lewis and J. R. R. Tolkien.
To ensure the triumph of beauty over ugliness—despite the fragile presence of beauty in modern life—was ultimately Vaughan Williams's most
cherished ambition.[113] That conviction, along with an idealization of a
premodern past and the virtues of the common human being, are the
overarching argument in Tolkien's *Lord of the Rings*, first published in
the mid-1950s. The constancy and survival of core values such as beauty,
goodness, friendship, generosity, and duty play the decisive role in
Tolkien's tale of the triumph of good over evil.

C. S. Lewis's 1950 *The Chronicles of Narnia* also foregrounded the triumph of the spiritual over the material in the battle between good and
evil in a manner somewhat akin to Vaughan Williams's final version of
The Pilgrim's Progress. But despite these resemblances, the suppositional
religiosity in Lewis's fantasy fiction overrides what might have been a
useful comparison with Vaughan Williams. Despite his Catholic faith,

Tolkien's engagement with a real and imagined past, and its many languages—echoes of George Borrow—demonstrated a resolute, universal, and essentially secular sensibility. That made Tolkien's outlook and aesthetic far closer to Vaughan Williams than that of Lewis's High Church Anglicanism. What Vaughan Williams's ambitions and career did share with the writings of both Tolkien and Lewis is a touching confidence in the ultimate arc of victory for good over evil, as well as in the role art and culture might play in that victory. All three sought to rescue the spiritual values they believed normative and which they identified with qualities uniquely English.

In Tolkien's account, the good and the beautiful are juxtaposed against evident emblems of modernity: industry, technology, the destruction of nature, the allure of untrammeled power, dominion over others, and brutal violence. In *Lord of the Rings*, the material stands sharply opposed to the spiritual. Vaughan Williams's—and certainly Trevelyan's— attachment to the distant rural past of England and its landscape is mirrored in Tolkien's rural Hobbits and their "Shire." Their simple, decent love of beauty, friendship, and kindness triumph over the perversion of science and the ruthlessness of the mechanical. Truth is located in honoring the past and listening to nature and preserving simple virtues. Tolkien's skepticism of modernity is framed in a morality tale that ends in some sort of triumph, albeit one shaded by an overriding sense of loss. By contrast, Vaughan Williams sought to compensate for the loss by integrating the past with the present.

Vaughan Williams's self-imposed distance from High Modernism and his loyalty to beauty as found in premodern folk traditions therefore did not lead him quite in the same direction as Tolkien. All too often, musical modernism simply sounded too much like all that Vaughan Williams wished would not triumph: soulless technology, materialism, elitism, intolerance, and violence. Any return to peace and tranquility and the spiritual virtues of beauty and goodness demanded a modified modernism without decrying it. Unlike Lewis, Vaughan Williams did not seek a restoration of Christianity, with its notions of sin, asceticism, and its epistemological and ethical subordination of the body to the soul. Rather, Vaughan Williams appropriated the virtues of Tolkien's protagonists and the moral of his imaginary history into new sounds. He sought the triumph of humanity in the capacity to redeem, in fresh and contemporary ways, the two central and intertwined secular and rational constant spiritual values, the good and the beautiful, and deploy them against the perils of modernity.

NOTES

I would like to thank Byron Adams, Daniel M. Grimley, Christopher H. Gibbs, Irene Zedlacher, Gary Hagberg, and Deirdre d'Albertis for their generous assistance and counsel in preparing this essay.

1. Ronald Taylor (1924–2013) was the author of many books, including one on Wagner, and the editor of a volume of writings by Wilhelm Furtwängler translated into English. He wrote on German culture and literature, not only on music, and was professor of German at the University of Sussex, 1965–86.

2. Ronald Taylor, "Vaughan Williams and English National Music," *Cambridge Journal* 6 (1953): 615–24.

3. John Foulds, *Music Today: Its Heritage from the Past, and Legacy to the Future* (London: Nicholson and Watson, 1934), 275–76.

4. Eric Taylor (1928–2016) was professor of music at Durham. Among his accomplishments was the introduction of the gamelan and the music of Southeast Asia to Britain and his overhaul of the teaching of music theory. I thank Byron Adams for this information.

5. Eric Taylor, "Vaughan Williams and the English Tradition," *Blackfriars* 36/417 (1954): 522–26.

6. The connection between ethics and aesthetics has a long history in eighteenth-century philosophy, particularly in England. The Earl of Shaftesbury was the most influential writer on this relationship. But as the discussion below on G. E. Moore's consideration of this link will argue, Shaftesbury's view of beauty as a normative virtue in art was based on a naturalist conception of the character of beauty, first in the link between beauty in nature and beauty in art, and second in the impact of human sentiment in defining and vindicating artistic beauty, thereby justifying the cultivation of taste as a means to moral betterment. A comparison of early twentieth-century thought on this issue with Friedrich von Schiller's views yields a similar contrast to Moore's and Vaughan Williams's ideas about the quality of beauty and its connection and resemblance to the quality of the "good." Moore was opposed to the "naturalist fallacy" in both ethics and aesthetics.

7. Ralph Vaughan Williams, "Local Musicians" (1939), in *Vaughan Williams on Music*, ed. David Manning (Oxford: Oxford University Press, 2008), 70–81, at 81. This formulation has an uncomfortable resemblance to the anti-Semitic rhetoric of the period. Vaughan Williams showed no tendency to anti-Semitism despite the awkward 1937 Hamburg Shakespeare Prize event which revealed his deep reluctance to contemplate a second war with Germany. This was shared by Trevelyan and made both late converts to Churchill's attack on appeasement. See Alain Frogley, "Vaughan Williams and Nazi Germany: The 1937 Hamburg Shakespeare Prize," in *Music as a Bridge: Musikalische Beziehungen zwischen England und Deutschland 1920–1950*, ed. Christa Brüstle and Guido Heldt (Hildesheim: Olms, 2005), 113–32; and Neil Wenborn, "'A desirable end': Vaughan Williams and the Refugee Relief Effort of the 1930s and 1940s," *Ralph Vaughan Williams Society Journal* 76 (October 2019): 9–11.

8. See Alain Frogley, "Tonality on the Town: Orchestrating the Metropolis in Vaughan Williams's *A London Symphony*," in *Tonality 1900–1950: Concept and Practice*, ed. Felix Wörner, Ullrich Scheideler, and Philip Rupprecht (Stuttgart: Franz Steiner, 2012), 187–202. What is striking about the opening is the "sharp juxtaposition" of "nature and the city," a synthesis of an archaic-sounding, premodern sonority with clearly contemporary harmonic practice. See also Frogley, "H. G. Wells and Vaughan Williams's *A London Symphony*: Politics and Culture in Fin-de-siècle England," in *Sundry Sorts of Music Books: Essays on the British Library Collections*, ed. Chris Banks, Arthur Searle, and Malcolm Turner (London: British Library, 1993), 299–308.

9. Adrian Boult, *On Music: Words from a Lifetime's Communication*, foreword by Bernard Shore, introduction by Vernon Hadley (London: Toccata Press, 1981), 63. See also Julius Röntgen's letter on *A Pastoral Symphony*, reproduced in the selection from Michael Kennedy's correspondence in this volume.

10. Karen Arrandale, *Edward J. Dent: A Life of Words and Music* (Woodbridge: Boydell Press, 2023), 509–10.

11. Bertrand Russell, *The Autobiography of Bertrand Russell, 1872–1914* (Boston: Little, Brown, 1967), 94–95.

12. The following have been invaluable resources: Eric Saylor, *Vaughan Williams* (Oxford: Oxford University Press, 2022); Ursula Vaughan Williams, *R.V.W.: A Biography of Ralph Vaughan Williams* (London: Oxford University Press, 1964); and Michael Kennedy, *A Catalogue of the Works of Ralph Vaughan Williams*, 2nd ed. (Oxford: Oxford University Press, 1996) and *The Works of Ralph Vaughan Williams*, 2nd ed. (Oxford: Oxford University Press, 1980).

13. George M. Trevelyan, *English Social History: A Survey of Six Centuries: Chaucer to Queen Victoria* (New York: Longmans, Green, and Co., 1942 [repr. 1944]), 569; and David Cannadine, *G. M. Trevelyan: A Life in History* (New York: W. W. Norton, 1993), 9.

14. Trevelyan, *English Social History*, 569.

15. See Jeremy Dibble, *C. Hubert H. Parry: His Life and Music* (Oxford: Clarendon Press, 1992). Parry had an aristocratic lineage, making his distrust of his own class complicated.

16. Ralph Vaughan Williams, "Sir Hubert Parry" (1918), in *Vaughan Williams on Music*, 295.

17. Vaughan Williams, "The Teaching of Parry and Stanford" (1955), in *Vaughan Williams on Music*, 316.

18. C. Hubert Parry, *Studies of Great Composers* (London: Routledge, 1904), 376.

19. Paul Levy, *G. E. Moore and the Cambridge Apostles* (New York: Holt, Rinehart, and Winston, 1979), 164.

20. G. E. Moore, "An Autobiography," in *The Philosophy of G. E. Moore*, ed. Paul A. Schlipp (New York: Tudor, 1952), 3–39.

21. See Nigel Simone, *Ralph Vaughan Williams and Adrian Boult* (Woodbridge, Suffolk: Boydell Press, 2022), 208–10.

22. The allure of a radical reformulation of Christianity toward a disciplined ascetic anti-authoritarian and anti-hierarchical ethics based on Jesus was widespread at the turn of the century, which suggests the impact of Tolstoy's writings from the 1880s and 1890s, including "What I Believe" (1884) and "The Kingdom of God is Within You" (1894). Tolstoy fascinated both Ludwig Wittgenstein and Max Weber.

23. Lytton Strachey, quoted in Levy, *G. E. Moore and the Cambridge Apostles*, 234.

24. Russell, quoted in ibid., 237–38.

25. Ursula Vaughan Williams, *R.V.W.*, 65.

26. The first movement of *A London Symphony* reveals polyphonic textures reminiscent of the music of the apprentices in Wagner's *Meistersinger*. See also the closing section of Vaughan Williams's essay "Some Conclusions," in *National Music and Other Essays*, ed. Michael Kennedy (Oxford: Oxford University Press, 1963), 72–73.

27. Interestingly, two decades after the premiere, the *Sea Symphony* earned a place in Aaron Copland's 1929 course "Forms of Modern Music" in a list of major choral symphonies alongside, among others, Schoenberg's *Gurrelieder*.

28. Henry Sidgwick, *The Methods of Ethics* (London: Macmillan, 1874). John Rawls contributed an introduction to the 1981 reprint of the *Methods* (Indianapolis: Hackett). He wrote "Sidgwick's originality consists in his conception of moral philosophy and of the way in which a reasoned and satisfactory justification of any moral conception must proceed from a full knowledge and systematic comparison of the more significant moral conceptions in the philosophical tradition." High praise for a work Rawls considered "the

most philosophically profound" defense of Utilitarianism (v, vi). See also David Phillip, *Sidgwick's "The Methods of Ethics": A Guide* (Oxford: Oxford University Press, 2022).

29. Sidgwick, *The Methods of Ethics*, 411–59.

30. Ibid., 373–84.

31. Ibid., 96–104.

32. See G. E. Moore, "Professor Sidgwick's Hedonism," in *Early Philosophical Writings*, ed. Thomas Baldwin and Consuelo Preti (Cambridge: Cambridge University Press, 2011), 87–94. On Moore see Thomas Baldwin, *G. E. Moore* (London and New York: Routledge, 1990), and the following essays in *The Philosophy of G. E. Moore*: C. D. Broad, "Certain Features in Moore's Ethical Doctrines" (41–68); Charles S. Stevenson, "Moore's Arguments Against Certain Forms of Ethical Naturalism" (69–90); William K. Frankena, "Obligation and Value in the Ethics of G. E. Moore" (91–110); and H. J. Paton, "The Alleged Independence of Goodness" (111–34). See also *G .E. Moore: Essays in Retrospect*, ed. Alice Ambrose and Morris Lazerowitz (London: George Allen & Unwin, 1970).

33. G. E. Moore, *Principia Ethica* (Garden City, NY: Dover Publications, repr. 2004), 92–94.

34. Ibid., 26–29.

35. G. E. Moore, *Ethics* (London: Oxford University Press, 1963), 146–47.

36. Moore, *Principia Ethica*, 182–225.

37. Ibid., 202.

38. Ibid., 201.

39. Levy, *G. E. Moore and the Cambridge Apostles*, 108.

40. On McTaggart, see Moore, "An Autobiography," 18–19; R. D. Ingthorssen, *McTaggart's Paradox* (London and New York: Routledge, 2016); C. J. Ducasse, "Moore's Refutation of Idealism," in *The Philosophy of G. E. Moore*, 223–52; and Russell, *Autobiography*, 166ff.

41. See Levy, *G. E. Moore and the Cambridge Apostles*, 191; and Morris Lazerowitz, "Moore's Paradox," in *The Philosophy of G. E. Moore*, 369–93. One might concede that human actions are somehow also part of the "absolute," which by definition is perfect. But by being part of a perfect absolute, must not anything within it also be perfect? Since there is little doubt that evil exists and we do not live in a perfect world, the claim that time does not exist appears absurd. If time is unreal, why develop valid ethical principles that help us, as imperfect beings, navigate the real world?

42. G. E. Moore, "The Defence of Common Sense," in *Selected Writings*, ed. Thomas Baldwin (London and New York: Routledge, 1993), 106–33.

43. Ibid., 119.

44. Ibid., 127.

45. Ibid., 119.

46. Ibid., 120.

47. Ludwig Wittgenstein, *Tractatus Logico-Philosophicus*, trans. D. F. Pears and B. F. McGuiness (London: Routledge & Kegan Paul, 1961), 145, 147, 151.

48. Percy Bysshe Shelley, *Prometheus Unbound, a Variorum Edition*, ed. Lawrence John Zillman (Seattle: University of Washington Press, 1959), 127.

49. "Palestrina and Beethoven" (1902), in Vaughan Williams, *Vaughan Williams on Music*, 125.

50. Ibid., 128.

51. Ibid.

52. Ibid.

53. "Bach and Schumann" (1902), in Vaughan Williams, *Vaughan Williams on Music*, 130.

54. "A London Symphony" (1920) in Vaughan Williams, *Vaughan Williams on Music*, 339.

55. It should be noted that Vaughan Williams's use of the term "absolute" is not related to the epistemological idea of the Absolute in McTaggart. Rather, it references the use of the term in the nineteenth-century debate triggered in part by Eduard Hanslick's 1854 *On the Beautiful in Music* and the distinction between program music and absolute

music, and therefore the tension between Liszt and Wagner and their opponents, primarily the circle around Brahms.

56. Vaughan Williams, "The Words of Wagner's Music Dramas" (1902), in *Vaughan Williams on Music*, 136.

57. Ibid., 146.

58. Ibid.

59. Vaughan Williams, "Preface to *The English Hymnal*" (1906), in *Vaughan Williams on Music*, 32.

60. Vaughan Williams, "*Ein Heldenleben*" (1903), in *Vaughan Williams on Music*, 162–63.

61. Vaughan Williams, "Hands off the Third" (1957), in *Vaughan Williams on Music*, 119.

62. Vaughan Williams, "The Justification of the Folk Song" (1941), in *Vaughan Williams on Music*, 247.

63. Vaughan Williams, "The Folk Song" (1932), in *National Music and Other Essays*, 22.

64. Vaughan Williams, "The Letter and the Spirit" (1920), in *National Music and Other Essays*, 122. The text of this essay is included earlier in this volume.

65. Ibid., 127–28.

66. Ibid.

67. Vaughan Williams, "Musical Autobiography" (1950), in *National Music and Other Essays*, 189–90.

68. It is interesting to compare these views with the end-of-career observations of the critic J. A. Fuller-Maitland. Writing in 1920, he described his difficulties with new music. In the end, Maitland, who liked Vaughan Williams's music, believed that the best of new music would take its place alongside the "classics," and by sustaining a common standard and widening the gap between first- and second-rate music, it would help consign all but the very best from the past to oblivion and so make room for the new. In Fuller-Maitland, *A Door-Keeper of Music* (London: John Murray, 1932), 230–31.

69. Michael Tippett, "Holst," in *Tippett on Music*, ed. Meirion Bowen (Oxford: Clarendon Press, 1995), 73–75. Tippett cites Paul Fussell's 1975 *The Great War and Modern Memory* (74).

70. Saylor, *Vaughan Williams*, 176.

71. Ibid., 168.

72. Vaughan Williams, "The Composer in Wartime" (1940), in *Vaughan Williams on Music*, 84. See also Daniel M. Grimley's essay on *A Pastoral Symphony*: "Landscape and Distance: Vaughan Williams, Modernism, and the Symphonic Pastoral," in *British Music and Modernism, 1895–1960*, ed. Matthew Riley (London: Routledge, 2010), 147–74.

73. Vaughan Williams, "Who Wants the English Composer?" (1912), in *Vaughan Williams on Music*, 40.

74. Vaughan Williams, "British Music" (1914), in *Vaughan Williams on Music*, 47.

75. Vaughan Williams, "Introduction to *English Music*" (1931), in *Vaughan Williams on Music*, 64.

76. Vaughan Williams was active in helping Jewish refugee musicians from Germany in the 1930s. His sympathy for Jews and Roma and their plight suggest the influence of George Borrow. See the discussion below on George Borrow.

77. Vaughan Williams, "The Folk Song" (1932), in *National Music and Other Essays*, 22.

78. Vaughan Williams, "Making Your Own Music" (1939), in *Vaughan Williams on Music*, 76.

79. Vaughan Williams's views on these matters overlap with the opinions of his friend, neighbor, and sometime collaborator, E. M. Forster. See Forster's *Two Cheers for Democracy* (New York: Harper Collins, 1962), 107–30, esp. 120 and 127–30.

80. Vaughan Williams, "Some Conclusions" (1932), in *National Music and Other Essays*, 68.

81. In this respect, Vaughan Williams can be compared to his American contemporary Charles Ives, who explicitly cited philosophy as a guide. Ives's debt to American

Transcendentalism was, by comparison, more extensive and direct than Vaughan Williams's debt to his contemporary British philosophers. Although Ives's music sounds on the surface radically different from Vaughan Williams's, the differences mask some fundamental similarities. Like Ives (and, indeed, like Mahler), Vaughan Williams integrated fragments and materials from the outside world—hymns, folksongs, marches—into his scores. Both composers responded to World War I through music. Both men held fierce, deep-seated commitments to democracy and to the ideal of the "common" people. Both were rather contemptuous of class distinctions and adhered to tenets of Christian ideals in a secularized form.

Unlike Vaughan Williams, Ives was a self-consciously experimental composer and far more contemptuous of Late Romanticism in music. However, both composers developed an anti-Romantic ideal of contemporary simplicity and clarity, even when they wrote music with complex rhythmic structures, polyphony that integrated fragmentation, and at times multi-layered sonorities. They both focused on their national communities as their preferred audience, a feature that was often conflated with parochialism. Both drew the new from the old, and by doing so, they expressed a not altogether optimistic sensibility about modernity that was rooted in suggestions of nostalgia. Of the two, Ives was the less generous and tolerant man, and more given to explicit chauvinism, particularly vis-à-vis Europe. At the same time, Ives and Vaughan Williams saw their role as composers as fostering the necessary advance of the democratic and egalitarian spirit.

82. See David Cannadine, *G. M. Trevelyan: A Life in History* (New York: W. W. Norton, 1993); and Laura Trevelyan, *A Very British Family: The Trevelyans and Their World* (London: Bloomsbury, 2012).

83. Vaughan Williams, "Introduction to *English Music*," 64.

84. Vaughan Williams, "Making Your Own Music."

85. George Borrow, *Lavengro* (London: John Murray, 1851), vi.

86. Ibid., 474. See also Roger Savage, *Masques, Mayings, and Music-Dramas: Vaughan Williams and the Early Twentieth-Century Stage* (Woodbridge, Suffolk: Boydell Press, 2014), 315; and his "Vaughan Williams, the Romany Ryes, and the Cambridge Ritualists," *Music & Letters* 83/3 (2002): 383–417.

87. Borrow, *Lavengro*, 7.

88. See ibid. See also the superb analysis by Deborah Epstein Nord, *Gypsies and the British Imagination, 1807–1930* (New York: Columbia University Press, 2008). The quote can be found on page 95. See also Lucille Herbert, "George Borrow and the Forms of Self-Reflection," *University of Toronto Quarterly* 40/2 (1970–71): 152–67.

89. Thomas Babbington Macaulay, *The Task of the Modern Historian* (New York: Doubleday, 1898), 178–79.

90. Ibid., 11. Macaulay's notion of the logic of history vindicated Vaughan Williams's notion of the potential role music could play in forming a national consciousness and character.

91. Trevelyan, *Social History*, 570.

92. Trevelyan, "The White Peril," *Nineteenth Century* 50 (1901): 1045.

93. Trevelyan, *Social History*, 588.

94. Ibid., 591–92.

95. Vaughan Williams, "Some Conclusions," 72.

96. Macauley, *The Task of the Modern Historian*, 7.

97. H. A. L. Fisher, *Frederick William Maitland* (Cambridge: Cambridge University Press, 1910), 31.

98. H. A. L. Fisher, *The Republican Tradition in Europe* (London: Methuen & Co., 1911), 276–77.

99. "planing down" as in "leveling down": ibid., 272.

100. Ibid., 271–72.

101. Quoted in Cannadine, *G. M. Trevelyan*, 153. See also the comment in Trevelyan's *Social History* from 1944.

102. G. M. Trevelyan. *The English Revolution, 1688–1689* (Oxford: Oxford University Press, 1938), 128.

103. Ibid., 129–30.

104. Ibid., 131.

105. Ibid., 130.

106. Ibid.

107. Trevelyan, *Social History*, 589–90.

108. H. A. L. Fisher, *A History of Europe* (London: Edward Arnold, 1937), v.

109. Ibid., vi.

110. Ibid., 1222.

111. G. M. Trevelyan, *History of England* (New York: Longmans, Green, 1956), 803.

112. See Alain Frogley, *Vaughan Williams's Ninth Symphony* (Oxford: Oxford University Press, 2001).

113. See Andrew Neill, "There Is Beauty in the Midst of Desolation," in *Let Beauty Awake: Elgar, Vaughan Williams, and Literature*, ed. Julian Rushton (London: Elgar Society, 2010), 18–31.

Index

Note: page numbers followed by "n" indicate chapter endnotes. Page numbers in italics refer to figures, tables, and musical examples. Throughout the index, RVW refers to Ralph Vaughan Williams.

Index of Names and Subjects

Notes on the Contributors

Byron Adams is a composer and musicologist. He has published essays in journals such as *19th-Century Music*, *The Musical Quarterly*, and *Music & Letters*, and has contributed chapters to volumes such as *The Cambridge Companion to Elgar* (2004) and *The Cambridge Companion to Vaughan Williams* (2013), *Jean Sibelius and His World* (2011), *The Music of Herbert Howells* (2014), *The Sea in the British Musical Imagination* (2015), and *Fauré Studies* (2021). In 2000, the American Musicological Society presented him with the Philip Brett Award. In 2007, he was appointed scholar-in-residence for the Bard Music Festival and edited the volume *Edward Elgar and His World*. He is an associate editor of *The Musical Quarterly*. Adams is Emeritus Professor of Musicology at the University of California, Riverside.

Leon Botstein is president and Leon Levy Professor in the Arts of Bard College and chancellor of the Open Society University Network (OSUN), as well as the author of several books and editor of *The Compleat Brahms* and *The Musical Quarterly*. The music director of the American Symphony Orchestra and The Orchestra Now, he has recorded works by, among others, Schoeck, Honegger, Szymanowski, Hartmann, Dukas, Foulds, Bruckner, Chausson, Richard Strauss, Mendelssohn, Popov, Liszt, and Shostakovich. He is co-artistic director of the Bard Music Festival.

Sarah Collins is a cultural historian and musicologist who has published widely on the relationship between music and literary aesthetics and broader intellectual and political currents in the late-nineteenth and early-twentieth centuries. She is the author of *Lateness and Modernism: Untimely Ideas about Music, Literature and Politics in Interwar Britain* (2019), and *The Aesthetic Life of Cyril Scott* (2013); editor of *Music and Victorian Liberalism: Composing the Liberal Subject* (2019); and co-editor with Paul Watt and Michael Allis of *The Oxford Handbook of Music and Intellectual Culture in the Nineteenth Century* (2020). Her research has appeared in the *Journal of the Royal Musical Association*, *Twentieth-Century Music*, *Music & Letters*, *Musical Quarterly*, *Cambridge Opera Journal*, and elsewhere. Sarah is associate professor, chair of musicology, and deputy head of school (research) at the University of Western Australia Conservatorium of Music. She has held visiting fellowships at Harvard University, the University of Oxford, and Durham University, and has received competitive research funding from a range of sources including the British Academy, the Australian Research Council, and the European Commission. She is a co-editor of *Music & Letters*; a fellow of the Australian Academy of the Humanities; and is on the council of the Royal Musical Association.

Annika Forkert is lecturer in music at the Royal Northern College of Music, Manchester. Her writings include a forthcoming monograph entitled *Elisabeth Lutyens and Edward Clark: The Orchestration of Progress in Twentieth-Century British Music* and articles in the *Journal of the Royal Musical Association*, *Twentieth Century Music*, and *The Musical Times*. Other academic work in English and German focuses on musical bricolage, collaboration, and modernism. She was a regular author of program notes for Bavarian Radio and other orchestras and ensembles and is currently co-writing a monograph on Franz Schreker's operas.

Alain Frogley is professor of music and dean of the School of Fine Arts at the University of Connecticut. He has also taught at Oxford, Lancaster, and Yale universities, and in 2005–6 was a fellow of the American Council of Learned Societies. He has written extensively on British music and on Beethoven; his research has centered on sketch studies, reception history, and the cultural contexts of musical nationalism, including imperialism and the modern metropolis. He has published three books on Vaughan Williams, and a critical edition of the composer's Ninth Symphony.

Daniel M. Grimley is a professor of music and head of humanities at the University of Oxford and a fellow of Merton College. A specialist in Scandinavian and Finnish music, early 20th-century English music, and music and cultural geography, his books include *Grieg: Music, Landscape and Norwegian Identity* (2006), *Carl Nielsen and the Idea of Modernism* (2010), and *Delius and the Sound of Place* (2018). His most recent book is *Jean Sibelius: Life, Music, Silence* (2021). He was principal investigator of the interdisciplinary Leverhulme International Research Network "Hearing Landscape Critically" from 2012 to 2016, and also has served as an editor of *Music & Letters* and associate editor of *The Musical Quarterly*. He broadcasts regularly on BBC Radio 3 and is a frequent speaker at the BBC Proms. In 2011, he was scholar-in-residence at the Bard Music Festival, editing *Jean Sibelius and His World*.

O. W. Neighbour (1923–2015) was a distinguished scholar who published on the music of Arnold Schoenberg, Ralph Vaughan Williams, and William Byrd. He matriculated at St. Catharine's College, Cambridge, becoming a friend of the novelist E. M. Forster. Neighbour joined the staff of the British Library in 1946, rising through steady promotion to the position of music librarian in 1976; he retired in 1985. Neighbour was elected a Fellow of the British Academy in 1982. His extensive collection of valuable music manuscripts, which included rare sketches by Fauré as well as manuscript scores by Ravel and Stravinsky, was quietly donated to the British Library in 2007. Among his several enthusiasms was traveling to see old English country churches, of which he was a connoisseur.

Ceri Owen is a prize-winning pianist, academic, and writer who is currently working on a new biography of the composer Ralph Vaughan Williams for Reaktion Books. She is also editing and writing for a book of essays about Vaughan Williams for Cambridge University Press. She serves on the faculty of the University of Birmingham. Projects as a performer include the creation and performance of a semi-improvised film score for the 1934 documentary *Man of Aran* with harper and sound artist Úna Monaghan and the singer Síle Denvir, for Belfast's Docs Ireland Film Festival, as well as recitals at some of the UK's leading concert halls, including the Barbican Hall, Kings Place, and St Martin-in-the-Fields, London, and as part of the BBC Proms Festival. She has made both live and recorded broadcasts for BBC Radio 3, both in performance as well as a speaker, and is regularly invited to give lectures and talks at national and international festivals.

Philip Rupprecht is professor of music at Duke University. His books include *British Musical Modernism: The Manchester Group and Their Contemporaries* (2015), the edited volume *Rethinking Britten* (2013), and *Britten's Musical Language* (2001). He is also co-editor of two essay volumes, *Tonality 1900–1950: Concept and Practice* (2012) and *Tonality Since 1950* (2017). Current research interests include the intersection of aesthetics and postwar bureaucracy in British symphonic genres of the 1940s and 1950s. Most recently, he has published essays on contemporary composers Thomas Adès, Simon Holt, and James Dillon. Rupprecht is co-editor (with David Beard) of the book series Music Since 1900, published by Cambridge University Press.

Julian Rushton is professor emeritus at the School of Music, Leeds University, where he was West Riding Chair of Music from 1981 to 2005. He previously taught at the universities of East Anglia and Cambridge, and was a fellow of King's College. His book publications include *Mozart* (*The Master Musicians*, 2006), *Mozart: An Extraordinary Life* (2006), *The Musical Language of Berlioz* (1983), *The Music of Berlioz* (2001) and as editor and contributor, *The Cambridge Berlioz Encyclopedia* (2018). He edited four volumes of the New Berlioz Edition, and has also edited works by Cipriani Potter, Elgar, and Vaughan Williams. He contributed the entry on Mozart to *The New Grove Dictionary of Opera* and several articles in *The New Grove Dictionary of Music and Musicians* and other reference works. He was general editor of Cambridge Music Handbooks, contributing volumes on Berlioz's *Roméo et Juliette* and Elgar's *Enigma* Variations. He was for twenty-five years chair of the editorial committee of Musica Britannica.

Eric Saylor is professor of music history at Drake University. He is the author of *Vaughan Williams* (2022) and *English Pastoral Music: From Arcadia to Utopia, 1900–1955* (2017), and co-editor of *The Sea in the British Imagination* (2015, with Christopher Scheer), and *Blackness in Opera* (2012, with Naomi André and Karen M. Bryan). His articles and reviews have appeared in the *Journal of the Royal Musical Association*, *The Musical Quarterly*, *The Musical Times*, *Musik-Konzepte*, *The Journal of Musicological Research*, *Music & Letters*, the *Journal of the Society for Musicology in Ireland*, and *Nineteenth-Century Music Review*. Saylor is the author of the Vaughan Williams entry in *Oxford Bibliographies Online* and has contributed chapters to *The Cambridge Companion to Vaughan Williams* (2013) and *Benjamin Britten in Context* (2022). He has also contributed to the *New Grove Dictionary of American Music* (2nd ed., 2013). He served as President of the North American British Music Studies Association (NABMSA) from 2016–2020.

Erica Siegel completed her PhD in musicology at the University of California, Riverside, in 2016. Her research focuses on 20th-century British music in relation to aspects of modernism, nationalism, and gender. She has delivered papers at meetings of the American Musicological Society and the North American British Music Studies Association, and has published on Vaughan Williams's students in *The Musical Quarterly*. Her monograph on the life and music of British composer Elizabeth Maconchy will be published in 2023 by the Boydell Press.

Franz Liszt and His World
edited by Christopher H. Gibbs and Dana Gooley (2006)

Edward Elgar and His World
edited by Byron Adams (2007)

Sergey Prokofiev and His World
edited by Simon Morrison (2008)

Brahms and His World (revised edition)
edited by Walter Frisch and Kevin C. Karnes (2009)

Richard Wagner and His World
edited by Thomas S. Grey (2009)

Alban Berg and His World
edited by Christopher Hailey (2010)

Jean Sibelius and His World
edited by Daniel M. Grimley (2011)

Camille Saint-Saëns and His World
edited by Jann Pasler (2012)

Stravinsky and His World
edited by Tamara Levitz (2013)

Franz Schubert and His World
edited by Christopher H. Gibbs and Morten Solvik (2014)

Carlos Chávez and His World
edited by Leonora Saavedra (2015)

Giacomo Puccini and His World
edited by Arman Schwartz and Emanuele Senici (2016)

Chopin and His World
edited by Jonathan D. Bellman and Halina Goldberg (2017)

Rimsky-Korsakov and His World
edited by Marina Frolova-Walker (2018)

Korngold and His World
edited by Daniel Goldmark and Kevin C. Karnes (2019)

Nadia Boulanger and Her World
edited by Jeanice Brooks (2020)

Rachmaninoff and His World
edited by Philip Ross Bullock (2022)

VAUGHAN WILLIAMS AND HIS WORLD

THE BARD MUSIC FESTIVAL

LEON BOTSTEIN AND CHRISTOPHER H. GIBBS
SERIES EDITORS